WITHDRAWN BY JUDITH

P9-CKL-457

Andrew Rollings and Ernest Adams on Game Design

Contents at a Glance

Andrew Rollings and Ernest Adams on Game Design

Andrew Rollings

Ernest Adams

New Riders

201 West 103rd Street, Indianapolis, Indiana 46290
An Imprint of Pearson Education
Boston • Indianapolis • London • Munich • New York • San Francisco

L.C.C. SOUTH CAMPUS LIBRARY

Andrew Rollings and Ernest Adams on Game Design

Copyright © 2003 by New Riders Publishing

All rights reserved. No part of this book shall be reproduced, stored in a retrieval system, or transmitted by any means—electronic, mechanical, photocopying, recording, or otherwise—without written permission from the publisher, except for the inclusion of brief quotations in a review.

International Standard Book Number: 1592730019

Library of Congress Catalog Card Number: 2002110543

Printed in the United States of America

First edition: May 2003

07 06 05 04   7 6 5 4 3 2

Interpretation of the printing code: The rightmost double-digit number is the year of the book's printing; the rightmost single-digit number is the number of the book's printing. For example, the printing code 03-1 shows that the first printing of the book occurred in 2003.

Shneiderman, B. *Designing the Web Interface: Strategies for Effective Human-Computer Interaction,* Third Edition, pp. 74 and 75, ©1998 Pearson Education. Reprinted by permission of Pearson Education, Inc.

Trademarks

All terms mentioned in this book that are known to be trademarks or service marks have been appropriately capitalized. New Riders Publishing cannot attest to the accuracy of this information. Use of a term in this book should not be regarded as affecting the validity of any trademark or service mark.

Warning and Disclaimer

Every effort has been made to make this book as complete and as accurate as possible, but no warranty of fitness is implied. The information is provided on an as-is basis. The authors and New Riders Publishing shall have neither liability nor responsibility to any person or entity with respect to any loss or damages arising from the information contained in this book or from the use of the programs that may accompany it.

Publisher
David Dwyer

Associate Publisher
Stephanie Wall

Production Manager
Gina Kanouse

Senior Product Marketing Manager
Tammy Detrich

Publicity Manager
Susan Nixon

Executive Development Editor
Lisa Thibault

Senior Project Editor
Sarah Kearns

Copy Editor
Krista Hansing

Indexer
Cheryl Lenser

Proofreader
Lori Lyons

Composition
Gloria Schurick

Manufacturing Coordinator
Dan Uhrig

Interior Designer
Kim Scott

Cover Designer
Aren Howell

QA
76.76
.C672
R65
2003

JUL 21 2004

To my wife, Stephanie Park, for putting up with me complaining about writing a book.

Andrew Rollings

To my wife, Mary Ellen Foley, for love, assistance, and unwavering support. Omnia vincit amor.

Ernest Adams

Table of Contents

About the Authors

Andrew Rollings has a B.S. in Physics from Imperial College, London, and Bristol University, and has worked as a technical consultant spanning the games industry and the financial industry since 1995. He is also the co-author of the highly successful book, *Game Architecture and Design*.

Ernest Adams is an American game design consultant currently based in England as a member of the International Hobo design consortium. He has worked in the interactive entertainment industry since 1989, and was most recently employed as a lead designer at Bullfrog Productions. For several years before that, Mr. Adams was the audio/video producer on the *Madden NFL Football* product line at Electronic Arts, and in a much earlier life he was a software engineer, first in the computer-aided design and then the computer game industries. He has developed online, computer, and console games for everything from the IBM 360 mainframe to the Sony Playstation 2. He is also the founder of the International Game Developers' Association, and is the author of the popular *Designer's Notebook* series of columns on the *Gamasutra* developers' webzine. His professional web site is at `http://www.designersnotebook.com`.

About the Technical Reviewers

These reviewers contributed their considerable hands-on expertise to the entire development process for *Andrew Rollings and Ernest Adams on Game Design*. As the book was being written, these dedicated professionals reviewed all the material for technical content, organization, and flow. Their feedback was critical to ensuring that *Andrew Rollings and Ernest Adams on Game Design* fits our reader's need for the highest-quality technical information.

Scott Crabtree started designing and building video games as a high school geek in 1980. He has professionally designed and managed development of entertainment software since 1995. Scott most recently founded Crabtree Media, an independent game development company working on multiple PlayStation 2 projects. An expert on design and project management, Scott has spoken at the Game Developer's Conference and been published on Gamasutra.com. He has designed and led production of dozens of games for major publishers such as Disney and Microsoft. Scott can be reached through Scott@CrabtreeMedia.com.

Jonathan S. Harbour has been been writing code for 15 years, having started with Microsoft BASIC and Turbo Pascal on a Tandy 1000. Jonathan graduated from DeVry Institute of Technology in 1997, with a bachelor's degree in computer information systems. He has since worked for cellular, aerospace, pharmaceutical, education, medical research, and healthcare companies. In his spare time, Jonathan enjoys spending time with his family, reading, playing video games, and restoring his 1968 Mustang. Jonathan has written several books, including *Visual Basic Game Programming with DirectX* and *Microsoft Visual Basic .NET Programming for the Absolute Beginner*.

Acknowledgments

It would be a rare developer indeed who had worked on every genre and style of game addressed in this book, and certainly neither of us can make that claim. When it came time to speak of subjects of which we had little direct experience, we relied heavily on the advice, wisdom, and support of our professional colleagues, for which we are immensely grateful. Five people in particular have given us permission to quote extensively from their writing, which has enriched the book enormously. We owe a special debt of gratitude to:

Jesyca Durchin
Scott Kim
Raph Koster
Brian Moriarty
Chris Taylor

Among our many other benefactors (here listed in alphabetical order) were:

Chris Bateman
Ellen Guon Beeman
Steve Beeman
Kim Blake
George Broussard
Charles Cecil
Charlie Cleveland
Noah Falstein
Geoff Howland
Amy Kalson
Dave Morris
Bill Roper
Jake Simpson
Tess Snider
Teut Weidemann
Russ Williams

We hasten to add that these people bear no responsibility for any faults in the work. Errors and omissions should be laid squarely at our own door.

In addition to our colleagues listed here, several other people deserve particular mention. Technical editors Scott Crabtree, Jonathan Harbour, and Brooke Monroe, all seasoned game developers, offered us important insights and commentary as they read through the entire manuscript. Mary Ellen Foley also read and edited large sections of the book, making hundreds of constructive suggestions to clarify our language while at the same time providing a valuable "outsider's" perspective. Our editors at New Riders, Stephanie Wall and Lisa Thibault, were unfailingly understanding and positive in the face of missed deadlines, incorrect formatting, and general grumpiness after two years of work on the project. And finally, we owe a great debt to our agent, Jawahara Saidullah of Waterside Productions, who helped us to rescue the book and find a new publisher after our first one went out of business.

To any whom we have inadvertently omitted, sincere apologies. We'll make sure your name gets into the second edition!

Tell Us What You Think

As the reader of this book, you are the most important critic and commentator. We value your opinion and want to know what we're doing right, what we could do better, what areas you'd like to see us publish in, and any other words of wisdom you're willing to pass our way.

As the Associate Publisher for New Riders Publishing, I welcome your comments. You can fax, email, or write me directly to let me know what you did or didn't like about this book—as well as what we can do to make our books stronger. When you write, please be sure to include this book's title, ISBN, and author, as well as your name and phone or fax number. I will carefully review your comments and share them with the author and editors who worked on the book.

Please note that I cannot help you with technical problems related to the topic of this book, and that due to the high volume of email I receive, I might not be able to reply to every message.

Fax: 317-581-4663

Email: stephanie.wall@newriders.com

Mail: Stephanie Wall
           Associate Publisher
           New Riders Publishing
           201 West 103rd Street
           Indianapolis, IN 46290 USA

Introduction

Every game player is a potential game designer, and that means you.

When you were a kid, you probably started many a game of whiffle ball or *Monopoly* with a little negotiation over the rules. "If the ball gets stuck in a tree, it's an out," "Chance and Community Chest fines go into a pool, and whoever lands on Free Parking gets the money," and so on. Kids don't hesitate to change the rules of existing games to make them more enjoyable. The participatory nature of playing a game encourages us to think about, and sometimes modify, its rules—that is, its design. And that's just as true of video games, too. We've all played games that we thought could be improved by a few adjustments.

But some people want to do more than alter the rules; they want to create entirely new games and even new kinds of games. Their heads are full of worlds to play in, characters to encounter, challenges to meet. Because you're reading this, you're almost certainly one of those people. Chances are that right this minute, you've got a great idea for a game your head—maybe half a dozen of them. But how do you turn a game *idea* into a game *design*?

From Idea to Design

We wrote this book to answer that question, specifically for people who want to design computer and video games. We discuss both the theory and the practice of game design: the why and the how. A design is much more than an idea; it's a blueprint for building an enjoyable and challenging game. We'll give you practical advice about how to design a game, what kinds of decisions you'll face as you go along, and how to write it all down in a design document. The design document communicates your intentions to the people who will build your game, and even if you plan to build it by yourself, you still need to keep a record of the choices you've made—and those you still need to make. By the end of this book, you will have the tools you need to design many kinds of games, and to create a professional-quality game design document.

What This Book Is (and Isn't) About

Andrew Rollings and Ernest Adams on Game Design contains our combined thoughts on the important issues that relate to designing games. We don't claim that it's the final word on game design. No book could be. We have chosen to address areas that we believe are important and under-served, and we don't expect everyone to agree with us on every point. That's the beauty and the terror of game design: There are no right answers.

We offer a game design methodology intended to spur your thinking and get your creative juices flowing. In this book, you will not find step-by-step instructions on how to create the next *Doom* or *Tetris* clone. Instead, we discuss the central issues that every game designer must face, and we pose a series of questions for you to ask yourself about the game that's in your head. The answers to those questions will move you along the path from idea to design.

One area that we have not addressed is level design. The reason for this is simple: There is no one standard way to design levels. Level design considerations are different for each genre of game, and we simply don't have the space to address them all properly. By examining the essential elements of a genre, we hope to give you the tools to design enjoyable levels, but the process itself is, as they say, "left as an exercise for the reader."

You are at the beginning of a voyage of discovery. Our book is a map with white space beyond the borders. We are sharing what we know about game design in order to enable you to navigate through the familiar regions and then to press on into *terra incognita*. We hope that you will in turn transmit your own learning to others, continuing to fill in the map and helping to push out the boundaries of game design. The journey begins here.

How This Book Is Organized

Andrew Rollings and Ernest Adams on Game Design is divided into two parts. The first eight chapters are about designing games in general: what a game is, how it works, and what kinds of decisions you have to make to create one. The next ten chapters are about different genres of games and the design considerations peculiar to each genre.

Part One: The Elements of Game Design

Chapter 1 provides an *introduction to game design*: what the designer needs to do and why. It also discusses the key talents and skills that game designers should have.

Chapter 2 is about *game concepts*: where the idea for a game comes from and how to refine it. The audience and the target hardware (the machine the game will run on) both have a strong influence on the direction the game will take.

Chapter 3 is about the *game's setting and world*: the place where the gameplay happens, and the way things work there. As the designer, you're the god of your world, and it's up to you to define its concepts of time and space, mechanics, and natural laws, as well as many other things: its logic, emotions, culture, and values.

Chapter 4 delves into the problems of *storytelling and narrative*: how to create a compelling storyline, and how to balance the inevitable tension between your desire for control as a designer, and the player's desire for freedom as an actor in your world.

Chapter 5 addresses *character design*: inventing the people, or beings, that populate your game world—especially the character who will represent the player there (his *avatar*), if there is one. Every successful entertainer from Homer onward has understood the importance of having an appealing protagonist.

Chapter 6 is about *user interface design*: the way that the player experiences and interacts with the game world. A bad user interface can kill an otherwise brilliant game, so you must get this right.

Chapter 7 discusses *gameplay*, the heart of the player's mental experience of a game: the challenges he faces and the actions he takes to overcome them.

Chapter 8 looks at the *internal economy* or *core mechanics* of a game, and the flow of resources (money, points, ammunition, or whatever) throughout the game. It also addresses the key issue essential to all games: *game balance*.

Part Two: The Genres of Games

Chapter 9 is about the earliest, and still the most popular, genre of interactive entertainment: *action games*.

Chapter 10 discusses another genre that has been part of gaming since the beginning: *strategy games*, both real-time and turn-based.

Chapter 11 is about *role-playing games*, a natural outgrowth of pencil and paper games such as *Dungeons & Dragons*.

Chapter 12 looks at *sports games*, which have a number of peculiar design challenges. The actual contest itself is designed by others; the trick is to map human athletic activities onto a screen and control devices.

Chapter 13 addresses *vehicle simulations*: cars, planes, boats, and other, more exotic modes of transportation such as tanks and mechs.

Chapter 14 is about *construction and management simulations*, in which the player tries to build and maintain something—a city, a theme park, a planet—within the limitations of an economic system.

Chapter 15 explores *adventure games*, an old and unique genre of gaming recently given new life by the creation of a hybrid type, the *action adventure*.

Chapter 16 examines a variety of other types of games: *artificial life*, *software toys*, *puzzle games*, and so on.

Chapter 17 is devoted to *online games*, which is not a genre but a technology. Online games enable people to play with, or against, each other in numbers from two up to hundreds of thousands. Playing against real people that you cannot see has enormous consequences for the game's design. The second half of the chapter addresses the particular problems of *persistent worlds* like *EverQuest*.

Chapter 18 takes a look at the *future of gaming* and where we believe the medium will go, both in the short and long term.

Part Three: Appendixes

Appendix A includes sample design documents and an extensive discussion of what they're used for.

Appendix B is a bibliography of works that either we used in writing this book, or that we find particularly useful in creating our own designs.

Non-Computer Games, Too!

This book is primarily about designing interactive entertainment: computer and video games of various kinds. You will notice, however, that we frequently refer to non-computerized games as well—card games like poker, board games like *Monopoly*, and so on. We do this for three reasons:

➤ First, those games are likely to be familiar to the largest number of people. Not all of our readers will have played computer games such as *Planescape: Torment*, and some will be too young to remember *Colossal Cave*, but everyone has heard of chess.

➤ Second, simpler, non-computerized games tend to be designed around a single principle, so they serve to illustrate that principle well.

➤ Finally, we believe that the essence of game design has little to do with the game's delivery medium. The principles that are common to all good games are independent of the means by which they are presented. A good game designer should be able to design board games, card games, pencil-and-paper games, and computer games with equal facility.

A Word About Pronouns

Because English doesn't include a gender-neutral pronoun applicable to humans, we have chosen to alternate, more or less randomly, between the use of "he" and "she" when speaking of indefinite individuals such as "the player" and "the designer." After we have designated "the player" to be male or female in a given context, we retain that usage throughout the section in order to avoid confusion. We feel that constructions such as "s/he" and "he or she" are awkward and distracting. However, if you find yourself pulled up short by the idea of a female player of sports games or a male designer of Barbie games, that's all to the good. We don't believe that games should be segregated into pink genres for women and blue genres for men, and as a designer you should be aware that your game could be played by anyone, male or female.

As for ourselves—well, we describe ourselves as "we." Andrew wrote some chapters and Ernest wrote others, and then we swapped them around and traded comments and suggestions. But we haven't identified who wrote what; we each take responsibility for the whole book.

Enjoy!

Part I

The Elements of Game Design

Chapter 1

What Is Game Design?

Humans have been devising and playing games for thousands of years. There is hot debate about which existing game is the oldest; some argue for Go (shown in Figure 1.1) and some for the African stone game Awari, but the first game ever devised is almost certainly lost to us today. The field of game design is as ancient as the human neocortex and is clearly related to our capacity to pretend, for pretending—that is, creating and playing in an artificial world—is at the heart of all games. Some, such as Go and chess, were perfected so long ago that their rules have not changed for centuries. Other games come on the market, enjoy a brief popularity, and fade away again. People are always interested in new games, so there is a constant demand for new game designs.

Figure 1.1 Go.

Game design is the process of:

> ➤ *Imagining* a game.

> ➤ *Defining* the way it works.

> ➤ *Describing* the elements that make up the game (conceptual, functional, artistic, and others).

> ➤ *Transmitting* that information to the team that will build the game.

A game designer's job includes all of these. In this chapter, we discuss what's involved in game design, why we do it, and what it takes to be a game designer.

In spite of the long history of game design, surprisingly little study has been devoted to the subject. Indeed, game design has been taken seriously as a subject worthy of academic interest only in the last few decades. But study requires funding; consequently, most game theory research has been directed toward economic principles and military applications. Little of this work applies to games intended for the consumer, and most of it requires an advanced knowledge of statistics to decipher. We concentrate on practical game design rather than formal game theory.

Art, Science, or Craft?

Many people consider game design to be an art, drawing on a mysterious wellspring of creativity possessed only by a talented few. They think of the "big names" in the game industry—Peter Molyneux, Brian Moriarty, Roberta Williams—as artists, and they admire the vision and originality that such people bring to their games. They imagine that game designers spend their time indulging in flights of imagination, and they ignore or are not even aware of the long and painstaking work that real design requires.

Other people who are more mathematically oriented see game design as a science. They concentrate on the methodology for determining the best rules of play, the intricate procedure of balancing a complex game. They think about equations, relationships, and the flow of resources. Game design to these people is a set of techniques, a process of thought.

We believe both of these views are wrong, or at least incomplete. Game design is not purely an art because it is not primarily a means of aesthetic expression. "Artistry" comes into envisioning the initial concepts and ideas, but once that is done, it's time for the real work of defining and refining how the game will function. Nor is game design purely a science; it doesn't posit hypotheses or seek truth. It's not bound by rigorous standards of logic or formal methods. The goal of a game is to entertain through play, and designing a game requires both creativity and careful planning.

Interactive entertainment is an art form, but like film, television, and theater, it is a collaborative art form, with no single person entitled to call himself the artist. In fact, most designers don't think of themselves as artists at all. Designing games is a *craft*, like cinematography or costume design in Hollywood. A game contains both artistic and functional elements: It must be aesthetically pleasing, but it also must work well and be enjoyable to play. The greatest games combine these attributes brilliantly, achieving a quality for which the only word is *elegance*. Elegance is the sign of craftsmanship of the highest order.

The Anatomy of Game Design

Game design cannot be reduced to a set of discrete instructions and processes. There is no formula that you can follow and produce a perfect game design, ready for your programming team to code into existence. However, you can take advantage of a set of common principles that apply to *all* successful games, and doing so can save you a fair amount of grunt work. Designing a successful game is not just random chance—although so many other factors besides design influence a game's success that it sometimes seems that way.

The Importance of Game Design

Game design (at least for the computer and console) is a very young field, and there is still much to be discovered. The movie industry and even the advertising industry know more about invoking atmosphere and mood than any game designer out there—and more important, they know how to apply their techniques effectively.

Take McDonalds, for example: Have you ever wondered why they use a predominantly red-and-yellow color scheme? Psychologists report that the color yellow influences the perceived hunger level of the subject, while red increases anxiety and the need to hurry. The result, according to the psychologists, is that you order more food, eat it quickly, and leave. The reasons for this appear to be deep in our ancestry. Red is the color of blood, signifying danger, and yellow is a predominant color in foodstuffs. In his book *ManWatching*, Desmond Morris goes into this and many other aspects of human behavior in a lot more detail. It makes for interesting reading, and we recommend it to any serious game designer. It's useful for the game designer to consider the ways that humans interact with each other and the subconscious stimuli that influence them. This and other kinds of understanding will take game design to a new level, resulting in richer, subtler, and ultimately better games.

Even though some people view game design as a mystical art, they can be peculiarly inconsistent in their attitudes: Nearly everybody who expresses an interest in the subject believes that he could be a game designer. The skill of game design is, so to speak, invisible. It looks as if anyone should be able to do it. After all, it's just a matter of writing a simple story, knocking up a design document or two, and telling the programmers what you want, right? No. That's about as realistic as expecting that anyone who can use a hammer and a saw should be able to produce a violin. Good game design is, as we said, a matter of craftsmanship.

If you want proof, just check any magazine that reviews games and see how often it marks down games for poor design. Games might be technically superb and look wonderful, but if the gameplay isn't there, it's not a game; it's a pretty demo. Even the original *Quake*, while lauded for its amazing technology, was slammed for the poor quality of its single-player gameplay (after the stunned awe had worn off). Sure, it looked great, but running around shooting poorly designed and badly placed enemies wore thin very quickly.

The creators of *Quake*, id software, acknowledged that the first *Quake* was just a technology demo. The gameplay was improved in *Quake II*, which presented a good single-player game, but with *Quake III*, we're back to the technology demo again. It was left to third parties (such as Valve, which developed *Half-Life* using the *Quake II* engine) to take the technology and make a game with it.

Given the amount of money routinely sunk into these technological powerhouse products, it seems amazing that more money is not spent on producing a decent game design. In many cases, the game design is an amalgamation of the "best" ideas of the development team. This works so rarely that when it *is* successful, the process is widely publicized and the publicity gives the impression that this is the best way to design a game. You might have heard the saying a camel is a horse designed by committee. Nowhere is this more applicable than the game industry.

Of course, for every rule, you can find a high-profile exception (otherwise, life would be a lot simpler—and duller). The designers of *Half-Life*, a truly excellent game, used a process like this, dubbed the *cabal process*. Valve was incredibly fortunate to have the right people in the right place at the right time. Most developers can't count on such luck. Valve can't even be certain that the cabal process will work again. History is on their side, but as they say in the financial industry, past performance is no guarantee of future success.

So what's the upshot of this? Although game design is a creative process requiring the ability to dream and imagine amazing worlds populated by strange and wonderful denizens, a great many practical principles also can be extracted and analyzed. When you thoroughly understand the techniques of game design, your imagination and intellect will be free to work together and concentrate on what's really important: great gameplay. Of course, in an ideal world, original and innovative gameplay would be equally important. Unfortunately, most publishers don't want games that are *too* innovative; they want something just like a recent hit, with a few more twists.

Seeking the Key Elements of Games

Our approach in teaching you how to design games centers on the idea that games are made up of certain key elements, and that the games in a given genre tend to have many of those elements in common. These elements include such things as the rules of the game, the player's role (pilot, athlete, general, spy, and so on), the challenges the player will face, and many others that we will introduce as we go along.

This doesn't mean that we think all games in a particular genre should be alike—far from it. Among cars, for example, all minivans (a genre of car, you might say) include seating for five or more people, have a rear door rather than a trunk, and stand up fairly high off the ground. Yet not all minivans look alike or have the same perform-ance characteristics. The same is true of games. Two war games can include many elements in common and still have completely different settings, units, and strategies, and be balanced in different ways.

We encourage you to adjust our elements as you see fit. The last thing we want to see is more games with different graphics but identical play mechanics; there are too many of those already. During the heyday of the Sega Genesis and the Super Nintendo, we saw too many side-scrollers, games about running and jumping on platforms; nowa-days store shelves overflow with too many first-person shooters in which players run through a 3D world firing at anything that moves. The game industry and our players don't need more games that look a little different but are essentially the same. That leads to creative stagnation among developers and eventual boredom and disinterest among customers.

The purpose of identifying common elements in a genre is not to encourage the devel-opment of cookie-cutter games, but to make sure that when you design a game, you have covered all the basics—the essential components that a game in a particular genre should have and without which is incomplete.

Okay, that's far enough. Before we continue, we need to discuss exactly what we mean by game design. After all, one of the most confusing aspects of the study of game design is that there's no official definition agreed on by the whole industry—different game designers might have different ideas of what comprises game design.

Laying Down the Ground Rules

For the purposes of this book, we have broken down game design into three specific areas: core mechanics, storytelling, and interactivity. Each is a distinct, complementary element of a game, and each makes up one part of a larger whole, as shown in Figure 1.2.

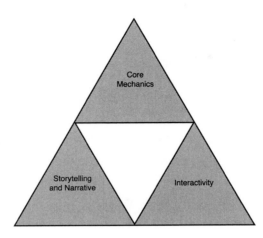

Figure 1.2   Core mechanics, interactivity, and storytelling.

Core Mechanics

The rules that define the operation of the game world make up the *core mechanics* of the game, or the foundations of gameplay.

The core mechanics are the translation of the designer's vision into a consistent set of rules that can be interpreted by a computer—or, more accurately, rules that can be interpreted by the people who write the software that is interpreted by the computer. Defining the core mechanics is the "science" part of game design. It is important not to confuse this with the technology of computer gaming. Although the core mechanics are implemented by creation of a mathematical (or computational) model of the abstract game world, the core mechanics describe the way the game works, not the way the software operates. In a noncomputerized game, we would simply call these the rules, but the rules of computer games are far more complex than the rules of any board or card game.

This is the heart and soul of the game—if the core mechanics aren't sound, you end up with a poor game. Unfortunately, this happens fairly frequently. It seems that the core mechanics are often the least-developed area in modern games. The reasons for this are many and varied, but the three most significant are as follows:

➤ Designer ignorance of game mechanics

➤ Marketing pressure

➤ Conflicting demands for impressive technology and good gameplay

Of these three, we can help with only the first and the third. Designer ignorance is what this book is intended to address. The second, marketing pressure, is beyond our control, much to our despair on a number of occasions in the past. We will also address the third, technology versus gameplay, in this book, although it's also partly brought on by market conditions. The technology race is analogous to the Cold War arms race: Technology produces eye candy, eye candy grabs customers' attention, and, in the viciously competitive arena of the software store and magazine page, attention is the most valuable commodity. Games have limited development budgets, and the money tends to go toward areas that will produce the most visible results. If technology sells products, then products will focus on technology. The core mechanics are often given short shrift in consequence.

Storytelling and Narrative

All games tell a story. The complexity and depth of that story depends on the game. At one extreme, in adventure games such as *Grim Fandango*, the game *is* the story. At the other extreme, it's the player who tells the story by the act of playing. Even *Tetris* has a story—a story created by the player as she plays.

Narrative, as we use the term, means that part of the story that is told by you, the author and designer, to the player. Narrative is the noninteractive, presentational part of the story. *Tetris* has a story, but it contains no narrative. Because playing games is an active process and listening to a narrative is a passive one, there is an inherent tension between interactivity and narrative. We discuss this tension in much more detail later.

Without a story, or some way for a player to implicitly form his own story, the game simply will not interest the player. As you probably remember from high school English classes, all stories feature *dramatic tension:* an unresolved issue, problem, or conflict that keeps the reader's attention and makes him want to read on. This is no less true of games than it is of novels or short stories. In the case of games, the dramatic tension often, though not always, arises from a challenge in the game that the player has not yet overcome. Whether the player makes up his own "story" or whether he reads or watches a scripted narrative, it's the primary hook that keeps the player playing. Many games try to aim for a middle ground: They provide a back story and let the player fill in the details—quite often by completing missions that drive the plot along.

Narratives in games are often quite linear, unaffected by the player's actions and unchanging from one playing to the next. Many designers see this as a limitation, impeding the freedom of the player. In recent years, there has been a lot of discussion about nonlinearity in computer games and the improvements it would bring. As with many "new and improved" features of games, a certain amount of smoke and mirrors is involved in bringing nonlinearity to nontrivial narrative-based games. Automated storytelling is the holy grail of computer game design. Chris Crawford, designer of *Balance of Power*, has performed some work in this area with his *Erasmatazz* project (www.erasmatazz.com).

There is still a long way to go before we have (or can provide) fully dynamic computer-generated stories. In the meantime, we'll have to continue to use the old-fashioned methods and let humans write the stories. Unfortunately, the effort involved in creating a nonlinear story grows exponentially with the number of story threads and typically weakens the story's impact. Hence, games with strong storylines are usually fairly linear. In fact, some genres suffer from *too* much scripting. Examples are flight simulators and strategy games that attempt to give the player an illusion of freedom beyond the bounds set by the scripting and consequently fail when the player does something unexpected that breaks the linearity.

A linear story does not have to be a disadvantage. The *Final Fantasy* series of games allows little room for variation from the main story—the only way to complete the game is to allow the story to carry you along, but they are still good games. Certain scripted events that are completely unalterable by the player push the story along—and the main challenge for the player is to fit in with these events, to become part of the story. Although this makes the story feel a bit unrealistic, it is nonetheless convincing enough to enthrall the player. We don't yet have the technology to create engaging and fully self-consistent nonlinear stories. We'll probably start to see real generic storytelling systems at about the same time we can say, "Good morning, computer," and expect it to understand and answer us!

Interactivity

For our purposes, *interactivity* is the way that the player sees, hears, and acts within the game's world—in short, the way the player plays the game. This covers a lot of diverse topics: graphics, sounds, user interface—everything that comes together to present the gaming experience. As a game designer, you will not create all these items yourself, but you will specify how the interactivity will work. It's up to the specialized members of your team to make it happen.

Interactivity has been a buzzword connected with computers and games for some time. It's often overused or used inappropriately. A few years back, some people thought that they could create a new kind of product by prefixing the word *interactive* to just about anything: interactive movies, interactive television, and so on. Don't let that turn you off: Interactivity is not just a buzzword in game design; it's the term used for making the game playable.

Poor interactive design ruins many products. For example, a badly designed user interface severely compromised *Warwind*, an otherwise promising *Warcraft* derivative. *Warwind* required players to negotiate an impossibly nested series of icon-based menus using only right-clicks. We're sure you can come up with your own list of similar games in which you've found critical design flaws such as these.

Interactivity (in the nonbuzz sense of the word) starts at the user interface. The user interface defines the "flavor" of your game. For example, the gameplay of *Mario 64* on the Nintendo 64 console is virtually identical to that of a 2D platform game such as the *Sonic the Hedgehog* games on the Sega Genesis (or Megadrive, to those of you in Europe). You run, jump, collect goodies, and avoid the baddies. The user interface—the buttons you push to play the game—made *Mario 64* stand out from its peers.

Taking this to the extreme, there is nothing in *Mario 64* that couldn't be implemented as a text-based game with type-in commands such as "run left," "jump right," and "take coin." Of course, it would be ridiculous to do this (even if the Nintendo 64 console had a keyboard)—the game would have sold close to zero copies. But the example shows that even though every other aspect of the game might be well designed (as it was in *Mario 64*), a good game requires a good user interface. Derivative games that arrived on the scene after the release of *Mario 64* didn't duplicate *Mario 64*'s excellent user interface and control system. Although they were similar in concept, they didn't reach that golden standard.

A game's graphics are also important parts of the interactive component, although designers disagree about how important they are. Unfortunately, the prevailing commercial pressure compels many designers to concentrate on appearances. In general, far too much time is spent on getting the look of a game right at the expense of tuning its gameplay. A lot of nostalgic gamers have called for a return to the values of the "golden age" of gaming—the 1980s, when hardware limitations forced developers to concentrate on gameplay. Nowadays, however, the capabilities of new machines require that more effort be spent on presentation. The more effort spent on presentation, the more the player expects to see in the next game, resulting in a vicious positive-feed-back cycle of player expectations boosting emphasis on presentation, which, in turn, boosts player expectations, and so on.

We've all had the experience of playing an action game really well, getting into a sort of "groove" in which your eyes and hands seem to meld with the machine. The best user interfaces allow you to immerse yourself in the game so deeply that you are no longer aware of the user interface at all—the infamous *Tetris Trance*. That's what well-designed interactivity does for a game.

Documenting the Design

As part of their job, game designers produce a series of documents to tell others about their game design. Exactly what documents they produce and what the documents are for varies from designer to designer and project to project—but they usually follow a common thread.

Why Do We Need Documents?

Beginning programmers, especially those who want to get into the game industry, often make the mistake of thinking up a game and then diving in and starting to program it right away. Programming is an immensely rewarding activity because you get to see the results of your work within seconds, and those programmers are seeking that reward as soon as possible. They can't wait to see at least some portion of their game up on the screen.

Back in the days when a single person designed and wrote an entire computer game, there wasn't really anything wrong with this. The programs were so small that even if the idea changed radically in the course of development, the programmer could modify the code within a few days. The games themselves were simple enough to be described in a page or two, so developers didn't feel any need for a formal design process.

In modern commercial game development, however, this kind of *ad hoc* approach is disastrous. Development teams often consist of 20 to 50 people. Millions of dollars are at stake. Critical release dates must be met to get the game on the shelves at a particular time—usually right before the Christmas shopping season. You can't build a game consisting of hundreds of megabytes of software, artwork, animations, movies, and sound files with a "let's try it and see" approach; a job of this scale calls for some sort of methodology. Different developers require different degrees of formality, but all serious game companies now insist on having some kind of written design before they start work.

As we said before, a key part of game design is transmitting the design to other members of the team. In practice, a lot of that communication takes place not through the documents themselves, but through team meetings, bull sessions, and conversations over lunch. That doesn't mean that there's no point in writing design documents, however. The documents record decisions made and agreed upon orally; they create a paper trail. More important, writing a document is a process of turning vague, unformed ideas into explicit plans. Even if no one reads it at all, an idea written down is a decision made, a conclusion reached. If a feature of a game is *not* described in writing, there's a good chance that it has been overlooked and that someone will have to make it up on the fly—or, worse, that each part of the team will work toward a different goal. It's far easier and cheaper to correct a design error before any code is written or artwork is created. Depending on the size of the game, wise developers will allot anywhere from one to six months for pure design work before starting on development, usually in combination with some throwaway prototype for testing out gameplay ideas.

Idea Versus Design Decision

Here's an idea: "Basilisks should protect their eggs."

Here's a design decision: "Whenever they have eggs in their nests, female basilisks will not move beyond visual range from the nest. If an enemy approaches within 50 meters of the nest, the basilisk will abandon any other activity and return to the nest to defend the eggs. She will not leave as long as a living enemy threatens the eggs, and will even defend the eggs to her own death."

See the difference? This is what creating design documents is about.

The Types of Design Documents

This section is a short introduction to the various types of documents a game designer might be asked to create. In chronological order, they are:

➤ High concept (2–4 pages)

➤ Game treatment (10–20 pages)

➤ Game script (50–200 pages)

The following sections briefly discuss these documents. Appendix A, "Sample Design Documents," contains samples (or pointers to samples) of each one and discusses their contents and formatting in much more detail.

The High Concept

Writing the *high-concept document* is the first step after scribbling down the initial idea. Its aim is to express the fundamental spirit of the game. Just as the purpose of a resumé is to get you a job interview, the purpose of a high-concept document is to get you a hearing from someone, a producer or publishing executive. It puts your key ideas down on paper in a bite-size chunk that he can read in a few minutes. Like a resumé, it should be short—not more than two to four pages long. The high-concept document should take, at most, a week to create, of which four days are spent thinking and one is spent writing.

If possible, try to begin the document with a single, punchy sentence—the high concept itself—that describes the game in a nutshell. Unfortunately, publishing executives have notoriously short attention spans and a great many calls on their time. You need to grab them as quickly as possible. The high concept for *Interstate '76* might have been, "Automotive vigilantes defend America's oil supply with heavily armed 1970s muscle cars in a high-octane, 3D action game."

The high-concept document covers these details:

➤ The premise of the game

➤ Its intended audience

➤ Its genre (if it belongs to one)

➤ Its unique selling points

➤ The target platform(s)

➤ The overall storyline

It must also describe the gameplay—what the player is supposed to do, what type of environment or scenarios he will encounter, and a general overview of the game flow. You might also want to include a description of any special technologies that will be used to build the game and any special hardware it might require.

If you plan to use the high-concept document as part of a sales pitch to a publisher, you might want to include a section containing short profiles of the development team members, with details of relevant past experience. You'll need to explain why they are the right team to build your game. You might or might not also want to include a budget estimate, depending on who will see it and what your relationship is with them.

The high-concept document need not be a sales tool; it's also worthwhile to write one for yourself, just to record an idea that you might want to work on in the future.

The Game Treatment

The purpose of the *game treatment* is to present the game in broad outline to someone who's already interested in it and wants to hear more about it. The treatment is designed both to satisfy initial curiosity and to stimulate real enthusiasm for the game. When you give a presentation about your game to a publisher, you should hand him the game treatment at the end so he'll have something to take away and look at, something that will float around his office and remind him of your game. Your goal at this point is to get funding of some sort, either to create a more thorough design or a prototype, or (preferably!) to develop the entire game.

You shouldn't try to cover all aspects of the game in rigorous detail. This isn't the game's design script. It can be a tool for selling the game to a potential publisher or investor; if you're assembling a team of developers, it's a good way to explain it to potential candidates. The treatment should fill in a few of the gaps and answer some of the questions left by the high-concept document. This is the place for mocked-up screen shots, background on the key characters, a brief description of the overall story arc, and anything else that's crucial to understanding what the game will look and feel like to play. You should also include an analysis of the competition and indicate the ways in which your game will be different—and better.

The initial treatment is still a simple document—almost a brochure that sums up the basic ideas in the game. A good way of picturing what to write in a treatment is to imagine that you are making a web site to help sell your game; then throw in some business and development details for good measure.

The Game Script

The *game script* (or "bible") is the largest and the last in this series. It's not a sales tool; it's much too large and comprehensive for that. It's intended to document design decisions, not to persuade anyone of anything. The game script is the definitive reference for all matters relating to the structure and organization of the game, what the player does and sees—the gameplay. It should also cover the game storyline, characters, user interface, and rules of play. It should answer all possible questions (except for technical ones) about the game.

The game script does not include the technical design. It documents the creative, conceptual, and functional aspects of the game, and it should include technical specifications where necessary. However, it does not address how the game is built or implemented in software. The technical design document, if there is one, is usually based on the game script and is written by the lead programmer or technical director for the game. Technical design is beyond the scope of this book. If you want to know more about technical design, read *Game Architecture and Design* (New Riders Publishing, 2004).

As a good rule of thumb, the game script should enable you to "play" the game. That is, it should specify the rules of play in enough detail that you could, in theory, play the game without the use of computer—maybe as a (complicated) board game or table-top role-playing game. This doesn't mean you should actually sit down and play it as such, but it should theoretically be possible to do so, just based on the game script document. Sitting down and playing paper versions of game ideas is a very inexpensive way of getting valuable feedback on your game design. For designers without huge teams and equally huge budgets, we heartily encourage paper-play testing.

Anatomy of a Game Designer

Many of the people working in game development aspire to be game designers. It's a highly sought-after position, and for good reason. Of all the jobs on the development team, game design is the one that offers the greatest scope for creative expression. In most cases, it is also the designer who gets the credit for a successful game and who gets the media attention. And if the designer's name becomes well enough known, fame can lead to fortune. Sid Meier, the designer of *Civilization* and many other titles, is now so famous that his name alone can increase the sales of a game. *Sid Meier's Alpha Centauri* (Firaxis Software) was actually designed by an ex-employee of Firaxis, Brian Reynolds, yet the publisher put Sid Meier's name in the title.

Like all crafts, game design requires both talent and skill. Talent is innate, but skill is learned. Skilled craftsmen know everything about the requirements of their job, the tools of their trade, the material with which they work, and the result they are trying to produce. For an effective game designer, a wide base of skills is required.

> *"One of the most difficult tasks people can perform, however much others may despise it, is the invention of good games...."*
>
> **—C.G. Jung**

Perhaps because the ideal skill set for an effective game designer is *so* extensive, diverse, and poorly defined, the requirements for the position of game designer are frequently underestimated. Many development groups treat game design as just one more task for a technical project lead, or as a communal process performed by the entire team. In practice, the skills required for effective game design are much more wide-ranging than you'll find in your average technical lead. This doesn't mean that a programmer can't become a game designer; it just means that you need far more than programming skills to be one.

The following sections discuss some of the skills that are most useful for the professional game designer. Don't be discouraged if you don't possess all of them. That does not mean that game design is not for you. It's a wish list—the characteristics we would like to see in a hypothetical (but certainly nonexistent!) "perfect designer."

Imagination

A game exists in an artificial universe, a make-believe place governed by make-believe rules. Imagination is essential to creating this place. Fortunately, this is not a problem for most people. Even if you feel that your imagination isn't your strongest point, it's possible to develop and improve it. Of course, this isn't a new concept. It's been around for hundreds of years, as can be seen in the following extract:

> *"Thou shouldst regard various walls which are covered with all manner of spots, or stone of different composition. If thou hast any capacity for discovery, thou mayest behold there things which resemble various landscapes decked with mountains, rivers, cliffs, trees, large plains, hills and valley of many sort. Thou canst also behold all manner of battles, life-like positions of strange, unfamiliar figures, expressions of face, costumes, and numberless things which thou mayest put into good and perfect form....*
>
> *Do not despise this opinion of mine when I counsel thee sometimes not to let it appear burdensome to thee to pause and look at the spots on walls, or the ashes in the fire, or the clouds, or mud, or other such places; thou wilt make very wonderful discoveries in them, if thou observest them rightly.... For through confused and undefined things the mind is awakened to new discoveries. But take heed, first, that thou understandest how to shape well all the members of the things that thou wishest to represent, for instance, the limbs of living beings, as also the parts of a landscape, namely the stones, trees, and the like."*
>
> **—Leonardo da Vinci**, *Treatise on Painting*

The imagination is like a muscle; with regular exercise, it grows stronger and easier to flex. Imagination comes in various forms:

➤ *Visual and auditory* imagination enables you to think of new buildings, trees, animals, creatures, clothing, and people—how they sound and their strange ways of speaking.

➤ *Dramatic imagination* is required for the development of good characters, plots, scenes, motivation, emotions, climaxes, and outcomes.

➤ *Conceptual imagination* is about relationships between ideas, their interactions and dependencies.

➤ *Lateral thinking* is the process of looking for alternative answers, taking an unexpected route to solve a problem.

A great example of a product that demonstrates all of these forms of imagination in abundance is Infogrames's *Outcast*.

Deduction isn't ordinarily thought of as imagination, but it can lead to new and unexpected ideas. *Deduction* is the process of reasoning from a creative decision you've made to its possible consequences. For example, if you design a preindustrial farming community with no beasts of burden, the size of the fields and the productivity of the agriculture must necessarily be limited. Horses and oxen can pull plows and carry loads much farther than humans can. The limited food supply, in turn, affects the population growth rate and so on. These details are arrived at by deduction.

Nor does imagination consist only of the ability to think of things that are completely new. It's also valuable to be able to look at an old idea and apply a new spin to it, to breathe new life into it with a fresh approach. Too many people in the game industry see something old and familiar and dismiss it. Instead they should think, "How can this be made better? How might this be more interesting?" J.K. Rowling does this brilliantly in her *Harry Potter* novels. They're full of imaginative twists on old ideas about witches and wizards. She still has witches flying on broomsticks, but she invented the sport of Quidditch, which is played while flying on them.

Technical Awareness

Technical awareness is a general understanding of how computer programs, particularly games, actually work. It isn't necessary to be a software engineer, but it is extremely valuable to have had a little experience programming, even if only in Blitz Basic (www.blitzbasic.com) or some other simple language. A computer game designer's delivery medium is the computer, so it behooves you to know how computers do what they do and also to have a general idea of what they're not good at doing. A designer with entirely unrealistic expectations of what a computer can do isn't going to get very far. For example, computers do not understand English well. If your game design requires that the machine be able to interpret complex sentences typed on the keyboard, your programmers are likely to throw things at you.

You must also have a basic knowledge of the technical capabilities of your target platform. At a minimum, you need to know whether you're designing a product for a home console, desktop computer, handheld platform, or more than one of these. Every feature that you specify must be possible on the machine that you're designing for. If in doubt, ask the programmers. Knowing the limitations imposed by the selected platform will result in an achievable design.

Analytical Competence

No game design is perfect from the start. Game design is a process of iterative refinement, which progresses from a rough draft to the finished *meisterwerk*. Consequently, you must be able to recognize the good and bad parts of a design for what they are. This requires a keen logical and analytical mind, and the ability to manipulate nebulous concepts with a high level of mental agility and critical analysis.

It is very difficult to effectively criticize your own work. You can be excessively hard on yourself and become convinced that all your work is worthless, or you can be blinded by familiarity and unable to analyze your own work in an unbiased fashion. Inexperienced designers often err in both directions, swinging wildly from one to the other.

There is no easy solution to these problems. Good self-analysis skills come with practice. As a reality check, you can try peer reviews (which are always a good idea anyway). See what your colleagues and co-workers think of your design. Try to choose people who are likely to give you an unbiased opinion. Friends and family are usually not good choices. They will be either too easy on you—after all, they are close to you personally—or too hard on you because they don't want to be seen as biased and, consequently, overcompensate.

A specific example of when analytical skills are particularly useful is in detecting dominant (that is, unbeatable or nearly unbeatable) strategies at the design phase and weeding them out before they get into the code, as in the infamous *Red Alert* "tank rush." The tank effectiveness in *Red Alert* was so out of balance that an experienced player could dedicate all production to cranking out a few tanks and then immediately storm the opposition base before the enemy had a chance to get a production line set up.

Mathematical Competence

Designers must have basic math skills (particularly statistical math skills) because balancing a game is largely a matter of math and can be a difficult task. In the case of a real-time strategy game or a war game, the apparently simple problem of ensuring that there are no dominant strategies or fighting units to unbalance the game is actually quite math-intensive.

That's not to say that you need a Ph.D. in mathematics—you're not going to be deriving complex equations from scratch. The only thing you'll need above basic math is some knowledge of statistical methods. Even so, in some cases, the math can be handled computationally. It's entirely possible that you can handle the math requirement simply by being good with a spreadsheet program such as Microsoft Excel.

Aesthetic Competence

Although you need not be an artist, you should have a general aesthetic competence and some sense of style. Far too many games are visual clones of one another, depending on stereotypes and clichés rather than real imagination. It's up to you (along with your lead artist) to set the visual tone of the game and to create a consistent, harmonious look.

Suppose you're designing a clever and calculating female assassin with nerves of steel. Many designers would clothe her in skin-tight black leather and give her a big, shiny automatic pistol; in other words, they'd opt for the stereotype, the easy way out. A slightly more imaginative designer might give her a miniskirt and a crossbow—still male-fantasy material, but marginally more interesting. A really good designer would realize that an assassin needs to blend in to her surroundings, to look like anybody else, yet still be visually identifiable to the player. He would think about her personality and create a unique visual style for her that is distinctive yet unobtrusive. Lara Croft is a good example of this kind of thing. Despite her ludicrous proportions, she's dressed appropriately but quite identifiably for her role as an explorer: shorts, tank top, hiking boots. More important, her shirt is a particular color that nobody else in the *Tomb Raider* games wears, which makes her stand out on the screen. If you're seeing that color, you're seeing Lara.

We encourage you to expand your aesthetic horizons as much as you can. Learn a little about the fundamentals of art: the principles of composition, and which colors coordinate and which clash. Check out classic art books and visit art museums. Find out about famous art movements—Art Nouveau, Surrealism, Impressionism—and how they changed the way we see things. Watch movies that are famous for their visual style, such as *Metropolis*. Then move on to the more practical arts: architecture, interior decoration, industrial design. All these things can contribute to the look of your game. The more aesthetic experience you have, the more likely you are to produce an artistically innovative product.

General Knowledge

Some of the best game designers tend to be ex-programmers or people with at least some formal scientific training—as long as they have broadened their sphere of knowledge outside of their narrow field of specialist expertise. A base level of general knowledge is valuable for a game designer, as is the ability to research what you might not know. It helps to be well-versed in mathematics, logic, history, literature, art, science, and current affairs. The more source material a game designer can assimilate, the better the final game design will be.

Make sure you watch a lot of movies and documentaries (The History Channel and The Discovery Channel are excellent resources). Read books, too, both for direct research and background material. The encyclopedia is a good place to start for any given subject. The information it contains might be too general for any detailed design, but it will provide a launching point. From there, you can increase your knowledge of a particular area by investing in other, more specialized books. They don't have to be particularly advanced—unless you're aiming for something such as a historically accurate simulation, you can often use books aimed at children to bone up on the background. After all, you don't want to risk alienating your audience. A game that is too true-to-life (and, hence, is likely to require specialist knowledge) will disappoint its players.

Let's take an example: Most people's idea of pirates comes from swashbuckling Errol Flynn movies, J.M. Barrie's (or even Disney's) *Peter Pan*, and the Muppets' *Treasure Island*.

If you're designing a game based on piracy on the high seas, then exact historical detail isn't going to be what they expect—a game based on venereal disease, scurvy, maggot-infested food that has to be eaten in the dark so the crew can't see what they're eating, starvation, brutality, and the "consequences" of dark and lonely nights on a female-free boat won't make a particularly interesting (or even tasteful) game.

On the other hand, if you have a game design featuring colorful, eye-patch wearing, wooden-legged pirates, gold, running deck battles, the Black Spot, the Jolly Roger, and buried doubloons secreted away on remote desert islands, then you probably have the seed of an entertaining game. Though, of course, if you'd stuck to the historically accurate literature, you wouldn't use the Jolly Roger (pure mythology) or the Black Spot (invented by Robert Louis Stevenson, author of *Treasure Island*).

Books aren't the only source of knowledge, of course. A game designer's first research stop is often the Internet, with its wealth of free information. It takes only a small amount of searching using a quality search engine, such as `www.google.com`, to unearth some useful information.

Writing Skills

The professional game designer *must* have good writing skills. This means being clear, concise, accurate, unambiguous, and, above all, readable. Apart from having to write several detailed documents for each design, you might be expected to produce the story narrative or dialogue—especially if the budget won't stretch to a scriptwriter.

Writing comes in several forms, and we briefly discuss some of these here. (We go into more detail in Chapter 4, "Storytelling and Narrative," and the appendixes.)

➤ *Technical writing* is the process of documenting the design in preparation for development. All possible questions on the game have to be answered unambiguously and precisely. For example, if a farm with one peasant produces one unit of food per week, does a farm with five peasants produce five units, or do the additional peasants consume additional food? Is the peasants' own food factored in? What is the maximum number of peasants that can work on a given farm? If all the peasants are killed in a raid, what happens to the farm? If it is not immediately destroyed, can the empty buildings be reoccupied by new peasants? How do farms get built anyway? Where do peasants come from anyway? At what rate?

Does the player have to manage the farming process, or do the peasants just get on with it? Can peasants fight? And so on and so on.

➤ *Fiction writing* (narrative) is useful for the manual, background material; character descriptions; introductory, transitional, and finale material; as well as other bodies of text, such as mission briefings.

➤ *Dialogue writing* (drama) is needed for audio voiceovers and cinematic material. Unfortunately, in most games the dialogue is even cornier than 1970s television shows, and the acting is as bad or worse. Try to avoid clichés, and use grammar and vocabulary that match each character's personality. If you have an ear for regional dialects, it can add real variety to your game, but, again, avoid stereotypes such as "dumb rednecks" or "brassy New Yorkers." The game *Starcraft* made excellent use of the subtle variety of southern American dialects, including proud aristocrats, gruff old generals, obnoxious bikers, and cheerful mechanics.

The greatest game design acumen in the world will be useless to you unless you can effectively communicate your ideas. As a designer, you will often need to evangelize your design at several different levels. In the professional setting, you will initially need to present your design to a publisher. Following that, you need to obtain buy-in from the team that will develop the game. This can be done in person or in writing, but the result is the same. You will need to be able to transmit your enthusiasm for the game as well as go into mind-boggling detail of its finer points to allow the development team to be able to create a game from your vision.

Drawing Skills

Some skill at basic drawing and sketching is highly valuable, although not absolutely required for a designer if you have a concept artist to work with. The saying "A picture is worth a thousand words" is never more true than when you are trying to impart a game idea. The vast majority of computer games rely heavily on visual content, and drawings are essential when pitching a product to a third party. Game-publishing executives will be interested in a hot concept, a hot market, or a hot license, but only pictures get them excited. The images are the hook on which the executives will hang everything else that they hear. Otherwise, you can talk about concepts forever and they won't remember a thing when you leave the room because they don't have a visual hook to hang it on. The images will remain in their memories long after they forget the details.

The Ability to Compromise

Probably the most important skill for a professional game designer is the ability to compromise on details and integrate a variety of opinions while preserving a consistent, holistic vision of the game. In an ideal world, we would be able to design whatever suited us and never have to worry about the demands of a publisher or the interests of the customers. Unfortunately, these external needs and interests do have to be considered, and, more often than not, the game designer is constrained by genre or license.

Different people on the development team and at the publishing company will have concerns about their own areas of expertise (programming, art, music, and so on), and their opinions will pull and push the design in different directions. As the designer, it's tempting to seek sole ownership of the vision, to argue that things must be exactly as you imagined them and to ignore other considerations. After all, there are plenty of other voices in your company advancing points of view about the other areas. But you must resist the temptation to do that, for two reasons:

➤ First, you must allow your team some ownership of the vision as well, or its members won't have any motivation or enthusiasm for the project. No one builds computer games solely for the money; we're all here so that we can contribute creatively.

➤ Second, a designer who gets a reputation as a visionary but who can't deliver a buildable, marketable game doesn't stay employed for long. It's your job to deliver an integrated design.

In many cases, you'll be given a brief that limits you to designing a genre clone or a heavily restricted licensed property. Being able to work within these limits to the satisfaction of the customer, whether your customer is the publisher, license holder, or end user, is essential. Unless you are one of the famous game designers who can guarantee success with your name alone, you are unlikely to be given a completely free rein. You may have designed the best text adventure game since *Colossal Cave*, but if the style of game is out of favor with the public, you're probably not going to get your game made—let alone published.

Putting It Together

This chapter puts forward the view that game design is not an arcane art, but rather a craft, just like any other, that can be learned with application.

Games are not works of art created by a mysterious, hit-or-miss process. Instead, they are a discrete set of rules and a presentation layer for those rules. We believe that by examining and documenting the fundamental similarities and differences between games of all types—computer and board, mental and physical—we can identify a valuable set of common elements that can be used to understand and, consequently, improve how great games are constructed.

As we said before, no one person is likely to have all these skills. We are talking about a hypothetical ideal game designer—the Superman of game design. It's no coincidence, however, that the best professional game designers possess a high degree of competence in many of these skills. They weren't born with them; they educated themselves and worked to develop them. We encourage you to do the same.

Chapter 2

Game Concepts

This chapter addresses the earliest stage of game design: getting and refining an idea for a game. Your goal at this point should be to write the high-concept document that we described in Chapter 1, "What Is Game Design?." To do this, you don't have to have all the details worked out yet. But you do need a clear understanding of what your game is about, and you must answer certain essential questions. When you've answered those questions to your satisfaction and have written down the answers, you have turned your idea into a *game concept*. At the end of this chapter, we've included a worksheet to help you out.

Getting an Idea

Game ideas come from almost anywhere, but they don't walk up and introduce themselves. You can't sit around and wait for inspiration to strike. Creativity is an active, not a passive, process. You have to put yourself in an inquisitive frame of mind and then go out and look for game ideas. Look everywhere. Some of the most mundane things could be hiding a game idea. Even delivering newspapers provided the basis for a successful arcade game, *Paperboy*, though developers spiced up the job by letting the player break windows with the newspapers and making him dodge cars on his bicycle.

One idea isn't enough. It's a common misconception that a brilliant game idea will make you a fortune. In fact, this occurs extremely rarely. You might think you have the game idea of the century, but concentrating on it without bothering to think about other game ideas is a little like pinning all your hopes on a single lottery ticket and not bothering to get up for work while you wait to see if your numbers come up. Unlike lottery tickets, ideas are free, so think about new ones constantly. Make a note of them and go on. If one seems especially promising to you, then you can start to expand and refine it, but don't let that prevent you from thinking about other games as well. When thinking up game ideas, more is always better.

Dreaming the Dream

Many game ideas begin as dreams. Not real dreams, but daydreams, things you think about when you're staring out the window or watching the clouds on a summer afternoon—these are the thoughts that you have when you let your mind roam free.

Computers can make dreams real. This is the unique characteristic of interactive entertainment that sets it apart from all other forms. Interactive entertainment can take you away to a wonderful place and there let you do an amazing thing. Books and movies can't do that. They can take you away to a wonderful place, but they can't let you do an amazing thing. Books and movies can create fantastic worlds and show them to you, but they can't let you be a part of them. Computer games create worlds, and they can let you live inside of them as well.

A lot of computer games are light entertainment, designed to while away a few minutes with a puzzle or a simple challenge. But larger, richer games begin with a dream. If you've ever thought to yourself, "I wish I could…" or "Imagine what it would be like to…," then you've taken the first step on the road to creating a computer game. The computer has the power to simulate reality (with varying degrees of accuracy), but, more important, it has the power to simulate dreams. Computers can create almost any sort of experience you can imagine visually, even experiences that are physically impossible in the real world. The design of a computer game begins with the question, "What dream am I going to fulfill?".

Perhaps it's a dream of exploring a dungeon infested with monsters. Perhaps it's a dream of coaching a football team. Perhaps it's a dream of being a fashion designer. But before you do anything else, you must dream the dream. Understand it. Feel it. Know who else dreams it and why.

Game Ideas from Other Media

Books, movies, television, and other entertainment media are a great source of inspiration for game ideas. The game *Interstate '76* (see Figure 2.1) was inspired by 1970s cop shows. Movies such as the James Bond series often inspire games. Any story containing an exciting action with something important at stake can form the kernel of a game. Think over the books you've read and the movies you've seen, and ask yourself whether any of the scenes in them could serve as the basis for a game.

Figure 2.1   *Interstate '76* was a great game inspired by another medium.

You can't, of course, go stealing other people's intellectual property. Even if the Pirates of the Caribbean ride at Disneyland seems like the basis for a great game, you can't go ahead and make it without Disney's approval. But you can certainly make a light-hearted game about pirates—as LucasArts did with its *Monkey Island* series.

You should also look beyond the usual science fiction and fantasy genres and beyond the usual sources. How about poetry? Beowulf's epic battle with the monster Grendel and then his even more terrible battle with Grendel's mother in a cave at the bottom of a lake sounds like the basis for a game. "The Charge of the Light Brigade" might make you wonder about cavalry tactics. What are the advantages and disadvantages? Would a game based on cavalry warfare be interesting to anyone? It's worth thinking about. The smash-hit game *The Sims* was partly inspired by a nonfiction book called *A Pattern Language*, which is about the way people's lives are affected by the design of their houses.

Game ideas can crop up in all sorts of unlikely places. Just as great scientists look at even the most common things in the world and ask how they work, great game designers are always looking at the world and wondering if it can be made into a game. The trick is to develop a game designer's instincts, to look for the fun and challenge even in things that don't sound like games at all.

Game Ideas from Other Games

A great many people who play computer games want to design them as well. Something about playing games stirs up people's creative juices. When you play a lot of games, you develop a sense of how they work and what their good and bad points are. Playing games is a valuable experience for a game designer. It gives insight and lets you compare and contrast the features of different games.

Sometimes we get game ideas through frustration. Most of us have had the experience, at one time or another, of playing a game that wasn't quite right somehow. The user interface was awkward, the game was too difficult, or the payoff was boring. We think, "If I had designed this game, I would have…." We have in our minds an imaginary ideal game, the one that would fix all those problems and the one that we would make if we had the chance.

To learn from other games, you have to pay attention as you play. Don't just play them for fun; look at them seriously and think about how they work. Take notes especially of things that you like or don't like and of features that seem to work particularly well or particularly badly. How do resources flow into the game? How do they flow out? How much is luck, and how much is skill?

As creative people, our instinct is to devise totally new kinds of games that have never before been seen. Unfortunately, publishers want games that they are sure they can sell, and that usually means variants on existing genres, perhaps with a new twist that they can use in marketing. This is why we keep seeing sequels and thinly disguised copies of earlier games. As designers, we have to learn to balance the tension between our own desire to innovate and the publisher's need for the comfortably familiar. Leonardo da Vinci warned against persistent imitation, however, in his *Treatise on Painting*:

"The painter will produce pictures of little merit if he takes the work of others as his standard; but if he will apply himself to learn from the objects of nature he will produce good results. This we see was the case with the painters who came after the Romans, for they continually imitated each other, and from age to age their art steadily declined... It is safer to go directly to the works of nature than to those which have been imitated from her originals, with great deterioration and thereby to acquire a bad method, for he who has access to the fountain does not go to the water pot."

There is a downside to deriving game ideas from other games. It tends to result in games that look or work alike. It's an evolutionary, not a revolutionary, approach. Deriving game ideas from other games is an excellent way to learn about games and gameplay, but if pursued exclusively, it produces similarity and, ultimately, mediocrity. The greatest games break new ground. They're unlike anything seen on the store shelves before. To achieve that, you have to dream.

From Dream to Game

A dream or an idea alone is only a start; it is not enough to make a game. A dream is a fantasy that you have by yourself. You can make computer games purely for yourself if you like, but most of us don't have the money to do that. A computer game is something that you make for someone else. You'll also discover after you've built a few games that playing a game that you worked on is a very different experience from playing a game that someone else has created. When you know what's on the inside and how it works, some of the fantasy is lost. Just as actors often don't watch their own movies, some game developers don't play their own games. For one thing, of course, if it's a single-player game, they already know how to beat it. But the experience, the dream, isn't quite the same when it's a game you built yourself. In your heart, you know it's an artificial simulation.

The chief purpose of a computer game is to entertain someone else. This means that you and your development team are the performers, the people who create the entertainment. An essential part of your job is communication, transmitting your dream to your audience, the players. If the game is in a well-known genre and setting (for example, a World War II flight simulator), you can be pretty certain that a number of people already share your dream. But if your game is in a new setting (a futuristic city of your imagination, for example)—and especially if it's in a new genre—you have to be very careful and thorough in communicating your dream to others. Some of the very first questions a publishing executive is going to ask you are "Why would anyone want to play this game?" and "What's going to make someone buy this game instead of another?".

But what does it mean to entertain someone? Many people think entertainment is synonymous with having fun, but even that isn't completely straightforward. People have fun in all kinds of ways. Some of those ways involve very hard work, such as gardening or building a new deck. Some of them involve frustration, such as solving a puzzle. Some, such as athletic competitions, even involve pain. One person's entertainment is another person's insufferable boredom. In building a computer game that entertains, it's important to understand *how* it entertains. And to do that, you have to know what a game really is.

The Elements of a Game

In this section, we give a formal definition of a game and describe the elements that comprise one. Remember that we're talking about any kind of game, computerized or not. We continue to use these terms throughout the book.

Games, Toys, and Puzzles

A *game* is a form of participatory, or interactive, entertainment. Watching television, reading, and going to the theater are all forms of passive entertainment. In those media, the entertainment is presented *to* you, and you're not expected to participate. In some plays, the audience itself has a role, but even then the actors are in control. The content of the entertainment is the drama, and the way you perceive it is by watching it. This mode is fundamentally passive: They act, you watch.

A game is a much more complicated thing. When people play a game, they are being entertained by actively participating. Although we use the term *interactive entertainment* to refer to computer and video games, any game is interactive if you're taking part in it, whether it's softball or postal chess. Active forms of entertainment are slowly gaining ground over passive forms; people are starting to play online role-playing games instead of watching TV. People love the feeling of involvement and empowerment that gaming gives.

A game takes place in an artificial universe that is governed by *rules*. The rules define the *actions* or *moves* that the players may make in the game, and also the actions that they may not make. In a computer game, most of these rules are hidden. Because you can interact with the game only through the machine's input devices, and the machine can ignore inappropriate inputs, you don't have to be told the rules explicitly. Computer games generally allow you to try anything you want; you can presume that anything you can do, you are allowed to do.

When you're playing a game, especially board games and computer games, you're often playing a role of some sort. Defining the player's role is a key part of game design, and we'll discuss it in more detail later.

Other kinds of interactive entertainment are not games. A *toy* is an object that you play with without rules. You can play a game with a toy if you make up some rules to play by, but ordinarily a toy does not come with rules.

Unlike a toy, a *puzzle* does have one definite rule: It has a correct solution that you are trying to find. Puzzles are normally worked by one person. Typically, they require problem-solving skills and the ability to think ahead, but they don't involve any role-playing and are not set in an artificial universe.

Challenges, Gameplay, and the Victory Condition

The rules also define the obstacles, or *challenges*, that the players must overcome to win the game. The challenges, together with the actions the players can take to meet them, make up the *gameplay*. Defining and tuning the gameplay is the largest and most difficult task in designing a game; this is discussed extensively in Chapter 7, "Gameplay."

Included with the rules of most (but not all) games is a special rule that defines the *victory condition*: a state of affairs in which one or more players are said to be the winner. Usually, the first player to achieve the victory condition is the winner and the others are the losers. These kinds of games are said to be *competitive*—that is, the players are trying to achieve the victory condition for themselves while preventing the others from doing so. Some games define the rules in such a way that all players must work together to achieve the victory condition; these are called *cooperative* games. If groups of players work together against other groups of players, the game is a *team* game. Most noncomputerized games—and many computerized ones as well— are *multi-player* games; if a game is played by one player alone, it is a *single-player* or *solitaire* game. Many video games sold at retail offer several different play modes: single-player, two-player competitive, two-player cooperative, and so on. Sports games are particularly well suited to these kinds of variations.

In addition to a victory condition, many games have one or more *loss conditions*. Sometimes the loss condition is implicit: If you aren't the first to achieve the victory condition, you lose. But in others, the loss conditions are explicit: Your character has died, for example, or you have run out of some vital resource.

Some computer games have no victory condition. These are often construction and management simulations such as *Sim City*. Rather than trying to "win" by achieving the victory condition, you can set your own goals for what you're trying to achieve. Or, you can just play around with the game without trying to achieve anything in particular. (*Sim City* also has some scenarios with victory conditions.) These kinds of games are sometimes referred to as *software toys*.

Many single-player arcade games, such as *Tetris*, are peculiar in that they have no victory condition. They are effectively unwinnable; the game just gets harder and harder until eventually you must lose. You do, however, get a score based on your ability, and your goal is to be listed among the top players. In effect, the victory condition is to do better than other people who play the game, but you can never actually win the game itself.

Setting, Interaction Model, and Perspective

A game also takes place in a *setting* or world. A sport such as football, for example, takes place on a field with defined boundaries. A board game takes place on and around the board. Even simple games with cards, dice, or dominoes take place on a tabletop, and the players implicitly agree that the table is the only legitimate playing surface. Because a computer screen has the capacity to display anything, a computer game can take place in any setting imaginable. We talk more about game settings and worlds in Chapter 3, "Game Settings and Worlds." For now, it's enough to know that a game's setting is part of its concept.

The way that the player interacts with the game world—takes actions to overcome the challenge—is called the game's *interaction model*. There are many different interaction models; some games have different models at different points in the game or allow the player to choose from a selection of models.

Two interaction models are particularly common in computer gaming. If the player plays in the game world by controlling a single character or piece that represents him, and if that character exists in a single place and can influence only the local area around him, that character is called his *avatar*. In Nintendo's *Mario* games, Mario is the player's avatar. On the other hand, if the player has the ability to view different parts of the game world, taking actions in many different places, the player is said to be *omnipresent* (even if parts of the world are hidden from him at times). This applies even if the player can act only by directing characters or units that belong to him; if he has the power to give directions to all of them independently, he is omnipresent. A good example of this kind of game is chess. The player can move any of his own pieces on the board, no matter where they are.

Perspective describes how the player actually sees the world on the screen. In war games, players usually have an aerial perspective above the battlefield. If the view is from directly above, like looking at a map, this is called a *top-down* perspective. Most old war games, as well as the original *Sim City*, used this perspective. Beginning with *Populous*, however, many aerial-perspective games adopted a more dramatic viewpoint. In this the view is at a 30- or 45-degree angle from the vertical, looking slightly across the landscape and not just straight down. The landscape is also rotated 45 degrees with respect to the bottom of the screen, so the player is always looking at one corner of rectangular objects such as buildings. This is called an *isometric* perspective. This viewpoint makes the player feel closer and more involved with events than the top-down perspective. It has the disadvantage that, if it can be rotated in 90-degree steps, the art team has to draw four different versions of everything that can appear on the ground, from each of the four angles.

Many games offer different perspectives or camera angles that the user can change. Not all camera angles suit all games; perspectives that are visually stunning to watch from can turn out to be impractical during actual gameplay. *Madden NFL Football*, for example, normally uses a perspective in which the camera is above and behind the ball carrier, looking somewhat downfield toward the goal. But it also provides a sideline camera, showing the field as it would appear to someone sitting in the stands. Although this is a very familiar perspective and is great for taking screenshots that look like real football on television, the game is quite difficult to play from this angle.

You're probably familiar with many common perspectives: *first person*, in which you look through the eyes of your avatar (most commonly found in first-person shooters such as *Half-Life*); *third person*, in which you follow behind your avatar in a three-dimensional world (*Tomb Raider* is one of the best-known examples); and *side-scrolling*, commonly seen in older video games such as *Sonic the Hedgehog*. With the introduction of 3D display engines, games can use any number of perspectives at no additional cost in art development time.

The Player's Role

When you're playing a game, especially board games and computer games, you're often playing a *role* of some sort. In *Monopoly,* you're playing a real estate tycoon. In *Goldeneye,* you're playing James Bond. Defining the player's *role* in the game world is a key part of defining your game's concept. If the player's role is difficult to describe, it might be difficult for the player to grasp as well, and it might indicate that there is a conceptual problem with the game. This doesn't mean that the role always has to be simple. In *Madden NFL Football,* for example, the player can be either a football player, a coach, or both. As the coach, he calls the plays that his team will run and makes player substitutions. As a player, he takes the snap, passes the ball, and runs with it. In fact, he's not controlling any single player; he's controlling whichever one happens to be in possession of the ball. On defense, he can switch from player to player to control whichever one has the best chance of tackling the ball carrier.

This works very well in a football game, where these roles, although different from one another in real life, are well understood by the game's audience and are exactly the ones they want to perform. But if a game takes place in a less familiar world with less familiar objectives, it's important for the roles to be clear. If the player's role changes from time to time—especially involuntarily—it's essential that the player know why it changed and be able to adapt quickly to the new circumstances.

The player's role also helps the player to understand what he's trying to achieve and what rules he's playing by. In Sierra Online's *Police Quest* series, for example, the player takes on the role of a real police officer. Real police officers can't just shoot anything that moves; they have to obey strict rules about when and how to use their guns. Tactical combat simulations such as *Rainbow Six* and *Counter-Strike* also implement these sorts of rules, placing the player in the shoes of a real Special Forces soldier. By telling the player what role he'll be playing, the player knows that his actions will have to be more cautious than in the usual frenetic shooter.

Modes and Structure

Some games, such as checkers, work the same way from beginning to end. The player is always trying to accomplish the same thing in the same way. Other games have distinct *modes,* in which the nature of the gameplay changes significantly from one mode to the next. War games, for example, might have a strategic mode in which you plan which battles you intend to fight and a tactical mode in which you actually fight the battles. Many things often change when the game switches modes: the interaction model, the perspective, the player's role, and some of the challenges.

In addition, many games have noninteractive modes that are interspersed with the interactive ones. War games, again, often have a briefing that occurs before the battle to explain to you what resources you have and what your objectives are, and a debriefing that occurs afterward to summarize what happened and tell you whether you won or lost.

The relationships between the modes and the rules determining when and why the game switches among them collectively form the *structure* of the game. The best way to document the structure of a game is with a *flowchart*, a series of boxes representing the modes with arrows from one to the next showing how the transitions occur. At the concept stage, this doesn't have to be detailed, but if you're designing a game with multiple modes, you should have at least a general idea of what modes you want and why.

Realism

When a game depicts a world, even an imaginary one, in such a way that the principles of real-world logic and common sense apply, we say that the game is *realistic*. *Microsoft Flight Simulator*, which tries to model accurately the behavior of real aircraft, is a good example. On the other hand, when a game has quite arbitrary rules and you cannot count on real-world common sense, as in *Pac-Man*, for example, we say that the game is *abstract*. We discuss realism in more detail in Chapter 3.

At the concept stage, you don't have to decide exactly how realistic your game is going to be. For example, in designing a war game, you might defer decisions about whether to allow friendly fire to harm your own troops. In real life, the military goes to great lengths to prevent friendly fire incidents, but tragically, they still do happen. In a war game, in which the player rarely has precise control over how each weapon is aimed, it might be placing too much of a burden on the player to handle the friendly fire problem. On the other hand, this might be an issue that you want to focus on. Play-testing can tell you whether it's manageable, but an experienced designer can usually predict gameplay problems before the game gets that far. At the concept stage, it's not that important to know whether your simulation will include the effects of friendly fire. It is useful, however, to have a general idea of whether your game is going to be abstract or realistic.

A Word About Story

Computer games lie in a peculiar middle ground between the purely passive, narrative media such as film and television and active, non-narrative games such as poker or dominoes. Some computer games, such as *Tetris*, have no narrative; others, such as the *Gabriel Knight* series, have a great deal. Some games tell linear, noninteractive stories interspersed with interactive episodes, others implement storylines that branch as the player makes decisions, and still others put their players in a setting where storylike adventures can take place and let them have at it. The relationship between the game and the story has been debated many times in the game industry.

It is our contention that, whether a game contains a great deal of narrative content or none at all, the player must ultimately live his own story through playing the game. The fundamental principle of computer gaming, its raison d'être, is interactivity: providing the player with something entertaining to *do*. It is not the business of the game designer to tell stories, but to create worlds in which stories take place around an active player.

A common error made by beginning game designers is to concern themselves with the story too early in the design process. The first concern of the designer is not "What am I going to show or tell my player?" but "What is my player going to do?". When conceptualizing your game, you don't have to know exactly what narrative content you want to include in your game. If you are working on it now, you are focusing your attention in the wrong place. All you need to know is whether you want a story and, if so, what its overall direction will be. You should be able to summarize it in a sentence or two, for example: "Jack Jones, leader of a secret DEA task force, will conduct a series of raids against the drug barons, ending in an apocalyptic battle in the cocaine fields of Colombia. Along the way, some of the people he encounters will not be quite what they seem." Remember that errors in the storyline are much easier to correct than errors in the gameplay, and gamers will forgive them more easily as well. Make sure you understand your game first; then build your story into it.

We discuss storytelling and narrative at length in Chapter 4, "Storytelling and Narrative."

Understanding Your Audience

In the previous section, we defined the elements of a game. But games don't exist in a vacuum; they're intended to be played by people. A common misconception among game designers is that all players enjoy the same things that the designer enjoys, so the designer only has to examine his own experience to know how to make a game entertaining. This is dangerous hubris. The reason for making a computer game is to entertain an audience. You have to think about who those people are and what they like.

Generalities are always risky, and misguided assumptions about players can result in games that no one will buy. Still, unless the game you're designing has been commissioned by a single individual, you are making it for a class of people, not for one person, and that class will be defined by common characteristics. Another important question a publisher will ask you is "Who will buy this game?". Think carefully about the answer. What things do they have in common? What things set them apart from other gamers? What challenges do they enjoy? More important, what challenges do they *not* enjoy? What interests them, bores them, frustrates them, excites them, frightens them, and offends them? Answer these questions, and keep the answers close at hand as you design your game.

Core Versus Casual

In our opinion, the most significant distinction among player types is not between console-game players and computer-game players, not between men and women, and not even between children and adults. The most significant distinction is between *core* gamers and *casual* gamers.

Core gamers play a lot of games. Games are more than light entertainment to them; they're a hobby that demands time and money. Core gamers subscribe to game magazines, chat on game bulletin boards, and build fan web sites about their favorite games. Above all, core gamers play for the exhilaration of defeating the game. They tolerate frustration well because of the charge they get out of finally winning. The greater the obstacle, the greater the sense of achievement. Core gamers thrive on competition. They don't like games that are easy; they like games that are challenging.

By comparison, *casual gamers* play for the sheer enjoyment of playing the game. If the game stops being enjoyable or becomes frustrating, the casual gamer will stop playing. For the casual gamer, playing a game must be entertaining, whether it's competitive or not. A casual gamer is simply not willing to spend hours learning complex controls or getting killed again and again until he finds the one weak point in an otherwise invincible enemy. To design a game for casual gamers, you have to challenge their minds at least as much as their motor skills.

In reality, of course, there are as many types of gamer as there are gamers; everyone has their own reasons for playing computer games. But the casual/core distinction is a very powerful one. If you design a game specifically for one group, you almost certainly won't have a lot of sales to the other group. A few very well-designed games manage to appeal to both: *Goldeneye*, for example, could be played happily by both core and casual gamers. Core gamers could set the game at the highest difficulty level and drive themselves crazy trying to cut 15 seconds off the last time it took to play a mission. Casual gamers could set the game at the easiest level and blast away, enjoying the game's smooth controls and visual detail.

Even at the concept level, you must have some understanding of who will play your game and what they will enjoy about it. A game concept is not complete without a statement describing its intended audience.

The Genres of Interactive Entertainment

As we said in the introduction, each genre of interactive entertainment displays a common pattern of challenges. In later chapters, we'll look at these genres in detail, examining each to see what can be learned from it:

> ► *Action games* normally include physical challenges, puzzles, races, and a variety of conflict challenges, mostly at the personal level. They can also contain simple economic challenges, usually involving collecting objects. They seldom include strategic or conceptual challenges.

> ► *Strategy games* tend to include strategic (naturally), tactical, and logistical challenges, in addition to the occasional economic ones. Once in a while, they have a personal conflict challenge thrown in for spice, but this often annoys strategically minded players.

> ➤ Most *role-playing games* involve tactical, logistical, and exploration challenges. They also include economic challenges because the games usually involve collecting loot and trading it in for better weapons. They sometimes include puzzles and conceptual challenges, but rarely physical ones.

> ➤ *Real-world simulations* include sports games and vehicle simulations, including military vehicles. They involve mostly physical and tactical challenges, but not exploration, economic, or conceptual ones.

> ➤ *Construction and management games* such as *Roller Coaster Tycoon* are primarily about economic and conceptual challenges. Only rarely do they involve conflict or exploration, and they almost never include physical challenges.

> ➤ *Adventure games* are chiefly about exploration and puzzle-solving. They sometimes contain conceptual challenges as well. These may include a physical challenge also, but only rarely.

> ➤ *Puzzle games* tend to be variations on a theme of some kind. *Sokoban* is about moving blocks around in a constricted space; *The Incredible Machine* is about building Rube Goldberg contraptions to accomplish particular tasks. The challenges are almost entirely logical, although occasionally there's time pressure or an action element.

Some games cross genres for some reason, combining elements that are not typically found together. The adventure game *Heart of China,* for example, included a small 3D tank simulator at one point. This is occasionally a design compromise between two people on the team who want the game to go in different directions. It's also sometimes an effort to appeal to a larger audience by including elements that both will like.

Although it can add flavor and interest to a game, crossing genres is a risky move. Rather than appealing to two groups, you might end up appealing to neither. Many players (and game reviewers) prefer particular genres and don't want to be confronted by challenges of a kind that they normally avoid. The wholesale buyers, who are planning to purchase a certain number of games from each genre for their stores, might not know which pigeonhole to put the game into and might shy away from it entirely.

However, you should not allow these genre descriptions to circumscribe your creativity—especially at the concept stage. If you have a wholly new, never-before-seen type of game in mind, design it as you see it in your vision; don't try to shoehorn it into a genre for the wrong reason. A game needs to be true to itself. But don't mix up genres purely for its own sake. A game should cross genres only if it genuinely needs to as part of the gameplay. A flight simulator with a logic puzzle in the middle of it, just to be different from other flight simulators, will only annoy flight sim fans.

The Types of Game Machines

Most game concepts should be fairly independent of the target platform. If you start thinking too early about the machine and its capabilities, you run the risk of designing a "technology-driven game," a notion that is discussed a little later in the chapter. Still, some genres of game are better suited to one kind of machine than another. It's valuable to know the strengths and weaknesses of the different types of machines and, even more important, how they are used by their owners.

Home Game Consoles

A *home game console* is usually set up in the living room or a child's bedroom. The player sits on a couch holding a dedicated controller in both hands, 3 to 6 feet away from a relatively low-resolution display, the television. This means that games designed for the home console machine cannot be as intricate as the typical PC game. The graphics have to be simpler and bolder, and the control method and user interface must be manageable with the provided controller. The kind of precision pointing that's possible with a mouse is much more difficult with most controllers, even those with analog joysticks. However, you are guaranteed that every machine will ship with a standardized controller; you don't have to cope with the huge variety of controllers and joysticks that are available for the PC.

Because the television is designed to be seen by several people at once, and because the console usually allows for at least two controllers, console machines are excellent for multiplayer games in which all the players look at the same screen. This means that every player can see what every other player is doing on the screen, which is a consideration in the design of some games. On the other hand, until recently, home consoles had no hard disk drives, so there was little space in which to store data between games. Games designed for consoles weren't very customizable and couldn't save complex states.

Home consoles tend to have very powerful graphics-display chips but slower central processing units and less RAM than personal computers. Because they sell for $200–$300, the manufacturer has to cut the hardware design to the bone to keep the cost down. This means that as computing devices, they are less powerful than personal computers and more difficult to program. On the other hand, their low price means that there are far more of them around, and a larger market for their games.

Personal Computers

A *personal computer* is usually set up away from the communal living space, on a computer desk. In this case, the player has a keyboard, a mouse, possibly a joystick, and (more rarely) a dedicated game controller like those on console machines. The player sits 12 to 18 inches away from a relatively small (compared to the television) high-resolution display. The high resolution means that the game can have subtle, detailed graphics. The mouse allows precision pointing and a more complex user interface. The keyboard enables the player to enter text conveniently and send messages to other players over a network, something that is nearly impossible with console machines.

The personal computer is quite awkward for more than one person to use. The controls of a PC are all designed for one individual, and even the furniture it usually sits on—a desk—is intended for a solitary use. PC games are rarely designed for more than one person to play on a single machine. On the other hand, a PC is very likely to be connected to the Internet, while consoles are just now beginning to get this capability. The PC is still the machine of choice for multiplayer networked games, but this could change soon.

The great boon of PC development is that anyone can program one; you don't have to get a license from the manufacturer or buy an expensive development station. Consequently, PCs are at the cutting edge of innovation in computer gaming. They're the platform of choice for small-scale, low-demand projects; interactive art; and other experimental forms of interactive entertainment.

The great bane of PC development is that no two machines are alike; because they're customizable, there are millions of possible configurations. In the early days of the game industry, this was a real nightmare for programmers. Fortunately, the Windows and Macintosh operating systems have solved many of these problems by isolating the programs from the hardware. Still, games tend to "push" the machine a lot harder than other applications, and configuration conflicts still occur.

Handheld Game Machines

Handheld game machines are a hugely popular and very inexpensive form of entertainment, mainly used by children. A given model is absolutely standard; there's no room for customization at all. These machines normally have a very limited number of controls and a very small LCD screen. They have little or no capacity to store data between games. Their CPUs are weak and slow by modern standards.

Many cheap handheld machines offer a fixed set of games that are built in, but the more versatile ones, such as the Game Boy Advance, accept games stored on ROM cartridges. Cartridges store far, far less data than the CD-ROMs or DVD discs that home consoles and computers use. Designing for a cartridge machine places severe limits on the amount of video, audio, graphics, and animation that you can include in the game. Because they're solid-state electronics, though, the data on a cartridge is available instantly. There's no delay for it to load the way there is with optical media devices.

The handheld game market is very lucrative, but creating a game for one will severely test your skills as a designer. With no room for fancy graphics or movies, you must rely on pure gameplay alone to provide the entertainment.

Other Devices

Games are showing up on all sorts of other devices these days. The more specialized the device is, the more important it is to have a clear understanding of its technical limitations and its audience. Text-based messaging on cellular telephones might breathe new life into a niche genre, the text MUD (multiuser dungeon or domain). Airlines are starting to build video games into their seats. Personal digital assistants (PDAs) are a great new platform for small, simple games. Video gambling machines are an entire industry unto themselves, one in which the random-number algorithms you use are closely monitored by state regulators. And, of course, there are arcade machines. Arcade games are subject to strange design limitations not seen on other devices. They have to maximize what the operators call "coin drop"—the amount of money that people put in through the front. Arcade operators care little for richness, depth, and the aesthetic qualities of a game as long as it makes a lot of money for them. This requires some fine balancing. If a game is too hard, people will abandon it in disgust, but if it is too easy, they will be able to play for a long time without putting any more money in.

Because these devices occupy niche markets with peculiar restrictions, we won't be addressing them in detail. This is a book about game design in general, so we concentrate on games for all-purpose game machines: home consoles and personal computers.

Motivations That Influence Design

Why build a computer game? The answer probably seems obvious: because it's a fun thing to do, to sell the game for money, or both. That's why most people get into the game industry—and probably why you are reading this book. But, in fact, there are a variety of reasons for building a game, and motivation has a powerful effect on the way a game is designed. Sometimes a game is built for several different reasons at once, and they're not always compatible with one another. Different motivations tend to pull the design of the game in different directions, which requires someone (usually the designer or the producer) to make a decision about which reason is most important.

Market-Driven Games

Most of the computer games in the world are built for sale. The publishing company wants to sell as many copies as it can. However, no one knows exactly what makes a game a hit, and unexpected hits such as *The Sims* continue to prove a lot of the conventional wisdom dead wrong. Still, certain genres and elements of games are generally thought to be popular with particular markets. Scantily clad women, big guns, and spectacular explosions, for example, are considered popular with teenage boys. Games with interesting characters, rich plots, and clever puzzles are thought to be popular with girls and women. These are, of course, stereotypes, but they are commonly held in the game industry. When a company chooses to build a game specifically for a particular market and to include certain elements in its design specifically to increase sales within that market, that game is said to be *market-driven*.

You might think that if publishers want to maximize sales, any game made for sale should be market-driven. Experience shows, however, that most market-driven games aren't very good. They do make a fair amount of money, but seldom enough to qualify as blockbuster hits. For one thing, the best games are expressions of the designer's vision and carry the designer's personal stamp, which makes them stand out from other games. Market-driven games do not reflect anyone's vision; instead, they reflect what the publishing company thinks the market wants. "Everybody knows" that boys like big explosions, so the publisher insists that the game include big explosions, whether they're really part of the designer's vision or not. As a result, market-driven games all tend to look alike because they're all designed according to the same stereotypes about the market. This results in a row of clone games on the store shelves. Because there isn't any particular reason to choose one over another, none of them becomes a blockbuster hit.

Another reason most market-driven games aren't very good is that they lack harmony, a concept that we discuss in more detail in Chapter 3. You can't make a brilliant game by simply throwing in all the popular elements you can think of. If you try, you get a game that doesn't feel as if it's about anything in particular. It doesn't hang together; it's merely a collection of pieces. Games don't sell only because they contain the "right" pieces; they also sell because the pieces fit together synergistically to make a coherent whole.

Finally, because market-driven games are designed to appeal to a stereotypical kind of gamer, they won't appeal to anyone who doesn't match the stereotype. If you make a game that is explicitly intended for teenage boys, you will not only turn off most girls who might otherwise like to play your game, but you'll also turn off any teenage boys who don't fit your stereotype. And if your stereotype happens to be wrong, you could end up making a game that appeals to nobody at all.

As a designer, you will, of course, make decisions with your players in mind. You will try to include elements that they will enjoy and avoid elements that they won't. That's entirely appropriate, and generally it's what your publisher wants you to do. But those elements must be consistent with your own vision of the game. If you include extraneous elements purely to boost sales but that don't really feel as if they belong there, you could end up doing your game more harm than good.

Designer-Driven Games

The opposite of a market-driven game is a *designer-driven* game. In designer-driven games, the designer retains all creative control and takes a personal role in every creative decision, no matter how small. Usually he does this because he's absolutely certain that his own creative instincts are the only right ones for the game and that his vision must rule supreme.

Relatively few games are designed this way. Few major publishers will grant a designer this much power unless he can claim a strong track record; there's too much money at stake to allow a single person to dictate everything. In practice, the design of most games is a collaborative process. The design includes not only the work of the lead designer, but also the input of others on the team. Producers, level designers, programmers, artists, and sometimes testers play a role in shaping the game. On the other hand, a good many small self-published games are designer-driven. Designer-driven games tend to be rather idiosyncratic. This might be harmful or it might be helpful; it depends on whether the designer's instincts are good ones.

The main problem with designer-driven games is that they're usually designed according to the designer's own notions of what constitutes a fun game, regardless of what play-testing shows. The designer invests too much of his own ego in his creation to allow other people to change it, even if changes would be an improvement. Also, when the designer insists on personal control over every decision, he often becomes a bottleneck in the development process. Other people on the team end up waiting around for the designer to make decisions for them, which wastes time and money.

A very small number of game designers—Will Wright and Sid Meier among them—have years of experience and proven track records, and can sell games on the strength of their names alone. They frequently turn out blockbusters even if the marketing department doesn't like or understand the idea. But even they are usually good at delegating. Micromanaging control freaks seldom make great designers. They're too busy cultivating one tree while the rest of the forest dies around them.

License Exploitation

Another reason that people make games is to exploit a particular intellectual property, a license. These games, often tie-ins with movies or books that have a highly recognizable brand name, can be enormously lucrative. Which do you think will sell better, a game about a suave, well-dressed British spy, or a game about James Bond? A game about a brilliant young star pilot, or a game about Luke Skywalker?

Working on a licensed game can be a lot of fun. As a designer, you will get to work creatively with characters and a world that you might already know and particularly like, and you'll be making a contribution to the canon of materials in that world. You might even get to meet some of the famous writers, directors, or actors who have brought that world to life in other media. When you say, "I designed a *Star Wars* game," people will be a lot more impressed than if you say, "I designed a game about a brilliant young star pilot."

One downside of designing licensed games is that you don't have as much creative freedom as you do designing a game entirely from your own imagination. You have to use the characters and settings provided by the license—but, more important, you have to conform to certain rules laid down by the original owners. They're usually very anxious to make sure their intellectual property isn't used in ways that conflict with their own marketing strategy or that would present their property in a negative light. The owners will almost certainly insist on the right to approve your game before it ships and to demand that you change things they don't like. If you had a license from the Walt Disney Corporation to make a Winnie the Pooh game, for example, Disney would never allow you to give Winnie the Pooh a machine gun. It would be a dumb thing to do, but it would also completely violate Disney's notions of what Winnie the Pooh is about—not to mention all the expectations buyers have when they see Winnie the Pooh on the box. Some intellectual property owners are lenient and don't really care what you do; most, however, are extremely strict and specify details right down to the precise vocabulary that you may use.

Licensed sports games have their own peculiarities. Usually, such games will have a license from the major league of the sport they are simulating—for example, Major League Baseball or the National Football League. These licenses will allow you to use the names and logos of teams in the league; they will also require you to display them properly and in the correct colors. The personal publicity rights of the players further complicate matters; some leagues do not have the right to license the players' names and images. We discuss these issues in more detail in Chapter 12, "Sports Games."

A great license doesn't guarantee success, however. A bad game with a famous license is still a bad game. The word will get around, and the players won't buy it. The most infamous example of this is the ill-fated *E.T.* game produced for the Atari 2600 machine during the summer of 1982. Atari manufactured millions and millions of cartridges in anticipation of huge sales, intending to take advantage of the success of the movie *E.T. The Extraterrestrial*. Unfortunately, it was a poor game, few people bought it, and, in the end Atari—which had paid an unheard-of $22 million for the license—ended up burying most of the cartridges in a landfill to take a tax write-off.

In short, designing a game with a license is a somewhat different experience from designing a game from scratch. You'll have both the original owners of the intellectual property and your own marketing department looking closely over your shoulder. Your publisher will probably put a lot of money into development and, having spent a lot to get the license, will want to make sure the game is good enough to earn it back. Of course, this means there's more at risk. If you do well and the brand is a popular one, your company stands to make a fortune. If you do a poor job and turn out a bad game, the owner of the license might refuse to renew it and will give it to some other developer instead. You will have cost your company millions in potential future revenue and put that money in your competitor's pockets.

Technology-Driven Games

A *technology-driven* game is one that is designed to show off a particular technological achievement, most often something to do with graphics. The original *Quake* was a technology-driven game. There wasn't much game there, but it helped to sell the *Quake* game engine to other developers. Sometimes the achievement is a piece of hardware instead of an algorithm. Console manufacturers often write technology-driven games when they release a new platform, to show everyone the features of their hardware.

Technology-driven games tend to sell well to hard-core gamers because those gamers are often technology-oriented themselves. Casual gamers can still recognize a big jump in image quality even though they're less impressed by performance statistics, and that will encourage them to buy a technology-driven game, too.

The main risk in designing a technology-driven game is that you'll spend too much time concentrating on the technology and not enough on making sure your game is really enjoyable. As with a hot license, a hot technology alone is not enough to guarantee a hit. If you're the first to market with the new technique and it really is spectacular, you could well have a meteoric success in the first few months. To last longer than that, your game has to be really fun to play as well. After the novelty of the technology has worn off, the gameplay will continue to sell the game.

Art-Driven Games

Art-driven games are comparatively rare. Just as a technology-driven game exists to show off a technical feature or achievement, an art-driven game exists to show off someone's artwork. These games are often designed by artists who have a strong visual sense but are new to the game industry. Although such games are visually innovative, they're seldom very good because the designer has spent more time thinking about ways to show off his artwork than about the player's experience of the game. If you want to design games to showcase your artwork, you must be aware that you need enjoyable gameplay as well as great visuals. *Myst* is an example of a game that got this right; it is an art-driven game with strong gameplay.

Entertainment and Integration

As we have shown, when a particular factor drives the development of a game, the result is often a substandard product. A good designer seeks not to optimize one characteristic at the expense of others, but to integrate them all in support of a higher goal: entertainment.

➤ A game must sell well, so the designer must consider the audience's preferences.

➤ A game must present an imaginative, coherent experience, so the designer must have a vision.

➤ A game with a license must pay back the license's cost, so the designer must understand what benefits it brings and exploit them to his best advantage.

➤ A game must offer an intelligent challenge and a smooth, seamless experience, so the designer must understand the technology.

➤ A game must be attractive, so the designer must think about the aesthetic style.

In designing an entertaining game, every element and every feature are tested against the standard: Does this contribute to the player's enjoyment? Does it entertain him? If so, it stays; if not, it should be looked at closely. There are reasons for including features that don't directly entertain: They might be necessary to make other parts of the game work or might be required by the licensor. But you should regard them with great suspicion and do your best to minimize their impact on the player.

Game Concept Worksheet

To turn your game idea into a fully fledged game concept, you need to think about and answer for yourself the following questions. You don't have to be precise or detailed, but you should have a general answer for all of them.

1. What is the nature of the gameplay? That is, what challenges will the player face? What actions will the player take to overcome them?
2. What is the victory condition for the game, if any? What is the player trying to achieve?
3. What is the player's role? Is the player pretending to be someone or something, and if so, what? How does the player's role help to define the gameplay?
4. What is the game's setting? Where does it take place?
5. What is the player's interaction model? Omnipresent? Through an avatar? Something else? Some combination?
6. What is the game's primary perspective? How will the player view the game's world on the screen? Will there be more than one perspective?
7. What is the general structure of the game? What is going on in each mode, and what function does each mode fulfill?
8. Is the game competitive, cooperative, team-based, or single-player? If multiple players are allowed, are they using the same machine with separate controls or different machines over a network?
9. Does the game have a narrative or story as it goes along? Summarize the plot in a sentence or two.
10. Does the game fall into an existing genre? If so, which one?
11. Why would anyone want to play this game? What sort of people would be attracted to this game?

Putting It Together

Now your idea is no longer just an idea. You've devised the essential elements of a game, and you know the answers to the vital questions that a publisher will ask. You have a game concept down on paper, and you're ready to show it to someone else for an opinion. The skeleton is assembled. Now it's time to put meat on the bones.

Chapter 3

Game Settings and Worlds

A game world is an artificial universe, an imaginary place whose creation begins with the (usually unspoken) words "Let's pretend...." Every game, no matter how small, takes place in a world. Most games have a physical, or at least a visible, manifestation of this world: a set of cards, a board, or an image on a computer screen. Even tic-tac-toe, one of the simplest games imaginable, has a world—a little diagram governed by rules and a victory condition. The boundaries of the diagram are the boundaries of the world. Any marks that you make outside of them are not part of the game.

The football field defines the physical boundaries of the football game's world. The football game's world is also bounded by time: It has a beginning and an end. When the clock runs out, the world ceases to exist; the game is over. The game can also be interrupted; during a timeout, the world freezes. It still exists in the minds of the players and the spectators— the game is still in progress—but no change can take place within the world until the timeout is over.

Not all game worlds have a visible component. The game Twenty Questions consists only of some basic rules and a victory condition, but it still has a world and the world has boundaries. If you're playing Twenty Questions and the questioner asks, "Wanna go surfing after work?," most people would say that the question lies outside the game world. It doesn't count as one of the 20 allowed. A text adventure is another game defined by words; the world is created in the player's imagination when he reads the text on the screen. A few master chess players can play in their heads, with no board at all—another example of a game world with no physical component.

The *setting* of a game is its fictional component, that aspect of the game that is a fantasy. Tic-tac-toe has no setting, nor does Twenty Questions; when you play them, you're not pretending to be anywhere else or to do anything besides what you're doing. Chess has just a scrap of a setting; although the board and the moves are abstract, the pieces have names that suggest a medieval court with its king and queen, knights and bishops. *Stratego* has even more of a setting. The pieces in *Stratego* are numbered, and you could play the game completely abstractly—my number 5 takes your number 6, and so on—but Milton Bradley has chosen to paint little pictures on them, encouraging us to pretend that they are colonels and sergeants and scouts in an army.

The Purpose of a Game Setting

Games exist to entertain, and the entertainment value of a game is derived from several sources: its gameplay, its story, social interaction (if it is a multi-player game), and so on. The setting also contributes to the entertainment that the game provides. In a game such as chess, almost all the entertainment value is in the gameplay; few people think of it as a game about medieval warfare. In an adventure game such as *Escape from Monkey Island*, the setting is essential to the fantasy. Without the setting, *Escape from Monkey Island* would not exist, and if it had a different setting, it would be a different game.

As a general rule, the more a game depends on its core mechanics to entertain, the less its setting matters. Mastering the core mechanics requires a kind of abstract thought, and fantasy can be a distraction. Serious chess players aren't interested in the shape of the chessmen; their shapes don't contribute significantly to the game. A serious chess player can have just as much fun with a $2 plastic travel chess set as with a $200 inlaid wooden board and solid pewter statues for pieces. As players learn to understand the core mechanics of other games, they stop thinking about the fantasy element as well. When players become highly skilled at a game such as *Quake III*, they no longer think about the fact that they're pretending to be space marines in a futuristic environment; they think only about hiding, moving, shooting, ambushing, obtaining more ammunition, and so on.

This process of *abstraction*—ignoring the game's setting—occurs only at a high level of play, however. To someone who's playing a game for the first time, the setting is vital to creating and sustaining his interest. One of the essential functions of a game's setting is actually to sell the game in the first place. It's not the game's mechanics that make a customer pick up a box in a store, but the fantasy it offers: who you'll be, where you'll be, and what you'll be doing there if you play that game.

The "Graphics Versus Gameplay" Debate

The relationship between the setting and the mechanics is the subject of considerable debate in the game industry, although it's usually characterized as "graphics versus gameplay." The graphics create the setting; the core mechanics, along with the user interface, create the gameplay—the challenges the player faces and the actions he may take to overcome them. In the early days of video gaming, graphics were seriously restricted by the weakness of the display hardware. The gameplay, as implemented by the programmers, was the source of most of the game's appeal. With the growth of modern display technology, the graphics have taken on much greater importance, and creating them consumes a large proportion of a game's development budget. Some designers and programmers, especially those who've been around since the early days, have become rather annoyed at the dominant role that graphics now play. They insist that graphics must be subordinate to gameplay in game design, and as proof they point to examples of games with great graphics and very little gameplay that offer poor value for the money.

This was a serious problem in the early 1990s, when Hollywood studios thought they could take over the game industry because they were better able to create impressive graphics than the game publishers. However, they failed. Hollywood didn't understand software engineering, didn't understand interactivity, and, most important, didn't understand gameplay. The public refused to accept games with bad gameplay, no matter how spectacular the graphics were. After a few false starts, Hollywood learned to work *with* game publishers rather than trying to *become* game publishers, realizing that the two groups bring complementary skills to creating games.

We believe the "graphics versus gameplay" debate is no longer a meaningful one. The truth is that graphics and gameplay must work together to produce the total play experience. The graphics create the setting, which both sells the game and involves the player in the game's fantasy. The gameplay provides the challenge and things for the player to do. Both are essential to the player's enjoyment of the game. The graphics bring in the player, and the gameplay keeps him there.

Immersiveness and Suspension of Disbelief

A key part of the experience of reading a novel or watching a movie is suspension of disbelief. *Suspension of disbelief* is a mental state in which you choose, for a period of time, to believe that this pack of lies, this fiction, is reality. This applies to games as well. When you go inside the game world and temporarily make it your reality, you suspend your disbelief. The better a game supports the illusion, the more thoroughly engrossed you become, and then the more *immersive* we say the game is. Immersiveness is one of the holy grails of game design.

Movies and novels try to create the impression that what they depict is real, though fantasy and science fiction novels rather test our patience in this regard. Few movies and novels specifically allude to the fact that they are fiction; they try to preserve the suspension of disbelief. Some deliberately play with the idea. Both the book and the movie *The French Lieutenant's Woman* specifically alluded to the fact that they were works of fiction, wrenching the audience out of the work's Victorian setting to encourage comparisons with today's world. The movie *The Stunt Man* similarly kept the viewer—and the movie's hero—off balance, unable to tell whether what we were seeing was supposed to be reality or merely a movie being filmed.

More often, however, suspension of disbelief is broken by poor design. This might occur if one of the people in the story does something that is wildly out of character, or if something highly improbable happens—a deus ex machina—and we are expected to accept it as normal. Another thing that frequently destroys a player's suspension of disbelief or prevents it from ever forming is a lack of harmony, which we discuss next.

The Importance of Harmony

Good games and game worlds possess *harmony*, a quality first identified by the legendary game designer Brian Moriarty. Harmony is the feeling that all parts of the game belong to a single, coherent whole. In his lecture "Listen: The Potential of Shared Hallucinations," Moriarty explained the concept of harmony so well that, with his permission, we use his own words to describe it:

Harmony isn't something you can fake. You don't need anyone to tell you if it's there or not. Nobody can sell it to you, it's not an intellectual exercise. It's a sensual, intuitive experience. It's something you feel. How do you achieve that feeling that everything works together? Where do you get this harmony stuff?

Well, I'm here to tell you that it doesn't come from design committees. It doesn't come from focus groups or market surveys. It doesn't come from cool technology or expensive marketing. And it never happens by accident or by luck. Games with harmony emerge from a fundamental note of clear intention. From design decisions based on an ineffable sense of proportion and rightness. Its presence produces an emotional resonance with its audience. A sense of inner unity that has nothing to do with what or how you did something, it has something to do with *why*. *Myst* and *Gemstone* both have harmony. They have it, because their makers had a vision of the experience they were trying to achieve and the confidence to attain it. They laid down a solid, ambient groove that players and their respective markets can relate to emotionally. They resisted the urge to overbuild. They didn't pile on a lot of gratuitous features just so they could boast about them. And they resisted the temptation to employ inappropriate emotional effects. Effects like shock violence, bad language, inside humor.

You know, the suspension of disbelief is fragile. It's hard to achieve it, and hard to maintain. One bit of unnecessary gore, one hip colloquialism, one reference to anything outside the imaginary world you've created is enough to destroy that world. These cheap effects are the most common indicators of a lack of vision or confidence. People who put this stuff into their games are not working hard enough.

Harmony is essential for a good game world. With every design decision you make, you should ask yourself whether the result is in harmony with your overall vision. Too many games have elements that seem bolted on, last-minute ideas that somebody thought would be "cool" to include. Although every game design requires compromises, as we said in Chapter 1, "What Is Game Design?," an important part of your job as a designer is to minimize the false notes or off-key elements that compromises tend to create. Try to find a way to make everything fit together into a coherent, integrated whole.

A good way to identify games with harmony is to look for those that have lasted far longer in the marketplace than their designers ever expected. This means that something about the game is striking a resonant chord with its players, a chord that continues to echo. For example, people continue to make modifications to *Half-Life* that are actually more popular than new games because *Half-Life* is such an elegant, harmonious game. *Tetris* is another case in point. Action games come and go, but *Tetris* has stood the test of time and might outlive us all.

The Dimensions of a Game World

A game's setting and world are defined by many different variables, each of which describes one dimension of the world, one of the aspects of the game's look and feel. To fully define your world and its setting, you need to consider each of these dimensions and answer certain questions about them.

The Physical Dimension

Game settings are almost always implemented as some sort of physical space. The player moves his avatar in and around this space, or moves other pieces, characters, or units in it. The physical characteristics of this space determine a great deal about the gameplay.

Even text adventures include a physical dimension. The player moves from one abstract "room" or other discrete location to another. Back when more people played text adventures, the boxes used to carry proud boasts about the number of rooms in the game. Gamers could take this as a very rough measure of the size of the world they could explore in the game and, therefore, the amount of gameplay that the game offered.

The physical dimension of a game is itself characterized by several different elements: dimensionality, scale, and boundaries.

Dimensionality

One of the first questions you have to ask yourself is how many dimensions your physical space is going to have. A few years ago, the vast majority of games had only two dimensions. This was especially noticeable in side-scrolling games such as *Super Mario Brothers*. Mario could run left and right and jump up and down, but he could not move toward the player ("out" of the screen) or away from him ("into" the screen).

It is essential to understand that the dimensionality of the game's physical space is not the same as how the game will *display* that space or how it will implement the space in software. Ultimately, all spaces must be displayed on the two-dimensional surface of the monitor screen, but that's a problem for a programmer, not a designer. How to implement and display the space are separate but related questions. The former has to do with technical design, and the latter has to do with user interface design.

Nowadays, a great many computer game settings have a three-dimensional space, even though the game might implement it in various ways. *Starcraft*, a war game, shows you plateaus and lowlands, as well as aircraft that pass over obstacles and ground units. *Starcraft's* setting is clearly three-dimensional, but the space is actually implemented in a series of two-dimensional planes or layers, one above another. Objects can be placed and moved within a plane with a fine degree of precision, but vertically, an object must be in one plane; there is no "in between." Flying objects can't move up and down in the air; they're always at the same altitude—in the "air layer."

When first thinking about the dimensionality of your game space, it's tempting to immediately assume that you want it to be three-dimensional because that offers the greatest flexibility or seems more real. But as with everything else, the dimensionality of your physical space must serve the entertainment value of the game. Make sure all the dimensions will contribute meaningfully. *Lemmings* was a hit 2D game, but *Lemmings 3D* was nowhere near as successful because it was much more difficult to play. The addition of a third dimension detracted from the player's enjoyment rather than adding to it.

It's possible to have more than three spatial dimensions, but, in general, we don't recommend it. A computer can display a distorted approximation of four-dimensional space in the two dimensions of the monitor screen, just as it can display an approximation of three-dimensional space in two dimensions. However, because humans are not used to dealing with 4D spaces, most of us have a hard time navigating through them. If you want to include a fourth dimension for some reason, you might consider doing it as an "alternate plane of reality" rather than an actual four-dimensional space. In other words, you have two three-dimensional spaces that look similar, but there is something different about them. For example, the game *Legacy of Kain: Soul Reaver* contained two three-dimensional spaces, the spectral realm and the material realm. The landscape was the same in each, but the spectral realm was lit by a blue light while the material realm was lit by white light; the actions available to the player were different in the spectral real from the material realm. Although they were both implemented in software by the same 3D models, they were functionally different places governed by different laws. In the movie version of *The Lord of the Rings*, the world that Frodo inhabits while he is wearing the Ring can be thought of as an alternate plane of reality as well, overlapping the real world but appearing and behaving differently.

Scale

By *scale*, we mean both the total size of the physical space represented and the relative sizes of objects in the game. If a game is purely abstract and doesn't correspond to anything in the real world, the sizes of objects in its game world don't really matter. You can adjust them to suit the game's needs any way you like. But if you are designing a game that is at least somewhat representational of the real world, you'll have to address the question of how big everything should be to both look real and play well. Some distortion is often necessary for the sake of gameplay; the trick is to do it without harming the player's suspension of disbelief too much.

With a sports game, a driving game, a flight simulator, or any other kind of game in which the player will expect a high degree of verisimilitude, you have little choice but to scale things to their actual sizes. In old sports games, it was not uncommon for the athletes to be depicted as 12 feet tall to make them more visible, but nowadays players wouldn't tolerate a game taking such liberties with reality. Serious simulations need an accurate representation of the physical world.

Similarly, you should scale most of the objects in first-person games accurately. Fortunately, almost all first-person games are set indoors or within very limited areas that are seldom larger than a few hundred feet in any dimension, so this doesn't create implementation problems. Because the player's perspective is that of a person walking through the space, objects need to look right for their surrounding area. You might want to slightly exaggerate the size of critical objects such as keys, weapons, or ammunition to make them more visible, but most things, such as doors and furniture, should be scaled normally. As screen resolutions continue to improve, we'll no longer need to exaggerate objects for visual clarity, unless we want to do so for a comic or cartoonlike effect.

If you're designing a game with an aerial or isometric perspective, you might need to fudge the scale of things somewhat. The real world is so much larger and more detailed than a game world that it's impossible to represent objects in their true scale in such a perspective. For example, in modern mechanized warfare, ground battles can easily take place over a 20-mile front, with weapons that can fire that far or farther. If you were to map an area this size onto a computer screen, an individual soldier or even a tank would be smaller than a single pixel, completely invisible. Although the player will normally be zoomed in on one small area of the whole map, the scale of objects will have to be somewhat exaggerated so that they're clearly identifiable on the screen.

One of the most common distortions games make is in the relative heights of people and the buildings or hills in their environment. The buildings are often only a little taller than the people who walk past them. To be able to see the roofs of all the buildings or the tops of all the hills, the camera must be positioned above the highest point on the ground; but if the camera is too high, the people would hardly be visible at all. To solve this problem, the game simply does not include tall buildings or hills and exaggerates the height of the people. Because the vertical dimension is seldom critical to the gameplay in things such as war games and role-playing games, it doesn't matter if it's not accurate, as long as it's not so inaccurate that it interferes with suspension of disbelief.

Designers often make another scale distortion between indoor and outdoor locations. When a character is walking through a town, simply going from one place to another, the player will want the character to get there reasonably quickly. The scale of the town should be small enough that the character takes only a few minutes to get from one end to another, unless the point of the game is to explore a richly detailed urban environment. When the character steps inside a building, however, and needs to negotiate doors and furniture, you should expand the scale to show these additional details. If you use the same animation for a character walking indoors and outdoors, this will give the impression that the character walks much faster outdoors than indoors. However, this seldom bothers players—they'd much rather have the game proceed quickly than have their avatar take hours to get anywhere, even if that would be more accurate.

This brings up one final distortion, which is also affected by the game's notion of time (see the section, "The Temporal Dimension"), and that is the relative speeds of moving objects. In the real world, a supersonic jet fighter can fly more than a hundred times faster than an infantry soldier can walk on the ground. If you're designing a game that includes both infantry soldiers and jet fighters, you're going to have a problem. If the scale of the battlefield is suitable for jets, it will take infantry weeks to walk across; if it's suitable for infantry, a jet could pass over it in the blink of an eye. One solution to this is to do what the real military does and implement transport vehicles for ground troops. Another is simply to fudge it and pretend that jets fly only four or five times as fast as people walk. As long as the jet is the fastest thing in the game, it doesn't really matter how much faster it is; the "strike and retreat" tactic that jets are good at will still work. Setting these values is all part of balancing the game, as discussed in more detail in Chapter 7, "Gameplay."

Boundaries

In board games, the edge of the board constitutes the edge of the game world. Because computers have a finite size, the physical dimension of a computer game world must have a finite size also. However, computer games are usually more immersive than board games, and they often try to disguise or explain away the fact that the world is limited, to maintain the player's suspension of disbelief.

In some cases, the boundaries of a game world arise naturally, and we don't have to disguise or explain them. Sports games take place only in a stadium or an arena, and no one expects or wants them to include the larger world. In most driving games, the car is restricted to a track or a road, and this, too, is reasonable enough.

Setting a game underground or indoors helps to create natural boundaries for the game world. Everyone expects indoor regions to be of a limited size, with walls defining the edges. The problem occurs when games move outdoors, where people expect large, open spaces without sharply defined edges. A common solution in this case is to set the game on an island surrounded by water or by some other kind of impassable terrain: mountains, swamps, or deserts. These establish both a credible and a visually distinctive "edge of the world."

In flight simulators, the boundaries of the world are even more problematic. Most flight simulators restrict the player to a particular area of the real world. Because there are no walls in the air, there's nothing to stop the plane from flying up to the edge of the game world, and the player can clearly see when he has arrived there that there's nothing beyond. In some games, the plane just stops there, hovering in midair, and won't go any farther. In *Battlefield 1942*, the game tells the player that he has left the scene of the action and forcibly returns him to the runway.

A common solution to the edge-of-the-world problem is to allow the flat world to "wrap" at the top, bottom, and sides. Although the world is implemented as a rectangular space in the software, objects that cross one edge appear at the opposite edge—they wrap around the world. If the object remains centered on the screen and the world appears to move beneath it, you can create the impression that the world is spherical. This was used to excellent effect in Bullfrog Productions' game *Magic Carpet*. In another Bullfrog game, *Populous: The Beginning*, the world was actually displayed graphically as a sphere on the screen, not just a wrapping rectangle.

Questions to Ask Yourself About the Physical Dimension

- Does my game require a physical dimension? What is it used for? Is it an essential part of gameplay or merely cosmetic?
- Leaving aside issues of implementation or display, how many imaginary spatial dimensions does my game require? If there are three or more, can objects move continuously through the third and higher dimensions, or are these dimensions partitioned into discrete "layers" or zones?
- How big is my game world, in light-years or inches? Is accuracy of scale critical, as in a football game, or not, as in a cartoonlike action game?
- Will my game need more than one scale, for indoor versus outdoor areas, for example? How many will it actually require?
- How am I going to handle the relative sizes of objects and people? What about their relative speeds of movement?
- How is my world bounded? Am I going to make an effort to disguise the "edge of the world," and if so, with what? What happens if the player tries to go beyond it?

The Temporal Dimension

The *temporal dimension* of a game world defines the way that time is treated in that world and the ways in which it differs from time in the real world.

In many turn-based games and action games, the world doesn't include a concept of time passing, days and nights, or seasons and years. Everything in the world idles or runs in a continuous loop until the player interacts with it in some way. Occasionally, the player is put under pressure by being given a limited amount of real-world time to accomplish something, but this is usually just a single challenge, not part of a larger notion of time in the game.

In some games, time is implemented as part of the setting but not part of the gameplay. Here time creates atmosphere and gives the game some variety, but it doesn't change the way you play the game. This usually feels rather artificial. If the player can do exactly the same things at night that she can during the daytime, and no one ever seems to sleep, then there's little point in making the distinction. For time to serve the fantasy, it must affect it in meaningful ways.

Baldur's Gate is a good example of a game in which time is meaningful. *Baldur's Gate* is a very large role-playing game implemented according to the *Advanced Dungeons & Dragons* rules. At night, shops are closed and the characters in the game run an increased risk of being attacked by wandering monsters. It's also darker and hard to see. Taverns are open all day and all night, which is reasonable enough, but the customers don't ever seem to leave and the bartender never goes off shift. In this way, the game's use of time is a little inconsistent, but the discrepancy serves the gameplay well because you can always trade with the bartender and pick up gossip no matter what time it is. The characters do need rest if they've been on the march for a long while, and this makes them vulnerable while they're sleeping. In the underground portions of the game, day and night have less meaning, as you would expect.

Variable Time

In games that do implement time as a significant element of the gameplay, as in books and movies, time in the game world usually runs much faster than in reality and often jumps, skipping periods when nothing interesting is happening. Most war games, for example, don't bother to implement nighttime or require that soldiers get any rest. In reality, soldier fatigue is a critical consideration in warfare, but because sleeping soldiers don't make exciting viewing and certainly aren't very interactive, most games just skip it. Allowing soldiers to fight continuously without a pause permits the player to play continuously without a pause also.

The Sims, a game about people living in a house, handles this problem a different way. The simulated characters require rest and sleep for their health, so *The Sims* depicts day and night accurately. However, when all the characters go to sleep, the game speeds up considerably, letting hours go by in a few seconds. As soon as anyone wakes up, it slows back down again.

The Sims is a rather unusual game in that it's chiefly about time management. You are under constant pressure to have your characters accomplish all their chores and get time for sleep, relaxation, and personal development as well. The game runs at something like 48 times as fast as real life, so you can play through the 16 hours of daytime in about 20 minutes. However, the characters don't move 48 times as fast. Their actions look pretty normal, about like real time. As a result, it takes them 15 minutes on the game's clock just to go out and pick up the newspaper. This contributes to the sense of time pressure. Because the characters do everything slowly (in game terms), they often don't get a chance to water the flowers, which consequently die.

Anomalous Time

In *The Settlers III*, a complex economic simulation, a tree can grow from a sapling to full size in about the same length of time that it takes for an iron foundry to smelt four or five bars of iron. This is a good example of *anomalous time:* time that seems to move at different speeds in different parts of the game. Blue Byte, the developer of *The Settlers*, tuned the length of time it takes to do each of the many tasks in the game to make sure that it would run smoothly. As a result, *The Settlers* is very well balanced at some cost to realism. However, it's doesn't disrupt the fantasy because *The Settlers* doesn't actually give the player a clock in the game world. There's no way to compare game time to real time, so in effect, the game world has no obvious timescale.

Another example of anomalous time appears in *Age of Empires*, in which tasks that should take less than a day in real time (gathering berries from a bush, for example) seem to take years in game time according to the game clock. *Age of Empires* does have a timescale, visible on the game clock, but not everything in the world makes sense on that timescale. The players simply have to accept these actions as symbolic rather than real. As designers, we have to make them work in the context of the game world without disrupting the fantasy. As long as the symbolic actions (gathering berries or growing trees) don't have to be coordinated with real-time actions (warfare), but remain essentially independent processes, it doesn't matter if they operate on an anomalous time scale.

Letting the Player Adjust Time

In sports games and vehicle simulations, game time usually runs at the same speed as real time. An American football game is, by definition, an hour long, but because the clock stops all the time, the actual elapsed time of a football game is closer to three hours. All serious computerized football games simulate this accurately. Verisimilitude is a key requirement of most sports games; if a game does not accurately simulate the real sport, it might not be approved by the league, and its competitors are bound to point it out as a flaw. However, most such games also allow the players to shorten the game by playing 5- or 10-minute quarters instead of 15-minute ones because most people don't want to devote a full three hours to playing a simulated football game. This is also a useful feature in testing; it would take far too long to test the product if you had to play a full-length game every time.

Flight simulators also usually run in real time. But there are often long periods of flying straight and level during which nothing of interest is going on; the plane is simply traveling from one place to another. To shorten these periods, many games offer a way to "speed up time" by two, four, or eight times—in effect, making everything in the game world go faster than real time. When the plane approaches its destination, the player can return the game to normal speed and play in real time.

Questions to Ask Yourself About the Temporal Dimension

- Is time a meaningful element of my game? Does the passage of time change anything in the game world even if the player does nothing, or does the world simply sit still and wait for the player to do something?
- If time does change the world, what effects does it have? Does food decay, and do light bulbs burn out?
- How does time affect the player's avatar? Does he get hungry or tired?
- What is the actual purpose of including time in my game? Is it only a part of the atmosphere, or is it an essential part of the gameplay?
- Is there a timescale for my game? Do I need to have measurable quantities of time, such as hours, days, and years, or can I just let time go by without bothering to measure it? Does the player need a clock to keep track of time?
- Are there periods of time that I'm going to skip or do without? Is this going to be visible to the player, or will it happen seamlessly?
- Do I need to implement day and night? If I do, what will make night different from day? Will it merely look different, or will it have other effects as well? What about seasons?
- Will any of the time in my game need to be anomalous? If so, why? Will that bother the player? Do I need to explain it away, and if so, how?
- Should the player be allowed to adjust time in any way? Why, how, and when?

The Environmental Dimension

The environmental dimension describes the world's appearance and its atmosphere. We've seen that the physical dimension defines the shape of the game's space; the environmental dimension is about what's in that space. Its two related elements, cultural context and physical surroundings, make up the visual implementation of the game's setting.

Cultural Context

When we speak of the *cultural context* of a game, we're talking about culture in the anthropological sense: the beliefs, attitudes, and values that the people in the game world hold, as well as their political and religious institutions, social organization, and so on. These characteristics are reflected in the manufactured items that appear in the game: clothing, furniture, architecture, landscaping, and every other man-made object in the world. The culture influences not only what appears and what doesn't (a game set in a realistic ancient Egypt obviously shouldn't include firearms), but also how everything looks. The appearance of objects is affected not only by their function in the world, but also by the aesthetic sensibilities of the people who constructed them: A Maori shield will look entirely different from King Arthur's shield.

The cultural context also includes the game's back story. The back story of a game is the imaginary history, either large-scale (nations, wars, natural disasters) or small-scale (personal events and interactions) that preceded the time when the game takes place. This historical background helps to establish why the culture is the way it is. A warlike people should have a history of warfare; a mercantile people should have a history of trading. In designing this, don't go into too much depth too early, however. As we warned in Chapter 2, "Game Concepts," the story serves the game, not the other way around.

For most game worlds, it's not necessary to define their culture in great detail. If the game is set in your own culture, you can simply use the things that you see around you. The *Sim City* series, for example, is clearly set in present-day America (European cities are rarely so rectilinear), and it looks like it. But when your game begins to deviate from your own culture, you need to start thinking about how it deviates and what consequences that has.

Physical Surroundings

The physical surroundings define what the game actually looks like. This is the part of game design in which it's most helpful to be an artist or to work closely with one. In the early stages of design, you don't need to make drawings of every single thing that can appear in the game world, although sooner or later someone is going to have to. But for the time being, it's important to create concept sketches: pencil or pen-and-ink drawings of key visual elements in the game. Depending on what your game is about, this can include buildings, vehicles, clothing, weaponry, furniture, decorations, works of art, jewelry, religious or magical items, logos or emblems, and on and on. Man-made items in particular are influenced by the game's culture. A powerful and highly religious people are likely to have large symbols of their spirituality: stone temples or cathedrals. A warlike nomadic people will have animals or vehicles to carry their gear and weapons suitable for use on the move. (Note that these might be future nomads, driving dune buggies rather than camels.)

Nor should you neglect the natural world. Too many games set in urban or indoor environments consisting entirely of man-made things feel sterile, artificially clean, and devoid of life. Think about birds and animals, plants and trees, earth, rocks, hills, and even the sky. Consider the climate: Is it hot or cold, wet or dry? Is the land fertile or barren, flat or mountainous? These things are all parts of a real place, opportunities to create a visually rich and distinctive environment.

If your world is chiefly indoors, of course, you don't have to think about nature much unless your character passes a window, but there are a hundred other issues instead. Where does the light come from? What are the walls, floors, and ceilings made of, and how are they decorated? Why is this building here? Do the rooms have a specific purpose, and if so, what? How can you tell the purpose of a room from its contents? Does the building have multiple stories? How does the player get from one story to another?

Physical surroundings include sounds as well as sights: music, ambient environmental sounds, the particular noises made by people, animals, machinery, and vehicles. Think about the sounds things make at the same time that you think about how they look. This will help you to create a coherent world. Suppose you're inventing a six-legged reptilian saddle animal with clawed feet rather than hooves. How does that sound as it moves? Its scales might rattle a bit. Its feet are not going to make the characteristic clop-clop sound of a shod horse. With six legs, it will probably have some rather odd gaits, and those should be reflected in the sound it makes.

The physical surroundings are primarily responsible for setting the tone and mood of the game as it is played, whether it's the lighthearted cheerfulness of *Mario* or the dimly lit suspense of *Thief: The Dark Project*. The sound, and especially the music, will contribute greatly to this. Think hard about the kind of music you want, and consider what genres will be appropriate. Stanley Kubrick listened to hundreds of records to select the music for *2001: A Space Odyssey*, and he astonished the world with his choice of "The Blue Danube" for the shuttle docking sequence. You have a similar opportunity in designing your game.

Detail

Every designer must decide how much detail the game world needs—that is to say, how richly textured the world will be and how accurately modeled its behavior will be. This is partly a question of "realism." Technical limitations and time constraints almost always determine a game's level of detail. No football game goes to the extent of modeling each fan in the stadium, and few flight simulators model all the physical characteristics of their aircraft. Detail helps to support the fantasy, but it always costs, in development time and memory or in disk space on the player's machine. In an adventure game, it should, in principle, be possible to pick up everything in the world; in practice, this just isn't practical. The consequence of this is that the player knows that if an object *can* be picked up, it must be important for some reason; if it can't be picked up, it isn't important. Similarly, in god games, it's common for all the people to look alike; they're often male adults. Bullfrog Productions once designed a god game with both male and female adults, but there wasn't enough time for the artists to model children as well. People simply had to be "born" into the world full grown. Lionhead's *Black and White,* on the other hand, managed to include men, women, and children.

Here's a good rule of thumb for determining the level of detail your game will contain: Include as much detail as you can to help the game's immersiveness, *up to* the point at which it begins to harm the gameplay. If the player is struggling to look after everything you've given him, the game probably has too much detail. (This is one of the reasons war games tend to have hundreds rather than hundreds of thousands of units. The player in a war game can't delegate tasks to intelligent subordinates, so the numbers have to be kept down to a size that he can reasonably manage.) A spectacularly detailed game that's no fun to play won't sell many copies.

Defining a Style

In describing how your world is going to look, you are defining a visual style for your game that will influence a great many other things as well: the character design, the user interface, perhaps the manual, and even the design of the box and the advertising. You actually have two tasks to take on here: defining the style of things *in* your world, and also defining the style of the artwork that will *depict* your world. They aren't the same. For example, you can describe a world whose architectural style is inspired by Southwestern pueblos, but draw it to look like a Warner Brothers cartoon. Or you could have medieval towns with half-timbered houses, but painted in a slightly fuzzy, Impressionistic style. You must choose both your content and the way in which you will present it.

Both decisions will significantly influence the player's experience of the game, jointly creating a distinct atmosphere. In general, the style of depiction tends to superimpose its mood on the style of the object depicted. For example, a Greek temple might be architecturally elegant, but if its style of drawing suggests a Looney Tunes cartoon, everyone will expect something wacky and outrageous to take place there. The drawing style imposes its own atmosphere over the temple, no matter how majestic it is.

Unless you're the lead artist for your game as well as its designer, you probably shouldn't—or won't be allowed to—do this alone. Your art team will have ideas of its own, and you should listen to those suggestions. The marketing department might insist on having a say as well. It's important, however, that you try to keep the style harmonious and consistent throughout your game. Too many games have been published in which different sections had wildly differing art styles because no one held and enforced a single overall vision.

Overused Settings

All too often, games borrow settings from one another or from common settings found in the movies and television. A huge number of games are set in science fiction and fantasy worlds, especially the quasimedieval, sword-and-sorcery fantasy inspired by J.R.R. Tolkien and *Dungeons & Dragons*, popular with the young people who used to be the primary—indeed, almost the only—market for computer games. But a lot more people play games nowadays, and they want new worlds to play in. You should look beyond these hoary old staples of gaming. As we mentioned in Chapter 2, *Interstate '76* was inspired by 1970s TV shows. It included cars, clothing, and music from that era, all highly distinctive and evocative of a particular culture. *Interstate '76* had great gameplay, but what really set it apart from its competitors was that it looked like nothing else on the market.

Especially if you are going to do science fiction or fantasy, try to make it distinctively different. At present, real spacecraft built by the United States or Russia look extremely functional, just as the first cars did in the 1880s, and the spacecraft in computer games tend to look that way also. But as cars became more common, they began exhibiting stylistic variation to appeal to different kinds of people, and now there is a whole school of aesthetics for automotive design. As spacecraft become more common, and especially as we start to see "personal" spacecraft, we should expect them to exhibit stylistic variation as well. This is an area in which you have tremendous freedom to innovate.

The same goes for fantasy. Forget the same old elves, dwarves, wizards, and dragons. Look to other cultures for your heroes and villains. Right now about the only non-Western culture portrayed with any frequency in games is Japanese (feudal, present-day, and future) because there is a large market for games in Japan, and Japanese style has found some acceptance in the West as well. But there are many more sources of inspiration around the world, most untapped. Around 1200 A.D., while the rulers of Europe were still holed up in cramped, drafty castles, Islamic culture reached a pinnacle of grace and elegance. Muslims built magnificent palaces filled with the riches of the Orient and majestic mosques of inlaid stone. Yet this proud and beautiful civilization seldom appears in computer games because Western game designers haven't bothered to learn about it or don't even know it existed. Set your fantasy in Valhalla, in Russia under Peter the Great, in the arctic tundra, at Angkor Wat, at Easter Island, or at Machu Picchu.

Sources of Inspiration

Art and architecture, history and anthropology, literature and religion, clothing fashions, and product design are all great sources of cultural material. Artistic and architectural movements, in particular, offer tremendous riches: Art Nouveau, Art Deco, Palladian, Brutalism. If you haven't heard of one of these, go look it up now. Browse the web or the art, architecture, and design sections of the bookstore or the public library for pictures of interesting objects, buildings, and clothing. Photocopy things that attract your eye and post them around your workspace to inspire yourself and your coworkers. Collect "graphic scrap" from anywhere that you find it. Try old copies of *National Geographic*. Visit museums of art, design, and natural history if you can get to them; one of the greatest resources of all is travel, if you can afford it. A good game designer is always on the lookout for new ideas, even when he's ostensibly "on vacation."

It's tempting to borrow from our closest visual neighbor, the movies, because in the movies someone has already done the visual design work for us. *Blade Runner* introduced the decaying urban future; *Alien* gave us disgustingly biological aliens rather than "little green men." The problem with these looks is that they've already been borrowed from many, many times. You can use them as a quick-and-dirty backdrop if you don't want to put much effort into developing your world, and players will instantly recognize them and know what they're about. But to stand out from the crowd, consider other genres. Film noir, the Marx Brothers, John Wayne westerns, war movies from the World War II era, costume dramas of all periods…. From the silliness of *One Million Years B.C.* to the Victorian elegance of *Wilde*, they're all grist for the mill.

Television goes through its own distinct phases, and because it's even more fashion-driven than the movies, it is ripe for parody. The comedies of the 1950s and 1960s and the nighttime soaps of the 1970s and 1980s all had characteristic looks that seem laughable today but that are immediately familiar to most adult Americans. That is one potential problem, however: If you make explicit references to American popular culture, non-Americans and children might not get it. If your gameplay is good enough, though, it won't matter.

Questions to Ask Yourself About the Environmental Dimension

- Is my game world set in a particular historical period or geographic location? When and where? Is it an alternate reality, and if so, what makes it different from ours?
- Are there any people in my game world? What are they like? Do they have a complex, highly organized society or a simple, tribal one? How do they govern themselves? How is this social structure reflected in their physical surroundings? Are there different classes of people, guilds, or specialized occupations?
- What do my people value? Trade, martial prowess, imperialism, peace? What kinds of lives do they lead in pursuit of these ends? Are they hunters, nomadic, agrarian, industrialized, even postindustrial? How does this affect their buildings and clothing?

- Are my people superstitious or religious? Do they have institutions or religious practices that will be visible in the game? Are there religious buildings? Do the people carry charms or display spiritual emblems?
- What are my people's aesthetics like? Are they flamboyant or reserved, chaotic or orderly, bright or subtle? What colors do they like? Do they prefer straight lines or curves?
- If there aren't any people in the game, what are there instead, and what do they look like and how do they behave?
- Does my game take place indoors or outdoors, or both? If indoors, what are the furnishings and interior decor like? If outdoors, what is the geography and architecture like?
- What is the style and mood of my game? How am I going to create them with art, sound, and music?
- How much detail can I afford in my game? Will it be rich and varied or sparse and uncluttered? How does this affect the way the game is played?

The Emotional Dimension

The emotional dimension of a game world defines not only the emotions of the people in the world, but, more important, the emotions that you, as a designer, hope to arouse in the player. Action and strategy games usually involve a narrow emotional dimension, but other games that rely more heavily on story and characters can offer rich emotional content that affects the player deeply.

The idea of manipulating the player's emotions might seem a little strange. Most computer games are pretty lighthearted and don't take themselves or their subject matter too seriously. For much of their history, games have been seen only as light entertainment, a way to while away a few hours in a fantasy world. But just because that's all they have been doesn't mean that's all they *can* be. In terms of the richness of their emotional content, games are now just about where the movies were when they moved from the nickelodeon to the screen. They're no longer just a few minutes' amusement; they are now capable of engaging their audience, and that means an emotional involvement as well as an intellectual one.

To affect a player's emotions, you have to make him care about something or someone, and then threaten that person or thing in a way that holds the player's interest. This is the essence of dramatic tension, whether we're watching Greek tragedy or reading *Harry Potter*. Something important must be at stake. The danger need not necessarily be physical; it can also be a social, emotional, or economic risk. Most of the young women in Jane Austen's novels were not in imminent peril of death or starvation, but it was essential to their family's social standing and financial future for them to make a good marriage. The conflict between their personal desires and their family obligations provides the tension in the novels.

A good many games set the danger at hyperbolic levels, with extreme claims like "The fate of the universe rests in your hands!". This appeals to young people, who often feel powerless and have fantasies about being powerful. To adults, it just sounds a bit silly. At the end of *Casablanca*, Rick said, "The problems of three little people don't amount to a hill of beans in this crazy world," but he was wrong. The whole movie, a movie still popular over a half century after its first release, is about the problems of three little people. For the duration of the film, these problems hold us entranced. It isn't necessary that the fate of the world be at stake; it is the fates of Rick, Ilsa, and Victor that tug at our hearts.

The Limitations of Fun

Most people think that the purpose of playing games is to have fun, but *fun* is a rather limiting term. It tends to suggest excitement and pleasure, either a physical pleasure such as riding a roller coaster, a social pleasure such as joking around with friends, or an intellectual pleasure such as playing cards or a board game. The problem with striving for fun is that it tends to limit the emotional range of games. Suspense, excitement, exhilaration, surprise, and various forms of pleasure fall within the definition of fun, but not pity, jealousy, anger, sorrow, guilt, outrage, or despair.

You might think that nobody in their right mind would want to explore these emotions, but other forms of entertainment—books, movies, television—do it all the time. And, in fact, that's the key: Those media don't provide only fun; they provide entertainment. People can be entertained in all sorts of ways. Movies with sad endings aren't "fun," but they're still entertaining. Although we say that we make "games," in fact, what we make is interactive entertainment. The potential of our medium to explore emotions and the human condition is much greater than the term *fun game* allows for.

All that said, however, bear in mind that most publishers and players want "fun." Too many inexperienced designers are actually more interested in showing how clever they are than in making sure the player has a good time; they place their own creative agenda before the player's enjoyment. As a designer, you must master the ability to create fun—light enjoyment—before you move on to more complex emotional issues. Unpleasant or painful emotions are a greater aesthetic challenge to address successfully, and they are commercially risky besides. For more on this topic, we recommend that you take a look at the book *Creating Emotion in Games*, by David Freeman (New Riders, 2003).

Questions to Ask Yourself About the Emotional Dimension

- Does my game have a significant emotional dimension? What emotions will my game world include?
- How does emotion serve the entertainment value of my game? Is it a key element of the plot? Does it motivate characters in the game or the player himself?
- What emotions will I try to inspire in the player? How will I do this? What will be at stake?

The Ethical Dimension

The ethical dimension of a game world defines what *right* and *wrong* mean within the context of that world. At first glance, this might seem kind of silly—it's only a game, so there's no need to talk about ethics. But most games that have a setting, a fantasy component, also have an ethical system that defines how the player is supposed to behave. As designers, we are the gods of the game's world, and we define its morality. When we tell a player that he must perform certain actions to win the game, we are defining those actions as good or desirable. Likewise, when we say that the player must avoid certain actions, we are defining them as bad or undesirable. The players who come into the world must adopt our standards, or they will lose the game.

In some respects, the ethical dimension of a game world is part of its culture, but we've broken it out for separate discussion because it poses special design problems. The ethical space of most game worlds is rather disjoint from ethics in the real world. Games allow, even require, you to do things that you can't do in the real world. The range of actions that the game world permits is typically narrower than in the real world (you can fly your F-15 fighter jet all you want, but you can't get out of the plane), but often the permitted actions are quite extreme: killing people, blowing things up, and so on.

On the whole, most games have simple ethics: clobber the bad guys, protect the good guys. It's not subtle but perfectly functional; that's how you play checkers. Not many games explore the ethical dimension in any depth. A few include explicit moral choices, but, unfortunately, they tend to be namby-pamby, consistently rewarding "nice" behavior and punishing "bad" behavior. Such preachy material turns off even children, not to mention adults. But you can build a richer, more involving game by giving the player tough moral choices to make. Ethical ambiguity and difficult decisions are at the heart of many great stories and, indeed, much of life. Should you send a platoon of soldiers to certain death to save a battalion of others? How would you feel if you were in the platoon?

Black and White was a game that included a certain amount of moral decision making. So are some role-playing games—you can choose to play as an evil character who steals and kills indiscriminately, but the game becomes more difficult to win that way because other characters will refuse to cooperate with you and might even attack you on sight. Rather than impose a rule that says, "Immoral behavior is forbidden," the game implements a rule that says, "You are free to make your own moral choices—but be prepared to live with the consequences!". This is a more adult approach to the issue.

All that said, we strongly discourage creating games that reward or even allow the player to do truly hateful things. One of the most repugnant games ever created was a cartridge for the Atari 2600 console called *Custer's Revenge*, in which the player's avatar, a cowboy, was supposed to try to rape a Native American woman who was tied to a pole. (The cartridge was independently published and was not supported or endorsed by Atari in any way.) This kind of thing is beyond bad taste; it's pathological. Games that expect a player to participate in sexual assault, torture, or child abuse will never sell well. They serve only to gratify their designers' sick fantasies while tarnishing the reputation of the rest of us. Although no one would condemn all cinema on the basis of one offensive movie, interactive entertainment is still a young-enough medium that it happens to us. Like it or not, what we each do individually affects us all collectively. The best way to avoid censorship is to exercise some judgment in the first place.

You must be sure to explain the ethical dimension of your game clearly in the manual, in introductory material, or in mission briefings. For example, some games that have hostage-rescue scenarios make the death of a hostage a loss condition: If a hostage dies, the player loses. This means that the player has to be extra careful not to kill any hostages, even at the risk of his own avatar's life. In other games, the only loss condition is the avatar's death. In this case, many players will shoot with complete abandon, killing hostages and their captors indiscriminately. In real life, of course, the truth is somewhere in between. Police officers who accidentally shoot a hostage are seldom prosecuted unless they've been grossly negligent, but it doesn't do their career any good. You can emulate this by penalizing the player somehow. To be fair to the player, however, you need to make this clear at the outset.

The ethical dimensions of multi-player games, whether online or local, are an enormous and separate problem. We discuss this at length in Chapter 17, "Online Games."

A Word About Game Violence

It's not part of our mission in this book to debate, much less offer an answer for, the problem of whether violent video games cause violent behavior in children or adults. This is a psychological question that will be resolved only after prolonged and careful study. Unfortunately, a good many people on both sides of the issue seem to have made up their minds already, and arguments continue to rage in the halls of Congress and elsewhere, supported for the most part by very few facts.

To you, as a designer, however, we do have a few suggestions. The essence of most games is conflict, and conflict is often represented as violence in varying degrees of realism. Chess is a war game in which pieces are killed—removed from the board—but nobody objects to the "violence" of chess; it's entirely abstract. American football is a violent contact sport in which real people get injured all the time, but there are no serious efforts to ban football, either. The only way to remove violence from gameplay would be to prohibit most of the games in the world because most contain violence in some more-or-less abstract form. The issue is not violence, per se, but how violence is portrayed and the circumstances under which it is acceptable.

Games get into political trouble when they have a close visual similarity to the real world but an ethical dimension that is strongly divergent from the real world. *Kingpin* was a game in which the player was encouraged to beat prostitutes to death with a crowbar, with bloodily realistic graphics. Not surprisingly, it earned a lot of criticism. On the other hand, *Space Invaders* involved shooting hundreds of aliens, but it was so visually abstract that nobody minded. In other words, the more a game resembles reality visually, the more its ethical dimension should resemble reality as well, or it's likely to make people upset. If you want to make a game in which the player is encouraged to shoot anything that moves, you're most likely to stay out of trouble if those targets are nonhuman and just quietly disappear rather than breaking apart into bloody chunks. Tie your ethical realism to your visual realism.

Computer games are about bringing fantasies to life, enabling people to do things in make-believe that they couldn't possibly do in the real world. But make-believe is a dangerous game if it is played by people for whom the line between fantasy and reality is not clear. Young children (those under about age eight) don't know much about the real world; they don't know what is possible and what isn't, what is fantasy and what is reality. An important part of raising them is teaching them this difference. But until they've learned it, it's best to make sure that any violence in young children's games is suitably proportionate to their age. The problem with showing violence to children is not the violence, per se, but the notion that there's no price to pay for it. For a detailed and insightful discussion of how children "process" violence, read *Killing Monsters: Why Children Need Fantasy, Super Heroes, and Make-Believe Violence* by Gerard Jones.

Ultimately, the violence in a game should serve the gameplay. If it doesn't, then it's just gratuitous and you should consider doing without it. A few designers, mostly young and male, seem to think that deliberately including gratuitous violence in their games is a gesture of rebellion against the antiviolence crusaders. We encourage these gentlemen to grow up and to remember who the game is for. Our customers don't buy games to see rebellious gestures; they buy them to be entertained.

Questions to Ask Yourself About the Ethical Dimension

- What constitutes right and wrong in my game? What player actions do I reward and what do I punish?
- How will I explain the ethical dimensions of the world to the player? What tells him how to behave and what is expected of him?
- If my game world includes conflict or competition, is that represented as violence or as something else (racing to a finish, winning an economic competition, outmaneuvering the other side)?
- What range of choices am I offering my player? Are there both violent and nonviolent ways to accomplish something? Is the player rewarded in any way for minimizing casualties, or is he punished for ignoring them?
- In many games, the end—winning the game—justifies any means that the game allows. Do I want to define the victory conditions in such a way that not all means are acceptable?

- Are any other ethical questions present in my game world? Can my player lie, cheat, steal, break promises, or double-cross anyone? Can he abuse, torture, or enslave anyone? Are there positive or negative consequences for these actions?
- Does my world contain any ethical ambiguities or moral dilemmas? How does making one choice over another affect the player, the plot, and the gameplay?
- How realistic is my portrayal of violence? Does the realism appropriately serve the entertainment value of the game?

Realism and Abstraction

As we said in Chapter 2, games can be divided very roughly into two categories, realistic and abstract. Realistic games make an effort to model the real world, and when playing them you can rely on real-world common sense. Abstract games bear little resemblance to the real world and have arbitrary rules that you have to learn somehow. However, it isn't really that simple. Realism is not a dichotomy, but a continuum. All games, no matter how realistic, represent an abstraction and simplification of the real world. Even the multimillion-dollar flight simulators used for training commercial pilots are incapable of turning the cockpit completely upside down. This event is (we hope) so rare in passenger aircraft that it's not worth the extra money it would take to simulate it.

Players and game reviewers often talk about realism as a quality of an entire game, but, in fact, it is a quality that differs in individual areas. Many games have highly realistic graphics but unrealistic physics, or realistic economic models but unrealistic user interfaces. For example, a good many first-person shooters accurately model the performance characteristics of a variety of weapons—their rate of fire, size of ammunition clips, accuracy, and so on—but enable the player to carry about 10 of them at once with no reduction in speed or mobility. Therefore, realism is not a single dimension of a game world, but a multivariate quality that applies to all parts of the game and everything in it. (If you're mathematically inclined, think of realism as a vector over every aspect of the game, with values ranging from 0, entirely abstract, to 1, entirely realistic. However, no value will ever equal 1 because nothing about a game is ever entirely realistic—if it were, it would be life, not a game.)

The realistic/abstract dichotomy is mostly useful as a starting point when thinking about what kind of a game you want to create. If you're designing a cartoony action game such as *Banjo-Kazooie*, you know that it's going to be mostly abstract. As you design elements of the game, you'll need to ask yourself how much realism you want to include. Can your avatar be hurt when he falls long distances? Is there a limit to how much he can carry at once? Do Newtonian physics apply to him, or can he change directions in midair?

On the other hand, if you're designing a game with a presumption of realism—a vehicle or sports simulation, for example—then you need to think about it from the other direction. What aspects of the real world are you going to abstract? Most modern fighter aircraft have literally hundreds of controls; that's why only a special group of people can be fighter pilots. To make a fighter simulation accessible to the general public, you'll have to remove or simplify a lot of those controls. Similarly, a fighter jet's engine is so powerful that certain maneuvers can knock the pilot unconscious or even rip the plane apart. Are you going to simulate these limitations accurately, or make the game a little more abstract by not requiring the player to think about them?

As we have said, every design decision you make must serve the entertainment value of the game. In addition, every design decision must serve your goals for the game's overall degree of realism. Some genres demand more realism than others. It's up to you to establish how much realism you want and in what areas. During the design process, you must continually monitor your decisions to see if they are meeting your goals.

The Save-Game Issue

Saving a game takes a snapshot of a game world and all its particulars at a given instant in time and stores them away somewhere. The player can then load the snapshot, return to that instant in the game world, and replay the game from that point. This might seem like a fairly straightforward thing to offer the player, but, in fact, it has consequences both for the player's experience of the game—the story he's creating as he plays—and for the way the player actually plays. Saving and restoring a game is technologically easy, and it's an essential tool for testing and debugging, so it's often slapped in as a feature without much thought about its effect on gameplay. As designers, though, it's our job to think about anything that affects gameplay or the player's experience of the game, and that includes the save-game feature.

Saving a game stores not only the player's location in the game, but also any customizations he might have made along the way. In *Michelle Kwan's Figure Skating Championship*, for example, the player could customize the body type, skin tone, hair color and style, and costume of the skater. The player could even load in a picture of her own face. The more freedom the player has to customize the avatar, the more data must be saved. Until recently, this has placed a limit on the richness of games for console machines. Games for personal computers could almost always be saved because PCs had disk drives available, but the feature came more slowly to console games. The oldest console machines, which simply emulated arcade machines, often had no way of saving games because they had no storage medium. If the player wanted to leave a game and come back to it later, he could only pause it and leave the console turned on. As a result, most of the games for these machines tended to feel a lot like arcade games as well. They were not designed to be played for a little while and then returned to a day or two later; they had to be played through in one sitting or abandoned.

Now that the Microsoft Xbox includes a hard disk drive, console machines can finally save games just as complex as personal computer games. This doesn't necessarily mean that Xbox games will be just like PC games—there are still important differences between consoles and PCs—but one significant barrier to rich gaming on consoles has been removed.

Reasons for Saving a Game

Three reasons exist for saving a player's game or allowing him to save it:

- ► **Allowing the player to leave the game and return to it later.** This is the most important reason for saving the game. In a large game, it's an essential feature. It's not realistic and not fair to the player to expect him to dedicate the computer or console machine to a 40-hour game until it's finished.

- ► **Letting the player recover from disastrous mistakes.** In practice, this usually means getting the avatar killed somehow. Arcade games, which have no save-game feature, traditionally give the player a fixed number of "lives" and chances to earn more along the way. Console action games have tended to follow the same scheme. Richer games, such as role-playing or adventure games, usually give the player only one life but allow him to reload a saved game if his avatar dies or he loses any possibility of winning the game.

➤ **Encouraging the player to explore alternate strategies.** Saving the game is a useful feature in turn-based strategic games because it lets the player learn the game by trying alternative approaches. If one doesn't seem to work, he can go back to the point at which he committed himself to one plan and try another approach.

Consequences for Immersion and Storytelling

Saving a computer game is not part of its gameplay. The act of saving a game takes place *outside* the game world, even if it changes the way the player plays inside the game world. It destroys the suspension of disbelief. If a game is immersive and tries to create the illusion that the player inhabits a fantasy world, the act of saving a copy of the fantasy world destroys the illusion. One of the most significant characteristics of real life is that you cannot return to the past to correct errors you have made. The moment you allow a player to do this, you acknowledge that the fantasy world is only a game.

The essence of a story is dramatic tension, and dramatic tension requires that something be at stake. Saving a game in a game with a branching storyline profoundly affects the player's experience of the story. In the real world, decisions are irrevocable. Some can be changed later, their consequences modified at some point in the future, but the original decision itself cannot be unmade. But when a player follows first one branch of a branching storyline and then goes back in time and follows another branch, he experiences a very unnatural, unreal phenomenon. Dramatic tension is reduced because if the future can be altered by returning to the past at any moment and changing it, then nothing is really at stake.

Ways of Saving a Game

Over the years, designers have devised a variety of different ways of saving a game, each with their own consequences for immersion and gameplay.

Save to a File or "Save Slot"

The most common way of saving a game is to allow the player to interrupt the play and save it either into a file on the hard drive that the player can name, or, more commonly, to allow the player to save it into one of a series of named "slots" that the game program keeps track of. When the player wants to replay the saved game, he tells the program to load it from the directory of files or slots. This mechanism is useful because it allows the player to keep several different copies, saved at different points, and to name them so that he can remember which one is which.

Unfortunately, it's also the method most harmful to the game's immersiveness. The user interface for managing the files or save slots necessarily looks like an operating system's file-management tool, not like a part of the fantasy world that the game depicts. You can make it prettier with appropriate graphics, but it almost always takes the player out of the world and destroys his suspension of disbelief. Some games improve this a little by calling it the player's "journal" and making it look as if the saved games are being kept in a book.

Quick-Save

Fast-moving games in which the player's avatar is in more or less constant danger (such as first-person shooters) frequently offer a quick-save feature. The player presses a single button to save the game instantly at any time, without ever leaving the game world. The screen displays the words "Quick saved" for a moment, but other than that, the player's concentration and immersion in the world are not broken. The player can reload the game just as swiftly by pressing a quick-load button. The game returns immediately to the place where the last quick-save was done, without going out of the game world to a file-management screen.

The disadvantage of quick-save is that it usually offers only one slot, although some games let the player designate a numbered slot by pressing the quick-save button and then a number key. He has to remember which slot is which by himself when quick-loading. Quick-save sacrifices flexibility to gain immersiveness and speed. It doesn't let the player name or manage multiple saved games, but it does allow him to save and load with minimal disruption to his suspension of disbelief.

Automatic Save

A few games automatically save the state of the game as it progresses, so the player can leave and return at any time without explicitly having to save it. Sometimes they save continuously, but more often they save intermittently at checkpoints, which may or may not be revealed to the player when they occur. This is even less disruptive than quick-saving because the player never has to do anything. However, if this is the only method provided, the player can't choose to save at certain points along the way. If the player wants to restart at an earlier point, he's out of luck; and if the checkpoints are a long way apart, he might lose a great deal of progress in the event of a disaster. Continuous-save prevents the player from going back and undoing disasters. On the other hand, he can play the game confident that he can interrupt and resume it at any point.

To Save or Not to Save

Here we look at the arguments for and against saving, and we present our own perspective on the matter.

The Argument Against

A few designers don't allow players to save their games at certain points, or even at all. If the player can save and reload constantly, he can solve puzzles or overcome other obstacles by trial and error rather than by skill or brains. If the designer wants him to solve them in an uninterrupted sequence, saving and reloading defeats that challenge. Some games (*The Legend of Zelda: Ocarina of Time*, for example) avoid this by saving a game only at checkpoints or particular locations, forcing the player to play the game again from that point when he reloads. Saving and reloading also enables players to avoid undesirable random events. If the event occurs, the player can simply reload the game repeatedly until it doesn't occur.

When you can save and reload at any point, nothing is at stake. Your avatar might die, lose money, or suffer some other disaster, but it can all be remedied simply by reloading the game. This takes away some of the challenge.

The Argument For

We believe that these arguments against saving are spurious and are the sign of a lazy designer. Making a game harder simply by preventing the player from saving the game is a cheap way of creating a challenge out of nothing. For example, you could set up a situation in which the player has no way of knowing which of several options to choose (for example, selecting one of three identical corridors to walk down). If two contain deadly traps and one does not, and the player is not allowed to save before walking down them, you've guaranteed that two times in three he will have to go back and start the game over, no matter how good he is otherwise. This isn't fun or even a fair challenge. If you really want to make the game harder, devise harder challenges. Forcing the player to replay an entire level because he made a mistake near the end wastes his time and condemns him to frustration and boredom. As a designer, it should be your goal to avoid those feelings, not create them.

If a player continuously reloads a game to avoid a random event or to solve some problem by trial and error rather than skill or intelligence, he is, in effect, cheating at solitaire. As the game's designer, you might not like it, but we don't feel that that is sufficient reason for denying the player the chance to save the game—he might need to save it for perfectly legitimate reasons. After all, cheating at solitaire says more about the player's character than anything else; if he wants to ruin the gameplay for himself, that's his business. Most games now recognize that players want—and even need—to cheat sometimes by offering cheat codes anyway.

The bottom line is that it's the player's machine. It's not fair to penalize him just because he has to go to the bathroom or because it's now his little brother's turn to play. Whether you implement save slots, quick-save, checkpoints, or continuous-save is up to you; there are advantages and disadvantages to each. But we strongly believe that players have a fundamental right to be able to stop playing when and where they want, without losing all that they have accomplished.

Putting It Together

At this point, you should know when and where your game takes place. You will have answered a huge number of questions about what your world looks like, what it sounds like, who lives there, and how they behave. If you've done it thoroughly, your game world will be one that a player can immerse himself in, an integrated harmonious fantasy that he can believe in and enjoy being part of. The next step is to figure out what's going to happen there. That's covered in Chapter 4, "Storytelling and Narrative."

Chapter 4

Storytelling and Narrative

Stories are as old as communication itself. Since the first protohominids daubed their paintings on the rough walls of their caves, stories have been told. Stories and games have been intertwined to varying degrees for almost as long.

Computer games generally have some sort of story attached to them as well. Sometimes it is a one-paragraph backstory. In other cases, it's a fully integrated story line—where the game *is* the story.

In this chapter, we discuss some guidelines for constructing compelling stories and integrating them into game designs. To some extent, the importance of story integration is dependent on the type of game you are designing: Some games require more integration than others. For example, a simple game such as *Space Invaders* requires only a one-liner: "Aliens are invading Earth, and *only you* can stop them." Why? It doesn't matter. The player's imagination takes care of that. At the other end of the spectrum, adventure games such as *Grim Fandango* and *Discworld Noir* have a detailed and involving story line, as convoluted and structured as any novel. And, of course, we have the middle range—games in which story is important but is not the overriding gameplay feature. This concept is illustrated in Figure 4.1. As we progress across the story spectrum from left to right, the importance of the story increases. Examples of games such as this include *Half-Life* and *Luigi's Mansion* (shown in Figure 4.2).

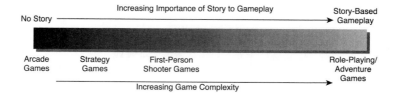

Figure 4.1 The story spectrum.

Figure 4.2 *Luigi's Mansion.*

In *Half-Life,* the story is an important part of the flavor of the game, but aside from acting as a mechanism to allow the player to become more immersed in the game world, it bears no relevance to the actual gameplay. (And by this we mean that the gameplay of *Half-Life* is virtually identical to that of any other first-person shooter; it's just the story and setting that give it the edge.)

Stories in Games

The use of stories in games is a fundamental part of game design. A game without a story becomes an abstract construct. Of course, for some games, such as *Tetris*, this is ideal, but the vast majority are much improved by the addition of a story.

Over the course of the 20th century, story form and design have been researched. As always, research gravitates toward money, so the most significant portion of this research over the last few years has tended to be about Hollywood and the movie industry. The rewards for a hit movie are usually much greater than the equivalent rewards for a best-selling book, so this is where we find the most accessible information.

The main focus of story-form research has been based on the concept of the *monomyth*: the fundamental story form that is common to most, if not all, accomplished literature and movies. We'll be discussing the structure of the monomyth a bit later. Of course, we are not saying that all stories conform to this formulaic approach. Many do, but not all. What we can say is that the concepts and ideas behind the monomyth are present in some form in virtually all nontrivial stories.

Previously, we mentioned the story spectrum as applied to games. At one end of the spectrum, we have the light backstory—usually a brief sentence or paragraph that sets the theme for a game. This is usually fairly trivial stuff, so we will not concern our-selves with it much. However, toward the other end of the spectrum, the importance of the story increases, culminating in those games in which the story *is* the game. In these cases, you will find the recurring elements of the monomyth, and it is in these cases that the structure and definition of the story is most important. Hence, it is this area that we will focus on.

Don't worry, though: All the concepts we discuss are equally applicable to the lighter end of the story spectrum. It's just that they are not as important for the success (or failure) of the game. If a game has a bad backstory, and the backstory has little impact on the game, then no one is really going to care. In fact, a number of games pride themselves on the absurdity of their (either real or implied) backstory. Consider Sega's *Super Monkey Ball*. The player's avatar is a monkey. In a ball. Collecting bananas. And as far as we can tell, that is the extent of the story, which is fine for that particular game. Any attempt to flesh it out further would be extraneous effort.

Simple Backstories

Not all games require a detailed and rigorous story. Often a couple of short paragraphs just setting the background are required. For example, a game such as *R-Type* doesn't need much of a story line. An evil galactic empire is invading, and you're the only one who can stop it. Original? No. Good enough for the purpose? Yes.

If a game doesn't require a detailed backstory, there is nothing to be gained by adding one. Think carefully before you decide this, though; consider the difference that the addition of a story made to *Half-Life*. (For those of you who don't know, *Half-Life* was the first decent attempt at a first-person shooter with a strong backstory.)

Games such as the *Mario* series often have simple backstories that are expanded upon during the game. The story line does not affect the gameplay to a restrictive degree, but it does provide direction and increases the interest level. By creating a loose story line that does not impact the gameplay, the designer increases the interest level by using the story line to involve the player in the plight of the characters.

Commonly, the backstory is used to provide a framework for a mission-based game structure. For the majority of games, this is the ideal approach. As the complexity of the game increases, the relative importance of the story to the gameplay can (but does not have to) increase. For example, the story line of a simple arcade game is a lot less important to the gameplay than in the case of a more complex game such as a role-playing game. This is shown in Figure 4.1.

Who Is the Storyteller?

It is important for the designer to consider who exactly the storyteller is. Who is the main driving force behind the narrative? Is it the designer or the player? Often a game designer falls victim to "frustrated author syndrome." The designer feels as if she should be writing a great novel and forces a linear and restrictive story line onto the player.

In other cases, the designer might swamp the player with reams of unnecessary dialogue or narrative. The player then has to fight his way through the excessive text, attempting to sort the wheat from the chaff.

The main distinguishing factor between games and other forms of entertainment is the level of interactivity. If players just wanted a story, they could watch a movie or read a book. When players are playing a game, they do not want to be force-fed a story that limits the gameplay. Stories generally are not interactive; the amount of branching available in the story tree is limited, so only a few alternative narrative paths are usually available. Hence, the story needs to be handled carefully. It should not be forced on the player, and wherever possible, you should avoid railroading the player down limited story paths because of your own frustrated author syndrome.

So what is the answer to the question of who the storyteller is? Simple. The players should be the primary storytellers. They are the stars of the show. The time they spend playing the game is their time to shine, not yours. Consequently, the game should be structured so that for the majority of the time, they are telling their own story.

The theme of a story is the philosophical idea that the author is trying to express. You can think of it as the "defining question" of the work. For example, can love triumph? Is murder ever justified? Are dreams real? Is death the end? We've said that the true author of a game narrative is (or should be) the player. Game design can steer the player toward the favored themes of the designer, but it's like leading the proverbial horse to water. You cannot force the players to think your way. Bearing these caveats in mind, let us continue with a discussion of story structure.

The Monomyth and the Hero's Journey

What is this construct that we are calling the monomyth? In 1949, Joseph Campbell published a seminal work called *The Hero with a Thousand Faces*, exploring the interrelationship among the legends and myths of cultures throughout the world and extracting a complex pattern that all of these stories followed. This pattern, the monomyth, is called "The Hero's Journey" and describes a series of steps and sequences that the story follows, charting the progress of the story's hero. The archetypal character types—those that occur across all cultures and ages—are incumbent features of the hero's journey. These powerful archetypes are so innately recognizable by all individuals through Jung's concept of the collective unconscious that they have a familiar resonance that serves to strengthen and validate the story. We cover these in detail in the next chapter. The following quote summarizes Campbell's belief in the universal story form.

"Whether we listen with aloof amusement to [a] ... witch doctor of the Congo, or read with cultivated rapture thin translations from the sonnets of the mystic Lao-tse; now and again crack the hard nutshell of an argument of Aquinas, or catch suddenly the shining meaning of [an] ... Eskimo fairy tale: it will always be the one, shape-shifting yet marvelously constant story that we find, together with a challengingly persistent suggestion of more remaining to be experienced than will even be known or told."

—**Joseph Campbell**, *The Hero with a Thousand Faces*, 1949

Despite the excellence of Campbell's book, it can be somewhat heavy going, and for all but the most story-intensive games, it could be considered overkill. *The Hero with a Thousand Faces* is recommended as an essential addition to the game designer's reference library. For the purposes of this chapter, we want to make use of a slightly lighter analysis, one that has been updated with modern considerations and that presents the concepts in a clearer fashion.

Fortunately, such a work exists. In 1993, screenwriter Christopher Vogler published the first edition of a book based on a seven-page pamphlet that he had been circulating around the Hollywood studio where he worked. This pamphlet, "A Practical Guide to the Hero's Journey," took the movie industry by storm, and the obvious step for Vogler was to expand the work and publish a book based on it. This book, *The Writer's Journey*, presents the concepts and ideas of the hero's journey in a concise and easily digestible form. It's not a perfect fit for our purposes, but it is an excellent start. As such, it forms the basis of our analysis of stories and comes heavily recommended. Any serious game designer needs to read this book thoroughly.

Note that we are not just trying to feed you the line that games are merely interactive movies. That is plainly not true. They are an entirely different medium. However, the ideas presented by Campbell and Vogler are universal. They transcend the medium of film and are applicable—at least, to some extent—directly to the field of game design, particularly where the story line is a major factor in the design.

Too Good to Be True?

One of the chief arguments against patterns—especially when related to design aspects—is that they stifle creativity, producing a lackluster and formulaic output. Of course, if you just take the basic interpretation and apply it, this can be true.

However, it should be realized that the monomyth is a form, not a formula. It is a set of guidelines for creating a rewarding and fulfilling story line, not a cookie-cutter template for autogenerating the same tired old story in a slightly different guise. Another important point to bear in mind is that we are using the term *hero* to refer to either sex. It could just as easily apply to a female hero as it does to a male.

With that in mind, let's take a look at this universal story form in more detail. The next few sections describe the stages present in Vogler's interpretation of the hero's journey. We will be careful to use the same terminology and notation as Vogler so that those of you who refer to his book will be able to use the same frame of reference.

Note that not all games use these structures for their story line. Some use just a few of them and miss out on key features (and, in some cases, their story usually feels somewhat unsatisfactory). For others, some of the steps are inappropriate and would add nothing to the game. For example, many games gloss over the introduction to the ordinary world and the hero's refusal of the call. Sometimes that is ideal—the player actually *wants* to be a gung-ho hero who is ready for anything, no matter how unrealistic that might be. There is no law, written or unwritten, that says that games have to conform to reality. They just have to be self-consistent.

The steps in Vogler's hero's journey are as follows:

1. The ordinary world.

2. The call to adventure.

3. The refusal of the call.

4. The meeting with the mentor.

5. Crossing the first threshold.

6. Tests, allies, and enemies.

7. The approach to the innermost cave.

8. The ordeal.

9. The reward.

10. The road back.

11. The resurrection.

12. The return with the reward.

We discuss these in detail and apply the ideas to game story design in the following sections.

The Ordinary World

All stories should start at the beginning (or thereabouts). The ordinary world is where the player first meets the hero and is introduced to her background and normal existence.

The ordinary world of the hero is used to set up the story, to provide a mundane canvas for the storyteller to contrast with the special world that the hero will be entering in the game. Often the introduction to the ordinary world of the hero is combined with a prologue. The prologue generally takes one of two forms:

➤ Explains the events that have happened to the hero so far, setting up the context for what is about to happen

➤ Provides a snippet of the special world, either by covering past events in the special world that are about to collide with the hero in the ordinary world or by foreshadowing an event to come

Care must be taken with the backstory and how this story is revealed to the player. Don't just blurt it out in one go. Nothing appears flatter than a straightforward monologue detailing the hero's background and motivations. It's far better to reveal the backstory gracefully. Make the player work a bit to put the pieces together. It's a more rewarding experience, and it makes the player feel as if he has achieved something in uncovering the story.

Foreshadowing is a powerful technique in storytelling. Consider an example from the introduction to Valve's *Half-Life*. The noninteractive opening scenes tell the story of Gordon Freeman, who has accepted a research position at the ultrasecretive Black Mesa research laboratory. As Gordon takes the underground monorail to the main security entrance, he gets a glimpse of the ordinary world of the research facility. At certain points throughout the journey, Gordon's attention is drawn to various constructs and facilities that will feature heavily in the special world when the catastrophic accident occurs. Another more explicit example of foreshadowing occurs at the point at which the accident occurs. When the experiment goes awry and the dimensional rift is opened, Gordon is transported to a variety of strange locations and glimpses strange alien landscapes and beings. This (unbeknownst to Gordon) is a taste of things to come.

Because foreshadowing is so powerful, it is very commonly used. Often in games that have boss characters, such as shoot 'em-ups, the boss character puts in brief cameo appearances throughout the level before appearing at the end of the level for the big confrontation. The various Star Wars games (an example of which is shown in Figure 4.3) that feature the Death Star often use this technique. The Death Star appears as part of the background graphics a couple of levels before the player is called upon to destroy it. As soon as it appears, ominously hanging in the distance like a small moon, the player knows that sooner or later he will be there.

Figure 4.3 *Star Wars: Rogue Squadron II.*

This foreshadowing is so effective because it contrasts the special world against the ordinary world. This confuses the player, and confusion eases the process of mental suggestion. Players who are susceptible to mental suggestion are easier to immerse in the game. The willing suspension of disbelief that the designer is aiming for becomes that little bit easier to achieve.

The "Ordinary World" section is the place to introduce the reasoning and motivation behind the hero's being who she is. Why is she even in this situation? What is the game actually going to be about? Here we discuss the best way to get that information to the player without being blatant and uninteresting.

This is where you introduce the hero to the player. You want to make the player identify with the hero. This is crucial—if you fail to do this, there is no compunction to play the game. There are many ways to do this, but probably the most effective way to get the player to identify with the hero is to play on the player's emotions.

We discuss non–story-based methods of creating the bond between the player and the hero in the next chapter. For now, let's consider how you can use the story to accomplish the same task. Often in classical literature, the hero has a flaw or some mental or spiritual wound that the reader can empathize with. This doesn't necessarily mean that the hero needs to be an inmate of a mental asylum (although some games have used just that mechanism—*American McGee's Alice*, shown in Figure 4.4, was set in the fantasies of a female patient).

Figure 4.4   *American McGee's Alice.*

An example is Gordon Freeman's inexperience in his new job. Gordon is a new employee in a top-secret lab. The player can empathize with this. We're pretty sure that the vast majority of *Half-Life* players would also feel rather overwhelmed in Gordon's position. The superb introductory sequence amplifies this sense of awe and transmits it to the player. In this way, a bond is created between the player and the avatar.

The Call to Adventure

The call to adventure is the first inkling the hero gets that she is going to be leaving the security of the ordinary world to enter the special world of the adventure ahead.

Now, bear in mind that the players already know they are going to be entering a special world, so it is very difficult to surprise them. It can be done—you can take the story line off at a tangent they would never expect—but the safer and easier approach is to make use of this expectation and build up the players' anticipation levels so that they can hardly wait to enter the special world. Don't try to maintain this buildup for too long, however. The player bought the game to play it, not to wait until the designer allows him to play it.

The call to adventure can take many forms. Infogrames's *Outcast* (see Figure 4.5) portrays the hero, retired Special Forces man Cutter Slade, sitting in a bar knocking back straight whiskies. As he is sitting nursing his drink, several G-men approach him and inform him that he is needed with the utmost urgency by Cutter's old commanding officer. This is his first call to adventure.

Figure 4.5   *Outcast.*

The call to adventure is often the catalyst or trigger that initiates the story line. It can take many forms, and we detail some of those here. In a few stories, the hero receives multiple calls. It then becomes the task of the hero to decide how to prioritize these calls—which to answer first or which to reject outright. In some cases, these priorities will already have been decided—or at least hinted at—by the designer.

Ultima VII epitomizes this concept. The avatar really leaves his own world through an obelisk into the fictional world of Brittania. In a sense, there are two dimensions to the fiction in the game because the "real world" is the initial setting of a fictional story. This extra dimension adds tremendously to the game experience, by adding yet another level to the suspension of disbelief. When playing *Ultima VII*, the player is fully engaged in the game world and the character. When players occasionally do think about the "real world," it is often thoughts of the avatar's "real world," not their own. They empathize with the avatar's wish to return home. In other words, they're sympathetic to the plight of a fictional game character!

Often the call to adventure is personal to the hero. Nintendo uses this technique a lot, particularly in the *Mario* series of games. For example, usually the Princess manages to get herself captured, and Mario, being the sterling sort of hero that he is, feels a burning urge to rescue her. This is a common thread running through the entire series of games. The call to adventure often involves family or friends in jeopardy. In *Luigi's Mansion*, Luigi is called upon to rescue his brother, who is lost inside a mysterious haunted house.

Of course, the call does not need to be on a level personal to the hero. External events are often used as a call to adventure. Some grand event happening on a large scale might act as the call. In these cases, only the hero's sense of decency (or other motivation, such as avarice) propels the hero into adventure.

Temptation can always be used as a call. Many forms of temptation exist, but in games, it usually comes in the form of greed. There are various reasons for this. One is that sexual temptation does not make a very good theme for a game. A few games have tried to use this, but they were, for the most part, poor games, and in some cases, verged on the extremely distasteful, with *Custer's Revenge* (which can be seen with a Google search) being a particularly obnoxious (and classic) example.

A far safer and more socially acceptable form of temptation is greed. (You've got to love capitalism!) For example, many games use the old "earn as much cash as possible" or "treasure hunting" paradigms as the call to adventure. Games such as *Monopoly Tycoon* (and, in fact, the majority of the tycoon-style games) use greed as the motivation to play. Remember, kiddies, greed is good! Even *Luigi's Mansion* uses treasure hunting as a secondary call (as do the majority of the other games in the series). The primary call is to rescue Mario, but the secondary call is to get rich in the process.

Sometimes the call comes in the form of a message from a herald, a character archetype. The herald does not have to be an ally of the hero. In fact, the character acting as the herald might reappear as another character archetype later in the game, such as the mentor or the shadow. Examples of the use of the herald to deliver the call are present in many games. The specific example we will use here is Lionhead's *Black and White*. In this game, two mentor characters representing the good and evil sides of the player vie for the player's attention. Both characters call the player to adventure—one on the side of good, and one on the side of evil.

In other situations, the call to adventure isn't an explicit call. It can be the result of a void felt by the hero due to a lack of or a need for something. What that "something" is can be the choice of the game designer. For example, in *Planescape: Torment*, the call for adventure is lack of knowledge on the part of the hero. The fact that he is referred to as the Nameless One indicates the magnitude of the call.

The call to adventure does not need to be optional. The hero isn't always given a choice (even if the player is: He can choose to play or not to play). In *Space Invaders*, the call to adventure is the need to destroy all the aliens to prevent the player's own destruction.

The Refusal of the Call

In the traditional monomyth form, the next stage after the call is the refusal. This is the representation of the hero rejecting the offer to leave her comfortable ordinary world. It does not have to be portrayed as a grandiose event—often the refusal amounts to little more than a quiet moment of personal doubt or a brief rebellious outburst on the part of the hero.

For a computer game, the call is usually not refused—especially if there is only one call. After all, if that were to occur, there would be no game. That is not to say that the refusal is never issued. Usually, however, it forms part of the initial background story, as is the case with Cutter Slade in *Outcast*. Cutter's response to the plea for assistance from the G-men is to turn away, slug back a shot of whiskey, and growl, "I'm retired." As an example of drama, this is far more involving than if he'd just leapt to attention and replied, "Yes sir, let's go." It's more believable and compelling, leaving the player wondering, "Will he or won't he?" even though we know he will. More important, it sets the stage for conflict. And conflict, as we all know, is interesting.

The refusal of the call is usually reserved for games that place more of an emphasis on story. For example, a call refusal would make little sense in a simple arcade game; it can be added to the backstory for additional flavor, but in general, it would have little effect on the gameplay.

Any games that offer multiple quests and subquests allow for multiple refusals. As long as the overall grand quest is attended to, the game designer can allow the hero to ignore some of the smaller quests without any serious penalty.

In the case of conflicting calls—when the hero is given two or more conflicting calls simultaneously—a dynamic tension automatically is created. The player has to decide which (if any) call to follow. The classic case is the choice between good and evil. In *Black and White*, the player is given the choice to be an evil god or a good god (and anything in between). The player's actions determine which call he has refused.

In some cases, refusal of the call can be seen as a positive action. The call to adventure can be a negative thing. For example, the hero might be offered a quest that involves partaking in some form of action that would result in unpleasant consequences. In the case of a role-playing game based on the familiar *Advanced Dungeons and Dragons* rules, a lawful good hero might be asked to perform an activity that would conflict with his alignment, such as killing a household of innocents. If the player sees it as advantageous in the long run to maintain his alignment, it would be wise to refuse this quest.

The Meeting with the Mentor

The character archetype of mentor is discussed at length in the next chapter. You've already seen an example of a mentor in the previous section, when we discussed *Black and White*. Another example is Morte, the first character that the Nameless One encounters in *Planescape: Torment*. At the start of the game, Morte's main purpose is to provide the Nameless One with information about his location and situation. As the Nameless One progresses further, Morte provides further tips and helpful suggestions until he is more familiar with his surroundings.

If the call to adventure is seen as the catalyst to the story, creating an impulse and motive where previously there were none, then the meeting with the mentor serves to give direction to these unleashed forces. When the hero decides to take action, it is the task of the mentor archetype to give the hero the information needed to choose which action to take.

Note that the mentor does not have to be a single character. Often the mentor is a clichéd wise old man, but there is no reason why this should be the case. The position of the mentor archetype can be filled by any combination of characters that give the hero information. In fact, the mentor does not even need to be a character. The hero can use past experiences, a library, a television, or any other information source. It's not important what or who fills the role of the mentor, as long as the information the hero needs is provided.

Crossing the First Threshold

After the hero has decided to leave the ordinary world, accepted the call to adventure, and discovered what needs to be done, she still has to make that first step and commit to the adventure. Vogler refers to this as "crossing the threshold" from the safe and comfortable ordinary world into the dangerous and strange special world of the quest ahead.

This step is not always optional. Sometimes the hero is thrust into the special world against her will. For example, in *Planescape: Torment*, the amnesiac hero wakes into the special world at the start of the game, with only a few tattered memories of the ordinary world from which he came.

To enter the special world, the hero must mentally prepare, garner her courage, and perform a certain amount of symbolic loin girding to confidently enter the strange and unknown experiences ahead. Often the hero expresses misgivings, concerns, and fears but makes the crossing anyway. This is a good time to bond the player with the hero by creating a sense of concern. The threshold guardian archetype often comes into play here. This could be manifested as the hero's own misgivings, the fear of the hero's companions, a warning from the enemy who the hero seeks to defeat, or any combination of these.

The opening scene of Midway's *Pac-Land* (shown in Figure 4.6) shows Pac-Man leaving the ordinary world of his home and setting out of a strange road full of danger and mystery. The act of leaving the house and heading off through the dangerous ghost-infested path is the crossing of the first threshold.

Figure 4.6   *Pac-Land.*

When the first threshold of adventure is crossed, there is no turning back. The next phase is entered, and the adventure into the special world truly begins.

Tests, Allies, and Enemies

The crossing of the threshold is the first test. In this phase, many more similar tests are thrown at the hero. This phase is often the longest phase of a game story and makes up the bulk of a game.

In this phase, the hero ventures forth into the special world and meets many of the character archetypes on the journey. For the majority of games, the character archetypes that the player meets are either allies, shadows, or tricksters. At the left edge of the story spectrum, you would expect to meet mainly shadows. For example, in *Space Invaders*, the player is alone against the alien onslaught—a hero surrounded by shadow.

Slightly more complex games often provide allies, such as the fairies at the end of each *Pac-Land* level. In arcade-style games—those that place more emphasis on the action than the story—these are likely to be the only archetypes present. The player will go through a series of tests with successively more powerful shadows, to be given a brief respite when an ally occasionally shows up to replenish the hero's spirit and resolve. In some cases, the player might even encounter the trickster and shape-shifter archetypes in the form of false allies who turn out to be shadows after all.

In a more complex game, where story is the biggest consideration, you would expect to see many more character archetypes during this phase of the game. For example, a role-playing game with a well-developed story line would be expected to use all of the major character archetypes many times over and in varying combinations.

The main purpose of this phase in the story is to test and prepare the hero for the grand ordeal that lies ahead. Here, the hero is expected to learn the unfamiliar rules and customs of the special world. During this succession of increasingly difficult tests, the hero forges alliances and makes enemies. Depending on the nature of the game, the opportunities available for the hero to actually make enemies or allies could be limited or predestined, as is the case with most games; the majority of characters the hero meets are already enemies, and allies are few and far between. This is not necessarily a disadvantage—an element can still add flavor to a game, even if it is noninteractive.

The Approach to the Innermost Cave

After the succession of tests, the hero approaches the innermost cave. This is the core of the story, where the hero will find the reward he seeks. Mostly, this is toward the end of the game, but in some cases, this occurs almost exactly in the middle.

The difference between these two alternatives is that the first—where the reward is close to the end of the game—doesn't pay too much attention to the journey back. The retrieval of the reward is the high point of the journey, and the return is assumed. This has its merits. In some cases, you would not want to force the player to retrace his steps back the way he came.

The second situation, in which the reward is close to the middle of the game, pays special attention to the journey back. In this case, retrieving the reward is only half the story. Now the hero actually has to escape with the reward and return to the ordinary world in one piece. For this style of game, the journey back is well integrated into the quest and should be significantly different than the journey that brought the hero to that point.

The traditional use for this story element is to help prepare the hero for the ordeal ahead. This is done by a number of means, including doing reconnaissance, gathering information, checking or purchasing equipment, or mentally preparing and girding loins for the coming tasks.

The Ordeal

The ordeal is the ultimate test: the fight with the nemesis. This is the culminating battle of the story. Until now, the hero might have dealt with some serious tests, but this is the real thing. The stakes are high, and the final reward is at hand.

Many games follow this pattern. In fact, any game that has a succession of levels punctuated by increasingly powerful boss enemies for the player to defeat follows this pattern. *Luigi's Mansion*, *Quake II*, *Half-Life*, *R-Type*, and *Diablo II* are some of these. We're sure that you can add hundreds to the list.

During the ordeal, you might try to cement the player's bond with the hero further. This is sometimes achieved by making it appear as if the hero is almost defeated, before fighting back from seemingly impossible odds to defeat the enemy.

In the ordeal, the hero faces the ultimate shadow. Defeat means failure, final and absolute. Victory means claiming the reward and the ultimate success. However, sometimes achieving victory is possible in many ways and at many levels, not all of them immediately obvious. For example, in the case of games such as LucasArts' *Jedi Knight* series, it could mean deciding whether to fight the ultimate nemesis.

The Reward

After the ultimate shadow is defeated, the reward can be claimed. The reward can come in many forms—and not all of them are positive. Sometimes the reward can be a negative option, something the hero would rather avoid but cannot, or simply was not, expecting.

More often, however, the reward is positive, even if it might not seem that way to the player. For example, the reward in *Planescape: Torment* is mortality and the promise of death. Although this might not seem like much of a reward to the player, to the hero—who has endured a long and painful cycle of continual death and rebirth—the ability to finally die and join his lover in the peace of eternal sleep is an ideal boon.

Many games end at this point. Some of these show the remaining story as a final cut scene. For other games, this is merely the beginning of the final phase.

Note that nothing says that the reward has to be the same one that the hero set out for at the beginning of the story. In *Half-Life*, Gordon Freeman initially sets out to escape from the alien-infested laboratory. By the end of the story, the stakes—and the potential reward for success—are much higher. The important thing is to make sure that the reward reflects the effort expended in reaching it. Nothing falls flat more than an insignificant reward—an excellent example of this being the ending of *Unreal*. After fighting the alien threat and escaping the planet, the player's avatar is left drifting in space as his escape pod runs out of fuel. The assumption is that you will eventually be rescued—or not (see Figure 4.7).

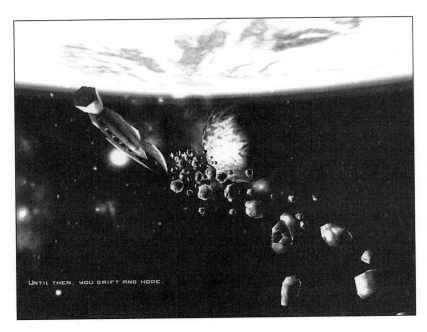

Figure 4.7 The ending of *Unreal*.

The Road Back

With the reward won, the hero now has to prepare for the journey back to the ordinary world. The experience of the adventure will have changed the hero, and it might be difficult (if not impossible) to integrate her successfully back into the ordinary world. As we've said, most games do not go as far as this in their interactive stories—instead, they leave this and the following two story elements to a final cut scene.

Interplay's *Fallout* (shown in Figure 4.8) used this particular element to good effect. In this post-apocalyptic role-playing game, the hero was tasked with finding a replacement chip to the water processor to allow the vault-dwellers to continue living in their underground vault. The hero was sent out into the radioactive wilderness to find this chip and, after many adventures, successfully returned with the reward. Upon his return, he was not permitted to re-enter the vault. The vault elders claimed that he had been so changed by his journey that he was too dangerous to be allowed to live in the vault with the others. Hence, he was turned away from his old ordinary world. His special world became his new ordinary world.

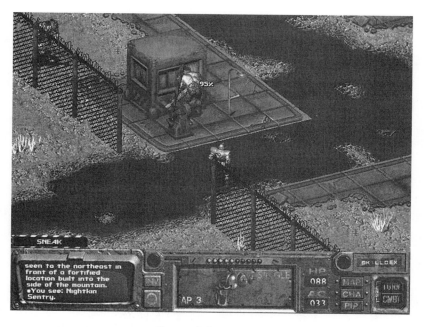

Figure 4.8 *Fallout.*

The Resurrection

The *resurrection* is the point in the story at which all outstanding plot threads are resolved. Any problems or consequences from the retrieval of the reward are (for the most part) resolved here. Does the story resolve itself? Are any questions left unanswered? Is this an oversight on the part of the designer, or are they deliberately left open for the sequel?

The resurrection is the final set of tests the hero faces before being able to enjoy the hard-earned reward fully. In conventional stories, this is comparable to the last-minute plot twist: Just when you think the story is over and the hero has won, the enemy resurfaces briefly for a final stand before dying.

Another purpose of the resurrection is so that the player can see clearly how the hero has evolved throughout the story. Has the hero changed? More important, does the hero have the answer to the question posed by the story?

The resurrection might also be in the form of an internal revelation for the character that the player might not have foreseen—a trick ending: "No, Luke...I *am* your father."

The Return with the Reward

Now the story is over, and the hero returns to his ordinary world to resume life as normal. The player gets to see the hero enjoy the benefits of the reward, and the story is over. This is the last stage in the circular story form. The story returns completely to its starting point so that comparisons can be drawn between the hero before and after.

However, a neatly tied-up story is not always desirable. Sometimes it is nice to leave a few questions open. One of the most popular forms of ending for a story is the "new beginning." In this type of ending, the story continues in the imagination of the player long after the game is completed. The player is left asking, "What happens next?" and the way is left open for a continuation or a sequel.

The most obvious example of this is *Half-Life*. The story line for this game contains a last-minute plot twist. Just when you think Gordon Freeman is about to escape, he is accosted by a man in black (who has been covertly watching Gordon during the entire game) and is offered two choices. We won't spoil the surprise for those of you who have not played the game to completion; suffice to say that it is certainly an unexpected twist. The reward in this case has mutated from freedom to something else entirely.

The Story Vehicle

The most common format for a story is the three-act structure. This is by no means the only structure, but it seems to be the most common structure. For example, some of Shakespeare's plays use different structures, such as five- and seven-act ones. However, most modern stories conform to the more common three-act structure, and that's what we'll concentrate on here.

The hero's journey is often used in a circular story form split into three acts. This does not mean that all stories return exactly to their starting point and circumstances. Often the manifestation of the circular form means that the hero's special world becomes his new ordinary world. How the hero's journey is related to the circular form is shown in Figure 4.9.

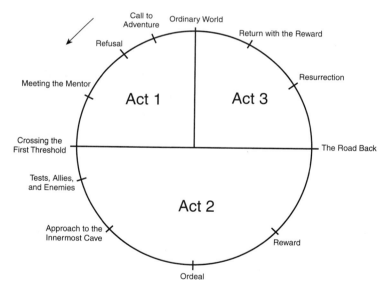

Figure 4.9   The circular story form.

Classically, this story form is used in literature and movies. It also applies directly to story-focused games and can be used as a guideline for games in which stories are present but are not the primary focus. Let's discuss the figure in some more detail.

The first act deals with the introduction of the hero and the ordinary world. The end of the first act is the point at which the hero prepares to cross the first threshold and enter the special world.

Act 2 is the longest act and takes place entirely in the special world. This act is often split into two parts, with the end of the first part coinciding with the ordeal. The second part begins with a change of pace; the story now begins to wind down, and the farthest point in the journey has been reached.

Act 2 ends with the road back, and the beginning of the third act heralds the return of the hero to the ordinary world, ending back where the story started in the ordinary world (although not necessarily the same one that the hero left).

The converse of the circular story form is the open-ended form. Here, the story is not tied up nicely as in the circular case. Plot strands are deliberately left open so that there is a sense of unresolved ambiguities and unanswered questions. This form is not often used in stories in Western culture and is often reserved for serials. Two classic movie examples of this form are Robert Zemeckis's *Back to the Future, Part II* and George Lucas's *The Empire Strikes Back*. In both of these films, we are left with many unanswered questions, leaving the way wide open for the sequels. Of course, the worst sin of the storyteller is to artificially include a fake plot element simply to force the circle to a close.

Plot Pacing

We previously mentioned that the plot can be paced in one of two main ways. The position of the crisis in the story makes the difference in the feel of the story: Whether the third act is a quick resolution or a slow wind-down of the story depends on it.

Given a conventional three-act structure in which the long second act is usually split into two parts, there are two main points at which the crisis occurs. How these are used is related to the pacing of the plot. The standard approach (shown in Figure 4.10) is to slowly build up to the ordeal at the end of Act 2 and move on fairly swiftly to the final climax. This approach is the more common one, both in games and in the movies. It allows the story to concentrate on the pre-ordeal story line, and after the reward is claimed, it tidies things up quickly.

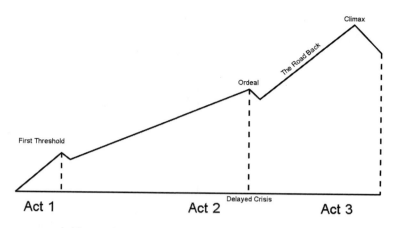

Figure 4.10   Delayed crisis in a three-act story.

That's one approach to plot pacing. The other common one is the central crisis. Here, Act 3 is lengthened so that the ordeal occurs roughly in the middle of the story, giving a symmetrical appearance. This approach allows for the consequences of the ordeal and the claiming of the reward to be expounded upon in more detail. Both halves of the story have equal importance, both pre- and post-ordeal. Often this can be used to give the villain a fighting chance to reclaim the reward and kill the hero, a sort of "just when you thought it was over" approach to the story. This form (shown in Figure 4.11) has not been used much in the games industry so far. This is a shame because it seems a bit naïve to assume that everything turns up rosy after the hero has claimed the reward. As we all know, sometimes that is not the case. For example, E.E. "Doc" Smith used an interesting variant of this in writing his *Lensman* and *Skylark* novels.

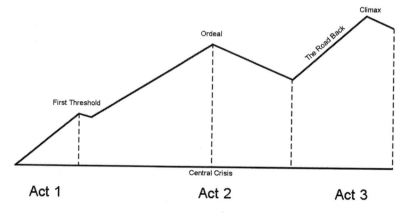

Figure 4.11   Central crisis in a three-act story.

Gameplay and Narrative

In this book, we've defined *narrative* to mean the noninteractive part of a computer game's story, the part in which you as the designer and author tell the player things without letting him do anything. This definition ignores literary theory and all the academic debate that surrounds modern creative writing, but it serves our purpose: to discuss the nature of storytelling in games and the relationship between interactive and noninteractive elements.

From this definition, you can see that a game's story content can be divided into interactive and noninteractive parts: the gameplay and the narrative. These exist in inverse proportion to one another: The more you have of one, the less you have of the other. A novel or a movie has no gameplay; it is entirely narrative. A simple arcade game such as *Space Invaders* has no narrative; it is entirely gameplay. The majority of home computer and console games lie somewhere in between; they seek to strike a balance between gameplay and narrative. You, as the designer, must decide where that balance lies.

The Role of Narrative

To make that determination, you have to ask what function narrative will have in your game. At first glance, it might seem to be pointless. A game is a form of participatory entertainment, and purists would say that any nonparticipatory elements are extraneous. A number of players feel that way, too: As soon as they are given some text to read or see a movie come up, they hit whatever button will skip past it and take them on to the gameplay. These kinds of players tend to be core gamers, motivated primarily by the challenges in the game and the desire to defeat them. To them, beating the game is its own reward, and they need nothing else.

Not all players are this eager to dive headfirst into the action, however. Casual gamers, who play for the enjoyment of being in the game's fantasy world, need to have the stage set for them. They need to feel part of something larger, a story that will excite their imaginations. Casual gamers also need rewards for overcoming the game's challenges. For them, it's not sufficient to know that they've defeated a dragon; there must be a reason to do it and a positive consequence for having done it. Both the reason and the consequence are given to them through narrative, expository material that tells them, "The dragon is eating all our herds and soon the peasants will starve" and "The King is greatly pleased with you."

The sights and sounds in your game, the graphics and audio, create the immediate physical embodiment of your game's setting, but that's not enough to establish a credible game world. Those sights and sounds should be informed by an underlying culture and a history that dictates not only *how* the world looks, but *why* it looks that way. If you don't design that culture and history, the game world will feel like a theme park: all false fronts and a thin, gaudy veneer over the game's mechanics. To establish the feeling of richness and depth, you must create a backstory, and some of that backstory must be revealed through narration.

Action games, sports games, and vehicle simulations seldom include much narrative. They emphasize the activity, or interactivity, of the moment; for the core gamer, that activity is its own reward. Even so, you can attract a larger audience if you offer a story line to maintain the casual player's interest. The casual player wants that story because the action alone doesn't do it for her. Consider two first-person shooter games: In one, you offer 25 different, unrelated levels of varying degrees of difficulty. All the player knows is that she has to kill all the enemies to win. In the other, each level is an episode in a larger story, tied together with narrative material that explains why the player is there and what her exertions are in aid of. The second will undoubtedly cost more to make, but it will also appeal to more people. Those who care nothing for narrative will ignore it, but those who need narrative to motivate them will be rewarded.

Too Much Narrative

If you offer too much narrative and too little gameplay, however, your game will feel as if it is a bad value for the money. A number of games have made this mistake. Players are paying for the opportunity to act out a fantasy. If most of your game's content is noninteractive, they'll feel cheated—they won't get the experience that they paid for.

The other problem with too much narrative is that it tends to make the game feel as if it's on rails. It's very linear, as if the only purpose the player's actions serve is to move the game toward a predestined conclusion. Of course, unless you've written a game with multiple endings, the conclusion *is* predestined, but the goal is to make the player feel as if he is in a story of his own telling. When you as the designer take over too much of the telling, the player feels as if he's being led by the nose. He doesn't have the freedom to play the game in his own way, to create his own experience for himself.

Balancing Narrative and Gameplay

The raison d'être of all computer gaming is *interactivity*: giving the player something to do that he cannot do in the real world. The trick, then, is to provide enough narrative to create the game world and motivate the player, but not so much as to inhibit his freedom to meet the game's challenges in his own way. Consider this paraphrase of the words of the wizard Gandalf in *The Lord of the Rings:* "We cannot choose the times in which we live. All we can decide is what to do with the time that is given us." The player cannot decide the world in which he plays; that is for you, the designer, to determine. But he must be allowed to decide for himself what to do within that world, or there is no point in playing. When you create your game's narrative segments, try to avoid seizing control of the player's avatar. In too many games, the player reaches a certain point and then the narrative takes over and makes the avatar do something that the player might not choose to do. It is fair to change the world around the avatar in response to the player's actions; it is less fair to suddenly take control of the avatar away from the player.

Multi-Part Stories

Not all stories are told in one session. The games industry has expressed much interest in the possibilities provided by episodic delivery. This can mean anything from a simple sequel to a hit game (as in the *Final Fantasy* series) or a properly episodic game such as the ill-fated *Majestic* from Electronic Arts.

There are three main forms for episodic delivery; these are indicated in Figures 4.12, 4.13, and 4.14 and are discussed in the following sections.

Series

A *series* is a limited sequence of episodes. Each episode is a self-contained story in which one major plot strand is resolved per episode. Usually, an overriding theme runs from the beginning of the series through to the end, as shown in Figure 4.12.

This is the format used in the majority of game series. Each game in the series contains a complete story set against the consistent world. The games in the series are often linked by a grand overarching plot. To get a handle on the concept, imagine a series of films such as *Die Hard* or *The Godfather* trilogy. Each film has a self-contained plot, and each can be viewed individually with little disadvantage, even though there is a consistent world and an overarching theme that ties the series together.

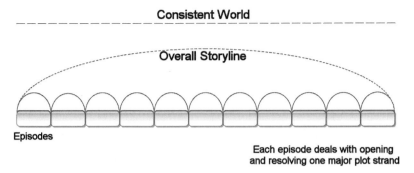

Figure 4.12 An example of series structure.

Serials

A *serial* is a (theoretically) infinite sequence of episodes. Serials are similar in nature to a series, except that the plot threads are not usually neatly resolved by each episode and there is generally no overarching story line—and, hence, no closure. To maintain interest, each episode generally ends halfway through the major plot strand, creating a cliffhanger situation that hopefully creates the "can't wait" feeling for the next episode.

Serials are designed to run and run. They rely on a large cast of characters, of whom a subset are involved in three or four different (and often quite independent) subplots at any one time. As one subplot ends, another one begins, using a new group of (formerly dormant) characters. Serials lack the grand sense of resolution that the hero's journey provides. Instead, they offer opportunities to observe different characters interacting under a variety of stresses. The cliffhanger at the end of each episode usually involves some shocking revelation that leaves us wondering how a key character will react to the news. One might say that serials are character-driven rather than plot-driven and involve a large number of archetypal characters: the bully, the good-hearted loser, the shrew, the plain but loving girl, the beautiful scheming woman, the ne'er-do-well, and so on. Occasionally, one of these characters will undergo a trauma so extreme that it produces a character transformation—for example, turning the noble young man into an evil schemer, which is, in effect, another plot twist.

If the serial comes to an end, it's usually because of the failure of the story, either because of falling ratings or sales or because the story writers ran out of ideas (although judging by some of the soap operas on television, some serials seem to have survived even beyond that particular death blow). The specific grisly fate that a serial comes to can be determined by how it ends. If it ends abruptly, with no attempt at plot resolution, it's a pretty good bet that sales or ratings fell. If some attempt at closure is made, the serial probably came to a natural end. Comparisons for serials are soap operas such as *Dallas*, or the old Saturday morning serials that most of you are probably too young to remember, such as *Rocket Man*, *Flash Gordon*, and *The Incredible Hulk*.

You might be wondering why we're going to such lengths describing something that seems to apply only to television. With the advent of games such as *Majestic* and the continued rumbling of the industry on the subject of episodic (or Webisodic) games, it's a fair bet that we're going to be seeing attempts at providing some sort of interactive serials over the next few years. How successful these will be is open to argument, but being able to charge a monthly fee for new material is a very appealing honey pot. (Witness the success of *EverQuest*, with roughly 400,000 subscribers each shelling out $10 a month for access.) Figure 4.13 is a depiction of the structure of a serial.

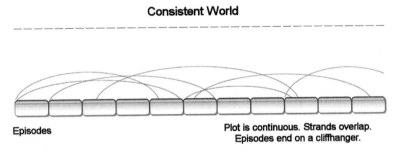

Figure 4.13   An example of serial structure.

Episodic Delivery

An *episodic delivery* is a cross between the serial and the series. Like the series, the episodic delivery contains a limited number of episodes, with an overall story line that is followed across the entirety. Unlike the series, however, there is often fairly tight integration between episodes and significant overlap of plot threads. This is similar to the serial, in which the plots thread across episodes.

Unlike the serial, this format doesn't rely so heavily on cliffhangers to end episodes and create interest in the subsequent episodes. Instead, the overall story line provides the driving interest, and the cliffhanger is used only as a secondary means of support (see Figure 4.14).

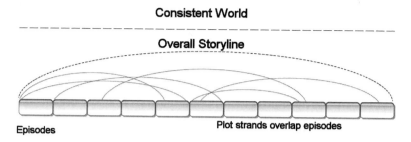

Figure 4.14   An example of episodic delivery structure.

Bearing in mind that we already have series-based games, we believe that episodic delivery is the form that most attempts at interactive episode-based entertainment will take, at least initially. If the medium takes off and is financially viable, we gradually might begin to see interactive serials, with no fixed episode count and a constantly evolving story. The only fly in the soup as far as this is concerned is the difficulty of sustained content creation. There will have to be some evolution in the methods used to create the content for such endeavors.

Storytelling and Narrative Worksheet

1. Does the game require a story, or is it entirely abstract? If it is abstract, would a story add to or detract from its appeal?

2. Can the story begin at the beginning of the game, or would the game benefit from a backstory as well?

3. Will the story make use of the monomyth? Which elements? If not, what form will it have?

4. Will the story have a three-act structure or something else, and if so, what? Will it be open-ended, leaving some plot threads unresolved?

5. How will the plot be paced? Graph out the major points of crisis, climax, rest, and resolution.

6. Will the game include narrative (that is, non-interactive) material? What role will it play—an introduction, mission briefing, transitional material, a conclusion, character definition? Is the narrative essential for the player to understand and play the game?

7. Will the narrative material be integrated seamlessly into the gameplay, or will it be a separate screen or interface element? Will the player be able to interrupt or ignore it?

8. What form will the narrative material take? Pages in the manual? Introductory text in the program? Movies? Cut-scenes?

9. Will the story be multi-part? How will the plotlines be handled: as a series, a serial, or episodically?

Putting It Together

The importance of story to a game tends to vary according to the complexity of the game. Of course, the importance of a story to a game is usually much less than the importance of a story to a movie. This is because of that magic ingredient, interactivity. Interactivity, at least currently, is at loggerheads with story. The more interactivity is desired, the less we can force the player to follow the story line.

Actually, that's not quite true. Apart from technical limitations, there is no reason why a story cannot be fully interactive and still be satisfying. *Star Trek's* holodeck often featured realistic characters and story lines, which adapted realistically to the characters. Of course, we're still a long way from that, even at the most basic level. Chris Crawford's *Erasmatron* (available from www.erasmatazz.com) makes bold strides in this direction, but there is still a long way to go.

As we've already stated, not all games need a well-developed story—or even a story at all. For those that do, the stories we've seen so far are generally not that strong. Even the best of them would not make good movies. Those games that have crossed over into movies have been (virtually without exception) poor. Consider the screen versions of *Final Fantasy, Mortal Kombat, Super Mario Brothers*, and *Tomb Raider*. Granted, the original story lines of the games were not that strong to begin with (with the possible exception of *Final Fantasy*), but watching the films, it becomes clear that they certainly weren't strong enough to support a film.

The techniques presented in this chapter are useful for guiding your story development. Remember, however, that story creation is not a formulaic activity. A fair amount of grunt work and creativity still is required. In the words of Christopher Vogler, the hero's journey is a *form*, not a *formula*. That is, it's a pattern (one of many) that can be used to develop your game story.

Chapter 5

Character Development

Using well-defined characters in games has been with us since the earliest days of computer gaming and is becoming increasingly sophisticated as time goes on. The days of anonymous blobs of pixels, such as the gunfighters in the early arcade game *Gunfight* (shown in Figure 5.1), are far behind us. Originally, it was fairly difficult to get any real characterization into a monochrome 32-pixel-high figure, but with the increasing capabilities of game hardware, the question of characterization becomes increasingly important. Note that text games had no such problem with characterization (but the graphical aspects were not at all important); the main practical limits that affected this particular genre were the skills of the author/designer.

Figure 5.1 *Gunfight.*

In this chapter, we discuss the method used to design compelling and believable characters for your game. It's important to realize that not all games require characters to be anything more than simple stereotypes (consider, for example, the *Mario* series of games). However, enough games out there require decent interactive characters to warrant a chapter covering the topic.

We've split this chapter into three fairly independent sections. Which is most appropriate for you depends on the type of game you are designing. The first section is for simpler games, in which the appearance of the hero and the characters is the most important consideration. The second is for those games in which the character and personality of the hero is more important. The third section concerns the supporting characters and their interaction with the hero.

You can design a character in two main ways: through art-sourced design or through story-sourced design. With art-based design, the appearance of a character is decided upon first, and then a background story is fleshed out to augment it if necessary. Generally, the simpler sorts of games—those that require superficial and simplistic characters—use this approach.

Art-Driven Character Design

Let's take a look at art-driven design in a little more detail. Historically, art-driven design was the main force behind character design. As we've said, the simpler games didn't rely so much on story, so the design emphasis tended to be visual.

Visual Design

The design of the central character in *Pac-Man* was purely artistic. The game designer, Toru Iwatani, was allegedly inspired by a pizza with one slice removed. Other famous game characters were also born this way: Lara Croft started life as the artist's dream girl and quickly became the "larger than life" heroine that we all know today. (This is despite the fact that somebody with those "proportions" would be unlikely to be as athletic as that—and would most likely run into a few lower-back problems in later life. But this is the games industry: Realism doesn't matter—self-consistency does.)

Characters that are developed from a purely artistic source tend to be far more superficial and one-dimensional than those sourced from a story-based design. In fact, we could say that they are the bimbos (or himbos—no sexism here!) of the games industry. This is not necessarily a bad thing. For many games, we simply do not need well-developed characters. It's far better to leave the character as a blank slate and let the player impose his own personality. This can aid the sense of game immersion greatly and is often the superior method, compared to trying to force a player to accept the role of a fully fleshed-out character. Even those games in which the player has a predefined character tend to be deliberately scant on background details, just so that the player won't have to change personalities to fit into the hero's skin. A small paragraph of backstory might give the player some direction, but trying to force a player into a role that does not appeal to her is futile.

At this point, we should mention that the second approach to designing characters is to develop a fully fleshed-out backstory before you even visualize their appearance. This approach tends to produce deeper and more realistic characters that the player will believe in more readily. Sometimes this can be a good thing, and sometimes not. It really depends on the result you are aiming for. For example, a fully detailed backstory for the aforementioned *Pac-Man*, detailing his likes, dislikes, hopes, and fears, certainly would not have added anything to the game. In fact, it would most likely have detracted from it. It would be as effective as replacing Heathcliff and Kathy from Bronte's *Wuthering Heights* with Kermit the Frog and Miss Piggy. We cover story-driven design later in this chapter.

The ultimate aim of the exercise, whether story-based or art-based, is to create a bond between the player and the hero so that the player is compelled to play the game. You should attempt to make the player genuinely care for the plight of the character under his control. A good, detailed backstory is certainly one way to get the player to empathize with the hero, but this is by no means the only way. In fact, the advantage of computer games is that the bond can be created in a number of ways (such as graphically) and is not restricted solely to abstract concepts and literary constructs.

Physical Design and Super-Sensuality

For example, let's consider some physical aspects. Sexual desirability is an often-used method. In Desmond Morris's *Manwatching*, he discusses the issue of super-senses. In advertising, certain features are often exaggerated to elicit a specific response in the viewer. The classic example is that the breast size and leg length of women are usually exaggerated by about 33 percent, their waists are too small to accommodate the required internal organs, and their hips are disproportionately wide. This apparently increases the sexual desirability of the subject (termed "super-sensory stimulation" by Morris). We've seen this many times in the game industry—I'm sure you can think of a couple of prime examples: Lara and Croft.

Cuteness works well, too. Some games attempt to bring out the player's protective feelings. In these games, the hero is almost supernaturally cute, and this causes the player to empathize with the hero much in the same way as he would empathize with a favorite pet or a baby.

Compared to fully grown animals, baby animals have large heads and eyes with respect to their body sizes. This can be exploited by a knowledgeable designer to create a "cute-appeal." Usually, this approach is aimed specifically at the younger game players. Targeting the younger gamer with the sexual approach would probably draw unwanted attention from the censors, so, for the most part, this is avoided. *Super Monkey Ball* (shown in Figure 5.2) uses the cute approach to good effect.

Figure 5.2 *Super Monkey Ball.*

The monkey characters follow Morris's super-sense guidelines—large heads; large, round eyes; and comparatively small bodies. Coincidentally (and rather perversely, to Western eyes), this is also the approach taken by Japanese ultra-violent Anime comics, an example of which is shown in Figure 5.3.

Figure 5.3 A Japanese-style character.

We realize that not all Anime is violent. Nevertheless, the artistic style emphasizes childlike super-sensuality while dealing with adult-oriented topics.

Art styles vary wildly among different cultures, particularly for characters. Japanese animation often uses huge eyes and tiny mouths for their characters, but the mouths sometimes swell to huge sizes when they shout, which looks grotesque to Americans. European cartoon characters often seem ugly and strange to Americans, too. Two exceptions to this include Asterix and Tintin.

Care must be taken with the super-sensuality approach to character design because it can backfire badly. We're sure a few of you will remember Bubsy the Bobcat. Bubsy fell out of that oft-forgotten (and rightly so) area of design—market-driven "me too" character design. At the time Bubsy was spawned, there had been a run of successful games based around cute characters. The end result was a hideously cynical "cute" character in a stereotypically poor platform game à la *Sonic*. Note that we believe that *Sonic* was a brilliant platform game, as platform games go—attractive, quite variable from level to level, and relatively nonviolent. The *Bubsy* series of games (see Figure 5.4) was a pale imitation of this, and the designers didn't understand exactly what made the *Sonic* games so good. The character of Bubsy simply wasn't appealing enough to save them. Contrast this with a game series such as *Crash Bandicoot*, in which the games are good *and* the character is appealing.

Figure 5.4 Bubsy the Bobcat.

Figure 5.5 shows a small selection of the virtually infinite variety of cute characters out there.

Figure 5.5 A selection of cute characters.

This form of design has a number of secondary contributing characteristics. The primary consideration is the limitations of the target platform. What looks great as a million-polygon rendered 3D model might not look so hot as a 64-pixel-high sprite. Hence, the appearance of an art-driven character is (obviously) influenced by the technology used to display it.

The design of the art-driven characters is dependent upon the flavor of the game. You have to consider the target audience when you're deciding upon the style of the characters. For example, the adjectives *cute* and *scary* will mean two different things to a 5-year-old and a 25-year-old. *Resident Evil*-style monsters certainly won't go down well in a *Mario*-esque style of adventure.

An interesting twist on this unwritten rule was presented in the form of *Conker's Bad Fur Day*, shown in Figure 5.6. Rare transplanted their cute children's characters into an adult-oriented game. Well, to be more accurate, it was a preteen vulgar, humor-oriented game but that's probably due to the difficulty of taking cute children's characters into an adult world. This form of toilet humor is very British in style and doesn't necessarily translate well to the rest of the world. Fighting the poo monster really appeals to only a certain subset of the intended audience. Note that the reverse would not apply—you couldn't put realistic *Resident Evil*-style characters in a children's game. It's a one-way transformation.

Figure 5.6   *Conker's Bad Fur Day.*

Another series of games that has attempted the same sort of thing (although without the humor quotient) is Nintendo's *Starfox* series. Here, the hero, Fox McCloud, and supporting characters are anthropomorphized animals. This is a common approach in literature. Many stories have used this approach, with *The Wind in the Willows* being a well-known example.

Cute Sidekicks

Art-driven character design gives probably the most prominent common element in game design: the cute hero with an optional sidekick.

This doesn't always jell as well as it should. For example, Sonic and Tails didn't work well together as a team because Sonic was much faster than Tails and kept running away from him. In other cases, alternative approaches give more success. Even though Banjo and Kazooie are separate entities, they were really only one player avatar; they just worked together inseparably. Link's fairy in the Zelda games served as a sort of tutorial and hint system. Morte in *Planescape: Torment* told the player a lot of background information in a funny, wise-guy style, but he was a character in his own right as well.

Unfortunately, for cute-style characters at least, art-based design seems to have degenerated into an unoriginal money-chasing exercise. "Can we appeal to the kiddie demographic? Can we get the right mix of cute with 'tude?" Switch on the Cartoon Network for 30 minutes, and you'll see all the evidence you need: *Powerpuff Girls, Dexter's Laboratory, Spongebob Squarepants,* and the rest. You name it, it's there. The evidence is there in the games industry as well. Everyone's looking for the next big cute phenomenon. Check out *Spyro the Dragon* and *Jak and Daxter,* or any one of the plethora of other examples. It wouldn't be so bad if it were a new concept, but it's been around since the dawn of the industry. Figure 5.7 shows a fairly early example.

Figure 5.7 Head and Heels from *Head over Heels.*

These two characters, Head and Heels, are buddies fighting against the evil emperor. The only difference between these two and the majority of today's examples is the originality in the relationship between the two characters: Head and Heels are both symbiotic creatures. Head can jump and glide, and Heels can run fast. When they are linked together, they combine their abilities and can solve problems that would be impossible to achieve individually. The difference between Head and Heels and the rest of the cute brigade is that Head and Heels actually had unique characteristics that made an original difference to the gameplay.

NOTE
To an extent, this was also true of Banjo and Kazooie. Even though they were implemented as a single avatar (much like Head and Heels when joined), each had individual abilities that complemented the other's.

Most of the examples from today are just minor variations on a rather old theme. At least try to inject some originality into it. Don't just go for the "It's like Sonic, except that he's called Phaser and he's a Porcupine!" approach.

If we might risk boldly stating our opinion at this point, we believe that this strain of "cute with attitude" character design is getting very clichéd. It also seems to be quite cold and calculating from a marketing point of view: The "cute" part attracts children, and the "with attitude" part alienates parents. With the recent troubles the games industry has had with the threat of censorship, a cute character spouting off attitude to other characters (especially those representing authority figures) probably isn't the best way to ingratiate ourselves with parents—and some of these parents are the people with the power to enforce regulation on the games industry. This doesn't mean that we should make our characters sugary-sweet and peachy keen, but we should be very aware of the age and developmental levels of our target audience.

NOTE
Don't forget that kids hate goody-two-shoes characters just as much as parents dislike characters with foul attitudes—but just because a character doesn't cop an attitude with authority figures doesn't make him a goody-two-shoes. The *Scooby Doo* kids are a pretty good example of nonattitude characters who nevertheless retain their appeal: intelligence, bravery, and resourcefulness. Scooby is funny, too, because despite his large size, he is a coward—hence, he helps make sure scary situations aren't *too* scary. In addition to this, because he's a dog and not a child, he doesn't get picked on or treated with contempt for being scared. This is actually a very clever solution. Notice also the *Archie* kids from the famous comic: You have the Everyman (Archie), the Goofball (Jughead), the Girl Next Door (Betty), the Fashion Plate (Veronica, whose beauty is offset by her vanity), and the Handsome Guy (Reggie, somewhat similar to Veronica in attitude). One common theme is that Jughead is pursued by an ugly girl, in a humorous (but actually slightly sexist) role reversal.

Story-Driven Character Design

The best approach to developing a well-fleshed-out character is to start with the story behind the character and develop the character's traits and personality before you even consider the appearance. Often artists prefer to work from a detailed description such as this; it allows them to really understand and visualize the character.

Even games that you would not expect to have fully developed characters can gain much by including them. Consider the multi-format title *SSX Tricky*, shown in Figure 5.8. This is an extreme sports snowboarding game that pays attention to character development. The player is allowed to make friends, foster rivalries, and enhance her character throughout the game. The addition of this storylike element enhances the game above the simple level of a straight sports game. The player chooses the preferred character and begins to identify with her. This causes a greater sense of immersion in the game—and best of all, it's not prescripted. The player can choose who to make friends with and who to antagonize, and it does have an effect on the gameplay. You can be sure that anyone who you make an enemy of will try their hardest to sabotage your run—and there will be a few sharp words exchanged at the finish line.

Figure 5.8   *SSX Tricky.*

Admittedly, it's not complex stuff—it could be taken further—but it's refreshing to see this sort of thing being attempted in the sort of games in which previously it was unheard of. Interaction between characters is one of the most interesting aspects of stories—sometimes more so than the actual plot. Although a plot details the path of a story (we cover this in the next chapter), the character interactions add a lot of flavor and subtlety that differentiate a well-crafted story from a fifth-grade English composition assignment.

One of the major problems with the games industry when it comes to character design and story content is our unoriginality. We are quite content to plagiarize our characters wholesale from other media, and we are almost afraid to develop original characters in their own right. For example, Lara Croft is simply a female version of Indiana Jones, except that she doesn't have anything like the depth of Indy—his vulnerability, weak spots, and so on. If he is two-dimensional, then she is one-dimensional. Lara eminently demonstrates that not only are we ripping off the movies, we're also doing a bad job of ripping off the movies, as far as characterization goes.

Joanna Dark (from *Perfect Dark*) is a female version of James Bond (or any other secret agent you prefer). As the industry gets bigger, game designers can no longer borrow ideas wholesale from other industries. They will need to carry themselves as an original art form, unless they want to suffer the same fate as the British movie industry—meagerly surviving on borrowed concepts (and borrowed time). Of course, this is a black picture to paint and is unlikely to come about in the extreme case. The games industry has survived one big crash so far, back when Atari went down the pan, and the resulting slow consolidation of the bulk of the industry into a small group of giant conglomerated corporations has done little to aid creativity.

Character Development

The primary indicator of good characters in any medium is how well they develop and adapt to changing circumstances.

Language is a key cue to a character's personality. His grammar and vocabulary send all kinds of signals—about his social class, education, ethnic origin, and so on. These, in turn, connect with patterns—or stereotypes, if you prefer—in the player's mind. This is also true of the character's accent. One of the most interesting uses of this in recent years was in *Starcraft*, which drew on a variety of American accents to create several different types of characters. Although they did include the "redneck Southerner" stereotype, which was regrettable but practically inevitable, they also included the "Southern aristocrat" and "Western sheriff" speech patterns for Arcturus Mengsk and Jim Raynor, respectively; the laconic, monosyllabic diction of airline pilots for the Wraith pilots; a cheerful, competent Midwestern waitress for the pilots of the troop transports; and a sort of anarchic, gonzo biker for the Vulture riders. This gave the game a great deal of character and flavor that it would have otherwise lacked if it has used bland, undifferentiated voices.

If a character is flat and one-dimensional, then it shows. Sometimes this can be the desired effect, especially in the case of comedic computer games. Consider Duke Nukem, a muscle-bound, blond-haired, misogynist killing machine. You would not expect him to develop his sensitive side and start calling his mother halfway through the game. In this case, his one-dimensionality is funny—it's used well as part of the game. It also allows the player to easily slot himself into the role, knowing that it will remain consistent. This works so well because the player is glimpsing only a limited part of the life of Duke. For the player, it is part of the fun for him to play the role of a thinly motivated hero.

Of course, this is also dangerous ground to tread upon. This sort of thinking landed *Doom* an (undeserved) starring role in the lawsuits following the Columbine tragedy back in 1999. Notwithstanding the fact that blaming the escapist world of a computer game for encouraging this sort of tragedy is simple witch-hunting, we should be aware that the games industry is a prime target for litigation. Computer games are still looked upon as "entertainment for children," and even though this is no longer true, we need to do more to encourage the maturation of the art.

One way to do this is to tackle serious subjects in a mature fashion, with the benefits of good character development and story lines. One way *not* to do it is to tackle serious subjects in an *immature* fashion, as *Postal* and, to a lesser extent, *Soldier of Fortune* did (see Figures 5.9 and 5.10).

"The most notable feature in Postal *is the violence, and this is definitely NOT a game for the kiddies. It even comes with the gaming version of an NC-17 rating, as well it should. You don't kill demon spawn or mutant dino-zombies. You're shooting at people, watching their blood spill onto the street, hearing them wail for mercy or to be put out of their misery. There's a button for execution; just stand over a victim moaning in pain and finish him off. And if things get too grisly, you can even end your own life via a shotgun to the head. This is really some unprecedented and uncensored violence, so parents beware."*

—Extract from a web review of *Postal* on `www.gamerevolution.com`

Figure 5.9   *Postal.*

Soldier of Fortune's main advertising thrust was the ability to accurately shoot individual body parts. It's fine to have this as a game feature, as long as it's appropriately marketed. It should not be the primary focus of the advertising because it does not add much to the gameplay. The focus of the marketing should be the story and gameplay, not the realistic deaths. The game would still play the same (a standard first-person shooter) with or without the accurate body part–shooting capabilities. It's the difference between marketing a mature game and a murder simulator.

Figure 5.10   *Soldier of Fortune.*

That doesn't mean we can solve all these problems by making our characters shed a tear when they kill. In general, though, treating these subjects with a bit more care and attention will improve their perceived value to the outside world.

Develop Believable Characters

Developing believable characters is not a straightforward process. Although there is no surefire method, there are three golden guidelines to developing effective, believable characters:

➤ The character needs to intrigue the player.

➤ The character needs to get the player to like him.

➤ The character needs to change and grow according to experience.

These rules are fairly obvious. If a character does not interest the players, they aren't going to play the game. Similarly, if the players don't develop an affinity for the character over time, they will not be particularly sympathetic to the hero's plight—and, consequently, won't be particularly compelled to take part. Generally, the first two guidelines are followed pretty well—or, at least, attempts are made. The previously mentioned Bubsy the Bobcat fails on all counts.

The third guideline is the one that seems to fall by the wayside. Although it is fairly easy to invent an interesting character that conforms to the first two guidelines, it's far more difficult to develop that character further so that it develops and grows realistically. If it were that easy, a lot more people would be writing best-selling novels.

Growth of the Character

One important consideration for realistic characters is based on the diagram shown in Figure 5.11. The growth and progression of the hero is an important part of the story—as important, if not more so, than the plot itself.

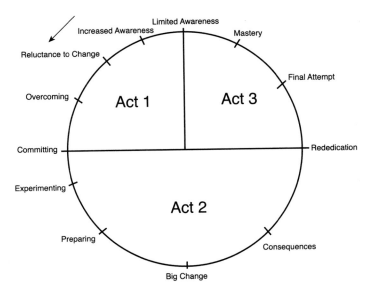

Figure 5.11 Character growth cycle.

The common character growth cycle that is tied in with the Hero's Journey advises how to manage the growth of the hero character. The hero starts with a *limited awareness* of himself and his situation. As the story unfolds, the hero's *awareness increases* to a point at which he realizes that a change is necessary. At this point, the hero often exhibits a *reluctance to change*—the point at which he would be leaving his ordinary world and entering the special world—and has to dedicate himself to *overcoming* his reluctance. The point at which the hero has *committed* himself to change usually signals the end of the first act of the story.

After the hero has entered the special world, he *experiments* with his new environment, trying to discover the rules and customs that will allow him to *prepare* effectively for his adjustment to the special world—his *big change*. This point usually marks the end of the first part of the second act. From this point, the story winds up toward the climax point of the second act by showing the *consequences* and setbacks of the hero's first attempt at change.

The third act starts with the *rededication* of the hero to the efforts to change. Here, he makes his *final attempt*, resulting in a *mastery* of the circumstances of the special world, closing the cycle and finishing the story—and the development of the character.

The various martial arts are a field full of Eastern traditions, with each style encompassing its own unique set of traditions, with many of these often traceable back to a single root. Common to most of these arts is the venerable black belt, the symbol of mastery of the art. These belts are constructed in such a way that over time, the black thread of the belt wears out and the white of the underlying material shows through. Contrary to initial appearances, this is not just a sign of shoddily made belts: It is representative of a tradition rich in symbolism. The painful transition from novice to master—from white to black—is a hero's journey. The symbolism of the black belt fading to white is to indicate that the master is, in fact, a novice at a new higher level. The master has an understanding of the physical aspects of the art; now he can start again and learn the spirituality behind them. The symbolism is beautiful: The master is still a novice, and the path to mastery is cyclic. In addition to this, martial arts tradition never originally called for colored belts. Rather, a white belt gradually became brown and then, over the years, black. This was a sign of experience. At the end of each session, the martial artist would wipe his sweat with the belt.

This same analogy is often applied to the hero's character development. That's why the diagram shown in Figure 5.11 is a circle. The hero, having achieved mastery of the special world, becomes a novice of circumstances in a new special world. This is the mechanism that is often used to create effective sequels.

This is a difficult concept to grasp, and it is even more difficult to implement well. Don't be too discouraged, though—some common techniques for effective character development are summarized at the end of this chapter. However, before we get to this new material, we need to cover some of the common character archetypes found in stories.

The Character Archetypes

According to classic literary theory, a number of character archetypes crop up in some form in most stories. This section covers these archetypes and describes their nature and roles.

These archetype definitions are taken from Christopher Vogler's *The Writer's Journey*, a treatment of Joseph Campbell's Hero's Journey aimed at screenwriters, as discussed in the previous chapter.

The common archetypes are not restricted to a single character in any particular story. The same character can play any number of different roles. For example, the character playing the mentor could also be an ally, a herald, a threshold guardian, or even a shadow at a different point in the story. This is how good drama is constructed.

Hero

The hero is traditionally the center of the story. In our case, the hero is the player's avatar. In literature, the hero is traditionally a character with one or more problems. The story tells how the character solves these problems. This apparently simple pattern is the basis for *all* stories. In general, stories revolve around a conflict and the resolution of that conflict. This is where the hero fits in.

The most important thing to do with the hero is ensure that the players can identify with the character. The hero should have qualities that the players can appreciate and empathize with. The hero's goals should become the player's goals. How you choose to implement this depends very much on the nature of the hero. For example, in *Oddworld: Munch's Odyssey*, the two heroes, Abe and Munch (shown in Figure 5.12), certainly don't win any beauty awards, but they still appeal successfully to the player.

Figure 5.12 Abe and Munch.

There are a number of possible reasons for this. Note that both Abe and Munch follow the super-sensuality guidelines mentioned earlier, with large eyes and big foreheads, echoing those of babies. Despite (or perhaps *because of*) their ugliness, and the fact that they are enslaved underdogs of a much uglier ruling class, they appeal to a wide range of players and have been a surprising success. It's surprising, that is, for the developers. However, close examination of the archetypes and the characteristics of Abe and Munch (as well as the quality of the games in which they were introduced) indicates that the success isn't as surprising as it might initially seem.

Of course, as we stated in our guidelines, after the initial interest has been created, it has to be maintained. One of the primary methods for doing this is to make sure that the hero changes and grows during the course of the game. Depending on the style of the game, this could be a real growth—in personality and demeanor—or a more straightforward approach, such as with power-ups and improvement of characteristics. The latter method is far more common in games, although some games do make use of the former to some extent. *Planescape: Torment* is a specific example that springs to mind, even though it uses standard stats-pumping growth, too.

The main defining characteristic of a hero in a story is that the hero performs most of the action and assumes the majority of the risk and responsibility. This doesn't mean that other characters can't take the mantle of hero temporarily. For example, in cut scenes, they might be shown sacrificing themselves for the hero.

Perversely, the hero doesn't necessarily have to be heroic: The antihero is also a classic motif. The *Dungeon Keeper* series of games uses this particular form, in which the aim of the game is to destroy the forces of good.

Heroes are not always on their own. In some games, the "hero" is represented by a group of individuals: the hero team. These are common in role-playing games. Often, though less frequently nowadays, character development in hero teams is limited; in the case of role-playing games, they are computer-generated characters created and customized by the player. However, when hero teams are used in multi-player games (such as *Diablo* and *Diablo II*), each player represents an individual hero. In single-player games, the player tends to pick a "favorite," and that character becomes her avatar. Sometimes games even mandate this choice for the player; examples of games that do this are *Baldur's Gate*, *Planescape: Torment*, and *Anachronox* (shown in Figure 5.13).

Figure 5.13 *Anachronox.*

In fact, Tom Hall's *Anachronox* is one of two excellent games that came out of Ion Storm. (*Deus Ex* is the other.) Unfortunately, by the time these games were released, the well had already been poisoned by the lamentable *Daikatana* (starting with the infamous "John Romero's about to make you his bitch" advertising campaign).

The hero of *Anachronox*, Sylvester (Sly) Boots, is a down-on-his-luck private detective who is being harassed by the local mob to pay back some debts. Sly Boots is a good example of a hero because, characteristically, a hero can be made more appealing by giving them a vulnerability. Heroes often have an inner problem and an outer problem. These can shift as the game progresses. The outer problem is the general quest that is the aim of the game. The inner problem is usually something personal to the hero. In Sly's case, his vulnerability is his debt. At the start of the game, Sly is being beaten to a pulp by a goon. His vulnerability is his lack of cash, so the first task for the player is to help him find a job. Initially, this is his outer problem. However, as the game progresses, this morphs into a grander quest to save the universe. Sly's inner problem is that he is a low-life. This affects the attitude of the other characters in the game toward him and serves to make the quest more difficult than it might have been otherwise. More important, it adds an extra dimension to the character that creates an air of believability.

In summary, the hero's outer problem can be stated as the aim of the game, whereas the inner problem is a character flaw or some other dark secret. The player might not even know the inner problem at the outset. *Planescape: Torment* uses this particular mechanism well.

Mentor

The *mentor* is the guide character. It can come in many formats: the clichéd wise old man or woman, the supernatural aid, or even the hero's own internal voice. The most familiar example of this that will spring to mind for most people is the character of Obi Wan Kenobi and his relationship with the would-be Jedi, Luke Skywalker.

Anachronox uses the mentor archetype brilliantly: Boots' mentor is his dead secretary. After she dies in some unspecified accident, Sly had her brain digitized and stored in a small device called a "life-cursor" (which also doubles as the player's game control cursor). This allows her to continue to function as a secretary, with the added benefit of being hooked into the world's computer systems. This also allows her to manage the adventure bookkeeping, providing timely advice and hints to Sly, and acting as a story guide to seamlessly keep the hero within the bounds of the designer's gameplay plans.

Mentors are not always positive. A mentor can also give bad advice deliberately designed to mislead the hero or to lead him down an evil path. A classic example of this form of "dark mentor" is the devilish advisor in Peter Molyneux's *Black and White*.

Higher Self

The *higher self* is the hero as he aspires to be. It is the ideal form of the hero. In many cases, the object of the game is to transform the hero into his higher self. Of course, this is not explicitly stated as a gameplay aim, and it usually happens as a side effect of completing the game.

There are many examples in role-playing of this particular motif. For example, the whole premise of *Planescape: Torment* is based on the transmutation of the Nameless One into his higher self. He is a character with amnesia but a distinct past, who seeks to regain his name and his memory. In the process of doing so, he might also have amends to make to people he has hurt in the past.

Allies

Allies are those characters placed in the game to aid the hero. Many games use the ally archetype. The aim of the ally is to aid the hero in the quest and help to complete tasks that would have been difficult or nearly impossible without aid. Han Solo is the classic example of the ally archetype that most people know.

We are sure you can think of many examples of this because it is one of the most common archetypes. An obvious example is the role of the scientists and security guards in *Half-Life*. In many instances, they team up with the hero, Gordon Freeman, to provide advice and help him get past obstacles, such as doors with retina scanner–based locks.

Shape Shifter

The *shape shifter* is the most elusive archetype used in stories. The role of the shape shifter is to appear in one form, only to be revealed later in the story as another. It's a catch-all transitional archetype that governs the transformation of characters.

For example, an ally or mentor could turn out to be a trickster or a shadow. A character that initially helps a player could turn out to have been acting in his own interests, finally betraying the hero when his aims are achieved.

An example of this archetype from classic literature is the evil queen in *Snow White*. She appears to Snow White as an ally and mentor (the wizened old woman with the apples) before revealing herself to be a shadow and a trickster when Snow White is poisoned. An example from a game is the White Lord from the old role-playing game

Dungeon Master. The White Lord initially acts as a mentor/herald, tasking the adventurers to enter a dungeon and seek out and destroy the Black Lord. If they achieve this, then upon return to the surface, the White Lord declares that they have been tainted by the evil of the dungeon and attempts to destroy them (becoming a shadow).

Threshold Guardian

The *threshold guardian* is another very common archetype used across the whole spectrum of game types. The role of the threshold guardian is to prevent the progress of the hero by whatever means are necessary—at least, until the hero has proven his worth. Sometimes the threshold guardian appears as a lesser form of the shadow archetype, maybe as a henchman or a lieutenant of the main shadow.

The most obvious example is the classic end-of-level boss used in virtually every arcade game since the Creation. A more subtle use of this archetype does not use force to dissuade the hero. It could be voiced by the hero's own self-doubt, or the warnings and ministrations of a mentor character. Consider the role of Yoda in *The Empire Strikes Back*. Although he acted as a mentor in training young Luke in the ways of the force, he also cautioned strongly against Luke leaving to face Darth Vader. Luke's training had not been completed, and he was not yet ready to face his nemesis.

Trickster

Tricksters are often neutral characters in storylines who delight in making mischief for the hero. They can also make an excellent (incompetent or otherwise) sidekick for the hero *or* the shadow, giving an easy opportunity to inject some comic relief to lighten the storyline.

There are many examples of trickster characters that we can draw on. For example, Bugs Bunny from Warner Brothers cartoons is one; Wile E. Coyote is a trickster, too, but his tricks always fail, or the Roadrunner out-tricks him. The trickster is someone who achieves his ends through cleverness, resourcefulness, or lateral thinking, especially in the face of superior force. Actually, this could be said of the hero in a fair number of adventure games; the puzzles represent the "tricks" in a way, especially if they're set up that way.

For example, the hero often has to trick a threshold guardian into leaving the threshold. In a way, this was the role of Bilbo Baggins in *The Hobbit*: He wasn't brought along on the adventure for his strength, but for his cleverness, which was eventually augmented by the Ring that made him invisible.

Shadow

The *shadow* is arguably the second most important character after the hero himself. In some stories, the shadow is elevated to the number-one rank. For example, Ritual Entertainment's *Sin's* main selling point was the shadow, Elexis Sinclaire, a beautiful, sexy CEO of a massive bio-tech corporation who happened to have a penchant for clothes and makeup that wouldn't appear out of place on a street-walking extra from the film *Pretty Woman*. Aside from the fact that the biographical details for Elexis Sinclaire (shown in Figure 5.14) are straight out of a (bad) schoolboy fantasy, the emphasis of the game is on her as the primary character in the game.

Figure 5.14   Elexis Sinclaire.

In other games, the shadow lives up to its designation—remaining mysterious until the story climax, when it is revealed in a flourish and a flash of lightning. This can add a lot to the gameplay, especially because part of the gameplay is often to find out the identity of the shadow. This can add a lot of dramatic tension and mystery to augment the gameplay.

The shadow is the ultimate evil, the great adversary that is responsible for the hero being in the predicament that he is in. Sometimes this is a personal decision: The shadow has a vendetta against the hero. In other situations, the shadow doesn't even know of the hero, and only the actions of the shadow affecting the hero on a personal level spur him to action. Of course, the shadow doesn't even have to be a concrete entity: It could be just a set of circumstances or feelings within the hero himself. His own dark side could be the shadow.

Herald

The *herald* archetype is used to provide the hero with a change of direction and propel the story in a different direction. The herald is often used to facilitate change in the story.

Princess Leia's message to Obi-Wan Kenobi that Luke discovers in R2D2's memory serves this function. It's unclear whether Princess Leia or R2D2 is the herald, but it doesn't really matter: Luke gets the message from a figure who provides his necessary "change of direction."

Another example is the voice of the narrator in *Dungeon Keeper.* This could be described as a herald: He describes the challenges to be faced in the level ahead and keeps the player appraised of the progress of the campaign.

The function of a herald is to provide a motivation to the hero to progress in the story. Heralds can be positive, negative, or neutral. It doesn't need to be the classic herald of Greek literature. In fact, the herald doesn't have to be a character at all: The call of the herald could simply be a set of tricks to mislead the hero into a certain route or path.

Character Development Worksheet

1. Are the game's characters primarily art-based or story-based?
2. What style is your art-based character drawn in: cartoon, comic-book superhero, realistic, gothic, and so on? Will your character be exaggerated in some way: cute, super-sensual, or otherwise?
3. Do your art-based characters depend upon visual stereotypes for instant identification, or are they more subtle than that? If they are more subtle, how does their appearance support their role in the game?
4. Can the player tell by looking at a character how that character is likely to act? Are there reasons in the story or gameplay for wanting a character's behavior to be predictable from his appearance, or is there a reason to make the character ambiguous?
5. If the game has an avatar, does the avatar have a sidekick? What does the sidekick offer the player—information, advice, physical assistance? How will the sidekick complement the avatar? How will the player be able to visually distinguish between the two of them at a glance?
6. With a story-based character, how will you convey the character's personality and attitudes to the player? Through narration, dialog, gameplay, backstory, or other means?
7. How does the character's grammar, vocabulary, tone of voice, and speech patterns contribute to the player's understanding of her?
8. Specifically in the case of avatar characters, what about the avatar will intrigue and interest the player?
9. What about the avatar will encourage the player to like him?
10. How will the avatar change and grow throughout the game?
11. Does the character (any character, not just the avatar) correspond to one of Campbell's mythic archetypes: the hero, mentor, ally, threshold guardian, and so on? Or does he have a less archetypal, more complex role to play, and if so, what is it?

Putting It Together

In any character design effort, some technical considerations need to be taken into account. For example, the player's avatar needs to have the largest number of animations, and they must be the smoothest animations of all because this is the character being watched all the time.

The avatar's movements must be attractive, not clumsy, unless that's part of the avatar's character. The player should be able to see the avatar easily: The avatar should be a distinct color that stands out from the background (at least, in action games) and should not be able to be mistaken for an enemy or a sidekick. When designing a group of human characters, consider useful ways of differentiating them: sex, hair color, general body shape, clothing, distinctive weapons or tools. You can also give them distinctive names and ethnicities, if appropriate. (The men of Sergeant Rock's Easy Company in the old DC Comics World War II series reflected the ethnic diversity of America, with names such as Dino Manelli, Izzy Cohen, and "Reb" Farmer—not to mention our square-jawed American hero, Sgt. Frank Rock.)

Of course, there is a flipside to this as well. Naming your characters in such a fashion lends a "cartoon-like" style to it. This is fine for some purposes, but for others it is not necessarily such a good fit. It's just not realistic, and if realism is your aim, then it cheapens the final result. Notice that we, the authors of this book, are not called Ernest O'Scribe or Andrew Penn-Wielder.

Names do not have to spell out explicitly the name of the character. For example, the name of the hero in *Anachronox*, Sylvester Boots, says little or nothing about the character. However his nickname, Sly, is altogether more revealing. Another example is Lara Croft. Although this does not immediately seem to indicate anything about the character, it does (to English sensibilities, at least) imply a degree of upper-class Englishness.

In short, the importance of character design on your game really depends on the nature of the game itself. However, the success of character-based franchises such as *Duke Nukem*, *Oddworld*, and the *Mario Brothers* certainly indicates that you should consider effective character design as one of your top game-design priorities.

Chapter 6

Creating the User Experience

A game is more than just the sum of its rules. It must interact with the players to immerse them in the game world.
To do this, it must project an aura of involvement that pro-
motes Samuel Coleridge's "willing suspension of disbelief."
Every element that the players' experience must contribute
to the whole. From the moment the player loads the software
and the first screen appears, he is in your world. Everything
that he sees, hears, and feels from that point on—every
audio, visual, and interactive element—must strive to convince him that the only thing that exists is the game. This is
not the easiest of goals to achieve; any slight discord can jar
the players out of their illusion. However, the best games
generally achieve this level of perfection, or close to it, and
the aim of this chapter is to discuss how you can attempt to
account for deep player immersion in your designs.

This chapter discusses some of the most relevant aspects of
user experience design (and note that by user experience,
we're talking about the whole thing: audio, visual, and interaction methods) for games. Even though we have stressed
the relative importance of flashy presentation as secondary
to gameplay, we would be foolish to discard presentation
entirely. The user interface is the first real glimpse the players will get of your game in action; it's your first chance to
suck them into the world presented by your game.

The user interface can make or break your game: It can give it the perfect air of consummate professionalism or the shabby appearance of an amateur effort. Although we would prefer to believe that the gameplay is the most important factor in the success of a game, the majority of commercial evidence seems to indicate otherwise. With few exceptions, two games that are functionally equivalent, with equally effective marketing and differing only in the quality of their user interface layers, will not perform equally in the market. It would be tempting to say that the game with the most visually and technically stunning user interface would sell better—and we know that would please a lot of developers and artists out there—but, all things being equal, that is not the case. In fact, given these two functionally equivalent products, the one with the interface that is most *fit for the purpose* will be the most successful. (Of course, you can publish all manner of tripe if you have a big name license attached to it. Some things will never change.)

What Is the User Experience?

User experience: The term sounds suspiciously like a couple of strung-together buzzwords you'd expect to see on poor advertising copy. Obviously, that's an impression we'd rather dispel as quickly as possible, so let's attempt to "debuzzify" the term by describing exactly what we mean.

We define the user experience as the total package presented to the player when she plays the game. It is the combination of three distinct areas of the design—the visual element, the audio element, and the interactive element—and is concerned with their impact on the user interface. The following sections give a brief précis of what we'll be covering in more detail.

> **NOTE**
>
> To read more details on user experience, see *The Elements of User Experience* by Jesse James Garrett (© 2003 New Riders Publishing).

The Interactive Element

The interactive part of the user experience is concerned with the way the player interacts with the game. This is tied in closely with the visual aspect but is more concerned
with the "feel" part of "the look and feel." Here, we are concerned with the functional
aspects of the user interface—the navigational pathways through the system—and the
physical controller setup. How the interface looks is considered only as far as it affects
the usability.

The Visual Element

The visual element concerns the "look" part of the "look and feel." Here, we consider
the overall impact of the artwork and how it meshes and combines to present an overall consistent picture to the player. This is closely related to the interactive experience—one has a direct influence on the other—but we will attempt to discuss the areas
separately and explain where there is crossover between the two.

The Audio Element

Often, the audio parts of a game are not considered in as much depth as the visual
"in-your-face" areas of the game. However, audio is just as important for both atmosphere and player feedback as the visual components. Even though sound is often in
third place after the visual and interactive elements, the fact that many games are
unplayable without it clearly indicates the importance of sound. (Although, strictly
speaking, no game should be designed that *necessitates* sound. That unfairly discrim-
inates against the hearing impaired.)

The Human-Computer Interface

Designing a good user interface is not about how beautiful and whizzy you can make
your buttons. In fact, the core essence of the user experience—enabling the player to
interact with the game world—doesn't need *any* fancy graphics or sound. The functionality that allows a player to interact with the game effectively could theoretically be
implemented using simple placeholder elements. In fact, while the interface is being
designed, this is the recommended approach—it's faster, and more resource-efficient.

As you may have already realized, we place more importance on the functional aspects of the user interface over the purely aesthetic aspects. Although we could argue that a perfectly functional user interface has a certain aesthetic appeal, we will not limit ourselves to this in our discussion. We would be foolish to completely disregard the aesthetic requirements—eye candy sells and certainly provides a more enjoyable, immersive experience—but they should be secondary to the functional aspects.

> *"When I am working on a problem, I never think about beauty. I only think about how to solve the problem. But when I have finished, if the solution is not beautiful, I know it is wrong."*
>
> —**Buckminster Fuller**, 1895-1983

The functionality of the user interface *is* the most important consideration. After all, what player is going to take the time to play a beautiful game if she can't figure out which exquisitely detailed picture is the button to start the game? Conversely, even with the most efficient user interface, few people will bother with the game if it's as ugly as sin.

Consequently, the discussions in this chapter take on a dual aspect: First, and most important in our view, we will concentrate on the functionality of the user interface. After we have discussed the functional aspects, we will concentrate on the aesthetics, paying particular attention to making sure that the aesthetics do not impact the functionality. Note that pure physical beauty is not the primary meaning of *aesthetics* for a user interface. Fitness for purpose is a far more important aesthetic consideration. This doesn't necessarily exclude having a beautiful interface, but we do insist that there should be more to the beauty than mere appearances. A butterfly may be prettier than a rubber life raft, but which would you rather have with you on a stormy sea?

Evolution of the User Experience

In order to set a context for the discussion in this chapter, it will be worth our while to take a brief look at how the user experience has progressed over the last 20 or so years.

Twenty years ago, each game had a different interface, although usually there was some influence from other sources—console games, arcade games, and other games in the same genre. It wasn't until the advent of the windowed operating systems that any form of homogeny was achieved. Nowadays, we don't even think twice before using the mouse to navigate and clicking the mouse button to press an onscreen button. It's a de facto standard now (on the PC at any rate), but it used to be a novelty.

Arcade Games

Initially, the game interface was simple. For arcade-style games, there would be a title screen with instructions (usually limited to a simple explanation of the controls) or a simple attract mode that cycled between two or three screens (title, instructions, and a high-score table). The game would remain in this state until the player pressed the Start button.

This soon evolved to include a fourth screen: the *demo mode*. For a small length of time (usually 30 seconds or so), a sequence was shown from the game in play, implemented either as a slide show of screens from various levels or as one of a selection of short snippets of gameplay.

Once the game was started, the in-game interface was usually very simple (see Figure 6.1). The playing area would take up most of the screen. There would be a score display, a high-score display, a level display (if appropriate), and a "lives remaining" display. These would be placed at the top or bottom of the screen. And for many years, that was about the extent of the arcade game interface. Of course, there were subtle variations on this theme—for example, a power level meter in addition to or instead of a "lives remaining" display, and the odd bit of pertinent information specific to the game, such as "number of lines" in *Tetris*.

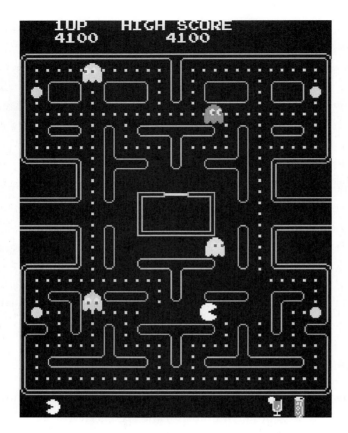

Figure 6.1 The standard arcade game interface (*Pac-Man Plus*).

Williams's *Defender* (shown in Figure 6.2) was arguably the first game to enhance this core interface by adding a minimap; it was one of the first games with a playing area larger than the visible screen.

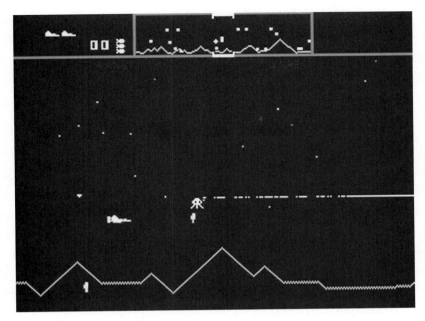

Figure 6.2   Williams's *Defender*.

Without waxing too lyrically about the nostalgia value of this proto-interface, it has to be said that there was a certain purity of purpose present. All the information that the player needed to be able to play the game was there at a glance. Of course, it wasn't that difficult to achieve, either; the limitations of the format pretty much dictated that the games be fairly simple. Any homogeny of interface was the result of the fact that there were only a few sensible ways of displaying the same information. The real progress occurred when the player needed to be fed too much information to be displayed on the screen at once.

Most arcade games *are* simple enough to be able to present all the necessary information on a single screen, and it's just as well that this is the case, because switching to an information screen in the middle of a fast-paced game is not a recipe for success. For those wanting to investigate some of these classic arcade games further, the MAME (Multiple Arcade Machine Emulator) web site, www.mame.net, is a good starting point.

Consider an example of interface evolution: the humble golf game. Presumably, you are familiar with the basics of golf: Take a stick, go for a walk, and hit a small ball toward a marginally larger hole with as much force as you possibly can. As enjoyable as that sounds, a good number of developers have injected even more fun into the sport by allowing you to simulate it while not moving from the front of your computer. Of course, golf has an element of skill in the aiming and timing of the swing. Walking from hole to hole is also an important part of real golf (socially speaking, anyway), but this would not translate well as a fun gameplay feature, and so it is usually skipped. Hence, it's a logical assumption that game designers made the actual swinging at and hitting of the ball the main focus of the game.

In fact, taking a look at the rough lineage of golf games, it can be seen that this interface was perfected early on (around the time of the original *Leaderboard* golf game, shown in Figure 6.3) and has only had minor tweaks since then, ignoring the odd short-lived "revolution" that has occurred in the meantime. The first button click started the power meter rising, the second button click set the power (whereupon the meter indicator would begin to fall), and the third determined the accuracy of the shot; it had to be clicked when the indicator returned to the starting position. Getting it exactly right resulted in a perfect shot. Apart from the switch from keyboard to mouse or trackball, there has been very little modification to this system; it's the perfect interface for the golf game and has been relied upon since then. Even fairly recent games, such as the latest effort in the *Links* series of games, have stuck to this basic mechanic for gameplay. Even *Golden Tee*, the latest in a long series of golf games, uses a trackball-based evolution of this original interface.

Figure 6.3 U.S. Gold's *World Class Leaderboard*.

This demonstrates an important point: Aside from the occasional flash of brilliance, the general progression of game interfaces has been an evolutionary, not revolutionary, one.

Adventure Games

Traditionally, adventure games were text-based. The player interacts with the system by reading a textual description of the location, and performing queries and actions based on that description.

The first adventures took their input in a *"verb-noun"* format. That is, "Take Food" would work, whereas "Take the Food on the Table" would be rejected. Movement commands generally took the single-word form—Up, Down, North, East, South, West—and could be abbreviated to U, D, N, E, S, W, NW, NE, and so on.

Adventure games used to be a popular and lucrative section of the games market. Over time, the sophistication of the parser allowed improvements in the nature of sentences usable with the games, and the quality of the writing correspondingly improved with the increasing capabilities of the target machines. Games such as *The Hitchhiker's Guide to the Galaxy* from Infocom (publishers of the original Zork series of games) and *Fish!* from Magnetic Scrolls are good examples. For the curious, a Java version of *The Hitchhiker's Guide* is available to play at Douglasadams.com (`www.douglasadams.com/creations/infocomjava.html`).

Eventually, simple graphics appeared to help enliven the textual description. This improved the atmosphere to a degree, but also coincided with a general decrease in the quality of the writing. The designers relied more on the graphics (it's easier to draw a good picture than to craft good text) to tell the story, and the writing suffered correspondingly. The graphics tended to be presented in one of two forms: as either a full-screen image that was displayed briefly on entering a new location before clearing to allow the text to be displayed, or as a split-screen style, occupying a portion of the screen (usually the top half).

Apart from general improvements to the parser, which is indirectly related to the quality of the game interface, this was the pinnacle of the adventure game interface. Today, text adventure games are not commercially viable, but they do live on in the form of MUDs (multiuser dungeons) and MUSHs (multiuser shared hallucinations). For those wanting to investigate MUDs and MUSHs further, a good place to begin is `www.mudcenter.com`.

Graphic Adventures

Graphic adventures are the spiritual successor to text adventures. Taking the maxim "a picture is worth a thousand words" as their rallying cry, designers began to take advantage of the increasing power of computers to create a fully graphical interface to the standard adventure game.

In many ways, this was unfortunate. We may lament the degradation of standards from the classic adventure game—similar to the preference of a significant portion of today's youth for watching cartoons over reading a good book—but we cannot argue with progress. Simply put, text adventures that required the player to type in their commands did not appeal to the consumer in the same way as a graphic adventure, which is, in effect, an interactive cartoon.

That aside, the point-and-click interface of the graphic adventure has changed very little over the years since the first appearance of the genre. From the earliest *Leisure Suit Larry* games (shown in Figure 6.4) through the latest in the *Monkey Island* series (shown in Figure 6.5), the interface has remained pleasingly consistent. The interface to a graphic adventure is a fairly simple construct. Most graphic adventures are 2D or pseudo-3D (that is, they use 3D graphics in a 2D scene-oriented fashion, rather like a stage show), and consequently, only a relatively simple game interface is required.

Figure 6.4 *Leisure Suit Larry II.*

Figure 6.5 *Escape from Monkey Island.*

There are two main paradigms for the interface that are currently in use. The first is the split-screen text- or icon-based interface, where the player selects actions in the selection area of the screen and watches the results in the results portion of the screen. An example of a game that uses this format is LucasArts's *Maniac Mansion: Day of the Tentacle*, shown in Figure 6.6.

Figure 6.6 *Maniac Mansion: Day of the Tentacle.*

The second paradigm, used by such games as *Myst* (shown in Figure 6.7), uses the whole screen as the interface. The player moves the cursor around the screen and clicks on objects or characters of interest. In this way, the story is visually progressed by player interaction. What this format loses in flexibility over the first system, it gains in atmosphere and immersion.

Figure 6.7   *Myst.*

We are not going to include games such as Ion Storm's *Deus Ex* in the category of adventure games. The action quotient in that game is too high to warrant inclusion, and we would prefer to class games of this type as a union of first/third-person shooters and role-playing games (even though it is a close call to make). Adventure games, on the other hand, are typically thought of as games that require pure thought and logic, and little in the way of reflexes. Thus, the game interface for the graphic adventure does not have speed as one of its main priorities, instead focusing on clarity of use.

Role-Playing Games

Role-playing games (RPGs), for the most part, have had roughly the same user interface since day one. This isn't necessarily a good thing. In fact, there is a lot about the standard role-playing game interface that we do not like, but aside from incremental improvements, it seems to be a case of using what works well enough, although a notable exception is the starting interface for *Morrowind*. Your character is defined by your responses to questions posed by interactive characters in the opening part of the game.

The generic role-playing game interface comes in three sections: the character generation screen, the in-game screen, and the inventory screen. These do not seem to have changed much since the inception of the genre, but their forms have been modified and refined somewhat.

Take, for example, an early role-playing game. *Out of the Shadows* from Mizar Software was released for the Sinclair Spectrum in 1984. Figure 6.8 shows the main game and character generation screen of this game. Pay particular attention to the character attributes on the right of the screen.

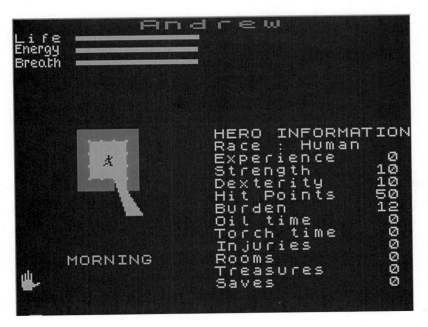

Figure 6.8   *Out of the Shadows* main game and character screen.

Now contrast this with the character generation screen from a more recent game, such as Black Isle Studio's *Planescape: Torment*, as shown in Figure 6.9.

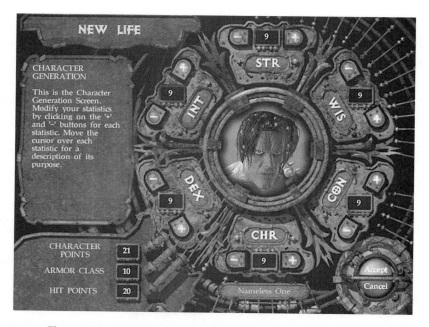

Figure 6.9 *Planescape: Torment* character generation screen.

Apart from the huge differences in the quality of the artwork and the capabilities of the target platforms, these screens are scarily similar in function. Sure, there are a few bells and whistles added to the latter example, but fundamentally, the functionality hasn't really changed in the 16 years between the two games. Note that we feel that *Planescape: Torment* is an excellent game, and we are not trying to imply otherwise by singling it out for our example. We merely want to illustrate how the basic character generation interface has not changed in functionality over the years.

You may be of the school of thought that believes this lack of change is a good thing. After all, it's a system that's been in use since the advent of paper-and-pencil role-playing games in the '70s. However, our view is different. Why use numbers at all in the game interface? They were a necessity in the paper-and-pencil role-playing games, but what a computer is very good at is dealing with numbers. Why bother the player with them? Having "Saving Roll +1" flash up onscreen when we've just dealt a mighty blow to a zombie does nothing except remind us that we're playing a dry game of statistics with some pretty graphics slapped on top. We know that this argument has been used before, and that some players actually prefer to deal with numbers—after all, it does allow the players to know exactly where they stand in the game. However, wondering how high your hit-points are while smiting a zombie jars your suspension of disbelief. Let those players who want to deal with numbers have them, but make them an option in the game. If you need to display numbers (maybe for the sake of accuracy), then at least display them as labels on some sort of bar chart or other graphical representation. To be fair, though, the user interface of *Planescape: Torment* does allow some limited hiding of the numbers, borrowing the technique of displaying graphical power bars from other genres, which is a neat way of sidestepping the problem.

Strategy and War Games

Like their cousin, the role-playing game, strategy and war games have their roots in board games. Hence, early efforts were often heavy on the numbers and played almost exactly like a computer-controlled board game. One of the first breakthrough titles that heralded the roots of the more accessible arcade-strategy genre was a title released for the Sinclair Spectrum back in 1984, called *Stonkers* (see Figure 6.10). This game presented simulated war in a more accessible arcade-influenced format and is arguably the very first RTS (real-time strategy) war game, introducing many of the concepts that are familiar in today's RTS and strategy games.

Figure 6.10   *Stonkers.*

More recent RTS games (such as *Sudden Strike*, shown in Figure 6.11), classic strategy games (such as *Civilization III*, shown in Figures 6.12 and 6.13), and the more traditional war games (such as *Sid Meier's Gettysburg*, shown in Figure 6.14) have a similar user experience—at least at a superficial level. All games of this type are concerned with the same basic set of actions: controlling large groups of units to solve a goal that could not be achieved by one unit alone. Of course, once you go beyond this superficial level, there is some variance in the user interface; for example, *Civilization III* has a diplomatic and city control interface that handles specific decisions at a wider level than those simply concerned with unit- and group-level decisions.

Figure 6.11 *Sudden Strike.*

Figure 6.12 *Civilization III* in-game interface.

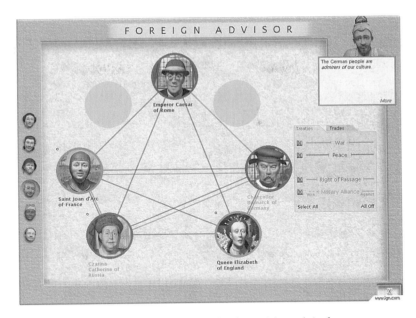

Figure 6.13 *Civilization III* foreign advisory interface.

Figure 6.14 *Sid Meier's Gettysburg.*

Because of its universal nature, the unit- and group-based interface has evolved to allow the player to control these groups easily. Games such as Blizzard's *Warcraft* and Westwood's *Command and Conquer* series have helped define the standard interface for RTS games that most games now follow. Left-clicking to select a unit, and then right-clicking on an object to select a context-sensitive action for the unit to perform on that object, have become familiar actions for most RTS gamers. More recently, the ability to click-drag select a group of units (a method borrowed directly from the Windows operating system) has been added to the repertoire.

However, as these games have become more complex, ways of managing that complexity become needed. This has prompted a divergence in the interfaces, especially with respect to the camera control mechanisms in those games that give the player control of the camera (although why the player would want to control the camera is beyond us—except in special situations, that should be a job for the computer).

Strategy games and war games are characterized by the strategic-level decisions the player is required to make. Consequently, the interface has to allow the player to make these strategic decisions. Note that a lot of these games (for better or worse) also include a fair amount of micromanagement of individual units, usually in the form of giving orders or training. This micromanagement is usually handled by a contextual iconic interface.

In order to be an effective interface, it has to seamlessly handle three levels of abstraction: grand strategy (as in Figure 6.13), group and unit navigation (as in Figure 6.14), and unit micromanagement (as in Figure 6.15). Not all these levels are necessarily present, depending on the strategic slant of the game. As a general rule, RTS games tend to focus on the latter two levels, group and unit navigation and unit micromanagement. More serious war games tend to use all three levels, usually with a focus on the grand strategic and the group and unit navigation levels. Pure strategy games (akin to computer-controlled board games), such as *Risk* (shown in Figure 6.16), focus on the grand strategic level, with varying levels of usage of the latter two levels. Of course, the best of these games allow the player to choose to what level he wants to involve himself—from the overseeing dictator figure all the way down to the bean-counting micromanager, and anywhere in between. *Sid Meier's Civilization* series of games are excellent in their use of the computer to handle such menial tasks at the player's request.

Figure 6.15 *Starcraft's* unit micromanagement interface.

Figure 6.16 *Risk.*

The more serious war games, which have traditionally been rather dry in their presentation, have started to use a number of these more "gamer-friendly" techniques. Previously, these games have focused on the accuracy of the war simulation, rather than any presentational niceties, and generally, that suited the players of these games perfectly. However, in order to attract new players, designers have learned lessons from the more accessible RTS-style games, which in turn were derived from the need to make war games more accessible to the average gamer. Nowadays, the hard-core war games are, in many cases, virtually indistinguishable from the RTS games that they initially inspired.

Components of the User Experience

So far, we've briefly covered a potted history of the user experience and how it has been implemented in game development. The trend has been toward increasing complexity and detail scaling with the capabilities of the hardware and the increasing sophistication of the game design. As the games become more complex, the required interface for the game has also become more complex. The only games that are released nowadays that use the original up/down/left/right/fire paradigm tend to be remakes of the old classics, such as the remake of *Ms. Pac-Man*, shown in Figure 6.17.

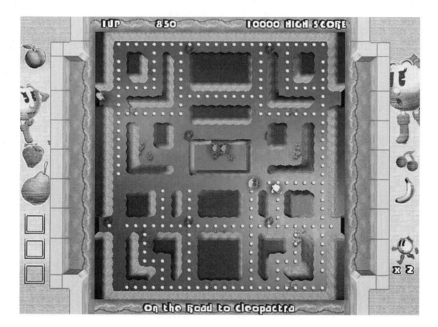

Figure 6.17   *Ms. Pac-Man: Quest for the Golden Maze.*

This increase in complexity is not just limited to the software. As the presentation layer has become more complex, so has the equipment needed to control it. Take a look at Figure 6.18.

Figure 6.18   Past to present: The Atari 2600 joystick versus the GameCube controller (not to scale).

The left-hand picture shows an Atari 2600 joystick. This joystick (circa 1977) was the pinnacle of home entertainment controllers in its day. What you see is what you get: one eight-directional digital stick and a single fire button. Compare it to the Nintendo GameCube controller on the right. This is arguably the most advanced (and well-designed) game controller to date. Take a look at what you get: three directional sticks (two analog and one eight-directional digital) and eight fire buttons. Clearly the sort of games that you can play with the GameCube controller will allow for a much finer degree of finesse in control than possible with the old Atari joystick. Of course, as with all evolution, there were dead-end branches—anyone actually use the Nintendo Power Glove or the Cheetah R.A.T.?

With this increase in complexity—both in hardware and software—comes a need for a more sophisticated approach to the user experience. It's not like it was in the old days, where the game *was* the interface. Today's gamers call out for a higher degree of sophistication and complexity, but paradoxically they want it simpler and easier to use than ever before. And they want the whole experience: sound, visuals, and ease of use in a nice simple package. No longer will they accept simple beeps and blips and the odd screen flash. Now they want CD-quality sound, dynamic music, and visuals that could be exhibited in an art and design museum. And if we don't provide them with what they want, we're in big trouble. Of course, it's not always easy, but perseverance pays off. As Edison put it:

"I haven't failed. I've found 10,000 ways that won't work."

—Thomas Alva Edison, 1847-1931

The Interactive Element

Aside from all the glitz and glamour, the main function of a user interface is to allow the player to play the game. From a purist point of view, that is its primary purpose. All else is secondary. We've lost count of the number of games we've played that have forgotten this simple rule. In these games, various interactivity problems prevent them from showing their true promise; the interface actually gets in the way of playing the game.

There are a couple of main ways in which this occurs. The first is that the interface is overly graphically obscure. The actual navigational pathways through the interface may be fine, and it may be a work of art by many standards, but if the player can't easily figure out how to perform the tasks required to play the game, that beauty is for nothing. Obscurity through artistic overenthusiasm is probably the most common reason for interface failure.

Another common problem that can occur in combination with or separately from the previous problem is an overly complex interface. Here, the player is overwhelmed by a vast wall of options and just does not know where to start. This problem occurs more often in the strategy end of the spectrum, rather than in the more "in-your-face" action games.

The converse of this is the overly simplistic interface. The choices available to the player are so limited, it restricts the gameplay to an "on-rails" experience. This particular flaw is not restricted to any particular genre. It is more commonly found in products that have been underdesigned or rushed through production. Often, the initial design was well fleshed out, but omissions and shortcuts taken during development left a hollow skeleton of the original game. We will be discussing these—and other—problems in the next few sections.

Navigation

Designing a user interface is not a trivial process. It's not just a simple matter of slapping a few buttons together and hoping for the best. The best approach (as with a lot of things) is to plan out everything on paper first.

Using graph paper, plot out a rough design for the user interface. It does not need to be artistic, but it should be an accurate flowchart of the main elements and menus required.

The important thing is to get it down on paper as early as possible in the game design process. Often, putting things on paper can crystallize your ideas and help stimulate new ones. Making sure everything works on paper can often help ensure consistency. When playing an otherwise good game, nothing jars more than interface non-sequiturs.

Bear in mind that you shouldn't feel that you are restricted to paper alone. There are plenty of good tools that allow decent interface prototyping, including graphics and sound, with minimal programming required. Macromedia Flash is one such tool, and—if you are willing to get your hands dirty with a little code—other game-making tools such as Blitz Basic (www.blitzbasic.com) will let you knock up a prototype interface.

Screen Layouts

Balancing between screen real estate and accessibility is a difficult but important task in user interface design. Ten years ago, technical issues were often a consideration; for example, *Ultima Underworld* had a relatively small game area, simply because the machines that it was designed to run on could not handle filling a full screen with texture-mapped polygons and scalable sprites. Thankfully, those days are behind us for the most part, and nowadays technical considerations are low on the list when we consider how much screen real estate to devote to the window on the game world. Except in the case where resolution is a fixed quantity, the only technical issue that rears its head nowadays is which screen resolution (or range of resolutions) to choose.

The screen layout delineates the primary purpose of various regions of the screen at a high level. It's important to get this decided upon as quickly as possible and then stick to that format where applicable throughout the game. Switching between screen layouts during play—particularly if the actual world window is shifted around—adds nothing to a game except momentary disorientation for the players.

The overriding guideline here is the KISS principle—or "Keep It Simple, Stupid." Keep the layout of the screen simple. Don't bother with lots of fiddly little overlays. Group all similar functionality together. That way, the player can take in the information she needs in a single glance, rather than having to roam all over the screen to gather the information she requires.

The human eye does not see consistently throughout its field of vision. There is an area immediately in the center of your field of vision where you see with the maximum amount of detail. This central vision area, the macula, is geared up to take in the visual information at the highest-possible resolution. The peripheral vision of a human does not sense the same amount of detail as the macula, but it is geared for detecting movement and change. If something changes in your peripheral vision, your first instinct is to turn and focus on the area concerned, to scrutinize it in more detail. This instinct can be exploited to focus the players' attention on an indicator if some important happening that they need to know about has occurred.

During our research for this chapter, we examined more than 2,000 screen captures of games, from the '80s right up to the present day. During that investigation, we noticed that there appear to be only nine main screen layouts used (not counting all of the symmetric variations thereof). These are shown in Figure 6.19. The gray area indicates status and other informational panels, and the white is the play area. Any one of these would make a good start for the layout of your user interface. We also noticed that the vast majority of screens we examined placed the most crucial information on the bottom-left quadrant of the screen. This is probably because the human eye is thought to focus on that particular area of the screen more than any other, which may have subconsciously influenced the layout design somewhat. Another important issue to consider is the changing demographic of game players. Older people are playing games now, and we hope this trend will increase as games become more accepted as a mainstream form of entertainment. As the human brain ages, it becomes less and less able to discern events that occur in the peripheral vision region, and becomes much slower at processing complex information too quickly. A too-complex interface will lose you an increasingly broad share of the market if you fail to find a way to appeal across the ever-widening demographic field.

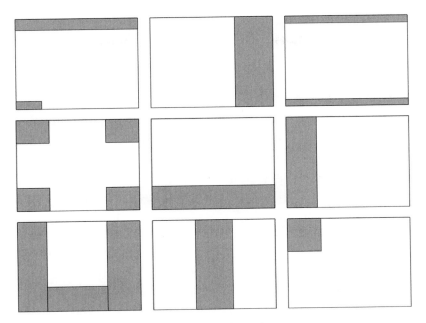

Figure 6.19   Layouts.

Note that we are certainly not claiming that these are the only layouts that have ever been used—if you find any other layouts in common use (not including those that are restricted because of technical considerations), feel free to email the authors, and we'll add them to the list.

Meeting Expectations

Originality is an important consideration, but not at the expense of other considerations. In fact, originality in general is to be much applauded—there is precious little remaining in the industry at the moment. However, there is a time and a place for originality, and the user interface is generally neither.

Although you will want your player to be amazed by the stunning originality of your gameplay, you most certainly do not want him to be amazed by the stunning originality of the control method and user interface. This is one place where the player will be happy to see the "same old, same old." Stick to what the player knows. If the standard method for controlling a first-person shooter works well enough, then use it. Don't foist a new one on the unsuspecting player. The player has a lot to learn when beginning to play a new game, and only a limited amount of time he will be willing to spend on it.

Our discussion will focus on the PC. Of course, there were games on other machines before then, but little progress was made in the development and design of user interfaces until the advent of Microsoft Windows and Mac OS (derived from the original Xerox research). Upon the rise of graphical operating systems, we started seeing some real progress in game interfaces and the beginning of the informal standardization efforts. Back in the bad old days of DOS, the interfaces for games differed radically from the interface for the more standard type of application, mainly because games had some form of graphics and business applications did not, but also because there was no standard for business application user interfaces. Every application (such as WordPerfect, QuickBasic, and so on) had a different way of interfacing with the user. There were no real standardization efforts and, consequently, no common ground on which to base a core game interface.

Unless your game is one that the players have been specifically waiting for, they won't spend too much time trying to figure out an unintuitive or noncooperative interface. And in the event that you do feel the need to inflict a brand-new interface on players (maybe it genuinely is an improvement and is sufficiently different so as to create a whole new learning curve), make sure that you provide a fallback position so that the players can switch to the "classic" interface if they prefer. Another important thing related to user interface is to make sure it doesn't take too many steps to do things. Any game that requires you to click several times and type in something every time you need to save the game is really annoying.

Generally, the only case where an interface should break expectations is if a significant improvement on the status quo can be made. Interface improvements are evolutionary, not revolutionary, so they can be introduced pretty much with impunity. Small chunks of progress are much easier to swallow than the complete deal. An example would be the incremental improvements in the interface of the average RTS game, which, spookily enough, now has many similarities to standard drag-and-drop file handling operations in Windows.

For better or worse, the growth of the games industry has caused games to be released to conform to a range of defined genres. These genres have evolved over time, and informal standards have been established. To the game designer, this means that although a fighting game controlled with a mouse-based interface might be a bold experiment, the game with the tagline "Click and destroy!" will probably be a commercial flop. When it comes to how they control their games, people simply *do not want change*.

A concrete example: In the '80s, a renowned programmer of hit games produced a series of highly successful soccer games for 8-bit computers. The control method used in these games was highly exacting. Unlike the soccer games of today, the player was given little or no assistance in controlling the ball. When the player's team member touched the ball, it bounced off. Hence, dribbling the ball was a matter of literally chasing the ball with the player's team member—a very tricky process when surrounded by opposing team members. Kicking the ball was even harder; it went in the direction of the kick. If the player wanted to kick the ball to another team member, it was the player's responsibility to ensure that the recipient was in exactly the right location.

In the late '90s, the programmer of this series was given an opportunity to produce an update of his classic soccer series for the PC and Sony PlayStation. Of course, in the meantime, the computerized soccer game interface had evolved, and certain interface features were considered standard (for example, autotargeted kicks, aftertouch, and autodribble). This meant that modern soccer games on the computer were less about controlling the ball, and more about the strategic flow of the game—more of "Are my players in the right formation to score a goal?" and less of "Argh! Where's the ball?".

The reasoning behind the programmer's new update was to eschew this namby-pamby "make it easy on the player" approach and take things back to the old days, where learning to control the ball was a player skill in its own right. Unfortunately, the game bombed. It was too difficult to learn, and too far behind the times. The original games were successful because they were state-of-the-art when they were released. Attempting to update the game without substantially updating the control interface to match modern standards was a bad idea from the start, appealing to no one except fans of the original games (most of whom had grown up and gone on to other things) or die-hard soccer freaks.

In order to be successful, a game has to be accessible to more than the hard-core fans. If your game is hotly anticipated (for example, if you happen to be writing *Doom III*), then more people will expend effort trying to learn it. If not, you had better make sure it's as accessible as possible. The best way to start is with the user interface.

Hardware Considerations

Whether designing a computer, console, or multiplatform game, hardware considerations should be foremost in your mind. The capabilities of the hardware—and specifically of the available controllers—will have a profound effect on your game design.

Game designers do not need to be technical wizards, but they do need to be aware of the capabilities and limitations of their target platform.

In the case of the PC, there is a plethora of available controllers. This is, in fact, one of the problems with designing games for a platform that is so variable. There are so many different controller configurations that you have to provide support for the lowest common denominator: the keyboard and the mouse. You can't even count on many PC owners having joysticks, let alone joysticks with force-feedback capabilities. You can, of course, provide support for more specific controllers—for example, racing games can support steering wheel and pedal kits, and flight simulators can support the full yoke system—but the usual approach is to make them an option rather than the default.

If a game has sufficient "weight" behind it, it can set the recommended default as a specific type of controller that would require a secondary purchase. An example of a game (in this case, a series of games) with the required clout to be able to pull this off is the *Madden* series of football games. The default controller in the instructions for the 2001 edition (and also referenced in-game) is a six-button gamepad. The game can be controlled with the keyboard and the mouse, but that is definitely the secondary mode of control. Requiring a specific controller is certainly not a recommended approach. It will alienate some of your potential players (who may think that they actually *need* a gamepad to play the game, and may not be willing to buy one), and sales will suffer as a result.

So let's consider the tools that we have available. On the PC, we have the keyboard and the mouse, and on the consoles, we have some form of gamepad-style controller. Obviously, the available controllers have an impact on the nature of the games that are created. On the consoles, you tend to get more action-oriented games. Those styles of games requiring more complex input—role-playing games, RTS games, adventure games, and simulation games—tend to appear on the PC, where the keyboard and mouse allow for more suitable input. That's not to say that crossover does not occur: *Starcraft* was released on the Nintendo 64, but it was not as easy to control—or indeed as successful—as the PC version because of the lack of a mouse. Of course, it would be naïve of us to insist that the sole reason for difference in game styles on consoles as compared to PCs is controller configuration—it also has a lot to do with player demographic (the sort of person who will buy a $200 console compared with a $1,500 computer).

Even though most games can be played using the standard controllers, some games are indeed better played with specialist hardware. For example, the games *Dance Dance Revolution*, Sega's *Bass Fishing*, and *Samba De Amigo* are much more enjoyable when played with a dance pad, a fishing controller, and maracas, respectively (shown in Figure 6.20).

Figure 6.20 Specialized controllers.

Steel Battalions by Capcom costs about $200 for the game, with a huge custom dual-stick controller with more than thirty buttons and foot pedals. It is considered to be an amazing gaming experience, but the player must be at least a passing mechwarrior freak in order to appreciate it.

Designing games to use specialized controllers is not an opportunity that many of us will get. Usually, the specialized controllers start off in Japanese arcades, follow through to the consoles, and then in a few (very few) instances, filter through to the PC. One case where a particular genre (or more exactly, one or two stand-out titles from that genre) has spawned a specialized controller is the first-person shooter (FPS). All the effort spent on creating the specialized FPS controller appears to be for nothing, however—the best controller for this particular genre still seems to be a combination of mouse and keyboard.

For a specialized controller to take root and become a standard, a critical mass has to be achieved. This can occur in a number of ways. One such way is for an incredibly successful game to offer better playability with the controller, such as in the case of *Dance Dance Revolution*. This introduces the controller into a lot of homes. Provided that the programming details of the controller are authorized public knowledge, there is no reason why your game cannot use the new controller if it has achieved a suitable level of ubiquity.

The effect of a controller on the user interface is profound. For example, controlling a pointer and clicking on buttons using a gamepad rather than a mouse always feels awkward. When a mouse is not available, a far better approach is to have the directional buttons on the gamepad highlight each button in turn. Obviously, there are many other ways that a controller can influence the usability of an interface. An interface suitable for keyboard or gamepad control needs modifications to be equally as usable with a mouse, and vice versa; hence, the capabilities of the selected controller must be taken into account when designing the interface. Again—as with many other aspects of user interface design—this task is made easier by informal genre standardization. You can take the root of your control system directly from other games that are similar in presentation to your design.

Simple User Interface Elements

User interfaces serve a primary function—interacting with the user—which is split into two main tasks. One of these tasks is to accept the player's commands. The second task is to inform the player of her status within the game and display the options available in as graphically clear a format as possible. There is a large element of graphic design in user interface design—even with something as simple as an arcade game.

There are certain standard elements of a user interface that we will discuss. These are divided into two broad classes: *in-game elements* and the *shell interface*, with the latter referring to the various menus and screens that allow the player to start, configure, and otherwise manage the game. The shell interface needs to provide functionality to allow the player to configure the video and audio settings and the controls; to provide access to a multiplayer lobby, where appropriate, and saved games; and to allow the player to exit the game. We will not discuss the design of shell interface in any great detail; suffice it to say that it should thematically and stylistically jell with the rest of the game and respond to the player quickly and smoothly. After all, there is no great secret to generic shell design—if you need inspiration, just look at another game, or even a standard Windows application, and base it on that. Make use of the millions of dollars Microsoft spent on user interface research, and don't bother reinventing the wheel.

"If you want to make an apple pie from scratch, you must first create the universe."

—**Carl Sagan**, 1934-1996

One very important point, however: The player should not be forced to spend too much time in the shell interface. Players should be able to get right into the action (fast-track style) by one or two clicks of a button if they so desire.

Now let's discuss the in-game interface. We will be concentrating on the tools and methods used to divulge information to the player while he is actually playing the game. We are going to try to assume nothing and start off by discussing the simplest constructs.

The player in a game needs to be aware of his status. The indicators are present to provide the player with the information to be able to set goals, increase the thrill level, and provide rewards when the player does well. That's what they *should* do. What they should not do is distract the player from the game, clutter the screen, confuse the player with unnecessary or extraneous information, or obfuscate vital information.

There are many indicators that are used to inform the player of his status, such as score, ammo count, power level, and level indicator. Some of these indicators are genre-specific, but many are pangenre. We'll cover a few of these here to give an example of the kind of things we are talking about. An exhaustive list isn't necessary, because in the first place, we'd be writing an entire book just on that subject, and in the second place, most of the elements are self-evident. Let's discuss some of them, and you'll see what we mean.

For example, the classic "score" indicator is virtually ever-present, especially on the console platforms. Although there have been many creative ways of displaying score, the usual approach is to display a numeric indicator. Of course, a score is a measure of success, and what use is a measure of success unless you have something to measure against? Hence, the high-score indicator—and associated high-score table—keep track of past scores and give players a yardstick by which to measure themselves. Sometimes, in order to add flavor, a score is accompanied by a rating. Thus, a low score may elicit a response of "You are pitiful!" while a more impressive score would give a slightly more encouraging response.

The score indicator is the simplest of the basic indicators. If score is a primary concern in the game, it's usually shown onscreen at all times. (If this is the case, the high score is often shown too, to act as a spur on to greater things.) In some cases, the score isn't really important during the game and is only totted up at the end of the level or the game. How you choose to track the player's progress is up to you or the conventions of the particular genre, but bear in mind that players generally play for a reason; they do want some indication of success (or failure).

Originally (and somewhat out of vogue nowadays), the score indicator was often accompanied by a "lives remaining" indicator. This would show how many chances the player has remaining, by showing either the correct number of miniature icons or a plain numerical display. Again, modern games seem to have eschewed the "number of lives" paradigm in favor of infinite respawns. Indeed, with the current trend of most games to allow saving of the game at almost any point, the concept of lives is pretty much irrelevant.

One small part of the "lives" concept that has managed to survive is the "power bar" indicator, shown in Figure 6.21. It usually takes the form of a horizontal bar that is colored in full. As the level decreases, the color drains from the right to the left. In this context, the player has only one life, but a limited amount of power. This power is drained until it is all gone, and then the player dies. The power indicator is still used in many other situations and can be found in many different types of games. In fact, it is often used in any situation where an attribute of the player's avatar has minimum and maximum values, and the value of that attribute can vary between them.

Figure 6.21   An example power bar.

Some games—particularly accurate flight or race car simulations or games that are aiming for a particular "analog" theme—use dials (see Figure 6.22). These are a variation on the power bar and are often modeled after the real thing, particularly in the case of accurate simulations.

Figure 6.22   Dials (*Microsoft Flight Simulator 2002*).

As we've said, we're not going to go through an exhaustive list of the possible user interface elements. You can see that they are fairly self-evident, and that consequently describing all the possible elements would be next to impossible. Fortunately, it's also not necessary. Most of the possibilities are combinations of the few basic elements mentioned in this chapter, and the remainder are clearly visible in context elsewhere—for example, in other games, or in the standard Windows interface. The only required skill is in deciding how to use them, which is mainly a matter of common sense. When designing the interface, work out which information the player needs at hand quickly and which can be put out of immediate reach.

Another very important consideration is consistency. Consistency makes your interface simpler and more predictable. When a player is trying to figure her way around a new interface, consistency will be a great help. When designing an interface, pay attention to matters of consistency. Make sure that your interface is stylistically consistent throughout. For example, switching between steam-punk brass and hi-tech chrome within the same context breaks the consistency rule.

Apart from stylistic consistency, it's also important to maintain navigational consistency. That is, the methods of accessing information and navigation between screens should be similar across the interface. If a slider is used to set a variable value, it should be used consistently throughout the interface, unless there is a good reason not to. Difference solely for the sake of difference is never a good idea—especially in the case of interface design.

As a small example of specifics, designers should strive for button consistency. The same button (on a controller) should always be used to select a menu item (for example, the green button), and the same button should always be used to exit the menu (for example, the red button). As another example, the use of defaults should always be consistent. Whether you choose to set the last item selected by the player as the default, or always set the first list item as the default, it should be reflected consistently across the interface.

Words and Pictures

Probably the most important interactive element of the user interface—present in virtually all games—is the icon, which often appears as a button or a label, sometimes in combination with or in addition to text. Information has to be presented to the player, and the main way to do this is visually. The adage "a picture is worth a thousand words" comes into play here—often a visual image can be interpreted and understood much faster than the equivalent text.

There is another reason for minimizing the amount of text onscreen: localization. Different languages have different scripts, grammatical structures, and sentence lengths. If everything onscreen is displayed as text, your localization team will soon run into a lexicographical nightmare trying to resolve the issues that come up with localization.

Most games contain a fair amount of text, all of which has to be localized if the product is going to go on sale in countries where English is not the native tongue. It makes sense, therefore, to minimize the amount of extraneous text that goes into areas such as the user interface. This does not entirely preclude the possibility of text in your user interface. That would be patently ridiculous. However, it makes sense to minimize it for both of the reasons mentioned here—the difficulty of assimilating text compared to representative images, and the issues with text localization.

Another issue that is sometimes overlooked when dealing with text is distinguishing between what is a text asset and what is an art asset. As a rule, you should never call upon the artists to embed text in a picture. This converts an easily managed text asset into a far less manageable art asset. To change text in a text file is trivial. To modify text added to an image at the design phase is usually not. It makes far more sense to maintain all text strings within the game as external resources and overlay them as needed within the game. Believe us: When you come to localize your game, you cannot imagine the headaches that doing this proactively will save you.

If you are going to display any significant amount of onscreen text, you need to make sure that it is easily readable. As a rule of thumb, the minimum height of text displayed on a screen should be about 12 pixels. There are exceptions to this rule, of course, but for the most part, it should be treated as an absolute. If the height of the text is any less than 12 pixels, the resolution and definition of the glyphs suffer—particularly if you require localization to non-roman alphabets, where you simply will not be able to get the detail you need in less than 12 pixels.

The formatting of your text is also important. Take some tips from standard publishing. Use mixed uppercase and lowercase letters—if you use all one case, it makes words harder to pick out. Trying to read all uppercase text has two problems. The first is that it looks as though the writer is SHOUTING, and the second is that IT CAN MAKE INDIVIDUAL WORDS HARDER TO PICK OUT THAN IF THEY WERE WRITTEN IN NORMAL MIXED CASE. It's just plain harder to read and it's ugly. Don't do it.

When selecting a font for your game, try to pick one font and stick with it. If you feel that you do have to mix fonts, be careful in how you mix them. Try not to use wildly differing styles together—unless you're specifically looking for that "ransom note" effect. It looks amateurish and unprofessional. In particular, don't use serif and sans serif together. If you're mixing, try and stay within the same class of font.

The development of the icon was precisely due to the problems with the efficiency of text as a communication medium. A clear, descriptive graphical image is easier to comprehend than text, but (and there is always a but) an icon can only be understood if there is a common cultural ground between the designer and the player. Let us provide an example. Consider Figure 6.23: The icon in this image will be immediately recognizable to an American, or to anybody who has spent some time in America, but it will probably not be familiar to anyone else. It's the symbol for a pharmacy, but you have to be familiar with American culture to know that. Nothing in the picture gives any clue as to its meaning. For that reason, it's a bad choice as an icon, unless your product is restricted to within the continent of North America. A better choice of icon would be a red cross on a white background, known widely as the symbol of the International Red Cross organization (or it would be good to use if it wasn't trademarked; id Software's *Doom* fell foul to this particular snafu).

Figure 6.23   Pharmacy icon.

Another example is to use a picture of a duck (the fowl) to indicate that your avatar will duck (the action). That relies on a visual pun that only works if you have a good understanding of English. Again, it automatically cuts you off from foreign markets and creates unnecessary localization issues. That does not mean that you are restricted to strictly representative icons. There is nothing to say that an icon has to specifically represent its intended action. The aim of an icon is to give a visual clue that can be easily understood *in the context of the situation.* You don't need to stress out trying to make sure that your icon cannot be mistaken for anything else under some strange circumstance. Your players will be a little more forgiving than that. The only real concerns are that your icons cannot be mistaken for another in the same interface, and that there is at least some conceptual link between the icon and the action that it represents.

There are some pan-cultural images that have been developed over a period of time that are now considered de facto standards. Consider the icons shown in Figure 6.24. All these symbols should be instantly recognizable to you. Even if they're not, you could easily make a guess at their probable meaning. Bear in mind that if any of them seems vague or ambiguous in the diagram, it is to be expected. You are viewing them in the rarified atmosphere of the printed page. There is no immediate context to set them against.

Figure 6.24   Universal icons.

Try considering some of these icons in context. For example, if the hammer and wrench icon was displayed on the opening menu of a game, you could assume that it allowed you to access the game configuration screen. On the other hand, if it was displayed on the control panel of an in-game vehicle in a racing game, you could assume that it served as a pit-stop button or some other mechanical function. The important thing is that the context makes the difference. As long as the icon is the only one of that type, the meaning is unambiguous. For example, having a separate hammer and a separate wrench as two icons on the same screen would cause confusion and should be avoided, unless the game specifically calls for those two tools separately, and the player had already been made aware of the distinction.

One good use for text in a game interface that relies on icons in some capacity is for "tool tips." Most people who have used a computer are now familiar with these, but for the uninitiated, tool tips are small balloons of text that appear when the pointer is hovered over a button for a short period of time without actually clicking it. Tool tips can be visual or audio (the function of the button is audibly announced), but the ideal situation is to have a visual *and* audio cue. Make sure the players can turn off this aspect of the audio if they want to.

Having good icons and representative images within your interface is a great start, but it's only half of the story. After a player has clicked on a button, she will want instant feedback. This doesn't mean that the corresponding action should happen immediately—that wouldn't always make sense, depending on context—but there should be a visual and an audio indication that the button has actually been clicked. In other words, tell the players that their request has been acknowledged and will be acted upon presently.

As with tool tips, the best method of acknowledging a request is audibly and visibly. The audio can be anything from a simple "click" noise to a function-specific "request acknowledged"-style announcement. The usual method for indicating that a button is pressed is to highlight it in some way, either by making it appear in the down position or by changing its color or contrast. Be careful with color usage. Bear in mind that about 8 percent of men are color-blind to some degree. If you are varying color as an acknowledgement, be sure to vary the contrast noticeably too—particularly if your colors have a large red/green component. This will allow players with diminished ability to distinguish color to play your game on equal terms with all other players.

Hiding Complexity

One of the problems with the increasing capabilities of game machines, and the resulting increase in sophistication of game designs, is that the issue of managing complexity rears its ugly head.

Some games have literally hundreds of options available to a player at any one time. Without some sensible scheme for managing the presentation of these options, we end up with a game that is very difficult to play—either because no one can remember all the options (think in terms of flight simulators), or because the screen is so crammed with icons and controls (think in terms of badly designed strategy games), there is no room to play the game.

A specific example of a game that handled complexity badly (by the designer's own admission, so you can't blame us for slinging mud) is the original *Dungeon Keeper*.

> "(Dungeon Keeper) *taught me to think even harder about design issues before starting the process of implementation. It also taught me how not to design an interface—the complicated interface meant that* Dungeon Keeper *was a missed opportunity."*
>
> —**Peter Molyneux**, designer of *Dungeon Keeper*

The user interface of *Dungeon Keeper* (shown in Figure 6.25) contains a status panel that Molyneux described as "terrible" and containing "too many icons" in his 2001 GDCE (Game Developer's Conference Europe) "Essentials of Game Design" presentation. In the opinion of Molyneux, *Dungeon Keeper* was a missed opportunity because of the bad interface. It sold 700,000 copies, which for most designers would be considered a great success. But when compared to the sales of *Populous, Theme Park*, and *Black and White* (also mostly designed by Molyneux) at 3.5 million copies each for the first two and 1.5 million copies for the latter, it's fairly clear as to why he saw *Dungeon Keeper* as a failure.

Figure 6.25 *Dungeon Keeper.*

What could he have done to mitigate the poor design and boost those sales? There are a number of approaches he could have taken, and we will detail some of these here (but bear in mind that hindsight is always 20/20).

When designing an interface that has as many options and features, as were present in *Dungeon Keeper*, we need to use some type of method to reduce the complexity. One thing to consider is the depth versus the width of the interface. How do we define the depth and width? In this sense, the width of an interface is the number of top-level options available to the player. For example, a menu with five buttons would have a width of five. The depth corresponds to the number of menus below the top-level menu. As a general rule of thumb (which is most certainly not valid in all situations), it is a good idea to make these values roughly equal (at least to within plus or minus 50 percent). As a guideline, count the total number of options available to your player and take the square root of that. That's the number you should be aiming for.

An interface that is too wide will overwhelm the player, whereas an interface that is too deep will be difficult for the player to remember where everything is. This, of course, assumes a static structure for the menu.

When deciding how to structure your menus, a good starting approach is to categorize the options by frequency of access. The most frequently accessed elements should be one or two steps away from the player at most. The least frequently accessed elements can be farther down the hierarchy.

A good set of guidelines, adapted from interface theory research performed by the University of Alberta, is as follows:

➤ **Be consistent.** The player should only be required to perform consistent sequences of actions in similar situations. The terminology used in prompts, menus, and game-screens should be identical. The use of color, capitalization, font, and layout should be consistent throughout logically connected sections of the game.

➤ **Enable hardcore players to use shortcuts.** To cater for hardcore players, provide abbreviations, special keys, hidden commands, and macros to enable them to play faster. Try not to unduly affect the game balance by making these shortcuts too powerful.

➤ **Give good feedback.** For every user action, the game should respond in some way. This one is obvious: When the player interacts with something, he will expect the game to respond—at least with an acknowledgment—immediately.

➤ **Design the interface to offer defined tasks.** The sequences of actions the player is performing should be arranged into a conceptual group of smaller subtasks, each with a defined beginning, middle, and end. Each task completion should be punctuated with an acknowledgment, so the player knows that his task has been completed.

➤ **Don't allow the player to make silly mistakes, and allow recovery from minor errors.** The player should not be able to make a serious error simply by typing or clicking the wrong thing. Check and validate all player input. If the player does make an erroneous entry that the game could not anticipate, then the player should be guided to graceful recovery. If the game requires a complex input method try and break the input into smaller tasks where appropriate.

➤ **Permit easy reversal of actions.** If a player makes a silly mistake, allow the player to reverse the action, unless it would affect the game balance adversely.

➤ **Remember that the player is the one in control.** Players want to feel in charge of the game—at least in regard to control of their avatar. Don't throw random uncontrollable events, or tedious or difficult input sequences (such as pointless jumping puzzles).

> ➤ **Don't strain the player's short-term memory.** Short-term memory is a finite resource. The player should not be overwhelmed by the information the game is provided. Provide ways to hierarchically (or otherwise if appropriate) compartmentalize information.

Another more advanced method of managing complexity is to have a fluid menu structure. By employing context sensitivity, we can show the player only options that are relevant to his current situation. For example, consider a hypothetical graphic adventure. Let's assume that our character is in the bathroom. There are only certain actions available to a player in the bathroom (and we won't dwell on those here), but there are many actions that are impossible. It would make no sense at all to give our player the menu option to, for example, cook something, so useless options such as these (which would normally elicit a response of "You can't do that here") can be culled from the available options. *The Sims* uses this particular approach to manage complexity. The caveat to using this form of context sensitivity is that it can make the gameplay more transparent if it is done badly. If the only options left available on the menu are the only actions that can be performed, it makes the adventure easier by automatically eliminating dead ends in the investigative process of playing the game. Thinking up solutions to the presented problems is part of the challenge to an adventure game, and presenting only the available actions to a player will reduce the level of challenge. This can be a good thing, reducing frustrating elements of play, as long as the challenge is not reduced to the level where only the correct solution is available as an option.

A valuable addition to the previous scheme is to allow the user to configure the interface to some degree. *Diablo* and *Diablo II* handled this admirably, by allowing the player to assign her favorite spells to hotkeys so that they could be accessed quickly in the heat of battle.

A related method, often used in graphic adventures, role-playing games, and other mouse-controlled games, is the context-sensitive pointer. The pointer will change its form when it is pointing to an object of interest. In the case of an RTS, it may change into a pickax when a peasant is selected and the pointer is over a collectable resource; or, if a warrior is selected, it may turn into a red crosshair when over an enemy, a yellow crosshair when over a neutral character, and a green crosshair when over a friend.

Another approach is to implement a beginner's mode and an expert mode. The beginner's mode only presents a simplified set of options that encompass the core set of necessary actions available to a player. The expert mode provides the same options, but divides them into a finer grain. For example, an RTS in beginner's mode may provide the option to attack, but in expert mode, it may allow the player to tailor the attack by providing reckless, cautious, or normal attacks, with the difference being the amount of punishment the unit will take before retreating.

More recently, the concept of the "invisible interface" has been touted around the industry. Of course, the invisible interface is one of many holy grails that the industry strives for. The most literal example of the invisible interface can be found in Lionhead's *Black and White*, shown in Figure 6.26.

Figure 6.26 *Black and White.*

In this game, the player's avatar is a disembodied hand that responds directly to the movements of the mouse. There is virtually no other status information displayed on the screen. There are no icons or buttons for the player to click on; every action that can be performed in the game is done by moving the mouse. For example, in Figure 6.26, the mouse has been moved in a star configuration. The game recognizes that as the pattern required to cast a spell; hence, the glowing star in the image. Similarly, if you want to punish your creature, you move your hand up and down in a vigorous fashion when it is over your creature. This results in the creature being slapped. Moving your hand more slowly results in you tickling and caressing your creature, rewarding it. To move your hand around the landscape, you move the hand ahead of you, grab the landscape, and "pull" the view forward.

Because there is no other interface to speak of other than the hand, this approach has been dubbed the invisible interface. From the overstuffed icon-fest of *Dungeon Keeper*, we have now reached the opposite extreme—no icons at all. We are not sure which approach is best—*Black and White* sure is difficult to play with a trackball—but the aim of the closely mapped mouse-to-hand movements is to attempt to immerse the player in the game with only the thinnest layer of interface separating him from it.

Another approach that implements the invisible interface is that taken by Hasbro's *Frogger 2*. Here, the game configuration menu is controlled by actually guiding the frog from island to island in a small "main menu" level. To configure the sound, you jump onto an old style gramophone; to start the game, you jump through a doorway (or something similar); and to play the old-style *Frogger*, you jump onto a *Frogger* arcade machine. This is a great approach to the invisible interface problem—it actually makes configuring and starting the game part of the fun.

However, in our opinion, an interface does not need to be nonexistent to be invisible. Our definition of an invisible interface would be one that fits the game so well that the player forgets that it is there. *Starcraft* is such a game. The interface is so well designed that the player performs her actions subconsciously. The interface efficiently transfers the player's desires into actions within the game world. With practice and experience, the use of the interface becomes second nature. This example of an invisible interface lacks the gimmicky (although effective) approach of the first two examples.

When designing your interface, if you want to achieve the invisible effect, you have at least these options open to you (and any others you may be able to think of). However, we prefer the third approach, and our design leanings are toward making an interface invisible by hiding it in plain sight—making it so intuitive that the player forgets it is there. This is the minimalist approach. Display what is needed to make the game fun and easy to control. No less and no more.

A major factor that will influence the effectiveness of your interface is the information density. For example, consider Figure 6.27. In each of these two examples, the first example on the top and the second on the bottom, the same information is presented in two different forms. One of the forms is quicker to comprehend than the other, and hence is more suitable for an interface. The top example compares an icon with the equivalent text. Obviously, the smiley face icon will be recognized by the brain more quickly than the equivalent text. The second example shows three numbers. Clearly, the second format shows the relationship between the numbers at a glance far better than the first format.

Figure 6.27   Optimal presentation of information.

One last important consideration—specifically for the PC—is to make sure that whatever interface you provide has keyboard shortcuts where possible. As players become more advanced in their game skills, they will often prefer to access a game function directly rather than through a hierarchy of menus or options. This is one major advantage that PCs have over consoles, and it makes our task as a game designer that little bit simpler. It's important to take every advantage given to you in order to make your game shine above others. The ability to offer an alternate "fast-track" interface for experienced players is one of those small touches that makes a difference.

The Visual Element

This chapter has focused on user interface, mainly from the functional and navigational point of view. However, we also have to consider the aesthetics. This will not be covered in as much detail as the navigational aspects, mainly because the topic is so large that to attempt to cover it all would be ineffectual.

Nowadays, the freedoms afforded by today's hardware—with millions of colors and high-resolution screens—allow the designer to let his imagination go with the visual appearance of a game. As with all freedoms, care must be taken to use it responsibly; the industry is littered with unsuccessful games that failed because of an inaccessibly beautiful interface. Consequently, we will discuss some of what we feel are the key issues surrounding the appearance of a game and its interface.

The 3D Versus 2D Argument

The 3D versus 2D argument is a contentious subject, and not everyone is likely to agree with our opinions. (That's why they are opinions—if everyone agreed with them, then life would become very boring.)

The industry has been moving toward more and more 3D games. Since the rise of 3D accelerator cards and consoles such as the PlayStation, Nintendo 64, and Dreamcast, there has been an inexorable increase in the use of 3D in every possible title. Even *Monopoly Tycoon*, a conversion of a board game, uses advanced 3D graphics. What's with this? Everybody is so caught up in the fact that they *can* that they haven't stopped to think whether they *should*.

We're not complete Luddites. We happen to play and enjoy a lot of 3D games, but we find ourselves wondering about some of the titles that appear to be released in 3D solely because 3D exists. Simply put, some games work better in 2D, and this is proved by the fact that these games usually have a default view that looks just like the old 2D view, except with the use of polygons. Polygons are pretty, to be sure, but we are not yet at the stage where polygons look prettier than well-drawn sprites. Compare a game such as *Sudden Strike* (shown earlier in Figure 6.11) to a polygon-based RTS game such as *Starship Troopers: Terran Ascendancy* (shown in Figure 6.28).

Figure 6.28 *Starship Troopers: Terran Ascendancy.*

Both games are similar in style, but the latter game, *Starship Troopers*, uses a polygon-based engine. It can be seen from the figure that the graphics are inferior to *Sudden Strike*: less detailed and more sparse. Of course, what you lose in detail you gain in flexibility—the player can rotate the camera view to get a different take on the action. The question is, "Why?" Does this improve the gameplay? The answer is probably not. The camera will just overcomplicate the interface, and most players will end up just playing it from the default overhead view anyway (in which case, sprites would look better).

Of course, if gameplay and clarity of interface were the only issues, most games would be in 2D. Obviously other factors, such as immersion and commercial expectations, influence the decision far more. Sometimes, however, the decision seems to be influenced by the commercial "because we can" instead of the practical "because we should."

What we are trying to say is don't use 3D for 3D's sake alone. Try to find some bona-fide justification for requiring that your title be 3D. (And, in case you are wondering, "because it sells better" is a valid response. It doesn't mean we have to like it, though.)

The Audio Element

We have already spoken a little about sound in our discussion of player feedback. However, this is not the only place where it should be used, or the playing experience ends up being very flat indeed.

This section covers some of the other areas and issues associated with sound design in games. We'll split our discussion into two distinct areas. The first will discuss sound effects, and the second will discuss music.

Sound Effects

Originally, sound was limited by hardware to beeps used as minor spot effects. Now, we expect CD-quality soundtracks and environmental audio surround sound with our games. Not only do we expect to be entertained visually and cerebrally, we also expect an audio feast for our ears.

The most prevalent use for sound effects in games is in *incidental effects*. These sounds correspond to the actions and events that happen in the game world—for example, a burst of gunfire, or the tight squealing of tires as a car slides sideways around a corner. Bear in mind that in nature, sound is often our first warning of an incoming event. You will often hear danger before you actually see it. Hence, it is fitting to use sound as the first indicator that something needs attention paid to it. Be sure to back it up with a visual indicator too, so that the player has somewhere to look and see what is going on. It's much easier to interpret an event visually that it is by audio alone.

As audio capabilities improved, sound effects were also used to provide feedback to the player. There are many examples of how this is done, and we have already discussed audio interface feedback previously in the chapter. Some examples include the ability to judge the need to change gear in a racing game by listening to the pitch of the engine, or knowing that an enemy is approaching because the player can hear his footsteps and heavy breathing as he rounds a nearby corner.

Beyond this, there is the issue of *dialog*. Many games—particularly adventures and role-playing games—rely heavily on scripted dialog. This is usually recorded by experienced voice actors, and it helps the player get fully immersed into the game world. Or at least it should. Bad voice acting does more to destroy immersion that no voice at all.

The original *Diablo* from Blizzard Entertainment was singled out for having particularly bad voice acting. However, computer games are a relatively new medium, and each new medium requires new techniques. It's entirely possible that these techniques remain to be discovered; in the years ahead, they might crack them, and we'll have convincing voice acting in games to look forward to.

Bear in mind that not all your players will have perfect hearing. Any time that a sound is used to notify a player of an event, a visual cue should be given, too. (This can be a configurable option, such as subtitles for spoken dialog.)

Music

No discussion of sound would be complete without a brief sojourn into the subject of music. Ever since the first strangled warblings of early sound chips, developers have attempted (with varying degrees of success) to get music into their games.

Initially, the player would usually be treated to a shockingly bad rendition of a familiar tune on the title screen. The practice of using familiar tunes took a dive, however, when copyright lawyers for the music industry started sitting up and taking notice. That's when the rise of the computer musicians started. These guys specialized in making original music for games. Some, such as Rob Hubbard (www.robhubbard.co.uk), even achieved a substantial level of independent fame in their own right, solely through their game music. Some of the more extreme fans even bought games solely for the music.

Once the hardware capabilities increased, games began to include in-game music. This led us to where we are today, where literally every game is expected to have a CD-quality soundtrack. When deciding on a soundtrack for your game, make sure that it fits thematically with the rest of the game. For example, a pentatonic scale guitar composition might sit well with a medieval Japanese adventure game, but it would certainly sound out of place in a futuristic war game.

Of course, discordance may be just the effect that you want to achieve. One of the most striking moments in the introductory movie for *Starcraft* was the use of classical opera as the audio backdrop, set against fierce battle scenes when the admirals calmly discussed the war situation as they prepared to abandon the men on the surface to their fate. The juxtaposition between the opulent calm of the admiral's bridge and the hell of war on the surface was accented excellently by the choice of music. Music is arguably capable of eliciting emotion more effectively than any other medium—and in this case, it worked well.

The music in the introductory movie for *Starcraft* was so effective because the mechanism was not overused. As a designer, you will want to give the player a musically appropriate experience the majority of the time. That way, when you bend the rules, it will have a greater impact on the emotions of the player. Of course, you won't be designing the music yourself—in most cases—but it is the designer's responsibility to tell the composer the effects and the emotions that the designer wants the player to be feeling by listening to the music.

Another holy grail of the industry (and there are many) is dynamically variable music, otherwise known as *interactive music*. This is a slight misnomer. We don't really need interactive music—what we need is *adaptive music*. The use of the word "interactive" implies an explicit two-way relationship: The player affects the music, and the music in turn explicitly affects the player. That's not what we'd want at all. Of course, the music may affect the player's emotions, which may in turn affect the way she plays, but that is just a secondary side effect and not the intended effect at all.

The aim of adaptive music is to play a constantly varying tune in the background, correctly anticipating the player's actions and upcoming game events so that the tune always accents the actions—similar to the way that music in a movie rises to a crescendo when an exciting or emotional climax is approaching.

So, is adaptive music the holy grail or merely fool's gold? After all, sound effects can do just as well at evoking mood, and in any nontrivial game (excepting those with "on-rails" gameplay), we don't know what's going to happen in the game. The algorithm forsuccessfully predicting the future when an unpredictable element (the player) is involved hasn't been perfected yet. We think that adaptive music in its current limited capacity is (or more specifically, will become) a valuable tool, but as yet, it is not quite ready for the prime time.

User Interface Worksheet

1. Roughly sketch out the major elements of the game's shell interface; then move on to the in-game experience. For the in-game experience, define each of the gameplay modes the game will require to be playable (including the pause menu, if there is one). Don't forget non-interactive modes such as movies or mission briefings.

2. Create a flowchart showing how the gameplay modes change from one to another, and what events (player actions or in-game events) cause each change.

3. For each gameplay mode in the game:
   a. Create its screen layout.
   b. Determine its perspective on the game world (or, if more than one is possible, determine all its perspectives and choose one as the default).
   c. Select its interaction model.
   d. Define what will happen when each button on the controller or keyboard is pressed and—if the game includes a pointing device—what will happen when an object in the game world is pointed to and selected.

4. If the interface includes multi-step actions (such as selecting units, and then giving them an order), create a flowchart indicating what happens in each step, and whether (and how) the sequence can be interrupted or cancelled.

5. Does the gameplay require a pointing or steering device? Should these be analog, or will a D-pad suffice? What do they actually do in the context of the game?

6. Does the function of one or more buttons on the controller change within a single gameplay mode? If so, are there visual cues to let the player know this is taking place?

7. If the player has an avatar (whether a person, creature, or vehicle), how do the movements and other behaviors of the avatar map to the machine's input devices?

8. Does the game's genre, if it has one, help to determine the user interface? What standards already exist that the player may be expecting the game to follow? Do you intend to break these expectations, and if so, how will you inform the player of that?

9. Does the game include menus? What is the menu structure? Is it broad and shallow (quick to use, but hard to learn), or narrow and deep (easy to learn, but slow to use)?

10. Does the game include text on the screen? If so, does it need provisions for localization?

11. What icons are used in the game? Are they visually distinct from one another and quickly identifiable? Are they culturally universal?

12. Does the player need to know numeric values (score, speed, health)? Can these be presented through non-numeric means (power bars, dials, brightness regions), or should they be shown as digits? If they are shown as digits, how can they be presented in such a way that they don't harm suspension of disbelief?

13. Will it be possible for the player to control the game's perspective (camera position)? Will it be necessary for the player to do so in order to play the game? What controls will be available? Will they be available at all times, or from a separate menu or other mechanism?

14. What is the aesthetic style of the game? How do the interface elements blend in and support that style?

15. How will audio be used to support the player's interaction with the game? What audio cues will accompany player actions? Will the game include audio advice or dialog?

16. How does music support the user interface and the game generally? Does it create an emotional tone or set a pace? Can it adapt to changing circumstances?

Putting It Together

In this chapter, we've covered a lot of diverse ground. By focusing on the functionality of the user interface, we've touched on a lot of other areas of game design.

This is not surprising in itself. The interface is the most important aspect of a computer game—it's the bottleneck between the player and the game world. It's the most important area of the game to get right. If anything goes wrong here, it doesn't matter what goodies you have hidden behind the interface. Your players won't even bother to go that far.

Chapter 7

Gameplay

Any game designer should agree that gameplay is the core of the game. Given an ideal world, designers would probably claim that gameplay should be put above all other considerations. And in a lot of cases, were it not for external pressures, these same game designers would attempt to treat the gameplay with the level of importance that it deserves. There's just one problem with this: There is no universally accepted definition of gameplay. Gameplay is an important, if nebulous, concept. Many times during discussions of games, we have heard comments such as, "This has great gameplay," followed by a detailed description of the particular aspect of the game. However, if instead you were to ask the question, "What is gameplay?", most answers would attempt to explain by example. Indeed, explanation by example can be helpful, but it requires that you infer a definition of gameplay by induction. Describing gameplay without using self-reference is similar to trying to explain the concept of red without reference to color. It is difficult to conceive, but not impossible.

There is a reason for this difficulty: The concept of gameplay is extremely difficult to define. Each designer has his or her own personal definition of gameplay, formed from exposure to many examples over the course of a career.

Gameplay is so difficult to define because there is no single entity that we can point to and say, "There! That's the gameplay." Gameplay is the result of a large number of contributing elements. The presence, or lack thereof, of gameplay can be deduced by examining a particular game for *indications* and *contraindications* of these elements. (These terms are borrowed from medical terminology: An indication is a positive sign that implies the existence of gameplay, and a contraindication is a negative sign that implies that gameplay does not exist.)

Use of Language

In other fields, such as engineering, architecture, and mathematics, the spread of ideas is facilitated by the use of a common language. Each engineer or mathematician knows how to express ideas—even brand-new ideas—in the given language of the craft.

The vocabulary and mechanism for expressing ideas is already there, formalized and developed over many years of practical use and theoretical study. As game designers, we do not have that luxury. Although there has been talk of defining a universal frame of reference for game designers, no such lexicon has been attempted in earnest. Any attempts that have so far been made have not gained major acceptance, and there is no real coordinated effort or cooperation between alternate factions (to the best of our knowledge).

This chapter attempts to define gameplay without reference to itself or reliance on examples of itself for definition. That doesn't mean that we won't give examples, but those examples will not serve as definitions. Instead, they will be used in their traditional role to illustrate the definitions previously laid out. This will give us the beginnings of our lexicon of game design. This might or might not become a standard, but it is at least a starting point that we can use to explain our ideas in this book.

Defining Gameplay

Although we briefly discussed (and loosely defined) gameplay in Chapter 2, "Game Concepts," we did so in terms of the player experience. To continue, we examine gameplay independent of the player experience. We examine the core concepts of gameplay, which are invariant with the player. To do this, we need to state a player-independent definition of gameplay. Sid Meier once defined gameplay as "a series of interesting choices." This is an excellent starting point and forms the basis of our definition of gameplay. We take this statement one step further with our formal definition of gameplay:

One or more causally linked series of challenges in a simulated environment.

On the surface, this does not seem that far removed from Sid Meier's original definition (although it's not quite as good of a sound bite). However, our statement is more precise and rigorous. To be fair, it's unlikely that Mr. Meier expected his original definition to be used for anything more than the off-the-cuff comment it was probably intended to be—a statement designed to challenge and spur further thinking on the subject. If this was the case, it certainly had its intended effect and served as an excellent starting point for our definition.

In the original statement, the use of the word *series* implies a number of sequential events. Although these events follow one another chronologically, there is no implication that they can be linked. For example, lightning strikes tend to come in a rapid succession of bolts, but there is no evidence to suggest that the strike order is anything other than chance. Hence, we need to define specifically that our gameplay events are linked by causality. Note that we do not say anything about whether the multiple series are required to be interlinked. In most cases, they are—for example, the multiple plot threads in an adventure game—but this is not a specific requirement.

The second half of the original definition uses the words "interesting choices." Although this is true, we feel that this is too broad of a definition. Choosing to visit the cinema, deciding what movie to watch, and thinking about whether to have caramel popcorn or salted popcorn is an example of a series of interesting choices, but it isn't an example of gameplay. So we replace this with "challenges in a simulated environment." The reason for the further restriction to a simulated environment should be self-evident: We stop playing when we quit the game.

Why are we using *challenges* in place of *choices*? Again, we feel that the word *choices* is too broad to be particularly useful. For example, we can make a decision to attempt to shoot the attacking robot, to avoid it, or to quit the game and play something else. All three of these are available choices, but only the first two are gameplay decisions. Consequently, we have chosen to use the word *challenges* because it more accurately describes the type of event that the player is subjected to.

Another example of a choice that is not directly a part of the gameplay is the prevalence of user-defined "skins" in games such as the *Quake* series and *Half-Life*. The player can choose any appearance, but it is purely a cosmetic choice and normally has little effect on gameplay (except when unscrupulous players use this to their advantage, either by deliberately choosing a skin that camouflages them too well—for example, in the extreme case, a moving, shooting crate—or by forcing all the opposing players to take on skins that make them more visible, such as pure white).

Odysseus faced many challenges on his 20-year voyage to return home to his wife, Penelope, in Homer's *Odyssey*. Gordon Freeman (and, by proxy, the player) faces many challenges on his quest to escape from the Black Mesa Research Laboratory in Valve's *Half-Life*. *Tetris* players face challenges in their attempts to attain a higher score. Even Pac-Man faces challenges in his attempts to eat all the pellets in the maze while avoiding the evil ghosts bent on his destruction.

The use of *challenges* is not perfect, but it'll do. An alternative to the use of the word *challenges* that we discussed in the past was *ordeals*, but this was found to be arguably too restrictive. Ideally, we'd like to use a word that indicates a concept somewhere between the two.

Pure Challenges

Pure challenges are the archetypal form of gameplay challenges. They are not often found in the wild in this form, but they form the basis for most, if not all, actual gameplay challenges. We first discuss the possible forms that pure challenges can take, and then we discuss how these can be applied to real gameplay situations.

Challenges come in many shapes and forms. Even within a genre, a good game presents a range of challenge types. The narrower the genre definition is, the narrower the range is, but this is usually not a problem. Game players who buy within genres tend to know what to expect. In fact, unless it is particularly well done and appropriate, they generally reject new forms of challenge as inappropriate to the genre in question.

An example is the inclusion of a fast-action, reflex-based arcade sequence in a traditional adventure game such as *Escape from Monkey Island* (see Figure 7.1). Handled properly, this can enhance the gameplay, giving a welcome break from the usual action. Handled badly, it can break the player's suspension of disbelief and effectively ruin the game.

Figure 7.1 *Escape from Monkey Island.*

A more concrete example of this phenomenon is found in Valve's *Half-Life* (see Figure 7.2), an excellent game that has rightly won many awards for its original and innovative gameplay and story line. (However, I also need to point out that the story line is excellent only when compared to other games within the same genre; it wouldn't be a best-selling novel or a blockbuster movie.) For the most part, playing *Half-Life* is a joy. In the first two thirds of the game, the sense of immersion and of actually being there as Gordon Freeman is unparalleled. You can imagine yourself squeezing through the confining corridors of the Black Mesa Research Laboratory out in the middle of the desert, avoiding the unwanted attentions of both vicious aliens out for blood and hostile government troops sent in to clean up the transdimensional mess. Then, as the story reaches the first climax point, you are catapulted into the alien dimension to take the battle into their territory.

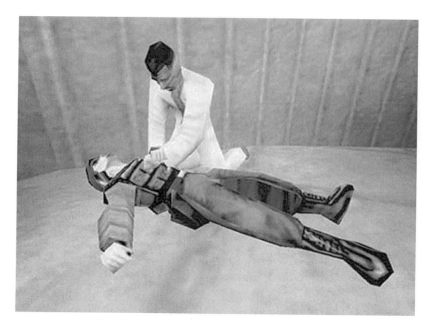

Figure 7.2 *Half-Life.*

In the alien dimension, things take a turn for the worse—at least, in terms of gameplay. Although it's not a game breaker by any means, the story line experiences a significant lull here. Initially, Gordon is required to jump from platform to platform in a sub-Mario platform game style. This abrupt change in the gameplay is a showstopper as far as the suspension of disbelief, which the designers had worked so hard to cultivate, is concerned. And as if that didn't deal enough of a blow, the subsequent levels are practically straight out of the original *Quake*, culminating in a showdown with the big, bad, end-of-game boss. Now, we don't mean to be unduly harsh on an otherwise excellent game, but the last third of the game is a real letdown in gameplay terms. All of the innovative and exciting features of the Black Mesa levels were replaced with a standard first-person jump'n'shooter. Even with the benefit of the intriguing and imaginative end sequence, the damage is done by this point: The suspension of disbelief is shattered and the player is left feeling somehow cheated. The inclusion of the platform-based level followed by the standard first-person fare is a classic nonsequitur that affects the enjoyment of the game.

Many types of challenges can be included in a game. In the majority of cases, these challenges are purely mental. In a few games, there is some degree of physical challenge, but this is usually understated—a simple test of reflexes or hand-eye coordination. In any case, they are localized to the hands and wrists.

> **NOTE**
>
> A high-profile exception is the recent spate of Japanese dancing games, such as *Dance Dance Revolution* (see Figure 7.3), which provide the player with a pressure-sensitive mat. The mat allows the player to dance in time to the music and dancers onscreen—an interesting gameplay innovation, but one that is hardly likely to amount to anything other than an amusing diversion.

Figure 7.3   *Dance Dance Revolution.*

A game can contain many challenges of each different type. To save us the insanity of trying to analyze the challenge content of a whole slew of games and concluding that they all have all the challenge types, it will serve our purpose to define two classes of challenge: *implicit* and *explicit*.

An *explicit* challenge is an intentional challenge specifically designed by the game designer. An example is the exact timing required to dodge the swinging pendulums in *Quake III Arena* (see Figure 7.4). This kind of challenge tends to be more immediate and intense than an implicit challenge.

Figure 7.4   *Quake III Arena.*

An *implicit* challenge is one that is not specifically designed in; in other words, it is an emergent feature of the game design. An example of an implicit challenge is figuring out the most efficient way to distribute items among your group in a traditional computer role-playing game (CRPG) such as Black Isle's *Baldur's Gate*. Implicit challenges tend to be more drawn out and less focused than explicit challenges.

Having stated that the challenges present in games are mostly mental, let us take a closer look at the many forms these challenges can take. It's important to note that the following sections describe pure archetypal challenges; that is, they can be categorized as a simple challenge type, such as logic-based or reaction time-based. Not all challenges can be categorized so easily: The "challenge space" is not populated by a set of discrete points representing the archetypal pure challenge types, but instead is a smoothly varying continuum. Challenges can be hybridized (for example, a logic-based puzzle requiring a fast reaction time) and rarely—if at all—appear in their pure form.

Logic and Inference Challenges

Logic and inference challenges test the ability of the player to assimilate information and use that information to decide upon the best course of action.

Logic is primarily used when the player is presented with perfect information, as in chess. In classical game theory, there are two broad classes of game: those of *perfect information*, with the complete state of play known to each player at all times, and those of *imperfect information*, with each player knowing only a fraction of the state of play (and not necessarily the same fraction for each player). For example, chess is a game of perfect information because the player is at all times aware of the state of the board and the position of all the pieces—both his own and his opponent's. Theoretically, given enough time and processing power, it is possible to analyze the game of chess to produce a perfect strategy. A perfect strategy is one that yields the maximum benefit to the player at all times. In the case of chess, this means that a user of that strategy would never lose. Of course, with the number of possible permutations of the chessboard and the move sequences, it would be beyond any human to blindly commit that strategy to memory, just as it is currently beyond any computer to calculate it.

When played in its puzzle mode, *Chu Chu Rocket* (see Figure 7.5), by Sega, is an example of a game of perfect information. The player is given a clearly defined win condition, a known playing field, and a known set of pieces to lay on that playing field. Hence, the player has perfect information. Knowing the rules governing the cat and mouse movement allows the player to predict (a *pattern-recognition* challenge) the paths of the cat and the mice and to place the playing pieces accordingly. Then the game is started and the results can be seen. If the win condition is not met, the player can replay the level.

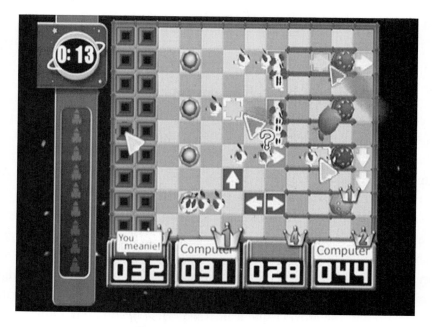

Figure 7.5 *Chu Chu Rocket.*

In games of imperfect information, logic is not sufficient. Logic cannot fully operate given an incomplete knowledge of the state of play. In these cases, the gaps in that knowledge must be filled using *inference*. In this context, inference is the ability to surmise, or guess, the incomplete knowledge based on extrapolation of the existing facts.

Microsoft Hearts (see Figure 7.6) is an example of a game of imperfect information. Initially, you do not know the contents of the hands of the other players, but a skilled player can work them out to a reasonable degree of certainty by using the information revealed by which cards are passed and what tricks are laid during the course of the game.

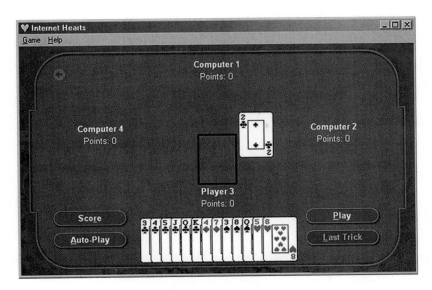

Figure 7.6   *Microsoft Hearts.*

Bridge is another classic example of a game of imperfect information. A player does not know the contents of his partner's or his opponents' hands. He must use his knowledge of the game to calculate the best estimate during the course of the game.

The classic real-time strategy game staple, the "fog of war" shown in Figure 7.7, is a way of graphically representing imperfect information of a battlefield. The player can see only enemy units that are within the line of sight of any of his units. When an enemy unit goes into the fog of war (usually represented by a grayed-out area as the terrain was last seen, or a black area where the terrain has never been seen), the player can estimate where his enemies are and, based on his knowledge of the battle-field, attempt to draw conclusions about their intentions and plan his counterattack against them.

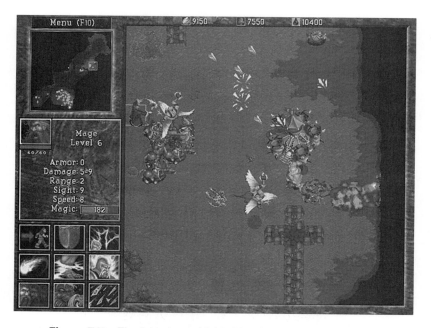

Figure 7.7 The fog of war (right side of screen) in *Warcraft II*.

Games of imperfect knowledge are much more common than games of perfect knowledge. This is because one of the key elements of gameplay is challenging the player to hypothesize about the game worlds, forming her own internal picture. The degree to which this picture matches the real thing depends very much on the logic and inference skills of the player. It is much harder to design a good game without the element of mystery. Only a few designers can achieve this with any degree of success. Mystery can be viewed as the easy way out. There is no better way to hook a player than to get her involved in a compelling mystery story. Human curiosity is a very strong attractor, and any game that successfully taps into this provides a strong gameplay element. *Half-Life* did this extremely well, putting the player in the role of a new scientist trying to escape after a hideous cross-dimensional experimental error at his first day of work.

One problem with games of perfect information is that, because of the difficulty of designing an engaging playing experience without hiding anything from the player, they tend to be very simple. Usually, they are implemented as computer board games or simple arcade games. *Archon* (see Figure 7.8) is an excellent example of a computerized board game that was popular in the 1980s.

Figure 7.8 *Archon.*

In *Archon* (and its sequels), the whole board was visible on the screen, and both play-ers had full knowledge of the game state. In many ways, *Archon* was a computer-age successor to chess, combining elements of board-game strategy and arcade action in a single game.

Lateral-Thinking Challenges

In some ways, *lateral-thinking challenges* are an extension of inference challenges. Certainly, they draw on the same core skills, but taken to the extreme. A lateral-thinking challenge tasks the player to draw on her previous experience and knowledge and combine them in a new and unexpected way.

This knowledge can be *intrinsic* or *extrinsic*. Intrinsic means that the knowledge was gained from within the game world—for example, figuring out a new combination of runes to cast a previously unknown spell, as was the case with the "flux cage" in FTL's *Dungeon Master* (see Figure 7.9). If the player figured out the meaning of the runes, it was possible to figure out roughly what purpose the unknown spell had, and the player needed to do that to win the game. No knowledge gained outside the game would have helped to figure out that particular problem (unless the player looked up the answer in a game magazine or on the Internet, but that's cheating).

Figure 7.9 *Dungeon Master.*

The converse of intrinsic knowledge is extrinsic knowledge. This means knowledge that was gained outside the game world, perhaps in real life. For example, a player could use his knowledge that wood floats to retrieve a key attached to a wooden block just beyond his reach at the bottom of a narrow container by filling the container with water. Or, for an example from a published role-playing game written many years ago by Dave Morris (co-author of *Game Architecture and Design* by New Riders Publishing, 2004), the player could use her knowledge that repeated rapid heating and cooling of a metal object causes it to become brittle. This was the required technique to break through a metal door, otherwise impervious to both weapons and magic. Of course, the player wasn't dropped into this situation unprepared. There were clues to guide the player toward this solution.

Half-Life made great use of extrinsic knowledge-based lateral-thinking problems. In one particularly memorable sequence, the player had to figure out that the giant tentacled monster was sensitive to sound and then could use that as a detection mechanism, necessitating extreme stealth or noisy diversionary tactics in its presence. Not only that, but the player also had to make the mental connection between the oxygen and fuel pipes running throughout the level and the ominous rocket poised directly over the seemingly invincible tentacle. There are many other such puzzles in *Half-Life*, but these are particularly notable (and ingenious) examples.

Memory Challenges

Memory challenges tax the player's memory of recent (and sometimes not so recent) game events. They are also purely intrinsic. That is to say, they rely specifically on the player's memory of events that have happened in the context of the game and do not rely on, for example, the player's memory of what he had for dinner a week ago.

Probably the best-known and most obvious example of a game based around a memory challenge is Milton Bradley's *Simon* (see Figure 7.10), a simplified electronic version of the classic children's game Simon Says. This game was very popular back in the 1980s. It had four buttons, colored red, yellow, green, and blue. When the player started a game, the computer flashed the buttons in a random sequence, although usually the game started with a single flash. After each sequence, the player had to repeat the sequence. If successful, the computer repeated the sequence again, adding one flash each time. The game was lost if the player made a mistake remembering the sequence. Many games—in particular, adventure games, role-playing games, and first-person shooters—make use of this particular memory-based challenge.

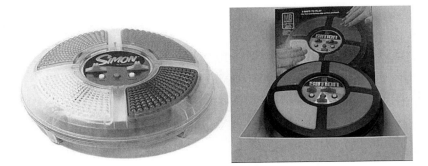

Figure 7.10   *Simon.*

Nowadays, memory-based challenges are commonly seen in children's software, and even then they are usually hybridized with other types of challenge.

In fact, at the most basic level, it could be said that memory challenges are present in virtually every game; for example, remembering the layout of the complex tunnels onboard the Borg cube in Raven's *Voyager: Elite Force* is an example of an implicit memory challenge.

Intelligence-Based Challenges

Intelligence-based challenges rely purely on the intelligence quotient of the player. This is extremely difficult to quantify and define, and, as far as we can tell, intelligence-based challenges do not exist "in the wild" in their pure form—at least, not in games.

In fact, the only place where this form of challenge exists in pure form is in official intelligence quotient (IQ) tests, such as those administered by Mensa, the organization for extremely intelligent people.

An example of an intelligence-based challenge, similar to those used by Mensa, is, given a sequence of similar shapes, to predict the next shape in the sequence from a choice of answers.

Intelligence-based challenges are included here as an archetype because they often form part of other challenges. Usually a more intelligent player will do better when playing a game using the more cerebral challenges.

Knowledge-Based Challenges

Knowledge-based challenges rely on the knowledge of the player. As we have already touched upon, there are two types of knowledge to consider: intrinsic and extrinsic. Intrinsic challenges rely on knowledge from within the game world. Extrinsic challenges rely on knowledge external to the game world.

In the case of knowledge-based challenges, the ultimate real-world example is *Trivial Pursuit* (see Figure 7.11). This board game, which most people are familiar with, relies on general knowledge to win. A player's progress is determined by his answers to a set of questions in various categories, the vast majority of which are simple and straightforward—provided that the player knows the answer. Of course, in some cases the player can attempt to answer questions that he isn't sure of by listening for the clue in the question—crossing over into the territory of a lateral-thinking challenge. Clearly, this is an example of a game relying on extrinsic knowledge-based challenges to provide the gameplay. *Trivial Pursuit* has also been released in computer versions for various platforms since its debut in the mid-1980s.

Figure 7.11   *Trivial Pursuit Millennium Edition.*

More recently, *You Don't Know Jack* (see Figure 7.12) tests general (hence, extrinsic) knowledge in a quiz game format. However, this is an example that does not use knowledge-based challenges in their pure form. Instead, the questions are mostly phrased as a humorous lateral thinking problem and are set to a time limit so that players can—in most cases—figure out the answer with some (admittedly rapid) careful thought. In a lot of cases, knowledge-based challenges are inextricably linked with lateral thinking–based challenges. Except in certain rarified environments such as quiz games, knowledge-based challenges rarely appear in their archetypal form.

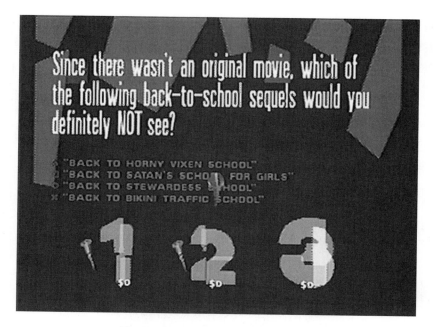

Figure 7.12 *You Don't Know Jack.*

Intrinsic knowledge–based challenges are found in practically all games. However, explicit, intrinsic knowledge–based challenges are more often found in role-playing or adventure games. Here, a good knowledge of the game world and the background story and characters is essential to progress in the game. In real terms, this means that if you were to start a new game of, for example, Warren Spector's *Deus Ex* by loading a saved game provided by someone else, and it started you halfway through the game, you would have a much harder time trying to progress through the game than you would if you had started from the beginning.

Pattern-Recognition Challenges

According to the theorists, the impressive abilities demonstrated by the human brain mainly stem from one basic ability: *pattern recognition*. In essence, our brain is a generalized pattern-recognition machine; our brain implicitly forms archetypes of objects and events and compares new experiences with these archetypes to recognize which category they fall under. For example, there are many different shapes and forms for tables, but somehow we always implicitly recognize a table when we see one, even if we have never seen that particular table.

According to some theories on learning, all types of learning are a form of pattern recognition and classification. When learning to speak, we are required to recognize and classify the sounds we hear as babies. In fact, to deal with everyday life, we are constantly recognizing patterns in events and using these to classify what is happening so that we can act according to past similar experiences. You know not to walk into a road without looking because you recognize the archetypal road, the archetypal event of walking across a road, and the possibility of the archetypal car or truck colliding with you and smearing you along several hundred yards of archetypal highway.

In this particular case, the human brain's ability to recognize patterns is sometimes overeager (for the technically minded, it uses a greedy algorithm) and can recognize patterns where there (arguably) are none. The name for this phenomenon is *pareidolia*, a type of illusion or misperception involving a vague or obscure stimulus being perceived as something clear and distinct. Human history is littered with examples of this: the constellations of stars in the night sky, the man in the moon, the whole field of astrology, and the articles that appear regularly in the *National Enquirer* proudly displaying the face of Jesus in a sesame seed bun. In fact, the Rorschach test, first published by Herman Rorschach in 1921, relies on the brain's overactive capacity for pattern recognition to attempt psychometric evaluation of the patient.

You can see this effect for yourself: Stare up at the clouds and see what they resemble (as an imaginative game designer, you should have no problem with this). For a slightly less subjective test, stare at the static on a television set for a minute or two, and you should begin to see imaginary structures pinwheeling about the screen. This is the brain attempting to find patterns where there are none.

A Google search on "nature versus nurture" and "pareidolia" will turn up lots of useful links on these subjects.

Figure 7.13 is a collection of common optical illusions. These illusions work primarily because of the way the brain's pattern recognition ability works. The top-left image is merely a set of straight lines with right angles, but we perceive it as an octagon with a square in the center. The top-right image could be taken from a Pac-Man conference, but we also see a phantom white triangle. The bottom-left image conjures up ghostly gray spots at the intersections. The bottom-right image appears to spin in different directions as you focus on the black dot in the center and move the page toward you.

Stare at the black dot and move
your face toward the page.

Figure 7.13 Pattern recognition: There is no spoon!

In some fairly unique games, the brain's ability to recognize patterns can be tuned into, to enhance the ability of the player. An example of this is *Tetris*. *Tetris* can be played consciously, examining each block as it falls and actively deciding where to stack the block for best effect. However, the best players don't seem to play like this, especially at the later levels, where blocks fall too fast to be able to make any conscious decision where to put them. Instead, these players seem to tune into the game at an almost subconscious level and enter what we call the "*Tetris* trance," a Zen-like state in which the players seem to lose all track of time and don't concentrate on the specifics of the game board. Instead the players defocus and appear to process the entire playing area as a whole, without considering the individual elements. In fact, if these players were in the *Star Wars* universe, the Force would be strong in them.

In reality, however, it appears that these players are tapping into their brain's subconscious pattern-recognition ability to improve their game. *Tetris* is not the only game in which this occurs. Pretty much any game that uses pattern-recognition challenges as the primary gameplay mechanism can be played in such a way, although we certainly believe that it helps if those games have a clear and simple presentation. Maybe that is because the area of the brain dealing with pattern recognition is quite primal and, to process information quickly at that level, needs the information to be presented clearly so that minimal preprocessing is required. Of course, this is pure speculation on our part, but it is no coincidence that many of the older games that are now considered classics are those that can be played in this fashion. The one thing that all of these games have in common (apart from their reliance on pattern-recognition challenges) is their simple presentation. Classic games such as *Robotron*, *Defender*, and *Sinistar* all exhibit this feature.

So, if the brain's primary cognitive function is to recognize patterns, what does this mean in terms of gameplay? Pattern-recognition challenges can make or break a game, depending on how they are used. If in an entirely deterministic game one or more of the players can determine the pattern of play, this allows them to make 100% accurate predictions about game world events before they actually occur. Although they should be commended on their acumen, this does not make the game fun for the other players. This could rapidly degenerate to the situation in which it is almost as if the predicting player is a god of the game world and the other players are mere pawns, with no free will of their own.

> **NOTE**
>
> Note that the opposing players can be either humans with limited play options or a computer opponent that has been programmed to respond in certain ways to specific inputs. We heard a story once about a game with an adaptive computer opponent; the opponent's skill level depended on the perceived level of skill of the player. Soon players discovered that the easiest way to progress past difficult levels in the game was to deliberately do badly in the levels immediately preceding the difficult level, whereupon the computer immediately eased up on the player, making the difficult level slightly easier. Although this is an ingenious and valid approach, it is probably not what the designer intended, even from emergent behavior. No battle in the field has ever been won by the enemy commander sympathizing with his opponents' lack of ability and "going easy on them." Note that in the context of gameplay, adaptive difficulty is a useful tool. Just don't make it so recognizable to the player that she can exploit it to progress in the game. This is one pattern that you do not want the player to recognize.

Plenty of basic pattern-recognition games exist. A simple example that combines pattern-recognition challenges with reflex/reaction time-based challenges is the card game Snap. In this game, the players take turns laying a card from their hands face up on the discard pile, making sure that it is unseen by *any* player until the last possible moment. When the card is turned face up, the players check to see if it matches the card underneath (and by *match*, we mean it is of the same face value). That's the pattern-recognition challenge. If there is a match, the first player to shout "Snap!" wins all the cards in the discard pile. That's the reflex/reaction time challenge. If any players run out of cards, they are out of the game. The winner is the last player remaining with any cards in his hand.

In the early days of computer games, patterns were a lot more prevalent (or, at least, more obvious) in games than they are today. There could be any number of reasons for this. Maybe patterns were the most efficient way to code for an interesting game, given the limited processing power of the target platform. Another option is that the patterns are always there in games, but in the older games they stood out in stark relief against the simplicity of the gameplay. Games such as *Space Invaders* and *Galaxians* made heavy use of patterns. In many cases, playing effectively was simply a matter of memorizing the patterns and reacting accordingly. This play method persisted through most of the shoot 'em-ups that were produced until recently. However, even *Iridion 3D* released on the Game Boy Advance is a shoot 'em-up that defines attack wave patterns that can be learned and dealt with accordingly. This is a very transparent use of patterns and temporal pattern recognition, and it would be considered a bit simplistic and naive for unmodified use in a game design today. However, it is certainly a useful starting point for the inclusion of pattern-recognition challenges in your own game designs.

Slightly more advanced use of pattern recognition is evident in many games that involved exploration. For example, in *Doom*, secret doorways could be found by searching for an area of wall that looked slightly different from the norm. Also, games such as the previously mentioned *Dungeon Master* relied on pattern-recognition challenges for the player to decipher the complex systems of runes governing spells and spell casting.

Platform games, such as the *Mario* series of games, often rely on pattern-recognition challenges quite heavily. Not only are the levels carefully scripted to be a repeatable (hence, learnable) experience, but the end-of-level bosses also tend to behave according to a certain pattern. Thus, in *Super Mario Advance*, you can defeat one of the end-of-level baddies by carefully counting how many flaming spit wads she ejects and then attacking in the interim. In this case, the pattern-recognition challenge is used to make the game more manageable. It is difficult enough to manipulate the player avatar on the platforms (an example of coordination, spatial awareness, and reflex/reaction time challenges), but trying to handle unpredictable enemies on top of this would detract from the gameplay. This is an example in which two distinct challenge types work together synergistically to improve the gameplay potential. The whole is more than the sum of the parts.

Moral Challenges

A *moral challenge* is a high-level challenge that can operate at several levels. Without delving too deeply into the field of metaethics, we can define these levels as universal, cultural, tribal, and personal. These levels are ordered from the all-encompassing to the specific. Each successive level affects a smaller moral area than the previous one. Usually, the lower levels have precedence, but that is not always the case.

Let us assume that there are no absolutes in morality. This implies that it is fundamentally incorrect to say that there is a definite right or wrong answer to a moral challenge; so much depends on context, emotional state, and past experience that an answer that might be correct for one individual would be totally wrong for another. An example: It is wrong to steal. But is it wrong to steal food if the only alternative is to starve? The answer to this depends on the individual.

But how does this example apply to games? In many games, the player is asked to make such choices. Raven's *Voyager: Elite Force* presents such a moral challenge early in the game: Should you save your teammate from the Borg and go against the captain's orders, jeopardizing the success of the mission?

We examine examples of the various forms that moral challenges can take in more detail. Before we can do this, however, we need to further define our various levels of moral challenge. Note that this is subjective: Exactly what defines the differences among universal, cultural, and tribal designations depends on context and the personal views of the observer. In the case of game design, it means that our definitions directly depend on the scope of the game. For example, a game set in America (with no mention of the rest of the world) would treat the whole of America as the universe. From here, the divisions of cultural and tribal entities would depend entirely on the game designers. They are under no compulsion to stick to reality—after all, it is their game.

A universal moral challenge is invariant no matter what the context is. By this, we mean that the correct moral outcome is independent of the entity making the choice. It would not matter if you were a human or a Zlerg from the planet Zlumpf—the correct choice would be the same. Universal moral challenges are concerned with the good of the universe as a whole. In the real world, they are most likely only a theoretical construct—a null container or superset for all the lower moral levels. They are extremely difficult to define and, as such, are a fairly rare form of challenge. In the limited context of a computer game, however, the cultural and universal morality levels are usually one and the same. (Often you will get a cultural moral challenge masquerading as a universal challenge; this is usually due to the game designer's inability to look outside her own backyard. This used to be a staple error in old sci-fi movies. Whenever the world was under threat, you'd see only America invaded—it was as if the rest of the world simply didn't exist.)

One of the main difficulties in defining a universal moral challenge is to define the limits. Do you say that the population of the world defines the moral universe, or is there life elsewhere in the universe governed by these morals? These are difficult metaphysical questions to answer, and the fact that games are set in a simulated universe does not make it any easier. Moral challenges are unusual in that they explicitly rely on the players' real-world experiences to provide their gameplay value. Hence, our views on the world directly affect our playing experience. For our purposes, we define the universal challenge as pertaining to all living beings in existence, within the confines of the game's simulated universe. With this definition in mind, we can infer that universal moral challenges are, at best, likely to be overly grandiose and, at worst, clichéd. As an example, imagine that the player is given a choice to go back in time to just before the birth of the universe and prevent it from happening. To simplify the choice, let's assume that the player's avatar is given amnesty from the effects of his choice: He would still exist and be able to live a (paradoxically) normal life, whatever the outcome. Given sufficient reasons for and against this would be a difficult moral choice to make. Should the player destroy all existence before it even comes into being, or should he allow things to happen as normal? (Obviously, you'd need a pretty good set of reasons for and against to make this into a difficult choice, but let's assume that the game designer has done a good job of setting that up for us.)

At a lower level than the universal challenge is the cultural challenge. Here we define a culture as a loosely affiliated collection of individuals all living by roughly the same standards; they do not necessarily have to be affiliated in any way other than their living standards and general lifestyle. For example, the Western world could be loosely viewed as a culture. If we wanted to take it down to a slightly finer grain, we could consider America as a culture. We could go further still and define Native American culture, Southern culture, Californian culture, and others.

Consequently, our definition of a cultural moral challenge is one that deals with the good of that culture as a whole. An example of dealing with the consequences of a moral challenge at the cultural level was provided in the 1988 film *Alien Nation*, directed by Graham Baker. In the opening scenes of this film, America (specifically, Los Angeles) is faced by a request for asylum from an escaped race of aliens genetically bred for slavery. The moral choice is whether to welcome the aliens into society, risking the dilution or destruction of human culture, or to turn the aliens away.

Fortunately for us, the smaller the scale of the moral choice is, the easier it is to define and give examples. Tribal moral choices are much smaller in scope. Note that the use of the word *tribal* is not intended to imply tribes in the full sense of the word; we use it here to mean any group of closely affiliated individuals. In a sense, a family unit can be considered a tribe, as can a role-playing adventure group and an American football team. Tribal moral choices are those that affect the well-being of the tribe. An example is the classic clichéd group decision in which all the group members have to decide which of them is going to have to perform some difficult—and, quite often, fatal—task to save the others. In fictional works, drawing lots usually solves this particular situation: a nonideal solution that avoids the difficult moral choice by abdicating the decision to the whims of chance.

Easiest of all to define, and perhaps the most familiar, is the personal moral choice. This is a moral choice made by an individual that has a direct outcome on that individual's own well-being and state of mind. There are no repercussions other than at the personal level for the player making the choice.

For example, in Will Wright's *The Sims*, the characters can earn money in a number of ways. A character can get a job and earn money the hard way, or he can become a professional widow: marry other characters and then kill them for the inheritance. The onus of this moral choice is really on the individual player. There are no lasting repercussions in the game world for murdering your husband or wife, and so (apart from the individual morals of the player) these are both equally valid methods of making money. This also depends on the player's level of involvement. It could be rendered more effective if there were unavoidable consequences within the game world. (The ghost of the dead Sim does not count; it can be removed by selling the tombstone.)

Moral dilemmas do not have to reside fully within one level. In fact, dynamically altering the priorities of these levels to force the player to decide between solving a moral dilemma within each fork in a different level can often lead to interesting and challenging gameplay. For example, we could posit a moral choice around the validity of the statement "The needs of the many outweigh the needs of the few."

So now we need some examples of real games that use moral dilemmas—but there is a problem. Until now, games have not sufficiently explored this area. Dealing with moral dilemmas has not traditionally been an area in which games excel. Morality in games has barely been considered at any level above simple "black and white" (no pun intended) playground morality. One reason for this is the difficulty of involving the player in difficult emotional situations; the willing suspension of disbelief required for the player to actively participate and believe in difficult emotional decisions is greater than that required for simpler choices. Hence, games that have employed moral decisions as a gameplay factor have relied on the simple "this is good, that is bad" approach. More recently, a game that has attempted (to some success) to deal with moral decisions in a more adult fashion is Lionhead's *Black and White*. Despite the title, the game attempts to deal with a moral spectrum. The player takes on the role of a god tending to the needs of her people. Aiding in the quest is a familiar, taking the form of a giant creature that can be trained to follow orders. The player is free to become any kind of god that she wants: from sickeningly good to terribly evil and anywhere in between. The nature of the god is reflected in the creature and the appearance of the land. How well this works in practice is open to discussion. So far, players have tended to gravitate directly toward total evil or total goodness. Although it cannot be strictly classed as a weakness or flaw, the cartoonlike nature of the game does undermine the seriousness of the moral decisions involved. This could be a good thing, of course— after all, you don't necessarily want your player to be racked by guilt for days after performing a questionable act. That would be going too far (if, indeed, it was possible).

Spatial-Awareness Challenges

Spatial-awareness challenges are usually implicit. Only a handful of games have relied on explicit spatial-awareness challenges, and, in most cases, they were 2D games, such as *Tron* (the light-cycles game) and *Snakes*. A 3D version on the Sinclair Spectrum (Sinclair Timex in the United States) was entitled *Knot in 3D* (shown in Figure 7.14) and was a 3D extension of the classic *Tron*-based game. A recent update of *Tron* is shown in Figure 7.15. Spatial-awareness challenges are a specialized hybrid of a memory challenge and an inference challenge.

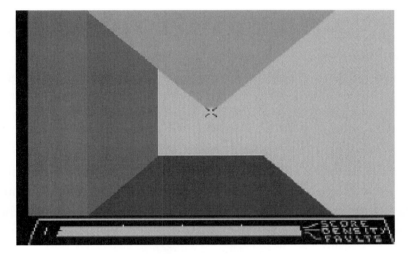

Figure 7.14   *Knot in 3D.*

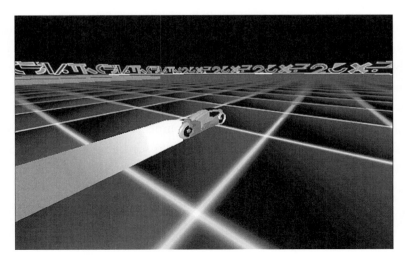

Figure 7.15   *glTron.*

Games that rely on spatial awareness are usually 3D games. The challenge of representing a 3D world on a 2D surface, and the challenge to the player to make sense of that representation form the bulk of the spatial awareness problem. In many cases, the player receives aid in the form of a computer-generated map, but in other cases, such as *Quake III*, the player is left to his own devices to find his way around the world.

The types of games that usually rely heavily on spatial-awareness challenges are flight simulators, space-flying games, and 3D combat games (particularly *Quake III* and *Unreal Tournament*). To a lesser extent, 2D games that involve large playing areas, such as *Age of Kings*, also use spatial-awareness challenges.

Coordination Challenges

Pretty much any game uses coordination challenges. Coordination challenges basically test the ability of the player to perform many simultaneous actions. They are almost always found in combination with reflex/reaction time challenges and are usually tightly coupled with them.

In its pure form, a coordination challenge is not dependent on any time constraints, but it isn't often found in the pure form. An example of a game (and there are many) that uses the coordination challenge to good effect (in combination with reflex/reaction time challenges) is *Super Mario*. Here, the player is expected to finely time jumps across wide chasms while avoiding circling enemies, requiring a plethora of accurately timed button presses from the player.

Shooting games of various sorts pose a challenge of accuracy: lining up a shot at a target, when the player or the target or both might be moving. Steering also requires accuracy. Flight simulators that properly model the behavior of aircraft, or racing simulators that accurately model the behavior of racing cars, require a high degree of precision. Airplanes, in particular, usually respond rather slowly to their controls. A player expecting an instant response will tend to overcompensate, pushing farther and farther forward on the joystick when the plane's nose doesn't drop right away, and then yanking it back in panic when it finally drops much farther than he intended in the first place.

Some games are forgiving about precision, allowing the player to be sloppy; others demand a delicate touch. Back before racing cars had airfoils to help hold them on the pavement, they flipped over very easily and required a much higher degree of skill from their drivers to keep them on the road. Papyrus Design Group accurately modeled this challenge in the game *Grand Prix Legends*.

Timing is the ability to overcome an obstacle by coordinating player moves with something else that is happening onscreen. Many video games present a weakness in an opponent's defenses for a limited period of time that, with practice, a player can learn to anticipate. Ducking under a constantly rotating hazard, for example, involves timing. Running and jumping across a chasm by pressing the Jump button at the last second is also an example of timing. It's related to reaction time, but instead of trying to do something as fast as possible, the player is trying to do something at exactly the right moment.

Many fighting games require complex sequences of joystick moves and button presses that, once mastered, will allow a "special move"—a particularly devastating attack, for example. These take a long time to learn and require very good motor coordination to achieve consistently. This sort of challenge is best suited to a player who can tolerate a high degree of frustration, or to a game that gives ample reward for this kind of persistence. Games that rely heavily on such techniques are difficult to balance. It is difficult to balance games that are based purely on physical dexterity. What one player might find easy, a different player might find impossible.

Reflex/Reaction Time Challenges

Reflex/reaction time challenges test the timing abilities of the player. The simplest example of a reaction time challenge (which we previously mentioned) is the children's card game Snap.

However, reflex/reaction time challenges are usually not used in isolation in games and are often found in combination with coordination challenges. The types of games that most commonly exhibit this type of challenge are platform games, fast shoot 'em-ups, first-person shooters, and pure arcade games such as *Tetris* and *Centipede*.

This type of challenge is a factor of most action games. Only turn-based games, adventures, and role-playing games tend not to rely on reflex/reaction time challenges.

In an action game, the speed at which you operate the controls often maps directly to the speed at which your avatar reacts. This is not always exactly true because your avatar might be displayed by animations that require a certain length of time to execute, but in general, the faster a player can move and the better his reaction time is, the greater advantage he has. Good speed and reaction time are particularly valuable in fighting games.

Physical Challenges

Physical challenges are extremely rare in games. The input methods available for computer games do not lend themselves to physical activity—at least, not without the purchase of specialized hardware.

Games such as *Samba De Amigo* and *Dance Dance Revolution* provide custom controller hardware, such as a special dance pad that enables the player to control the game by dancing on the pad. Others, such as Konami's *Hypersport*, don't use specialized hardware, relying on a standard joystick and, consequently, focusing the physical challenge to the hand and lower arm of the player.

Physical challenges are not often found in their pure form, and because of the expense and difficulty of including them in games, they are not often found at all.

Applied Challenges

You will recall from Chapter 2 that gameplay consists of the challenges the player faces, plus the actions she can take to overcome them. As we said previously, designing the gameplay is one of your most important design tasks. To some extent, the nature of the challenge suggests the nature of the player's response. The best games, however, allow the player to think creatively and use unconventional actions to meet the challenges.

At the concept stage, you don't have to define precisely what challenges the player will face, but it's good to have an idea of what *kinds* of challenges you want in the game. *Applied challenges* are the application and use of the pure challenge forms we have discussed thus far. An applied challenge is a combination of one or more pure challenge forms applied to a given gameplay situation or style.

Races

A *race* is an attempt to accomplish something before someone else does. It doesn't have to be a physical race through space; it can also be a race to construct something, to accumulate something, or to do practically anything else. Normally we think of races as peaceful, involving competition without conflict, but, of course, they can be combined with conflict as well. Because races put time pressure on the player, they discourage careful strategic thought and instead encourage direct, brute-force solutions. If the player has only 15 seconds to get through a host of enemies and disarm a bomb, he's not going to pick them off one by one with sniping shots; he's going to mow them down and charge through the gap, even if it means taking a lot of damage.

Puzzles

Far too many kinds of puzzles exist to list here, but a *puzzle* is primarily a mental challenge. Often a puzzle is presented as a sort of lock that, when solved, opens another part of the game. The player is presented with a series of objects—often objects that are related in ways that are not directly obvious—and he must manipulate them into a certain configuration to solve the puzzle. To solve the puzzle, it's necessary to understand the relationship among the objects, usually by trial and error and close observation.

Players normally get all the time they need to solve puzzles. Because different people have differing amounts of brainpower, requiring that a puzzle be solved within a time limit might make the game impossible for some players.

A few games offer puzzles whose correct solution is not made clear at the outset. The player not only has to understand how the puzzle works, but also has to guess at the solution she is trying to achieve. We consider this a case of bad game design: It forces the player to solve the puzzle by trial and error alone because there's no way to tell when she's on the right track. *Infidel* was one such game. In the final puzzle at the end of the game, to open a stone sarcophagus, the player had to find 1 of 24 possible combinations of objects. There were no hints about which combination was correct; the player simply had to try them all.

Exploration

Exploration is a key element of many games and is often its own reward. Players enjoy moving into new areas and seeing new things, but exploration cannot be free of challenge or it will just become "sightseeing." Sightseers can exhaust the entertainment of your game in such a short time that they won't perceive the value in the game; it will fail to entertain them for long. To prevent this, we design obstacles that make the players work for their freedom to explore.

The simplest sort of obstacle to exploration is the locked door. We don't literally mean a door with a lock in it, but any device that prevents the player from going on until he has done something to unlock it. You can require the player to do an infinite number of things: find a key elsewhere and bring it to the door; find and manipulate a hidden control (usually unmarked) that opens the door; solve a puzzle that is built into the door; discover a magic word; defeat the doorkeeper in a test of skill, either physical or mental; and so on. The trick is to make the challenge interesting and fresh.

Another common obstacle is the trap. A *trap* is a device that somehow harms the player's avatar when triggered—possibly killing her or causing damage—and, in any case, discouraging her from coming that way or using that move again. A trap is like a locked door with higher stakes: It poses an actual threat to the player. Traps can take a variety of forms:

➤ Some fire off once and then are harmless.

➤ Others fire but require a certain recycle time before they can fire again.

➤ Still others respond to particular conditions but not to others, like a metal detector at an airport.

A player might simply withstand some traps if they don't do too much damage; other traps can be disarmed or circumvented in some way. If a player has no way of detecting a trap and can find it only by falling into it, it's really just the designer's way of slowing the player down. It's not much fun for the player. For players, the real fun comes in outwitting traps: finding and disabling them without getting caught in them. This gives players a pleasurable feeling of having outfoxed you, the designer, even as you were trying to outfox them.

Yet another example is the maze. A *maze* is an area where every place looks alike, or mostly alike, and the player has to discover how the places are related to get out, usually by wandering around. Good mazes are implemented as a sort of puzzle, in which the player can deduce the organization of the maze from clues found in the rooms. Poor mazes simply put the player in an area and let her find the way out by trial and error.

Illogical spaces are a variant on the maze theme. In old text adventure games, it was not uncommon that going north from area A took you to area B, but going south from area B did not take you back to area A. The relationships among the spaces were illogical. This challenge requires the player to keep a map, because he can't rely on his common sense to learn his way around. In modern games with 3D engines, illogical spaces are more difficult to implement than they were in text adventures. Illogical spaces are now considered an outdated technique, but they still crop up from time to time. If you're going to use them, do so sparingly, and only in places where there's an explanation for it: "Beware! There is a rip in the fabric of space-time!" or some similar excuse—although preferably more original than this one.

Teleporters are the modern equivalent of illogical spaces. A *teleporter* is any mechanism that suddenly transports the player from where she is to someplace else. Teleporters are often hidden, which means that players trying to explore an area get caught in them and moved elsewhere without warning. If there are many hidden teleporters in an area, they can make it very difficult to explore. Teleporters can further complicate matters by not always working the same way, teleporting the player to one place the first time they are used, but to somewhere else the second time, and so on. They can also be one-way or two-way, teleporting players somewhere with no way to get back, or allowing them to teleport back again.

Conflict

Conflict is a central element of a great many games because it seems almost inherent in the notion of winning and losing. To win a game, you have to beat the other players. The question is how you beat them. If you beat them by attacking them directly in some way, the game is about conflict. This doesn't necessarily mean combat or violence; checkers is a completely bloodless game, but it's still about conflict.

The challenges associated with conflict depend on the following:

> ➤ The scale of the action (from individuals to whole armies)

> ➤ The speed at which the conflict takes place (from turn-based, allowing all the time you want, to frenetic activity)

> ➤ The complexity of the victory conditions (from simple survival to complex missions with goals and subgoals)

Strategy is the mental act of planning: taking advantage of your situation and resources, anticipating your opponent's moves, knowing and minimizing your weaknesses. A strategic challenge is one in which the player must look carefully at the game and devise a plan of action. In a strategic game, the player's chance of winning depends greatly on the quality of her plan. Chance (luck) and missing information interfere with strategy. Chess is the classic strategy game because it contains no element of chance and offers complete information to both players. Nine Men's Morris and Tic-Tac-Toe are also pure, if simple, strategy games. Backgammon is a game with some strategy, but it also depends a great deal on luck.

Pure strategy games favor the player with a certain type of talent, and they appeal most to the kinds of people who have that talent. Because computer games are usually aimed at a broader audience, relatively few offer pure strategy games. They tend to include elements of chance and missing information as well.

Tactics involve putting a plan into *execution*, the process of accomplishing the goals that strategy calls for. Tactics are also about responding to unexpected events or conditions, which can include new information or bad luck. Even chess has tactics: The unknown quantity is your opponent, and she might make moves that you did not anticipate. Responding to them requires tactical skill.

It's possible to design a purely tactical game with no strategy. A small-squad combat game in which the soldiers are always moving into unknown territory contains no opportunities for strategy—you can't plan if you don't know where you're going or what you're up against—but many for tactics, such as keeping your soldiers covered, taking advantage of their particular skills, and so on.

The business of supporting troops in the field and bringing fresh troops to the front lines is called logistics. Most war games don't bother with logistical challenges such as transporting food and fuel to where they're needed. These activities are generally considered boring and distracting from the main purpose of the game, which is combat. Real armies have whole teams of people responsible for logistics and could never win without this support; computer games have only the player to handle everything, so it stands to reason that he should be concentrating on more exciting tasks such as attack and defense.

However, modern real-time strategy (RTS) games have introduced one important logistical challenge: weapons production. Unlike board war games, in which the player commonly starts with a fixed number of troops, RTSs now require the player to produce weapons and to research new ones from a limited amount of available raw material. The production facilities themselves must be constructed and then defended. This has changed the entire face of war-gaming, adding a new logistical challenge to what was formerly a purely combat-oriented genre.

In role-playing games, the limited size of the characters' inventories presents another logistical challenge. The player must frequently decide what to carry and what to leave behind. Equipping and balancing a party of heterogeneous characters with all that they need to face a dangerous adventure occupies a significant amount of the player's time. Of course, sometimes this is the fault of a badly designed inventory system, in which an apple takes up the same amount of space as a single coin.

On a smaller scale, personal conflict, as a one-on-one or one-on-many challenge, is a key feature of many action games. The player controls an avatar who battles directly against one or more opponents, often at very high speeds. The challenge of personal combat is immediate, exciting, and visceral.

The fundamental challenge in any game based on conflict is survival. If characters can be removed from the field of play by death or any other means, it is essential to preserve their lives or effective playing time, or you cannot achieve the victory condition. In a few games, survival is itself the victory condition and no other achievements are required, but in most, survival is necessary but not sufficient to win.

Survival is about defending one's self, but many games require that the player defend other things as well, especially things that cannot defend themselves. In chess, this is, of course, the king. This challenge requires that the player know not only the capabilities and vulnerabilities of his units, but also those of the thing he is protecting. He must be prepared to sacrifice valuable units to protect the vital item. *Lemmings* was an excellent game about sacrificing some units to preserve others.

Another important gaming challenge, first used extensively in *Thief: The Dark Project*, is stealth—the ability to move undetected. This is an extremely valuable capacity in almost any kind of conflict, especially if the player is the underdog. War games occasionally pose challenges in which the victory condition cannot be achieved through combat but must be achieved through stealth. *Thief* was designed entirely around this premise. Players had to achieve their missions by stealth as much as possible and had to avoid discovery or combat if they could.

The element of stealth introduces considerable complexity into the design and gameplay of war games. The simplest war games are traditionally games of "perfect information," in which both players know everything about one another. Imagine how difficult chess would be if there were an invisible piece somewhere on the board that could be discovered only by accident.

Economies

An *economy* is a system in which resources move around, either physically from place to place, or conceptually from owner to owner. This doesn't necessarily mean money; any sort of resource that can be created, moved, stored, earned, exchanged, or destroyed can be involved. Most games contain an economy of some sort. Even a first-person shooter has a simple economy: Ammunition is obtained by finding it or taking it from dead opponents, and it is consumed by firing your weapons. Health points are consumed by being hit and are restored by medical kits. The designer can make the game easier or harder by adjusting the amounts of ammunition and medical kits available, and a player who is running short must meet the challenge of obtaining more somehow.

Economic challenges are defined in terms of the flow of resources. Some games, such as *Theme Park*, consist only of economic challenges; others, such as first-person shooters, combine both economic and conflict challenges.

In many games, the challenge is simply to accumulate something: wealth, points, or any-thing else of intrinsic value. The object of the game might be to accumulate more money, plutonium, or widgets than your opponents. This is the basis of *Monopoly*, of course, and many other games. The game challenges the player to understand the mechanisms by which wealth is created and to optimize them to his own advantage. In the case of *Monopoly*, it's helpful to mortgage low-rent properties and use the cash to purchase high-rent ones because high-rent properties are the real source of wealth toward the end of the game. Players who understand this are at an advantage over those who don't.

Requiring your players to achieve balance in an economy gives them a more interesting challenge than simply accumulating points, especially if you give them many different kinds of resources to manage. *The Settlers* is a series of games involving complex inter-actions among resources: Wheat goes to the mill to become flour, which goes to the bakery to become bread. Bread feeds miners who dig coal and iron ore, which goes to the smelter to become iron bars, which then go to the blacksmith to become weapons, and so on. All of these resources have to be produced and transported to establish a balanced economy. Produce too little of a vital item, and the whole economy grinds to a halt; produce too much, and it piles up, taking up space and wasting time and resources that could be better used elsewhere.

A peculiar sort of economic challenge involves looking after a person or creature, or a small number of them, as in *The Sims* and *Creatures*. Unlike a large-scale simulation such as *Caesar*, in which the player must build and manage an entire town, these smaller-scale simulations focus on individuals. The player must meet the needs of each individual and take into account the unique characteristics that differentiate each one from other individuals. The challenge is to make sure their needs are met and perhaps to improve their growth in various ways. The creatures often behave unpredictably, which adds both to the challenge and to the charm.

Conceptual Challenges

Conceptual challenges are those that require the player to understand something new. To the game designer, conceptual challenges are the richest and most interesting to design because they offer the broadest scope for innovation. They can also be difficult to design and even more difficult to program. Conceptual challenges often occur in construction and management simulations, in which the game is simulating processes that the player must come to understand. In *Sim City*, for example, there is a direct relationship between an efficient transportation system and economic prosperity. The player who does not deduce this will have difficulty with the game. *Sim City* challenges the player to comprehend this and many other relationships involved in town planning.

Another sort of conceptual challenge occurs in mystery or detective games, in which the object is not merely to accomplish certain feats, but also to examine the evidence and deduce who committed the crime and how. The game *Eagle Eye Mysteries* is an excellent example of this: Players follow clues, ignore red herrings, and arrive at a theory of the crime, assembling the relevant evidence to demonstrate proof. *Planescape: Torment* also offered significant conceptual challenges and had several different endings, depending on how the player interpreted a complex and bizarre series of events.

Gameplay Worksheet

1. What types of challenges do you want to include in your game? Do you want to challenge the player's physical abilities, his mental abilities, or both?
2. Game genres are defined in part by the nature of the challenges they offer. Have you selected a genre in advance, and if so, what does that imply for the gameplay? Do you intend to include any cross-genre elements, challenges that are not normally found in your chosen genre?
3. Does the game include implicit challenges (those that emerge from the design), as well as explicit challenges (those that you specify)?
4. If the game has a story, how does the story influence the gameplay, and vice versa? Do they operate in tandem, or are they effectively separate pieces?
5. If the player has an avatar, how does the gameplay influence the avatar's appearance and capabilities?
6. Is the game's collection of challenges a related group, or is it a compilation of unrelated elements? If the latter, does that have any effect on the player's suspension of disbelief?
7. Given that not all players enjoy the same kinds of challenges, how does the game's target audience influence the challenges it includes? What challenges will you deliberately exclude?
8. Will the player be required to face more than one challenge at a time? Which ones?

Putting It Together

As we have discussed in this chapter, there is no single aspect of any game that we can point to and identify as the gameplay. That is because gameplay is not a singular entity. It is a combination of many elements, a synergy that emerges from the inclusion of certain factors. If all of those elements are present in the correct proportion and style, we can be fairly sure that the potential for good gameplay is there; consequently, we can presume (but not be certain) that we have a good game. The gameplay emerges from the interaction among these elements, much in the same way as complex automata emerge from the simple rules of *Conway's Game of Life*.

There is a particular paradox known as the *Sorites Paradox* or *Heap Paradox*. It concerns a pile of sand. An observer is asked whether sand is a pile, and the answer is yes. Then a grain of sand is taken away. The question is repeated, and the answer is still in the affirmative. This process continues, and then at some point, the observer will say that it is no longer a pile. The question then posed is to ask why one grain of sand makes a difference between a pile and a nonpile. Can the observer state a specific number of grains of sand that define a pile? It's back to the familiar "argument of the beard": Why is the observer's definition any better than another observer's definition?

The same applies to gameplay, although on a smaller and coarser-grained scale. In a *gedanken experiment*, we can look at a game and take away an element (or part thereof) of gameplay. (For example, we could disable Mario's ability to turn left in *Mario 64*.) We can then pose the question "Does it still have gameplay?" We can continue to remove elements or sub-elements and pose the same question. At some point, the game will be sufficiently crippled for the observer to say that it no longer has gameplay. This point will be different for every observer. Whose opinion is best? That's a question for the philosophers. In short, we cannot define exactly how many gameplay elements are required to make a game. We cannot even state with certainty which are required and which are superfluous. We can only state that, to have gameplay, we need some or all of these elements; to have a pile of sand, we need some or all of these grains.

Much the same way that we can expect to find elements indicating gameplay, we can expect to find opposing elements that indicate the absence of gameplay. By this, we mean that the inclusion of the particular element could be detrimental to the gameplay or, more rarely, that gameplay is not present at all. The game in question might have included all of the elements expected to indicate good gameplay, but it might have also muddied the mix by including extra unwelcome elements that detracted from the positive effects of the good. We have all played games that were almost perfect, apart from one or two annoying flaws: Maybe the difficulty level ramped too quickly, maybe the controls were unwieldy, or maybe the collision detection was slightly suspect. Whatever the cause, it has the overall effect of taking a potentially superb game and knocking it down a peg or two, reducing it to the rank of failed contender. This determines the difference between the excellent and the merely good.

It would seem fairly obvious to the game designer that she is including some suspect elements to the gameplay and, therefore, would make efforts to eliminate them from the design. This has happened. A particular case of note is Blizzard Entertainment's *StarCraft*. This game was continually tweaked right up until the point of release, to ensure that the gameplay and unit/unit balance was as good as possible. Even so, they didn't quite get it right, and so the expansion pack, *Brood War*, made further changes to the unit/unit balance—the most notable being an increase in usefulness of the Terran marine and an overhaul of the air-air and air-ground combat units.

The presence or absence of these elements of gameplay can often be inferred only by the existence of their indications or contraindications. We examine these in more detail in the genre-specific chapters.

Chapter 8

The Internal Economy of Games and Game Balancing

This chapter is an introduction to the tools and techniques that we will use in later chapters when discussing the balancing of specific game genres. Different genres require different modes of balance, but in many cases, the common thread that binds them is the same.

The methods discussed in this chapter provide a basis for us to examine the issue of balance in games:

➤ What exactly do we mean by balance?

➤ How do we define balance?

➤ How can we say that one game is well balanced where another is not?

These are not easy questions to answer; an answer that may be correct for one person may be completely incorrect for another. In some ways, there can be no definitive answers to the questions. Like so many other questions in game design, the answer contains an unknown quantity: the player.

Although we can attempt to anticipate what sort of people will play our game, we will never be able to satisfy all of them. However, as fallacious as it may seem, we have to start somewhere. In balancing a game, we have to assume the existence of an average player and target the balance to suit that player. Remember, however, that your average player will not be anywhere near as skilled at computer games as you and your team. Don't fall for the extremely common mistake of "making a game that you enjoy playing." This statement has been the epithet for many promising games. The danger of aiming to make a game that you enjoy playing is that you run the risk of making a game that *only* you enjoy playing. A significant level of "dumbing down" may be required to make your game as accessible as possible to the average player. Do not be alarmed by this; you can cater for extremes by providing different difficulty settings, as necessary. So with this in mind, let's explore the subject of game balancing in more detail.

What Is Game Balance?

Many games are released each year that commit fundamental game design errors. These games are fatally flawed from the outset, and short of a monumental marketing campaign and a small spate of miracles, they are doomed to failure. There are many obvious reasons for this kind of spectacular failure, such as bad coding, buggy software, poor quality control, and substandard graphics.

However, on many occasions, the cause of failure is not so immediately obvious. The game may *look* okay, *sound* okay, and even to some extent *play* okay, but it still fails commercially. One of the reasons for failure (and the one we are going to concern ourselves with here) is poor game design. In Chapter 7, "Gameplay," we introduced the elements of gameplay that we expect to find in games. We also touched a little on the subject of game balance. Including all the expected elements in a game does no good if they are not in balance with one another and with the player.

But what exactly do we mean by a balanced game? A *balanced game* is one where the main determining factor for the success of the player is the skill level of that player. That does not mean that random events cannot occur, but a better player should ordinarily be more successful than a poor one unless he has an unusually long run of bad luck.

Traditionally, game balance has been very much a trial-and-error process. The game is played, the game is tweaked, the game is played, the game is tweaked, and then finally, when time runs out, the game is released (and usually tweaked further in the form of patches).

So why are there no formalized, scientifically rigorous methods of game balancing? Well, for a start, it's an extremely difficult and complex process. Essentially, game balancing is a problem involving a fantastically large number of independent variables. It's an optimization problem in n-dimensional space where n is a very large number. No formal rules govern game balancing, except in a very small number of abstract mathematical scenarios.

Classical game theory is simply not suited to this kind of problem. Most areas of research concern themselves with games in which there are discrete player turns and a limited number of variables. This type of theory is ideal for analyzing games of chance, such as poker and coin-toss games, but it would be nearly impossible to use for the analysis of more complex games, such as computer games, which are more often continuous and have hundreds, if not thousands, of independent variables. Also, the majority of game theory is concerned with finding the optimum way to *play* a game. Using game theory to balance a game would be like playing a twisted version of *Jeopardy*—starting with the answer and working back to the best possible question. (It's possible that one day there might be some sort of "game calculus" invented to handle these problems, but we're not going to hold our collective breath. Besides, that still doesn't solve the problem of how to break down the game into a list of strategies and variables to fit into the equations.)

This sort of n-dimensional optimization problem occurs in many areas of science, and it is from these areas that we can borrow techniques to help us solve the problem. This is not to say that all game-balancing problems can be solved by the blanket application of a sterile algorithm. A healthy measure of human finesse is still required in order to make a game feel "just right." Just because a result is mathematically correct does not automatically make it aesthetically pleasing.

In fact, the tweak-play-tweak method of game balancing is a valid approach (and is pretty much the only approach so far). The only problem is that this method is time- and resource-intensive and is extremely prone to error. Worse still, balancing a game is a very difficult concept to grasp. After all, what are you balancing it against? Are you balancing it against itself? The player? And how exactly are you balancing it? Are you balancing it so that it is a fair game? Are you balancing it so that it provides a consistent experience to the player no matter what her ability? The answers to these questions are—at least to some degree—subjective and depend upon the nature of the game. For example, a historically accurate simulation of the Anglo-Zulu wars would not be a fair game. The Zulus would have to lose, which would be a bit depressing for the Zulu player.

Even a nonrealistic game has to take some liberties in order to obtain balance. For example, a hypothetical game that simulates the invasion of modern-day Earth by a race of aliens has to give the humans a chance to win. And in spite of what you've seen in films like *Independence Day*, any race that is advanced enough to move huge ships across hundreds or thousands of light-years probably wouldn't have much difficulty mopping up a small planet like ours—and they certainly wouldn't have computers that interfaced with an Apple Macintosh, conveniently allowing us to destroy their whole operation. In order to base a game around such a scenario, we'd have to stretch credibility to the breaking point, in that with today's technology we could actually defeat a race of advanced aliens whose sole specialty is enslaving entire worlds. Human "pluck" will only take us so far.

Before we get into the gritty detail, we should briefly describe what it is that we are actually balancing. There are several ways of implementing balance in a game, centered around how the equilibrium is maintained. In particular, there are two broad classes of balance that we will be discussing: *static balance* and *dynamic balance*. Traditionally, balance has not been differentiated in this fashion; when game balance is referred to, it is usually referred to as a whole, comprising both the static and the dynamic balance. Often, you will hear discussion in terms of the opening, the midgame, and the endgame, much as you would in chess. This is a perfectly valid, if a little rudimentary, approach; it's fine for the discussion of a game that has already been written, but when we are designing a new game, we would like to be able to go to a finer grain of detail. It has often been said, however, that the degree of understanding of a subject is directly proportional to the sophistication of the available language used to describe it. For our discussion, referring to balance as a whole rather than distinguishing between the two areas of balance is an unnecessary handicap that we would rather avoid.

Static Balance

Static balance is concerned with the rules of the game and how they interact with each other. These are specifically time invariant. In other words, these are the rules of the game that can be written down and documented to aid play—the usual strategy guide fodder.

A concrete example would be a comparison of the relative strengths of units in a war game, or the average jumping distance of Mario in relation to the average distance between platforms. Generally, when game balance is spoken about, most people are unconsciously referring to the static balance (sometimes mixed with a little of the dynamic balance).

Static balance is the classic game balance that is talked about in other books, including *Game Architecture and Design*, also from New Riders (although we did delve somewhat into the subject of dynamic balance in that book, without specifically naming it as such). This is the process whereby we ensure that the game is fair and all elements interlock seamlessly to avoid dominant and recessive strategies that can ruin a game.

Randomness and Average Values

In the following few sections, we are going to discuss balancing gameplay elements using payoff matrices to demonstrate some of the points. Payoff matrices are used to illustrate the balance between elements of the game.

For example, let's take a symmetrical game involving two players: red and blue. Each of these players has two strategies that it can use: R1, R2, B1, and B2.

Let's say that R2 beats B1 with a payoff of 3, B2 beats R1 with a payoff of -2, B1 draws with R1, and R2 draws with B2, as shown in Table 8.1.

Table 8.1 A Simple Net Payoff Matrix

	B1	B2
R1	0	-2
R2	3	0

Note that negative numbers indicate a win to blue, and positive numbers indicate a win to red.

This doesn't have to mean that for each play of the game, R2 beats B1—occasionally the converse could occur. It depends on the nature of the game. What it is generally taken to mean is that the *net* payoff is that value. In some cases, the strategy B1 could pay more or less against the strategy R1 (subject to the whims of chance), but the average value of the payoff over time would tend to the specified value.

This is especially important to realize when we are considering net payoff strategies for computer games. We have to deal with a large number of random events that do not necessarily all have the same result, but that will tend toward a certain value; hence, the net payoff tends toward a discrete value. If we were to attempt to examine each of the separate results as an individual strategy, rather than taking an average of all similar events (for example, knight versus archer combat), then the analysis would soon become unmanageable (and without meaning).

Dominant Strategies

Dominant strategy is a term from classic game theory. A dominant strategy is one that surpasses all others by being the best one to choose under any circumstances. That does not mean that it guarantees winning, but it should guarantee not losing. (To be exact, a *strongly* dominant strategy guarantees winning, while a *weakly* dominant strategy guarantees not losing.)

A strongly dominant strategy is never desirable, but care should be taken when excising weakly dominant strategies—sometimes they can be valuable (for example, forcing a draw in chess). When eliminating a weakly dominant strategy, make sure you're not throwing the baby out with the bath water.

The difficulty in applying these concepts from classic game theory to real games is the massive increase in complexity. A typical game theory example deals with a simple game with known parameters, such as the tossing of a coin, whereas a game such as Westwood's *Command and Conquer: Red Alert* has many hundreds of variables—too many, in fact to be able to deal with rigorously—and the values that they take are effectively continuous, not discrete like the heads or tails of a coin toss. To us, this means that the labeling of strategies as dominant takes on a bit of fuzziness. There is no discrete boundary. What would be a dominant strategy in the hands of one player is a guaranteed loser in the hands of another.

The ideal solution to this would be to talk in terms of an idealized perfect player who only makes perfect decisions. Unfortunately, although that would result in mathematically correct games, they almost certainly would not be fun. The players of our games are real people, with different attitudes, abilities, likes, and dislikes, and we would be doing them (and ourselves) a great disservice by trying to shoehorn them into a particular box to fit some theory. And that's the biggest problem we have in balancing a game: No matter how much perfect math and science we can apply to the problem, it will only take us so far. The rest is up to us, as game designers. In fact, it's this final stage of game balancing that really distinguishes the greats of game design, such as Shigeru Miyamoto, Brian Reynolds, Sid Meier, and Dani Berry.

Let's look at a trivial example of a dominant strategy and then look at some real-world games that also have dominant strategies.

You're returning home from a busy day at the office, when suddenly you wonder whether it's your wife's birthday today. Should you buy flowers or not?

The risks you take are as follows: If it is your wife's birthday, and you buy flowers, you win 10 brownie points, because you remembered her birthday. If it's not her birthday, you will win 20 brownie points, because you have surprised her with your thoughtfulness.

Alternatively, you could decide that it is *not* her birthday and you don't need to buy any flowers. In this case, if you are wrong and it actually *is* her birthday, you take a big hit in brownie points—you lose 100 of them. If it's not her birthday and you don't buy her flowers, then everything is normal when you get home, and you neither gain nor lose any brownie points.

The net payoff matrix for this game is shown in Table 8.2.

Table 8.2   The Wife's Birthday Conundrum

	Wife's Birthday	Not Wife's Birthday
Buy Flowers	10	20
Don't Buy Flowers	-100	0

Quite clearly, the dominant strategy is to always buy flowers, because you will always get a positive payoff. (An even more obvious strategy, although outside the bounds of this example, is to make sure you *remember* your wife's birthday in the first place.)

The second strategy—don't buy flowers—would be immediately discounted by any rational game player; the strategy only guarantees a zero payoff at best, and a massive loss in the worst-case scenario.

Of course, to turn this example into a *real* game decision (by eliminating the dominant strategy), we would have to attribute some cost to the flowers so that buying flowers when it is not her birthday results in a negative payoff. We'd also have to figure out the exchange rate between dollars and brownie points.

Unfortunately, only the most trivial examples can be broken down into a simple payoff matrix. For a more complicated example, we should examine the previously mentioned *Red Alert* (see Figure 8.1). This game is famed for a particular dominant (or near domi-nant) strategy, which has become known as the tank rush (a name that has spread to similar strategies in other games).

Figure 8.1 *Red Alert.*

An experienced player playing as the Soviet side could devote all of her energies to producing a large force of tanks in the early part of the game, and then use those tanks to attack the nascent enemy base en masse. Against an unprepared opponent, this almost always guarantees a victory. Of course, because of the immense number of variables involved, we cannot say with certainty that this *is* a dominant strategy—that is, it may not be the best strategy to play regardless of what the opponent does—but it is certainly near dominant.

Another real-world example, again from a real-time strategy game, occurred because of relative unit strength mismatches. In the original *Warcraft* game from Blizzard Entertainment, the Orc player was almost always guaranteed victory if he was able to produce warlocks (see Figure 8.2). Once a warlock was in play, it could be used to create an army of powerful demons. This almost always guaranteed a win for the Orc player and was a strategy worth playing, whatever the opposing player did. In fact, we found that the only way to guarantee a fair game in the original *Warcraft* was to explicitly agree to disallow any magical warfare.

Figure 8.2 *Warcraft.*

These examples are both from real-time strategy games. This type of game is often the easiest to analyze, because it so closely matches the areas of research in conventional military game theory. However, we don't want to give the impression that we are only concerned with real-time strategy games, so our last example of a dominant strategy is one that affected an old side-scrolling space shooter game on the Nintendo Super NES. In this game (which we will not name to prevent embarrassment on the part of the individuals responsible), it was possible to make your way through the entire game by upgrading your weapons to a certain level and then, going as low on the screen as possible, keeping your finger on the fire button. In this position, you were invulnerable to the enemy attacks and could finish the game on a single life. This is a clear example of a dominant strategy.

All these examples show why dominant strategies are a bad thing, and why we must strive to avoid them in our games. They ruin gameplay. The presence of a single dominant strategy is enough to render a good portion of our intended gameplay obsolete. All other strategies that may potentially be used in the same circumstances are recessive strategies, and no rational player would choose to use them.

An interesting point to examine is where to draw the line between a valid (but undesirable) dominant strategy and plain cheating. For example, some players may view the strategies mentioned earlier as cheating, whereas others would be of the view that if the game system allows it, it is a valid strategy. The question is, where does this leave the classic "God Mode" present in virtually all first-person shooters since the original *Wolfenstein 3D* (see Figure 8.3)? Taken from a game theory purist point of view, the obvious dominant strategy is to use the God Mode when playing the game. Why? Because it guarantees that you will not lose and is consequently the best approach to take, regardless of what the opponent is doing. However, this extreme case also demonstrates effectively how a dominant strategy ruins gameplay: You are not experiencing the game as the designer intended (and it's also the reason why we disapprove of cheat modes in games, but that's another story entirely). Of course, this assumes that people play just to win. However, for most people, a major reason for playing is to have fun, not just to win.

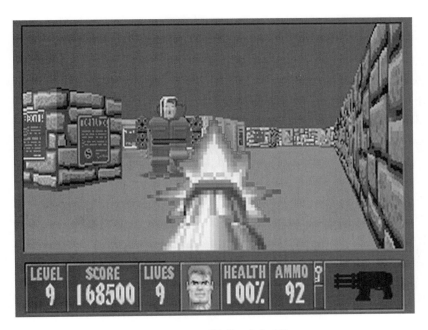

Figure 8.3   *Wolfenstein 3D.*

Occasionally, a bug in a game can be exploited to the benefit of the player. For example, in the game *Super Turbo Street Fighter 2*, the secret character Akuma is completely out of balance with the rest of the characters in the game (see Figure 8.4). This character has an unbeatable attack, the air fireball, which is so superior to the rest of the characters' attacks that they don't stand a chance. Using Akuma is the dominant strategy—if the opponent chooses any other character, she is pretty much assured a loss. If the opponent chooses Akuma also, then given equal skill levels, a draw is the likely outcome. The only option to ensure a fair result is to ban the use of that character in any serious competitive game. It's not that this is the only game that has an unbalanced character, but in other games, the superior character isn't so far out of balance that it ruins the game for other players.

Figure 8.4 *Super Turbo Street Fighter 2.*

Traditionally, the only way to remove dominant strategies in nontrivial examples is thorough play testing. Unfortunately, there is always some chance that flaws will slip through the net. This chapter covers some of the ways that we can try to prevent this from occurring.

Symmetry

Symmetry is the simplest way of balancing a game. Each player (including the computer) is given the same starting conditions and abilities. This ensures that the outcome of the game is dependent only on the relative skill level of the players. Sounds ideal, doesn't it?

Unfortunately, this approach only works in abstract games such as chess. Can you imagine simulating a real battle with the infantry, knights, and archers lined up facing each other over a perfectly symmetrical field? It would feel unnatural and would quickly become boring. Even though pure symmetry is limited in use to the abstract, there is a way that symmetry can be used to ensure balance without appearing to be contrived.

Pure symmetry works very well for sport simulations. You would expect that two teams playing the same game would be very similar to one another in both form and function. However, the highly standardized world of sport is about the only situation where this pure symmetry is appropriate. In a real-world situation, pure symmetry stands out like a sore thumb.

In *Game Architecture and Design*, we talked about functional symmetry. This is a form of symmetry where the abilities of the player are roughly—but not exactly—mirrored. That is, they are functionally equivalent, not exactly equivalent.

The example used in *Game Architecture and Design* concerns a real-time strategy game with various types of landmass—water, mountain, and plain. We can use this as the basis of our example here. All units can travel over the plain, but only air units can travel over mountains, and only water units can travel over water (assume that they are hovercraft that can travel over plain as well as water). Do you see the functional symmetry? Each side has units that are functionally equivalent, but depending on the layout of the level (one player could be surrounded by mountains, the other could be bordered by sea), the way and the proportions in which those units would be used would be different.

Symmetry is mainly useful in balancing *n*-player games. It can also be used in balancing single player games; it's a good starting point to ensure that the computer-controlled entities are roughly in balance with the player. However, symmetry is a fairly unsophisticated approach and leads to a limited number of directly confrontational strategies. The player runs the risk of being restricted to a simple game of tit-for-tat. The computer throws *X* at me, so I have to respond with *Y*, which encourages the computer to throw more *X* at me, and so on. This does not lead to particularly interesting gameplay, and it shuts out a number of the more interesting gameplay dynamics we could expect if we were to use a more advanced balancing technique in conjunction with functional symmetry.

Transitive Relationships

In a nutshell, a transitive relationship defines a one-way relationship between two or more entities. A can beat B, B can beat C, and C cannot beat anyone (and hence, by implication, A can beat C), as shown in Figure 8.5 and Table 8.3.

Figure 8.5 Transitive relationships.

Table 8.3 Net Payoff Matrix for A, B, and C

	A	B	C
A	0	1	1
B	-1	0	1
C	-1	-1	0

Taken at face value, it would seem that transitive relationships are not very useful. Why would anyone want to use C when they could use A? That's where the balancing comes in. So how do you balance the relationship? The more effective entity comes at a higher cost. Note that we don't necessarily mean a direct dollar or points or score cost; the cost could be in the lives of the people sent to fetch the prized entity, or the trials and difficulties that the player has to endure to reach the entity. There is no way of directly quantifying these indirect costs—known as shadow costs—but they should be sufficiently high as to justify the reward. Note that shadow costs are the end result of a number of other factors. They can be measured, but cannot be directly modified.

Pure transitive relationships, without shadow costs to balance them out, lead to trivial and undemanding gameplay choices, which serve to undermine balance. However, shadow costs, together with the possibility of being knocked back down the ladder, allow for an interesting progression/regression dynamic that can lead to some taut and suspenseful gameplay. Care should be taken to ensure that the player can reestablish her previous level. Games such as *Diablo* from Blizzard Entertainment do this by allowing the player to retrieve her possessions from the corpse of the previous incarnation.

Transitive relationships are very common in games, especially games such as first-person shooters. Think back to the original *Doom* from id Software. The player starts the game with a relatively weak pistol. Sure, the player can get a little way with it, but each monster takes more than one shot to dispatch, and initial progress is tricky. A little way into the game, the player finds a shotgun, which is a much more effective weapon. The player can now dispatch the monsters with relative ease, allowing him to get further into the game. Now the monsters become harder to kill, and shotgun ammunition becomes scarce.

We're back where we started—with a relatively weak weapon—and we need to search for another stronger weapon to make the same progress we were making before. This is how the game draws us in and impels us to keep playing.

Transitive relationships are mainly used in games with a need to continually drive the player forward toward a goal. The player responds to that need and is rewarded with upgrades and progress, until eventually she reaches the goal, and the game is over.

As such, transitive relationships are only really useful in games that have a definite end point (which is most of them). They are rarely (if at all) used in open-ended games without some way of closing the loop and returning the player back to square one. An example is in the multiplayer arenas of games such as *Quake III* and *Unreal Tournament*. Here, the loop is closed by the death of the player, as he is respawned with only the basic weaponry and has to fight his way back up the transitive relationship ladder.

Any game that involves upgrading or augmenting the player's capabilities within the game makes use of transitive relationships. We can think of plenty of examples of games that operate in this fashion. For example:

➤ **Super Mario.** A series of side-scrolling platform games (see Figure 8.6). The progression is of Mario's abilities. With the first mushroom, he doubles in size, and with subsequent items, his abilities improve further to include flying and invulnerability. These abilities are lost in stages when Mario collides with an enemy.

Figure 8.6 *Super Mario Advance.*

➤ **Legend of Zelda.** A series of top-down arcade style role-playing games (except for the Nintendo 64 and GameCube versions, which were full 3D), as shown in Figure 8.7. Link (the hero) collects items to enhance his skills and stamina. The basis of the game is to solve the overall quest by adventuring through a series of dungeons. In general, the prize for each dungeon is a magical item that enhances Link's abilities. A nice little game design touch is that the ability upgraded is the ability that would have been most useful in traversing the dungeon in which it was secreted.

➤ **R-Type.** A side-scrolling space-based shoot 'em-up (see Figure 8.8). As the player defeats enemies, they drop pods containing weapons upgrades for the player's ship. The cumulative upgrades are lost when your ship is destroyed.

Figure 8.7 *Legend of Zelda.*

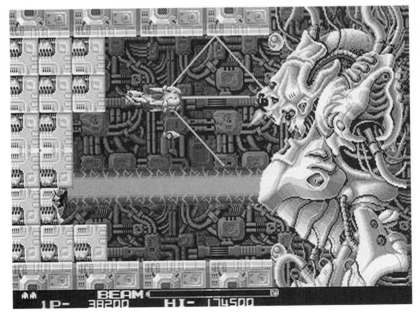

Figure 8.8 *R-Type.*

➤ *Diablo.* An isometric 3D action-adventure game (see Figure 8.9). As the player battles through the dungeons, the innovative skill and leveling systems allow you to spend experience points, gained while adventuring, on improving your character.

Figure 8.9   *Diablo.*

➤ *Doom,* *Quake,* *Half-Life,* **and so on.** First-person shooters (see Figure 8.10). As you progress through the game, successively better weapons can be found that scale the player's firepower with that of the enemy. You lose the advanced weapons when your avatar is killed.

➤ *The Sims.* A "family simulator" that lets the player build and furnish a house and manage the family living within it (see Figure 8.11). For each household item you can purchase, there are upgrades available that function more efficiently. The more money you spend on an item, the more efficiently it does its job—it could take up less space, be prettier, or perform a double function.

Figure 8.10   *Doom.*

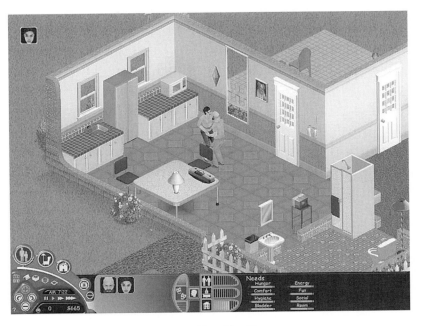

Figure 8.11   *The Sims.*

Intransitive Relationships: Rock, Paper, Scissors

Almost everyone is familiar with the children's game Rock, Paper, Scissors (sometimes called Scissors, Paper, Stone). For those of you who managed to miss this one, the rules are basically summarized as follows: scissors cut paper, paper wraps stone, stone blunts scissors. Two players, the red player and the blue player, choose one of the three glyphs and score the game depending on the rules.

This gives us a balanced, three-way intransitive relationship, as shown in Figure 8.12.

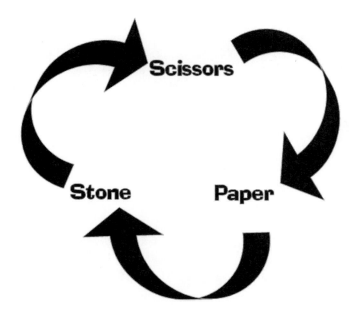

Figure 8.12 Three-way intransitive relationship in Rock, Paper, Scissors.

The net payoff matrix for Rock, Paper, Scissors is shown in Table 8.4.

Table 8.4 Rock, Paper, Scissors

	Scissors	Paper	Rock
Scissors	0	1	-1
Paper	-1	0	1
Rock	1	-1	0

Rock, Paper, Scissors is a *zero sum game*. That is, if the red player wins, the blue player has to lose. If the blue player wins, the red player has to lose. And if the blue player draws, then the red player has to draw as well (and vice versa). Most interesting games are zero sum: The player wins (or player team wins) and the computer (or opposing player/team) loses—or at least, that's the idea.

The three-way intransitive relationship of Rock, Paper, Scissors has been the model for most real-time strategy game balancing and has also been used in other game genres, such as racing games and role-playing games, for many years. Static intransitive relationships—although more aesthetically pleasing than transitive relationships—do not lead to innovative gameplay. It's far too easy for the player to learn the simple relationships between units and figure out the best strategy to use. The game becomes a one-trick pony. The solution to this is to dynamically vary the relationship.

The other problem with the three-way intransitive relationship in its unmodified form that can lead to uninteresting gameplay is that each strategy tends to be used equally, and the pattern can become predictable. In order to make the decisions more interesting, we can vary the shadow costs to alter the likelihood that the particular strategy is chosen.

Let's consider an example of altering shadow cost to affect the relationship. Imagine a confrontation between two craft, A and B. These craft are capable of operating as aircraft or submersibles. Craft A is optimized for flight and is more efficient in the air than in the water. Craft B is optimized for submersible operation and is not as maneuverable in the air. In an air combat situation, A can regularly defeat B. In a submerged combat situation, B regularly defeats A. By altering the environment (and hence, the shadow costs of operating the craft), we introduce an interesting dynamic in the relationship between them. Now, this is just a binary relationship (imagine it as a isolated link in an *n*-way intransitive relationship); that is, A beats B or B beats A. However, it is not difficult to imagine how this binary relationship could be stretched out over a continuum. For example, if we transferred both craft into a hypothetical semifluid environment that was neither air nor water, where the abilities of both craft cancelled out, we would get a stalemate between them. From here, we could vary the medium's properties one way or the other, giving one of the craft a variable advantage over the other.

Trade-Offs

Not all relationships between entities are a transition between an inferior and a superior entity. One entity might be better than another in some ways and not in others, but a general improvement can sometimes be gained by the transition, depending on the circumstances. (For example, a pistol is great on land compared with a harpoon, but the roles are reversed underwater.)

A good trade-off example can be found in *The Sims*. When the player earns money and chooses to upgrade the living environment for her Sims, she has a choice of many items of household furniture. Some of these items are better than others in some areas and inferior in others. For example, an expensive couch could improve the appearance of a room (making it more aesthetically pleasing for the Sims), but could be less comfortable than a slightly cheaper and less beauteous couch. The player then has to decide which of the two parameters to maximize.

This sort of balancing act (or *stats juggling*, as it's affectionately known) is very common in role-playing games. First, the player usually has to generate a character to play with. This is done with a combination of simulated dice rolls and the distribution of a number of points among a number of attributes, such as strength, stamina, and intelligence. After this is done, the player is normally allowed to shift points from one area to another in order to balance out the points.

As a method of achieving balance, point distribution has some merits. Note that it does not have to be restricted to role-playing games and other such number-crunching games. In fact, the player does not even need to know that there has been a point distribution system used. It can be hidden behind the scenes. In most games, there is no need for the player even to be aware (except at the most superficial level) that there is any such distribution of points in place. For example, consider a simple platform game where the player is pitched against a number of different enemies. For each level, the enemies could have a fixed number of points to divide between two attributes, speed and jumping power. This would give us a nice range of enemies of different abilities. In order to ramp up difficulty as the player progresses through the game, the fixed number of points available to distribute could increase with the level. Some of Nintendo's *Mario* platform games use something close to this approach: The player is given a choice of several characters to play—such as Mario, Luigi, Toad, and Peach—and each character has different levels of ability in jumping, running, and floating.

A few caveats need to be considered, however. In order for the point distribution system to work effectively, all of the attributes must be orthogonal. That is to say, they must be independent attributes. An attribute should not affect the domain of another attribute. Having two closely related attributes, such as weight and floating ability, undermines the point system. The player (or designer) should not be able to gain the same effect by pumping points into one attribute as she could by pumping the points into another.

You also want to make sure that spending a point on one attribute has a similar magnitude of effect as it would on any other attribute. This means that, for example, adding a point to strength should increase the character's strength by the same factor as spending the same amount on improving the character's intelligence.

Combination

Transitive and intransitive relationships don't necessarily have to involve single entities. That is to say, you don't have to specify that one archer beats one unit of infantry. In some cases, two or more entities can be treated as a single entity when balancing a game. For example, even though one unit of infantry may not be enough to beat one archer, you might be able to use a unit of infantry in combination with another unit.

As a designer, you wouldn't necessarily be expected to explicitly design in all of the possible combinations of entities within your game. You do, however, have to be aware of them and to balance the more troublesome ones by modifying the entities themselves and using shadow costs to equalize them. The previously mentioned tank rush from *Red Alert* could have been avoided by modifying the shadow costs of tanks so that they were much more expensive to produce in the early stages of the game. In the single-player game, this was attempted by disallowing certain units in the earlier levels (a clumsy approach), but multiplayer games are a free-for-all, and the imbalance comes to the fore.

In general, combinatorial effects in your game will not be a significant problem if you pay attention to the basic balance. If your foundation is strong and balanced, the chances are good that you won't run into any major difficulties with combinatorial effects and emergence.

Emergence

Emergence is the action of simple rules combining to produce complex results. The classic example in the computer world is Conway's *Game of Life*. In this cellular automata simulation (which the majority of people will be familiar with), a few simple rules produce some astoundingly complex results.

> *"We ended up with a game that I didn't know how to win. I didn't know which were the best strategies or tactics, even though I designed all the game's systems. That is what makes a good strategy game."*
>
> —**Julian Gollop**, referring to *X-Com: UFO Defense*

Of course, the phenomenon of emergence is not restricted to the domain of the computer. Emergence is ubiquitous in nature. Literally everything you see, touch, taste, hear, and feel is a direct result of emergence. From a few simple rules, the amazing complexity of the universe emerges. The motion of the planets is accurately predicted by the general theory of relativity, our genetic code determines our body shape and size, and a few simple electrochemical interactions in our brains produce our consciousness and personality.

In Chapters 1, "What Is Game Design?" and 2, "Game Concepts," we encouraged you to look for inspiration from many diverse sources. The use (or more accurately, the taming) of emergence is a prime example of this directive. Emergence is a natural phenomenon in its own right. It occurs everywhere, and games that use it effectively are among the best of their type. A good reference work for this phenomenon is Steven Johnson's book *Emergence: The Connected Lives of Ants, Brains, Cities, and Software* (Touchstone Books).

Let's consider a simple example to illustrate the point. Imagine that our character is on one side of a locked wooden door and wants to get to the other side of the door. There are a number of ways to approach this, ranging from the obvious to the obscure. First, we could find the key and open the door. That's the simplest solution. But let's say we cannot find the key. Let's try picking the lock—no luck there, because we're not skilled enough. Okay, another approach: We'll try and cast our magic Open Sesame spell and open the door magically. Nope—we're fresh out of magic.

In most games, that would be as far as we get. If our progression in the game depended on our getting through that door, we would be stuck and consequently would be forced to go and search for the key, find some way of improving our lock-picking skills, or find a way to replenish our magic and try the spell again. (See the section "Avoiding Stagnation," later in this chapter.)

However, in reality, we know that there would be other ways to get through the door. We could attempt to break it down with an axe or a mace. We could attempt to burn through it using fire or acid. We could try casting a spell to turn it to stone or glass and then shatter it. We could attempt to unscrew the hinges or the lock. We could attempt to use acid to burn through the hinges or the lock. We could try and break our way through the wall *next* to the door. We could attempt to cast a "ghost" spell on ourselves that lets us pass through solid objects. And these are just the first ideas that came to us—just imagine what else your players will think of.

As game designers, we get away with allowing only a small range of free will for one main reason: The power of the world simulation is limited by hardware and software considerations. We're going to ignore the argument that restricting the range of game-play choices can also improve gameplay; it's valid in some cases, but here it would be sophistry.

So what does this have to do with emergence? Imagine that we designed our simulation so that we took into account a limited subset of fundamental properties of matter and handled our interactions between objects in that fashion. Then we would consider the door as a collection of connected objects: the hinge, the door itself, and the lock. The door is made of wood. Wood has a set of properties somewhat like this: flammability (high), resistance to acid (average), and strength (average). That takes care of the door. We've stated that it can be burnt, that it can be destroyed with acid, and that it's possible to smash through it, provided that the physics engine handles things at this level. Similarly, the lock and hinges would be made of metal. Metal would have the following properties: flammability (low), resistance to acid (poor), and strength (high). Hence, we could not burn the lock or hinges, but we could melt them with acid, and good luck trying to smash them. Similarly, you could assign properties to the stone wall holding the door that detail whether it could be broken through or not.

This is not a rigorous example, but it forms the basis of a workable system. What we are demonstrating here is the power of emergent properties. You don't need to go overboard trying to cover every conceivable property of matter—just choose a few that make sense within the bounds of your world model. We took three simple properties (flammability, resistance to acid, and strength) and showed how they could determine a wide range of behaviors. In fact, they would let us get to the other side of the door in a number of ways that we may not have even thought of. And that's the power of emergence: complex behaviors resulting from a simple model. Imagine if we had a model that had a few more properties—which would pretty much cover every conceivable way of getting through the door—including bombarding it with frozen marshmallows, if the fancy took us.

As with all tools, emergence has to be used with care. In the prior example, the fact that the player could imagine ways that we haven't considered in order to get through the door makes it difficult for us to control the gameplay directly. If we wanted the door to be a particularly tricky puzzle, we risk undermining the gameplay by providing the player with the freedom to figure out his own way through the door. Emergence is both the bane and the savior of game design. In our opinion, it is the single most valuable tool for taking your game beyond the ordinary, but it can be a double-edged sword. Emergence has its dark side, and in the wrong place, it can undermine gameplay, leading to undesirable dominant strategies or, worse, fatal gameplay flaws.

For example, a series of artificial life games, the *Creatures* series from CyberLife, relies heavily on emergence (see Figure 8.13). The behavior of the life-forms, the Norns, is determined by a neural network. Although this is a prime example of emergence, it also gives us an example of why emergence isn't the universal panacea it is claimed to be. The problem stems from the fact that Norns learn by positive and negative reinforcement: If something feels good, they'll keep doing it, and if something feels bad, they won't. There's nothing *inherently* wrong with this—in fact, it's probably the only sensible approach, because it seems to work well enough in the real world. However, within the simplified world of the Norns, it has some unfortunate side effects.

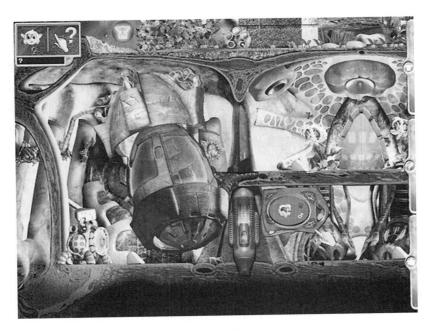

Figure 8.13 *Creatures.*

For example, in one of the games, there is a still that produces alcoholic beverages. The pleasure reward from drinking at the still is so immediate that all Norns who find their way to the still would simply stay there and get drunk. Unfortunately, this is not nearly as entertaining as it sounds (well, not for long anyway). They get drunk. They fall down. And that's about it. Clearly, this is an undesirable example of emergence. It does not add anything interesting to the game and, in fact, detracts from it.

Feedback Loops

The basic progression of a game is that it starts statically and dynamically balanced and then gets out of balance, first one way and then the other. It goes backward and forward like a seesaw, with one player ahead and then the other, until someone eventually gets so far ahead that it is impossible for the other to catch up.

Often, being ahead tends to make things easier for the player in that position and harder for the other. This is positive feedback that helps the leading player. That is, "the rich get richer and the poor get poorer," as in *Monopoly*. The more money you have, the more hotels you can put up, which produces more money, and so on. This is a desirable trait as long as it doesn't happen too fast and doesn't leave the player who's behind with no way to catch up. In chess, taking an opponent's piece gives the taker a slight advantage: The other side doesn't have that piece to play with anymore. But in Japanese chess, when you take an opponent's piece, you move it to your side of the board, and it becomes your piece (although it turns into a weaker piece). This confers an *additional* advantage: Not only does the enemy not have that piece, but you have an extra piece to play with. If you did this with Western chess, the games would be very short indeed.

Therefore, you want positive feedback so that the game will end eventually, but not too much. Most war games, for example *Warcraft*, don't let you take and use enemy factories; they only let you damage and destroy them. If you could use enemy factories to build armies, the game would become unbalanced too quickly.

You need the keep the players in the balance sweet spot for as long as is practical in order to keep the game fun and let the underdogs have a chance to catch up. A game where the slightest advantage leads to a runaway victory for one player would not be fun. In summary, if you are going to use positive feedback loops in your design, make sure they have a reasonable response time delay before they kick into action.

Or you can counter positive feedback with negative feedback, as well. Suppose taking an enemy piece enables you to use it, but there is a price to be paid for it: It must be supported somehow. This means that taking it is not "free." This was found in *Dungeon Keeper*: You could torture enemy creatures to convert them to your side, but once you did, they had to have food and money and a place to sleep. The process of converting them also took time, and if you weren't careful, you might kill them without converting them. As a result, it wasn't a strongly dominant strategy. It was a weakly dominant one that was well worthwhile but not absolutely necessary (we won't comment on the morals of simulated torture of imaginary creatures).

Another example is the venerable game of 8-ball pool: The more you get ahead, the more difficult it is to keep sinking shots because you have less balls to target and your opponent has more balls to get in the way.

Another solution to too much positive feedback is to include a random factor that gives the player who's behind a chance to catch up just through sheer luck: throwing double sixes in backgammon, for example. Of course, if the random factor is fair, it might put the player even further behind, too, but at least it adds variety and uncertainty to the game. But the random factor must not be too great, or it overrides the value of good play in the first place and discourages a good player. Why play well if the result amounts to flipping a coin anyway? Poker is a good example of a game with a well-balanced random factor: In any given game, randomness plays a large role, but smart players don't bet large amounts on a single game. Rather, they count on the cumulative effect of good play over many games to reward good players and take money from poor ones. The major factor that determines winners (averaged over a statistically significant number of games) is player skill.

Summary of Static Balance

Static balance boils down to the fact that the balance in most games is simply a dynamic tension (by means of feedback loops) between the transitive and intransitive relationships and the shadow costs for obtaining and transitioning between entities.

Static game balance is only half the story. Setting up the static balance ensures that the initial starting position for the game is in equilibrium. And then along comes a player whose sole aim is to destroy your carefully constructed balance by actually *playing* the game. So now it's time to set the machine in motion. The next section on dynamic balance covers how to handle balance issues while the player is interacting with the system.

Dynamic Balance

Dynamic balance covers the opening, midgame, and endgame of classic game analysis on a much finer scale. Rather than treating the game as three discrete phases, which is fine for postgame analyses, we have to consider the fully continuous spectrum of play, from start to end. This differs from the static balance, because we have to consider the interaction of the player or players with the statically balanced system. We are concerned with not only static balance, but also dynamic balance—how the balance changes with time and player interaction.

We have to consider *passive balancing*, that is, keeping the system in balance with the player, without actually moving the equilibrium point. We also need to consider *active balancing*, shifting the equilibrium dynamically in response to the player's actions, either to increase difficulty or to adapt the game to the abilities of the player.

What Are We Balancing?

The word *balancing* suggests the act of restoring a system to an equilibrium position. Consequently, our discussion of game balance revolves around the hypothesis that a game is a system (or collection of systems) that needs to be restored to equilibrium. This is, in fact, the case, but these systems need to be balanced in slightly different ways, depending on their nature and function.

In some ways, this is a moot point—part of balance is the player herself—and we don't necessarily want to have to implement handicaps for a good player so that a rank newbie can hold her own. You can take play balancing too far. If a player is willing to work fairly within the bounds of the system in order to gain a competitive edge (such as those players of *Starcraft* who memorize statistics and use the user interface shortcuts to the fullest to gain an advantage, as shown in Figure 8.14), she should be allowed that privilege.

Figure 8.14 *Starcraft.*

The objective of balancing a game is to provide a game that is internally consistent and fair, without allowing players to exploit flaws and weaknesses to gain advantages. The other aim (of course) is to make sure that the game is fun.

A game system should initially be in a state of static balance, but once it is set in motion, a different form of balance, the dynamic balance, is maintained. The success or failure of the game designer to manage dynamic balance defines the gameplay. A good dynamic balance provides the impetus of the gameplay.

There are several ways that the player can interact with the dynamic balance, depending on the aims of the game. (Note that these interactions do not have to be at the global level; the player can be assigned different interaction models for different subgames.) The following three interaction models are available. The player can:

➤ Restore a balance.

➤ Maintain a balance.

➤ Destroy a balance.

Restoring a Balance

If the task of the player is to restore the balance, the object of the game is to move the game system back to an equilibrium point. The gameplay is derived from the player's attempt to restore the initial unbalanced state of the system back to a more ordered state.

The opposing unbalancing force is not strong enough to counteract the player's attempts to restore order. Either the force has stopped interacting with the system before the player intercedes, or else it interacts so weakly that the player is able to force the system back to a balanced state.

An example of a simple game that uses this particular interaction model is a sliding block puzzle. The system starts in a chaotic (unbalanced) state that must be restored to an ordered (balanced) state. The win condition is when the system has been restored.

Maintaining a Balance

If the task of the player is to maintain a balance, the object of the game is to prevent the opposing unbalancing force from overrunning the system.

The difference between this interaction model and the previous one is that the unbalancing force is still very much active. For each action of the player, the opposing force attempts to provide an (at least) equal and opposite reaction to counteract and defeat the player's attempts to force the system back to an ordered state.

If the player was to stop interacting with the system, the unbalancing force would win. The gameplay is defined so that the ideal state is a position of equilibrium between the two opposing forces. There is no win condition in this sort of game. Given a steadily increasing opposing force, it is only a matter of time before the player loses.

An example of a game that uses this interaction model is *Tetris* (see Figure 8.15). The player must attempt to keep the playing field clear of blocks, and the opposing force relentlessly tries to fill the playing field with blocks. Success depends on maintaining the balance between the opposing forces. As the difficulty level increases, the speed with which the opposing force attempts to fill the playing area with blocks increases, and the player must work faster and harder to maintain the balance.

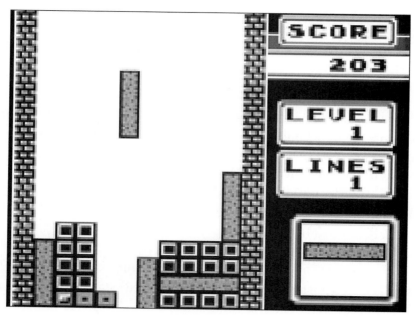

Figure 8.15 *Tetris.*

Destroying a Balance

If the task of a player is to destroy a balance, the object is a reversal of the first interaction model. In this case, the player takes on the role of the unbalanced force, and the opposing force attempts to balance the system.

Actually, this is almost identical to the first interaction model. It's really just a matter of semantics. It depends on who is defining whether a system is balanced or not. It is, however, still useful to retain the distinction. Note that destroying a balance does not necessarily mean that the system has to be plunged into chaos—although that is a valid interpretation and has been used in a good number of games. Additionally, it could also mean that the player has to shift from one equilibrium point to another.

An example of a game that uses this interaction model is *X-Com: Enemy Unknown* (see Figure 8.16). The Earth has been invaded by evil aliens (aren't they all?) who seem intent on using it for their own nefarious purposes. This is the first equilibrium point. The task of the player is to rid the Earth of the evil aliens, hence moving the system to a new alien-free equilibrium.

Figure 8.16   *X-Com: Enemy Unknown.*

As we've already hinted, this could also fit the description of the first interaction model. However, we prefer to use that for game systems where there is no discernible initial equilibrium point from which the player is transitioning.

Balanced Systems

The aim of game balancing is to set up a balanced system for the player to experience. Consequently, gameplay should be set up to do the following:

➤ Provide a consistent challenge

➤ Provide the player with a perceivably fair playing experience

➤ Avoid stagnation

➤ Avoid trivialities

➤ Allow setting of difficulty level (where appropriate)

Let's examine how we can achieve these aims in our game design. The following sections describe each point in some detail and discuss methods of implementation.

Providing a Consistent Challenge

The game should scale in difficulty smoothly as the player progresses into it. A number of games seem to miss this particular point, and in some cases, the midgame experience turns out to be substantially more difficult than the endgame.

One of the major things to be checking for is that the game's difficulty increases smoothly and does not peak or spike irregularly. This is definitely something we need to avoid; the damage that it does to the pacing of the game is irreparable, because the player will feel that anything after that point is anticlimactic. In other words, if you show off your strongest hand too early in the game, anything after that is a disappointment. This highlights the importance of thorough play testing.

Providing a Perceivably Fair Playing Experience

A major factor in whether a player enjoys a game is whether she perceives it to be fair or not. Note that it does not actually matter whether the game *is* fair. What is important here is the player's *perception* of fairness.

For example, if you are going to allow the computer opponents to cheat, you should do it subtly. Blatant cheating is a throwback to the days of minimal processing power; the only way the player *could* expect a decent opponent was if the computer cheated, and there was not enough spare processing power to even attempt to hide it. Nowadays, of course, we cannot use this excuse. Blatant cheating by the computer is seen as a sign of laziness on the part of the designers and developers.

A number of measures can be used to help ensure that a game is fair. This is integral to good design technique. For example, no good designer would knowingly design a game where a player destroys all chances of winning by taking an action earlier in the game and not finding out until later in the game.

A classic example of this is *Monty on the Run* by Gremlin Graphics (see Figure 8.17). This was a maze-based platform game for the 8-bit ZX Spectrum computer released back in the '80s. The object of the game was to guide the hero to freedom and to escape the long arm of the law. One of the unique selling points of this game was the "freedom kit." When the player started the game, he had to choose five items to take along. These items would help get past various obstacles throughout the game. The problem was that the player was given no clues as to which were correct and which were not. The only way to discover this was by trial and error. Thus, the player was effectively doomed from the start unless the correct choice was made at the beginning of the game. This is clearly not fair. This is an extreme example; not many games so blatantly flout fairness in this way. However, even though this is an old game, there are still more recent games that do similar things. How many times have you forgotten to pick up an item that is necessary later in the game? The only choice is to restart the game or to painfully pick your way back to retrieve the item.

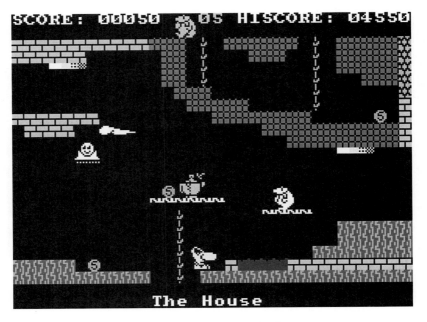

Figure 8.17 *Monty on the Run.*

This example also breaks another of the cardinal rules of game design fairness: informing the player of everything needed to play the game and not using unknowable or unguessable information. The choice of the freedom kit items is not intuitive. The player is given no information of which is the best choice to make. In fact, the only way to be sure of making the correct choice is to cheat—either by reading it in a magazine or finding out from friends. Any game that requires reading a strategy guide or searching on the web, rather than the player's natural ability to play it successfully, is fundamentally flawed.

Another important consideration for ensuring fairness—particularly in multiplayer games—is to protect new players while they are finding their feet in the world. Here, we can take a lesson from nature. Most animals protect their young in some form or another. We need to ensure that our new players are protected in a similar manner. Nothing is more discouraging than joining a new game only to be slaughtered for fun or profit by an experienced player. This protection can be provided in a number of ways. The opportunity to practice in a single-player game is the best way to enable this. First-person shooters tend to implement this well; the single-player game provides a good training ground for players to prepare for joining the multiplayer online mêlée. Purely online games, such as *EverQuest* and *Ultima Online*, need to take a different approach (see Figure 8.18). Here, special training areas should be set aside for new players. There should also be a guiding principle that says that an 8-foot 300-pound barbarian giant cannot be killed by an ordinary rat. Where's the balance in that? *Anarchy Online* does provides specific training areas for new players—where you *can* get killed by a rat!

Figure 8.18 *EverQuest* and *Ultima Online*.

The question of balance in an online game is an ongoing one, as you have the opportunity to respond to "real play" situation in a way that a standard single-player game can't—until the expansion pack, at any rate. *Asheron's Call* does this on a regular basis—and yet it's still fundamentally unbalanced in favor of magic users. It seems to be that way because that's what the magic users want, and obviously the publishers want to hold their audience. Suddenly, game balance is more about ongoing sales and politics than it is about the game play—but it's something that you have to consider as a designer.

Nothing is more frustrating for a player than having to repeat actions over and over again. This is a cardinal (and unfortunately common) sin for a computer game. Surely everyone has screamed in frustration at the save-die-reload cycle that causes the player to replay a section of the game already completed. Worse still are those games that send you back to a distant "checkpoint" on death. Game designers need to learn an important lesson here. Nobody wants to be forced to repeat completed sections of the game. Give them the choice, by all means, but don't force it on them.

Last, but certainly by no means least, the concept of fairness extends to how the player's avatar dies. At no point in the game should the players feel as if events and their consequences are out of control. The players should be made to feel as if every event in the game is under their control. If they fail to control it, they should feel that it was a failure to act on their part, and not just a random arbitrary event that they had no way of avoiding. Instant death syndrome is the most concrete manifestation of this. *Deathtrap Dungeon*, published by Eidos, was guilty of this (see Figure 8.19). Many of the traps were completely unavoidable. The only way to even know that the traps were there was to trigger them and die. Then your next incarnation would know better. Good game design? Maybe not.

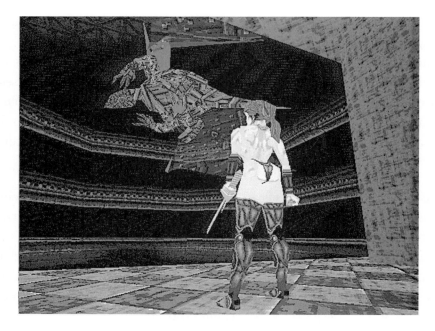

Figure 8.19 *Deathtrap Dungeon.*

The worst thing about fairness is that everyone has a different concept of what *fair* is. The task that the game designer faces is finding a common ground that will keep as many people happy as possible. The old adage is true: You can fool some of the people all of the time, and all of the people some of the time, but not all of the people all of the time. Harsh though it may be, as a game designer, you are trying to fool as many people as possible into thinking that your crude simulation of a real world cares enough about the players to ensure that they get a fair experience.

Avoiding Stagnation

Stagnation is generally as unpleasant as it sounds and smells almost as bad in a game design as it does in water. Stagnation occurs when players are playing a game and reach a point where they appear to be stuck, with no way to go on. There is nothing worse than running round a level of the latest and greatest first-person shooter trying to find that last hidden switch that opens the level exit. Of course, it's not just that type of game that is guilty of this offense (although it is a persistent offender). Any game that leaves the players in a position where they simply do not know what to do next is stagnating.

In some cases, this is very difficult to avoid. A sprawling action-adventure has so many different combinations and configurations that it is difficult to anticipate exactly what the player may or may not try and do. However, it is still possible to give the players positive and negative feedback as they progress. The problem of stagnation can be tackled passively; that is, the designer can make sure that the clues about how to proceed are hidden in plain sight. The other alternative is to tackle stagnation actively: Have the game work out whether the player has been wandering around aimlessly and provide a few gentle nudges to guide him in the right direction.

The key point is never to let the player feel bewildered. The players should always feel as if they know what their next move should be. It is no fun to bang your head up against a brick wall simply because you are completely and utterly stuck in a game. This ties in with our earlier piece of advice about making sure the player is adequately provided with information. If a player has to resort to outside assistance—whether by cheating, reading a strategy guide, or looking up the answers on the web—the game designer should view that as a failure of the design.

Avoiding Trivialities

Not many players actually want to be bogged down in the minutiae of myriad trivial decisions when they can be directing the big decisions at a higher level. Forcing the player to decide where the gold is stored when she is trying to build an army and plan a grand strategy is a form of slow torture. Who cares where the gold is stored—just store it.

A trivial decision is a no-brainer decision. Any decision that has only one logical outcome, or where the outcome has no real effect on the game world, is trivial. The player should not be bothered with these. Let the computer handle it and, if necessary, inform the player afterward.

Sid Meier's Alpha Centauri handled this magnificently (see Figure 8.20). In this game, the player can choose to handle every decision in the game, from grand strategy all the way down to unit production and direction. In addition, the player can let a computer-controlled manager control the bases, and the player's units can be set to automatic control. The player has the choice to micromanage every aspect of the game, from the movements of an individual unit all the way up to the overall control of the planet. The important thing here is that the player is given the *choice*. Other games force the player to do all the micromanagement, whether they want to or not.

Figure 8.20 *Sid Meier's Alpha Centauri.*

Worse still, there are games that force completely trivial decisions on the player. If the player wants to choose whether to wear the blue tunic or the red tunic, then fine, but don't force that decision on him as a gameplay choice, unless it has some sort of direct relevance to the gameplay. For example, if the player's avatar needs to be disguised as a guard in the enemies' Red Guards, the blue tunic wouldn't help matters.

To be fair, this sort of trivial decision doesn't crop up as blatantly as this; usually it appears in a more subtle form, disguising the fact that the decision has no value. Note that if this is done well, the trivial decision can actually *add* to the gameplay. It can add depth and flavor to an otherwise shallow game. If you do choose to use it, though, make sure that you use it with care. If you are caught, it will undermine your gameplay.

For an example of how you could use trivial decisions, consider a fictional cops and robbers game. Your officer is patrolling the city as usual, on the lookout for crime, when suddenly he spots a group of suspicious-looking characters on the corner. He stops the car and they immediately run down an alleyway and vanish. Behind the scenes, these people never had any part in the gameplay; they were just flavor to give the impression of a bustling city. The player is not led *too* far down the wrong path—she is just given the impression that there is more to the city than meets the eye.

Setting the Difficulty Level

The first time the players of your game come across balance is when they select the difficulty level. The standard for difficulty levels seems to have evolved into three (or sometimes four) distinct settings: *easy*, *normal*, *hard*, and *nightmare* (or similar assignations), popularized by the original *Doom* from id Software.

Traditionally, not all games have difficulty level settings. For example, adventure games tend to have only one difficulty level—for no good reason, as far as we can see—as do online-only games, although for more sensible reasons. After all, how do you assign a difficulty level to a world made up of avatars for real people? You could segregate players with different experience levels into different areas, graded according to their abilities with tougher monsters and tougher spells, but this doesn't really solve the problem—it just sidesteps it.

Other games have taken a more original approach to the difficulty level problem: self-adjusting games. These games tailor themselves to the player; the more skilled the player, the harder the game gets. *Max Payne* by Remedy Entertainment is a game that claims to implement this (see Figure 8.21). The only problem that we can see with dynamic difficulty level adjustment is the possibility of abuse of the system. After all, what is to stop a skilled player deliberately playing badly just before he gets to a really tough section of the game so the game will go easier on him when he gets there? After he's through the softened-up section, he can resume blasting with his prior skill level until he comes up to another tough section.

Figure 8.21   *Max Payne.*

Generally, the standard difficulty levels are implemented by making the enemies tougher, and they are usually applied as a global modifier for all enemies. Another commonly used approach (sometimes in tandem with increasing toughness) is to make the enemies more numerous. For example, on a normal level, the statistics and number for an enemy might be equivalent to the easy level plus 15 percent, the hard level might be equivalent to the easy level plus 30 percent, and the nightmare level might be equivalent to the easy level plus 50 percent. That is to say, on the normal, hard, and nightmare levels, the enemy toughness or density increases by 15, 30, and 50 percent, respectively. Bear in mind that these are just arbitrary numbers plucked out of thin air; they may not be suitable or even applicable to your game. If you are designing a quiz game, for example, the idea of making the opponents 50-percent tougher is absolutely meaningless. Your only option is to grade questions for difficulty—which is not as easy as you may think, because of subjectivity—and group them into sets based on the difficulty levels that they have been assigned.

Yet another mechanism is to increase the intelligence of enemy creatures by one means or another. In AI research conducted by Dr. John Laird at the University of Michigan, he was able to demonstrate that shortening the intervals between "looking around" on the part of *Quake*-bots contributed more to their success as players than any other tactic. They didn't have to have smarter strategies; they just had to have faster reaction times.

Usually, deciding how to design and implement difficulty level settings is not particularly tricky. In most cases, there is either a de facto standard set of guidelines in place that the game designer can draw on, or it's obvious to the designer based on her knowledge of the design. In any case, choosing how to implement difficulty level settings is by no means the most taxing task the game designer faces.

Tools for Balancing

We have spoken at some length about the act of balancing games. In order to round off this chapter, we are now going to cover some of the techniques that the game designer can use to actually perform this balancing. We will also be exploring some new ideas for balancing games that, even though they are not currently in use, might be useful in the future.

It is beyond the scope of this chapter to go into more than cursory details of these techniques. In some cases, however, they are adequately documented in other places and repeating that information here would be superfluous. Where this is the case, we will attempt to provide pointers to more information on the subject in the appendixes.

Design for Modification

When designing a game, it is sensible to design a core set of rules that the game adheres to and then design the game entities to conform to those rules. This is often a simpler and more intuitive approach than designing entities that each requires its own special considerations. Not only does this make matters simpler when it comes to programming the game—the developers can concentrate on implementing the core rules and then adding entities on top of those core rules, rather than coding each entity separately—it also simplifies tweaking the design.

As long as the core rules are balanced, tweaking them slightly will probably not affect the balance in wild and unpredictable ways. However, if each entity adheres to a separate set of rules, then in all but the simplest games, modifying one entity is independent of any of the others, which could potentially cause balance problems.

Take a game such as Ensemble's *Age of Empires* (see Figure 8.22). All the game entities are governed by the same rules; they have a large set of parameters used to configure those rules to distinguish each entity class. A change to one of these parameters does not require a corresponding code change. During development, the parameters were stored in a Paradox database. This allowed the designers to tweak parameters easily.

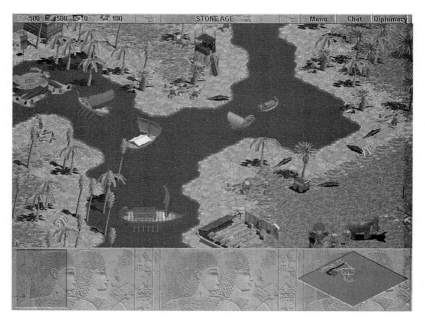

Figure 8.22   *Age of Empires.*

This is an excellent technique to facilitate the easy modification of game balance. Describing implementation techniques is beyond the scope of this book, but this separation of code and data also helps to enforce good development technique. The parameters can be stored in a database during development and then migrated into a custom format for the final release.

Tweaking and Experimental Methods

One of the most important rules to bear in mind is that tweaking parameters randomly is an inefficient and wasteful way to modify balance. A brief digression into correct experimental method is required to ensure that you are making the best use of your time.

The first, and most important, point to remember is to modify only one parameter at a time. Although it may be tempting to tweak a whole bunch of parameters in order to force a result, unless you are extremely lucky, you won't get anything useful. And even if you do, you will have no idea which of the parameter tweaks got you there. Correct experimental method dictates that one parameter should be modified, and then the results should be checked. When initially modifying parameters, don't bother with small changes; Brian Reynolds (of Big Huge Games) suggests doubling or halving the parameter and seeing what it does. From there, you can iteratively move toward the ideal value as efficiently as possible. This makes sense. By changing by such a large factor, you can easily zero in on your optimum setting.

Design Prototyping

Developing a prototype of the gameplay in a simple yet powerful programming language such as Blitz Basic (`www.blitzbasic.com`) can act as a very useful test bed for new gameplay techniques.

There are two main reasons for using a language such as Blitz Basic for prototyping gameplay instead of a more complex language such as C++. The first of these reasons is the ease of use: C++ is complicated and has a steep learning curve. Blitz Basic is simple and has a low-entry barrier. It's easy to learn and is fairly intuitive for the nonprogrammer. A designer could reasonably be expected to pick up the basics in less than a week, and the benefits of being able to test out gameplay concepts without taking time away from developers are incalculable.

The second reason is that it is always a dangerous practice to code any form of prototype in the same language as the main development. The temptation to incorporate the prototype code into the main project can sometimes be overwhelming and is, without fail, a recipe for disaster.

Future Potential

We're going to finish this chapter with a little bit of a blue-sky wish list that we'd like to see. In the games industry, much effort is expended on new technology, but most of this effort is spent on producing in-your-face flashy results. Plumbing—the infrastructure and grunt work of development—just isn't considered as sexy.

Consider this: Manually tweaking parameters to balance a game is, at best, tedious and, at worst, an inefficient use of resources. Although we have not heard of any previous attempts to do so, we feel it would be worth considering the possibility of automating the process to some degree.

In a number of cases, including most of the games that Blizzard Entertainment has produced, the patches for those games have addressed balance issues. One thing that we have considered—and we know of no companies that have tried this—is the possibility of collecting gameplay statistics from players and uploading them (with the player's permission, of course) to a central server, where the results from all the players can be analyzed to determine how well the game is balanced. A further feature could be the automatic downloading of any tweaks to the balance to the player's machine.

In a sense, half of the technology is already in place. Many games now feature auto-patching technology that automatically upgrades a game as soon as an update is available. It's not impossible to imagine that this technology could be implemented as a worthwhile investment if it were produced as a reusable module. There is certainly no reason why it couldn't even be used to customize the data downloaded for each player, based on a profile the player specifies: shift the balance to a harder position for the more advanced players, and vice versa for the novices.

Whether any system such as this has been or will be implemented is not clear, but we feel that it would be a useful tool in the game designer arsenal. After all, it's very difficult to get game balance exactly right on the first few passes. A method by which we could continually tweak a game after release with minimal intervention would be an extremely exciting and useful development.

Internal Economy Worksheet

1. If the game involves conflict between opposing forces, are the capabilities of the forces symmetric or asymmetric? If they are asymmetric, in what ways do they differ, and how will they be balanced? By adjusting costs? By changing rules or probabilities to compensate?
2. Will the starting conditions be symmetric or asymmetric?
3. Are the relationships in the game largely transitive, intransitive, or a mixture? Do you intend to assign shadow costs to balance your transitive relationships?
4. Try to devise a payoff matrix for your game, if possible. Do any dominant strategies appear?
5. Are the challenges in the game solvable only by predefined means, or can they be solved by emergent means?
6. Does the game include positive feedback? If so, what features will it include to avoid runaway victory for the first player who gets ahead? A time delay? Negative feedback? A random factor?
7. Is the player's goal in the game to restore, maintain, or destroy a balance of some kind?
8. Do the game's challenges increase steadily in difficulty, or are there peaks and troughs, or spikes, in the difficulty level? If so, where are they?
9. Does the game contain any elements that the player might perceive to be unfair? If the game must cheat in order to provide a decent challenge, can you disguise the cheating in such a way that the player does not notice it?
10. How will the player know what to do next? What features does the game include to prevent stagnation?
11. To what degree is the player required to micromanage the game? Is the player obliged to look after trivia? Are there mechanisms by which the player can delegate some of these responsibilities to an automated process? If so, can the player be confident the automated process will make intelligent choices?
12. What mechanisms, if any, will there be for changing the game's difficulty level? Hints? Shortcuts? Cheats? A difficulty setting? How will the difficulty setting change the nature of the challenges offered? Will it make the enemies tougher or weaker, smarter or more stupid? Will it add or remove challenges entirely?

Putting It Together

Balancing a game is a complex and demanding task. This chapter has discussed a number of approaches to the problem of balancing gameplay. The following list summarizes these points.

A balanced game should:

➤ Be internally consistent.

➤ Ensure that victory is determined by player skill, not random factors.

➤ Ensure that all players have access to the same or functionally equivalent core options.

➤ Ensure that attributes for which the player pays with points are orthogonal.

➤ Ensure that combination and emergence don't destroy the balance.

➤ Provide a consistent challenge.

➤ Provide the player with a perceivably fair playing experience.

➤ Avoid stagnation.

➤ Avoid trivialities.

➤ Allow setting of difficulty level (where appropriate).

We're not even going to pretend that this chapter is an all-encompassing, thorough treatment of game balance. The subject could take up a whole book by itself. What we have put forth here is a brief summary of the areas that interest us. There is no guarantee that you will find them as valuable as we have—in fact, it's probable that you have other methods for game balancing that work just as well, if not better, or that cover different situations that we have not covered because of space considerations. Our main aim in this chapter (and, in fact, in this book) is to get you thinking about these issues. Then, even if you don't agree with our conclusions (and feel free to email us stating your case), our aims will have been achieved.

Part II

The Genres of Games

Chapter 9

Action Games

The designation "action game" covers a wide range of game styles, both 3D and 2D. But all games categorized under this label invariably have one aspect in common—they are all twitch games. The key skills tested by the gameplay are reaction time and hand-eye coordination under pressure. Action games tend to be simpler than most other types because there is only so much information and complexity that the average brain can interpret in unit time. As a general rule, this relationship can be stated as an inverse proportionality between the speed of a game and the complexity.

Action games are the oldest genre—the very first arcade games were mainly action games, because the nature of the beast is exemplified in its simplicity. The game mechanics and gameplay are very simple and, provided the presentation layer is correspondingly simple, they are ideally suited to the lower spec (and older) machines.

Action Game Genres

For the purposes of discussion, the "action game" genre can be further divided into two sub-genres: those with shooting and those without. These sub-genres can be further divided, but at this point we would start to get into technology based distinctions—that is, the divisions are dependent on the technology used to present the game. For example, some people consider that the first-person shooter (FPS) is a genre in its own right. We can see this point of view, and it is a valid one under some circumstances. However, the key skill used in a FPS is reaction-based, and hence we'll be approaching all games that rely on reaction times as their key playing hook as a single genre. This is not as useless as it may seem. The fundamental patterns of action games—whether 2D, 3D, shooting, or non-shooting—are the same, no matter what the presentation layer.

So, given that we could argue that any distinctions within the action genre are pretty much arbitrary, we'll bravely soldier on with our basic division into shooters and non-shooters. Characteristically (and rather stereotypically) shooter games tend to appeal more to the male demographic, and non-shooters tend (although much more loosely) to appeal to female gamers more. (Consider that *Pac-Man* was one of the first wildly successful games to have a roughly equal male/female player split. However, it's clear that this is not the only factor—*Centipede*, a game that certainly involved violence, was also fairly successful with females.)

Dividing the genre into shooters and non-shooters is useful, but it's still not quite fine-grained enough to be able to discuss the genre fully. The elements and rules can, for the most part, still be applied to just the two divisions, but there are certain issues that need to be covered in specific areas. Let's look at each of these divisions in a little more detail, and cover some of the types of game that are included in each of the divisions.

Almost all action games use a number of common elements that are covered in this chapter, such as **lives**, **reaction tests**, and **hand-eye coordination tests**. Many of them also use the **levels**, **waves**, and **power-up** design elements. Less common nowadays, but originally very common (possibly due to hardware limitations), is the **single-screen** element.

We will be discussing all of these elements later in the chapter. Before we do that, we will examine each of our initial genre divisions in turn, starting with the shooters.

Shooters

Shooters make up the majority of action games. Shooter games (despite their designation) don't always involve explicit shooting, but they do focus on violence as a major game mechanic. Shooters generally—but not always—focus on the actions of the avatar using some sort of weapon. Usually, this weapon is a gun, or some other long-range weapon. A smaller portion of these makes use of local effect weapons, as in the case of fighting games, ranging from games such as the *Street Fighter* series to the modern tour de force of *Dead or Alive 3*. Screens from both are shown in Figure 9.1.

Figure 9.1   Fighting games.

Usually, this particular class of game presents a similar interface, showing both fighters onscreen at once. Even if a fighting game is portrayed in 3D, the main playing region is the vertical 2D plane defined by drawing a straight line between the two fighters. Thus, almost without exception, the "3D" fighting game is still played in a 2D sense, no matter how much eye candy is thrown your way. Of course, 3D isn't the main area of innovation in fighting games, although the added realism it can provide is certainly worthwhile. For the most part, the area of innovation in fighting games is in the realism of the characters, (including their interactions with each other and their reactions to injury), and the methods used to control the fighters—especially when considering how to handle special moves and combos. The main elements found within fighting games are variants of rock-paper-scissors (to handle the outcomes of playing certain moves against another) and the **combo move**.

Of course, the majority of games involving violence are actually "shooters." There are two broad classes that we will consider here: first-person shooters (FPS) such as *Quake III*, *Unreal Tournament*, and *Return to Castle Wolfenstein*, and 2D shooters such as *R-Type*, *Space Tripper*, *Commando*, *Gauntlet Legends*, *Space Invaders*, *Robotron*, *Defender*, *Uridium*, and *Centipede*. Even though this list of games seems to include many that are not similar to the others, they all share the common attributes of an avatar, one or more ranged weapons, and a varying number of enemies. Each of the games take place in an arena designed to require a strategic use of the weapon(s) and of any other tools that the player's avatar may be provided with. Figures 9.2 to 9.5 show a selection of these games.

The reason that this particular range of 2D games has been chosen is that the gameplay has been enduring enough to have inspired modern updates. This implies that these games have some admirable qualities that we would do well to emulate. Of course, not all the updated versions have succeeded in capturing the gameplay of their parents as well as the designer might hope; in other cases, however, the gameplay matches or exceeds the original.

The original versions of the games were all completely 2D, because they were all written way before the hardware to support advanced 3D graphics had even been conceived of. With so little hardware power, the focus couldn't really be on the graphics or flashy effects, so all the focus went into the gameplay. Fortunately, the developers of the updated versions realized this, and for the most part, they succeeded in the difficult task of preserving the gameplay while updating the appearance to keep up with modern standards.

The original *Gauntlet* was one of the first games that provided the option for cooperative multi-play (see Figure 9.2). Each player could take on one of four avatars (Warrior, Wizard, Valkyrie, and Elf), and adventure through an (almost) endless series of dungeons, searching for treasure and food. This game introduced (more or less) many of the common action game elements we will be discussing later, such as the **locked door and key**, **monster generators**, **team play**, and **dungeon exit**.

There have been many updates for the classic *Gauntlet*, starting with the immediate sequel, *Gauntlet II*. Some have been more successful than others. The most recent of these updates, *Gauntlet Legends*, brings the graphics and environment up to date, adding a backstory and some extra features, but still manages to maintain the core of the old game mechanic.

Figure 9.2 *Gauntlet* and *Gauntlet Legends*.

Similarly, the original *Robotron 2084* was a classic game when it was released into arcades back in 1982 (see Figure 9.3). The sole object of this game was to defend the last human family against wave upon wave of killing machines bent on their destruction. Another notable feature was the ability to shoot independently of the direction in which the avatar was moving. This was controlled by a second joystick.

The strength of the *Robotron* gameplay meant that for many years, updates just didn't happen. In fact, you can still get pixel-perfect versions of *Robotron 2084* for the PC, Gameboy Advance, and other consoles. The first updated version (that we know of) was more of a tribute to the original *Robotron* than an update—*Super Smash TV*, based around a TV show where the contestants battled hordes of attackers in single-screen arenas.

The first "official" update of this game, *Robotron X*, heralded the start of the "retrogaming" fad, and updated the graphics to 3D. The gameplay (apart from a few extra bonus levels) was barely touched, but the shift to 3D negatively impacted the playability.

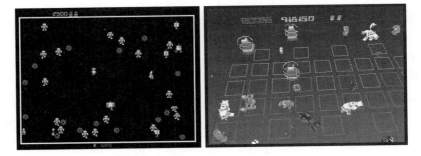

Figure 9.3   *Robotron 2084* and *Robotron X*.

The advantage of the original *Robotron* was that all the action could be viewed onscreen at one time (using the **single-screen** design element). The 3D update, with its swooping camera, often obscured parts of the playing area. This meant that occasionally you would be killed by an enemy that suddenly appeared from an off-camera region—an impossibility in the original game. This detracts from the playability because it is not the player's fault that he cannot see offscreen. In the original *Robotron*, if the player died, it *was* his fault—all the information was there to be interpreted, so he had no excuses if he failed to react to the situation quickly enough to avoid the danger.

Centipede is yet another classic arcade game from the early days (see Figure 9.4). This game is often lauded as an example of near-perfect gameplay. The elements of the game are set up in such a way as to balance out perfectly and exhibit many interesting emergent properties. The player has to make informed choices about when and how to clear the mushrooms—too many, and the centipede has an easier time reaching you and is harder to hit; too few, and more enemies appear to add more mushrooms.

Hasbro, flushed with the success of their *Frogger* remake, which sold millions of copies, decided to try again with a new remake. The remake of *Centipede* added 3D graphics, and a story. Unfortunately, something was lost during the process, and the gameplay suffered as a consequence. Even the inclusion of a pseudo-3D version of the original arcade game failed to save this attempt at retro-chic. One of the keys behind the playability of the original *Centipede* (and, in fact, a consistent theme running through all successful action games) was that the player did not have to *think* in order to interpret what was on the screen. It was easy, and took place at a subconscious level: The centipede is one color, mushrooms are another color, and spiders are yet another color. Unfortunately, this use of color to provide information was lost in the update, where the emphasis was on the graphics appearing realistically textured and interesting. Unfortunately, that meant that the players' subconscious had to work that much harder to be able to determine what was happening onscreen. Combine this with the shift from a 2D fixed play-field to a fully scrolling 3D world, and it becomes fairly easy to understand why this update failed to maintain the standards set by the original.

Figure 9.4   *Centipede* and *Centipede 3D.*

As shown in Figure 9.5, the space shooter is one of the oldest styles of games. From the venerable *Space Invaders* through to modern masterpieces such as *Space Tripper*, this has been a class of game that is consistently popular. One of the fondly remembered classic games from the days of 8-bit computers is *Uridium*, a game that puts the player in a

Manta assault craft on a one-man attack run against a fleet of enemy space stations. As the Manta flies from left to right, waves of aliens and missiles launched from the stations converge on the player. The space stations were huge, spanning several screen-widths, and so the player had to be aware of what was happening not only on the visible screen he could see, but also in the much larger region that he could not. This was a mechanic lifted straight from Williams' *Defender*, although *Uridium* is played from a top-down view, not a side view. This class of game requires extremely good reflexes on the part of the player, and additionally, the ability to form a mental model of what was happening outside the bounds of the screen. There are two main classes of scrolling shooter—those with fixed scrolling, where the screen would continuously scroll in one direction such as Irem's *R-Type*, and those with variable scrolling, where the player had some degree of control over the scroll direction.

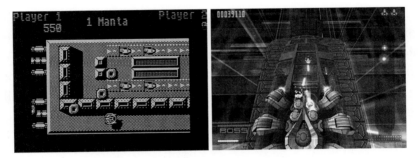

Figure 9.5   *Uridium* and *Space Tripper*.

Usually the degree of control was limited. Common configurations included horizontal, vertical, 4-way, 8-way, and multi-way scrolling. For players to be able to form the mental model required for successful play, a different technique is required for each of these types. The fixed scrolling games relied more often than not on memory. As well as reaction-time challenges, they also used memory challenges. A player learned the game as she played; if she got killed in a particular spot once, then she would learn the pattern of enemies for the next time around and hopefully wouldn't suffer the same fate. This was also used (although not to the same all-encompassing extent) in the variably scrolling games. In most cases, it certainly did the player no harm to remember the rough order of enemy attack, but the gameplay was not centered on that as a core mechanism. Instead, this class of game often provided players with a **mini-map** that displayed the game world in miniature, giving them an idea of what to expect to appear next on the edge of their screens. *Space Tripper*, from PomPom (www.pompom. org.uk), is a modern update of the archetypal scrolling shooter using 3D graphics and focuses on the core gameplay of the genre. Similar in concept to *Uridium*, it succeeds by using the 3D graphics solely as a presentation method. The actual game makes little use of the third dimension—except occasionally for dramatic effect—and remains, for the most part, a 2D game. This is what makes it so effective—the developers have not succumbed to the temptation to make 3D an important part of the gameplay. For this style of fast-action game, it's hard enough maneuvering in 2D—to do so in 3D would be an order of magnitude more difficult.

Figure 9.6 shows two examples of the logical extension of the 2D shooter—the 3D FPS. This is the ultimate expression of the shooter side of the genre. Fully 3D FPS games are an entirely different animal from their 2D ancestors. For a start, they are bound by hardware limitations to a much greater extent than 2D games. This can be clearly seen from the early 3D FPS games such as *Battlezone*, where there were no more than two or three enemies at one time. Even more recent games, such as *Quake III*, have comparatively few enemies present. Of course, this is not just due to hardware issues (which will become much less of an issue over the next few years). It's also due to perspective issues. The player can only interpret and handle so much information at one time, and shifting the perspective to full 3D complicates this. This will be explained in more detail in the later section on game perspectives.

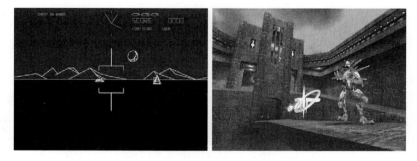

Figure 9.6 *Battlezone* and *Quake III*.

Non-Shooters

Many games—particularly in the early years of the industry before commercial pressures intervened to the levels they have today—were non-violent. This proliferation of non-violent games with strange themes is often likened to the early days of the movie industry, where creativity was the highest driving force, before the big money moved in.

Today, most games seem to be aimed at the typical male 25-35 demographic, but there are still notable exceptions. As we've already stated, the non-violent games seem to appeal more to the female demographic. One of the reasons for this, we feel, is that by removing the easy option of violence, the designer has to think a little bit harder about how to provide the gameplay hooks.

Notable "non-shooter" action games include *Marble Madness*, *Lode Runner*, *Pac-Man*, *Chuckie Egg*, the *Mario* games, *Q*Bert*, *Super Monkey Ball 1 and 2*, *Pong*, *Donkey Kong*, and *Frogger*. All these games have the same non-violence motif running through them (although the latter two *are* arguable). The primary reason for this is because the games were (to a greater or lesser extent, depending on the game) designed to be appealing to children, particularly in the case of the *Mario* series of games.

Frogger, shown in Figure 9.7, was originally a highly successful arcade game released back in 1981. The aim of the game was to get the world's only non-swimming frog family across a busy road and a logging river infested with crocodiles and fickle turtles. From these humble beginnings sprang one of the most successful series of remakes of all time. Hasbro's remake of *Frogger* (also shown in Figure 9.7) sold millions of copies, and was a mainstay of the software charts for many months after release. Interestingly enough, the developers focused on keeping the gameplay virtually unchanged, and just updated the presentation, increasing the variety of the levels available to the player. *Frogger 2*, released several years later, introduced a more structured game, while still remaining faithful to the core gameplay of the original.

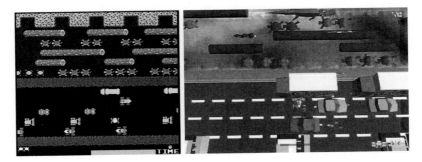

Figure 9.7   *Frogger* and *Frogger 3D*.

Of course, the phenomenal success of the *Frogger* remake caused a scramble for licenses for further remakes, which the publishers viewed as a license to print money. Consequently, there have been a number of ill-advised and hastily conceived remakes released onto the market. *Pac-Man* was one of the most successful games of its generation. Obviously, it could not escape being remade. One of the (many) remakes was *Pac-Man: Adventures in Time*. This update brought new additions to the game, including a story and a set of themed levels. Unfortunately, much in the same way as with *Centipede*, these additions diminished rather than added to the gameplay. However, *Pac-Man World 2* on the Gamecube is an excellent use of the license.

Another phenomenally successful game was *Q*Bert*, initially released in 1982. This game placed a strange orange character on a pyramid of cubes, who was then chased by enemies including a cascade of balls and an evil snake named Coily. The object of the game was to change all the cubes to a target color by landing on them one or more times. The remake (shown on the right in Figure 9.8) followed the familiar pattern of adding a story and updating the presentation. Fortunately, due to the quasi-3D appearance of the original game, the gameplay translated well to the update, and the story doesn't affect the gameplay negatively, aside from minor issues caused by the entire playing area not being visible on the screen at one time.

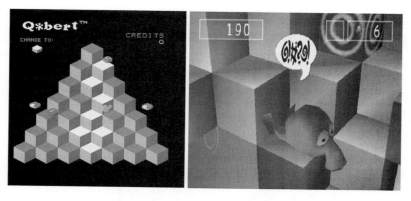

Figure 9.8 *Q*Bert* and *Q*Bert 3D*.

Design Elements

Action games are a good source of distinct design elements, mainly because their relative simplicity makes analysis of their game mechanics fairly easy compared to the more complex genres.

What we are attempting to do when we are extracting design elements from games on a genre-by-genre basis is to form the basis of a genre-describing "meta-game." What we mean by meta-game is a description of an archetypal action game. Of course, such a construct is purely hypothetical. It would be pretty much impossible to actually produce a fully comprehensive document. So with this in mind, let's start with an analysis of the design elements that govern the rules of the game. These design elements are only a small subset of the whole, but the aim is to give a starting point for your own investigations into the gameplay mechanics of action games.

The Rules

The rules of an action game describe the basic game mechanics. They are usually very simple because of the frenetic nature of the gameplay. Fundamentally, action games are games that require skill as the primary factor for play, not rote memorization of complex rules.

There are many design elements that we can examine here, and the following few sections will cover some of these. Note that words in bold indicate references to other design elements within this chapter.

Levels

Action games are often split into a succession of levels. A *level* is a specifically defined area in the game arena, in which the objective for the player is to complete a specific task. When the task is finished, the level is complete. Each level is played until complete, and upon completion the player's avatar is moved to the next level, and play continues. Generally, the difficulty will increase with each subsequent level.

Often, levels are grouped by theme. All the themed levels in the set will have a similar appearance and set of enemies. A set of themed levels usually ends with an encounter with a **big boss**. In some cases, the boss has to be defeated with the use of **power-ups** and/or skills that the player gained during the preceding level set.

Checkpoints

If the nature of the game is such that the player progresses through a level, then the position that the player's avatar appears in after a **life** has been lost is often determined by the use of checkpoints.

The most straightforward form of checkpoint is that the avatar appears in the same location where it died, or in the case where that is impossible (for example, Mario falling into water), then it appears in the last safe location before it died (for example, the last platform that Mario was on before he fell in the water). The state of the level is unchanged—the avatar just reincarnates, and play continues.

Other (more difficult) games, such as *Space Tripper*, simply restart the level from the beginning upon avatar death. This particular form is fairly rare, because it increases the game challenge significantly, and often causes player frustration. It requires that the player play a "perfect" level in order to progress to the next one.

The final form of this design element is an amalgam between the first two. As the player progresses through the level, he reaches a number of predefined checkpoints. When the avatar dies, the level is reset to the last checkpoint that the player success-fully achieved. An example of a classic game that uses this form is *Moon Patrol*, shown in Figure 9.9.

Figure 9.9 *Moon Patrol.*

Lives

The player's avatar is usually given a small number of reprieves from death. Initially, the number of lives provided usually ranges from between three and five. A life is lost by collision with an enemy or some other dangerous structure. Extra lives can be earned either by picking up a **power-up** or reaching a certain **score** threshold multiple. The player's avatar is usually invulnerable for a few seconds when reappearing after losing a life, in order for the player to gather his bearings. When all lives are lost, the game is over.

Often, this design element appears in conjunction with the **energy** design element. If this occurs, then the avatar isn't destroyed immediately on contact with the enemy. Instead, energy is drained from the avatar. When all the energy is drained, a life is lost. When all lives are lost, the game is over.

Energy

The player's avatar is given a limited amount of energy, some of which is depleted when the avatar is injured. It can often be partially, or even fully, replenished by the use of a **collectible** or a **power-up**. When the avatar's energy is depleted, the game is over.

This design element is sometimes used in conjunction with the **lives** design element. In this case, when the avatar's energy is depleted, one of the lives are lost. Sometimes the energy is spread over a number of physical features—for example, it can be a limited resource that is shuffled between shields and fuel, requiring the player to carefully balance resources.

Time Limit

The time limit design element is indicated by the use of a timer that counts down from some initial value to zero. When the timer reaches zero, an action occurs that causes a major event in the game.

The time limit is normally used in one of three ways. The first way is as a **level** timer. The player has a limited amount of time to complete the level, and if he fails to do so, the level is reset, and the player has to start again. Often, this is accompanied by a life loss and, if the level is finished with time left over, then this excess time is multiplied by a constant as a **score** bonus.

The second use of the time limit design element is as the countdown to a catastrophe. The player has to achieve some task before the timer runs out, or the task will become much more difficult to achieve. This particular form is used in *Sinistar*. When the timer runs out, it means that the eponymous Sinistar has been built, and the player is in a lot of trouble.

The third use of the time limit design element is to limit the effectiveness of **power-ups**. When the timer runs out, the temporary power-up that it governed is removed, and the player's avatar reverts to the normal state. *Pac-Man's* power pellets, which allow the Pac-Man to eat the ghosts for a limited time, are good examples of this form.

Score

One feature that is often specific to action games is the score indicator. Often in an action game, the only indicator of progress is a score. It is how the player is intended to measure her success against others. Many types of games do not use the score pattern, but action games are pretty much centered around it.

Scores are recorded in high-score tables for posterity, and to provide bragging rights for the very best players. Many games also reward skillful play with bonus scores and multipliers. The classic example of the score multiplier in action can be found in *Pac-Man*: After getting the power pill, the first ghost eaten earns 200 points, the next earns 400 points, then 800, and then 1600 respectively. Hence, skillful play is rewarded with higher and higher scores.

Power-Ups

One of the staple design elements of action games is the power-up. As a reward for progress, the player is given the opportunity to increase the strength of his avatar. In the case of a shooter, this can come in the form of stronger weapons or shields.

Power-ups come in two main strains: permanent and temporary. A permanent power-up is one that remains with the avatar for the remainder of the game (or at least the current life or level). *Space Tripper* (and many other shoot 'em-ups) uses this model. *Space Tripper* is unique, however, in that when the avatar dies, only power-ups gained on that level are lost.

Temporary power-ups are usually short lived (anything from a few seconds up to a couple of minutes) and provide the avatar with a powerful advantage for a short time (such as shields). The general rule is that the more powerful the advantage, the shorter the time it is available for. The Quad Damage power-up in *Quake III* is a perfect example of this. An alternative to the time limit is to allow a certain amount of usage. For example, shields may be used up after they are powered on for a certain period of time, or after a certain number of hits.

One interesting aspect of power-ups that is used in quite a few games is the concept of power points. The player is awarded a certain number of "points" to spend on an upgrade, and then to a certain degree, the player is allowed to decide how he wants to upgrade his avatar. *Space Tripper* has two main weapons; the weapon that is currently selected is the one that is upgraded. Successful play requires that the player balance the upgrade points between both weapons.

A specialized case of the power-up is the **combo move**. This is more often found in fighting games, and is a power-up that relies on the skill of the player to execute a sequence of commands with exact timing. The reward for success is a special move that devastates the opponent's defenses. The effectiveness of the move is often related to the difficulty of execution—a period of time in which the avatar is open to attack. Thus, more difficult combos carry higher risk.

Collectibles

Collectibles are bonus objects that allow the player to augment his score. They are not essential to the game, and are often used just to augment the player's score. The player is not penalized for failing to collect them, but if he can justify the risk, then the rewards are high.

In some cases, collectibles can unlock secret levels or cause special bonus events. For example, in *Rainbow Islands*, one means by which the player could kill enemies was by collapsing rainbows onto them. Enemies killed in this fashion deposited crystals that could be collected for bonus points. If these crystals were collected in the right order (red, orange, yellow, green, blue, indigo, violet), then a doorway to a secret level would be opened, which gave the player a huge score and a permanent secret **power-up**.

Smart Bombs

Defender was the first game to introduce the concept of the smart bomb (see Figure 9.10). Smart bombs are used to get the player out of a difficult situation when no other options are available.

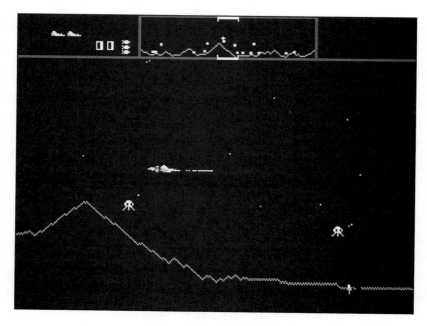

Figure 9.10   *Defender.*

Usually, the player is given a strictly limited number of smart bombs, and opportunities to replace them are either extremely rare or non-existent. The function of the smart bomb is to clear the area immediately surrounding the player of enemies. Usually, this means that the visible area is cleared entirely of enemies, but the range cleared does vary dependent on the game. Smart bombs should be used by the player only in dire emergencies when there are no other options available. The scarcity of availability is the primary mechanism available to enforce this.

Hyperspace

Hyperspace is another mechanism for getting the player out of trouble. However, unlike the **smart bomb**, the hyperspace design element is just as likely to land the avatar in an equally difficult situation as it is to get it to safety.

The first commonly known game to make use of the hyperspace element was *Asteroids*, shown in Figure 9.11. When the avatar was in immediate danger of being destroyed by an oncoming asteroid, the player could hit the hyperspace button, which would instantly move the player to another part of the screen. The amount of times the player can hyperspace is unlimited. This is because the usefulness of the hyperspace is balanced out by the chances that the avatar could appear in a worse situation than before. Hence, the choice of whether to use the hyperspace is tempered by the risks involved in doing so. Ironically, the more necessary it is to use it (the more debris of the playfield), the more risk there is to the player.

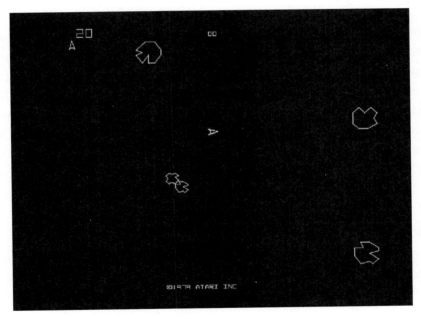

Figure 9.11   *Asteroids.*

Waves

During a level, the enemies that confront the player's avatar can be introduced in a number of ways (generally called *waves*). There are two common ways that this is achieved. The difference between these two methods is in how the enemies appear.

With the first method, the layout and scheduled appearance times of the enemies are (for the most part) pre-scripted. There are very little (if any) random materializations of enemies. This has been used in games from the original *Space Invaders* to more recent games such as *Max Payne* and many others. In these types of games, the points at which the enemies appear are predefined, and an integral part of the level design. Of course, once they do appear, they can either follow a previously scripted attack formation, or rely on their own AI to locate and attack the player.

The second way of approaching wave formation is to make the enemies materialize randomly. Usually, there is some sort of algorithm determining which sort of enemies will appear, in order to maintain some sort of smooth difficulty progression. Often, the location and type of the enemy is selected from a small pool of variants for the particular level, as defined by the designer.

With both methods, the general usage is as follows. Throughout a level, the enemies arrive in some sort of formation. These formations will vary in composition to include a selection of enemies appropriate to the current challenge level. As the game progresses further, the formation composition will include stronger enemies. In some cases, the earlier weaker enemies will be phased out of the line-up, because they will no longer provide an effective challenge to the player. The enemies increase in difficulty and numbers as the player progresses in an environment, reaching a peaked frenzy at the end of the level. After this point, the environment changes and the intensity reduces to the initial point or somewhere just a bit higher.

The Big Boss

A traditional staple of action games are the boss characters. In many games, the end of a group of themed levels is guarded by a large enemy—the boss character—who is significantly harder to fight than any of the previously encountered enemies.

Defeating the boss takes the player to a new set of levels, with a different theme. Boss characters often can't be hurt by normal methods and require a special attack method to be damaged. For example, they could be invincible at certain times (i.e., Piranha Plants in *Super Mario Sunshine* can be hurt only when their mouths are open) or can be hurt only by certain weapons.

Often, the boss character is themed after the environment (or vice versa). For example, the first set of levels in *Parasol Stars* are themed after musical instruments. The left side of Figure 9.12 shows the first boss, which is in keeping with the musical theme.

Another boss design element that is used fairly frequently is to use a much bigger and stronger version of an enemy that the player has already encountered. The right side of Figure 9.12 shows a classic example, taken from *Rainbow Islands*. The first set of levels are garden themed (with the enemies being mainly insects and birds). One of the first enemies encountered is a spider. The boss character is simply a much larger version of that spider. This enhances the gameplay by allowing the player to predict some of the boss behavior, and gives him a small advantage in knowing what to expect—an advantage that would not be there if the boss was entirely unfamiliar, and the player had to learn his behavior from scratch.

Figure 9.12 The first bosses in *Parasol Stars* and *Rainbow Islands*.

Of course, many games aren't suited for such an unsubtle set of themed levels, but even so, the themed level and big boss are one of the mainstay design elements of action games. The pattern of a succession of levels increasing in difficulty and challenge to a climax with the boss, before starting again at a slightly lower difficulty level, is present in virtually every level-based action-based game today. This is shown in Figure 9.13.

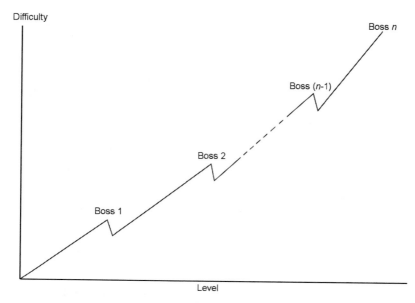

Figure 9.13   The general progression of an action game.

Wildcard Enemies

In order to break up the predictability of predefined waves, many games use a randomly spawned wildcard enemy to provide a fresh challenge to the player, and break up the predictability of wave-based gameplay.

For example, the Atari game *Asteroids* has predictable waves because, once they have appeared, the movement of the asteroids are completely deterministic—except at the instance where they are shot and break up into smaller asteroids. However, at random points during the wave, an enemy UFO appears and follows a non-deterministic path, shooting at the player.

Another example is the *Galaxian* dive-bombers that break away from the main body of the wave and swoop down on the player's avatar. Wildcard enemies are usually a completely different class of enemy from level bosses, in that they are normally mixed in with normal enemies, and behave in a somewhat random or unexpected way.

Locked Door and Key

The player encounters a locked door that requires a key to open it. The key (which is not necessarily a physical key) is hidden somewhere in the level, and must be found in order to open the door.

This is a common method used to partition levels, and to control the player's progress in order to manage the gameplay delivery. This particular design element is often strung together in a sequence of several overlapping instances, where a key is used to open a door to give access to another key, which in turn opens another door that the player encountered previously. *Doom* is a particularly good example of this.

This design element should be used with caution. If it is used too liberally, then it tends to make the gameplay feel clichéd, tedious, and old-fashioned. However, it can be very effective if some originality is applied to the design element, specifically in terms of how you implement the door/key mechanism. Remember, it doesn't have to be a traditional door and key. That would be boring, and has been done too many times. A door and key are just a conceptual representation of a construct that requires an effort (the key) on the part of the player to pass an obstacle (the door). A slightly more creative example is the use of this design element in *Grand Theft Auto III*. To open up new cities for play, certain difficult missions must be completed first.

Monster Generators

Gauntlet (and its various sequels) was one of the first games to feature a monster generator. The concept of a monster generator is simple: It's an object that generates fresh enemies to confront the player.

The monster generator isn't always visible: for example, enemy spawn points in games such as *Doom* are not explicit objects. Instead, the monsters just appear out of thin air in a flash of green light—usually out of the sight of the player.

The difference between the use of monster generators in *Gauntlet* and *Doom* is substantial. In *Gauntlet*, monster generators are an integral part of the gameplay—destroy the monster generators, and no more monsters will appear. Hence, the player has two main strategies: Fight the monsters, or destroy the generator. In terms of survival, the dominant strategy is to destroy the monster generators before they can spawn too many monsters, but if players are aiming for the high score, then they may hold off on destroying the monster generator until they have boosted their scores sufficiently. You can see in this case that the monster generators are not only an integral part of the gameplay, but they can play a strategic role too.

In *Doom*, however, the monster generators are much more behind the scenes. All players know is that monsters are appearing—they are not given the opportunity to destroy the generators to prevent this from happening. The only sensible strategy under these circumstances is to avoid or destroy the monsters, and get to the level exit as quickly as possible.

Monster generators—whether represented by a physical object or not—can have other attributes too. The most obvious of these is whether the generator will spawn an infinite number of monsters or just a limited amount before being spent. If the monster generator spawns infinitely, then you may want to consider the possibility of allowing the player to destroy it.

Another consideration is whether the monster generator will spawn only one type of enemy, or whether it has a range of enemies at its disposal. This can either be a static relationship or can be tied in with the difficulty level.

Dungeon Exits and Level Warps

The dungeon exit signifies a transition within the game. Usually, this transition involves progressing to a new level, or a new area within the current level. The dungeon exit design element often is used as a goal or sub-goal of the current level. In other cases, it is merely an enabler, allowing the player to move between different areas while she attempts to complete other goals.

The dungeon exit is usually guarded by enemies and/or is well-hidden. The strength of the guard force and the difficulty in locating an exit is usually in direct relationship to the benefits of locating it. A common variant on this element is to provide more than one exit to a certain level. One of these is the standard exit, which takes the player to the next level. The second is a warp exit, which will jump the player ahead several levels. This second exit (often visible when you find the first) is difficult to reach, and requires extra sacrifice on the part of the player. The reward is usually proportional to the level of sacrifice, and this particular variation has been used in many games—from *Defender: Stargate* (allowing experienced players to warp ahead to the more challenging levels) to *Gauntlet* (where alternative exits would jump the player ahead by a few levels for the same reasons as *Stargate*) to games such as *Luigi's Mansion* and the *Super Mario* series (where some levels have hidden exits that lead to secret areas). If there is a hidden exit, you may want to give the player a subtle clue. For example, in *Super Mario World*, levels with secret exits are shown as flashing red dots (rather than flashing yellow dots) on the world overview map.

Mini-Maps

As action games became more complex, the play area began to span multiple screens of action, although the player still needed to be aware of what was going on in the game-world not visible onscreen.

The solution to this was to place a small dynamically updated map or radar display in the status display. There are several common configurations used for this. The original configuration was used in *Defender* and showed the entire game world to the player. Another configuration does not show the entire game world to the player, merely showing a zoomed-out view of the area surrounding the player. Williams' *Sinistar* used this approach, augmented with a text status line to notify the player of important events occurring outside of the scanner range.

A third configuration that we'll mention here—although it is used more often in other genres that are not so action oriented—is to have the map build up as the player explores. Areas that the player has not yet visited do not show up on the map. When the player visits them, they are drawn, and the map remains in the same form and is not updated further until the player revisits the area.

Victory Conditions

Action games—being among the first of the genres—benefited well from the early experimental years of the industry. The plots and settings of the early action games were many and varied, usually very original, and with the amount of extraneous story kept to a minimum; consequently, the nature of the victory conditions were for the most part simple and clear. The vast majority of games have a clear set of victory conditions, which are made clear to the player from the outset. In some cases—particularly in the case of action games—these victory conditions are illusory. For example, the accompanying blurb for *Space Invaders* talks about the player saving the Earth from the evil alien invaders. However, as anyone who has played the game is aware, after you've saved the Earth from one wave of evil invaders, another appears to take their place. And so on, ad infinitum, with each wave getting faster and more aggressive, until the player is overwhelmed.

Case Study 9.1   A Flawed Victory Condition

In some games, the victory condition is a result of a bug that prevents the player from progressing any further. This is surprisingly common, due to the fact that the developers of such games usually didn't test that far into the game. The most well-known example of this is probably *Pac-Man*.

For years, people have been attempting to get a perfect score on *Pac-Man*. In July of 1999, Billy Mitchell of Fort Lauderdale, Florida scored a perfect 3,333,360 points on a *Pac-Man* machine in Weirs Beach, New Hampshire. The perfect score is achieved by playing for six hours, through 256 levels of *Pac-Man*, eating every pellet, power-pill, blue ghost, and piece of fruit on every single level, without dying once. After the 256th level, the game freezes.

When he stepped away from the game after beating it, he said "I never have to play that darn game again…".

What can be derived from this is the observation that action games generally have one or zero victory conditions. They are split into two broad classes: those that are possible to win, and those where it is possible only to attain the highest score. Most early action games were of the latter class—mainly due to memory constraints. In later years, when the processing power and storage capabilities increased, developers began incorporating structured stories into their games—and with stories, come endings. Games such as *Golden Axe* (shown in Figure 9.14) had definite endings where, after the defeat of the big bad end-of-game boss (in this case, Death Adder), the players' avatars lived happily ever after (until the inevitable sequel comes along, of course).

Figure 9.14   *Golden Axe.*

As such, action games are unusual because the victory conditions are either crystal clear and known to the player in advance, or completely non-existent, being wrapped in an amorphous goal that can never be attained, such as the previously mentioned *Space Invaders*. Finding something between these two extremes is rare, mainly because it pushes the game away from being a pure action game into another genre entirely.

Interaction Model

The primary model in action games is based purely on fast interactions—hand-eye coordination and reaction speed. The ability to think quickly and analyze situations almost instantaneously is favored as well. The player is usually given direct control over a single avatar. In order to efficiently translate the player's intent into actions within the game, the control methods for action games are usually extremely simple. Even so, various action games have attempted to implement more complex control schemes. The success of these games depended on the lengths to which players were prepared to go to learn the system. Games that succeed in this are usually the games that set the standards for new genres. For example, the *Doom* and *Quake* modes of interaction for FPS games are pretty much ubiquitous nowadays. Similarly, the *Super Mario 64* control system has become the de facto standard control system for most console-based 3D platform games.

Often, the ability to analyze the situation in a particular game is a learned process developed through playing that particular game. In some cases, the skills learned playing one game can be applied to other games, with varying levels of transferability. For example, the skills learned when playing *Space Invaders* can be transferred wholesale over to other games such as *Galaxians* and, to a lesser extent, *Centipede*. There are several levels to the nature of the skills developed by playing certain games, and these levels are linked to how domain-specific the skills are. For example, the skill of picking off the spider in *Centipede* is not that useful in many other action games. Conversely, the skill of navigating the player's avatar and picking off a target further up the screen is useful in a much wider range of games. Obviously, if similar games use similar control systems, then the cross-game transfer of these skills is that much easier.

Of course, the ability to analyze a complex play-situation instantaneously is of limited use if the player has poor hand-eye coordination and reaction times. Studies tend to be conflicted on whether games improve or reduce these attributes in regular players. Common sense seems to indicate that exercising a skill tends to improve it, but what the official line is on this matter depends on the flavor of this month's study.

Perspective

Action games, whether directly or indirectly, are intended to be played from the viewpoint of the avatar. This is obvious when it comes to 3D FPS games such as *Quake*. You are looking through the eyes of your character—there's no other way to interpret it. Unfortunately, despite protests to the contrary, the FPS 3D view is probably one of the most unrealistic views possible. We do not dispute the aesthetics of this viewpoint—in fact, we believe it is excellent for immersion in a game world, but in strictly purist terms, it is simply not realistic.

The average human has 120 degrees of vision and can detect movement in the peripheral field at up to 180 degrees laterally. The average game of *Quake* shows a 30-degree view—not to mention the fact that your ability to control the character is solely provided via a keyboard/mouse interface. Compared to the freedom of view and subtle nuance of movement in the real world, in the game world, your avatar is a tunnel-visioned paraplegic in an electric wheelchair.

Some 3D games, such as *Super Mario Sunshine*, *Max Payne*, and the *Tomb Raider* series, offer a third-person view. The player can see her avatar onscreen. Aside from niggling issues with camera control, this is probably the closest perspective to natural vision. Players can see clearly ahead of them, and they also are provided with limited awareness of what is behind and to the side of them. The only fly in the ointment as far as this particular scheme goes is the camera. A good camera can make or break a third-person view game. If the player is to feel as if she is part of the action rather than a disjointed observer, then the camera must be as unobtrusive as possible. An obvious camera adds an extra degree of complexity for understanding the world—another obstacle in the way of gameplay. Giving the player control of the camera is not a solution—it's merely a quick patch of a broken feature.

For an action game, sometimes it's just not enough to give the player a view that is close to reality. In order to make the game manageable, it's necessary to give the player super-human vision. That sounds like a good justification for the 2D viewpoint, but really it is just a rationalization after the fact. 2D action games were often so frenetic simply because of the super-human viewpoint that they offered the player.

Humans are creatures capable of thinking in three dimensions. Hence, displaying a representation of a system in 2D instantly confers an advantage. There is an order of magnitude less complexity for the player to cope with in terms of object positioning. This means that 2D action games can afford to throw a lot more at the player before overwhelming them than an equivalent 3D game.

User Interface Design

In principle, user interface design for action games is extremely straightforward. It should follow the KISS (Keep It Simple, Stupid) principle to the letter. The user interface should be as minimalist as possible. In order for the player to be able to effectively play the game, he needs to able to accurately and quickly assess the play environment.

All the information that the player needs to be able to access in order to be effective at the game should be immediately present onscreen. Most action games require only a limited amount of information, so this isn't difficult to achieve. For example, the HUD (Heads-Up Display) for *Quake III* shows the minimum amount of information. Basically, it shows the player's current health, weapon, and amount of ammo. Don't try to show too much information to the player at one time. Not only does the player have to contend with the frantic action in the game, but he also has to pay attention to the indicators in the status panel. He should be able to do this at a glance, without having to work to interpret the information. Use simple schemes to get the required information across. One way you can do this is to use colors wherever possible to indicate changing situations, rather than textual or numerical methods. Another important situation to consider is when the player's attention needs to be attracted quickly to a changing status panel, especially when the panel is outside the main field of peripheral vision of the player; then he will be concentrating on the in-game action, not the status panel. If you need the player to notice something in the status panel, then you'll need to take appropriate measures. Within the main focus of view of the player, the eyes are sensitive to color and shape. Outside of this region, the eye is attuned to detect changes in contrast or color, so the easiest way to draw the attention of the player is to use a flashing or flickering indicator.

In some cases, additional information (too much to appear comfortably in one small status panel) is required. This should be avoided whenever possible, but when it is not possible to avoid, it must be handled carefully so as not to disrupt the flow of the game to the detriment of the player. If the player loses out by having to switch to a secondary map or status screen, then the enjoyment of the game is impacted. For example, in many FPS games, the level map is shown on a separate screen that obscures the main view. This means that the player has to be in a safe position to look at the map safely. Other games use a transparent overlay to display the same map information. Often, this is the ideal presentation method, as it allows the player to clearly see both the surrounding environment and the map. However, its effectiveness is limited if the map is so complex that it obscures the main view too much.

Another golden rule for action games is that the player avatar must be extremely easy to pick out. In the case of FPS games, this is easy—the avatar is the player, looking out through the screen. This is the exception, however. In every other type of action game, the avatar is displayed onscreen. In almost all cases, the avatar *looks* unique—it has a unique shape or position onscreen. However, the most effective way of ensuring that an avatar is easily discernable is use of color. For example, Lara Croft is the only entity onscreen in *Tomb Raider* wearing a light blue shirt. This means that if the player can see a splash of that particular light blue on the screen, then he is looking at Lara. This also means that Lara is immediately identifiable onscreen without any conscious thought process on the part of the player. In other games—for example, in the case of two-dimensional scrolling games—the avatar is often distinguished by position. It is always in the same absolute position—or at least on the same horizontal or vertical line—onscreen, and the world moves around it. This gives players a fixed point of reference about which to orient themselves.

Not only is it important to be able to pick out the avatar, but it is also extremely important to be able to quickly identify enemies. There are several mechanisms in use for this. The majority of action games use color schemes to achieve this. As mentioned previously, the avatar is often a unique color. An extension of this scheme is to ensure that enemies follow a common scheme of color or appearance. Think of the film *Tron*—you can easily identify the bad guys because they're the ones in red. The good guys are in blue. This is a throwback to the old spaghetti westerns where the good guys wore white and the bad guys wore black. A similar scheme can also be used for collectible items. In fact, an often-used scheme is to have the avatar predominantly one color and all collectibles another color, with the majority of the background yet another color. Anything else is an enemy. Of course, this is mainly used in older games, and is often tied to hardware limitations (as in *Pac-Man*). There is no reason to use this particular configuration, however, and it can be shuffled around, as long as it is consistent. For example, each level of *Space Tripper* uses unique color schemes for the enemies, collectibles, and avatar designed to have maximum contrast with the level scenery. In this way, it is easy for the player to analyze the playing environment as easily as possible. The only problem with this is the issue of color-blindness. Relying solely on color as a differentiating indicator excludes a significant section of potential game players. Use form and contrast in tandem with color to maximize the differentiation methods available to players. Of course, color blindness typically affects only 10% of males (and even fewer females), and usually only affects the ability to differentiate red from green (and dependent colors). Other colors (with little or no red/green component, such as shades of blue) are safe to use.

Action games (with one notable exception) require simple controls. Because of the fast-action nature of these games, the controls should, wherever possible, directly translate to avatar actions—pushing left on the controls makes the avatar go left, pushing right makes the avatar go right, and so on. For 2D games, this is a fairly simple endeavor, but for first- or third-person 3D games, there is an additional complication caused by the third dimension. There will always be an extra level of indirection for the player to deal with, and the controls will not be as intuitive as a 2D game. *Quake*-style games, even though they have standardized on a fairly logically consistent control system, are by no means simple for a complete beginner. Learning to use the *Quake*-style interface is the biggest barrier to mass-market success for first-person 3D games. For example, consider the success of the Mario series of games on the early Nintendo console systems. *Super Mario World* on the SNES was a system-seller. On the strength of that game alone, Nintendo sold many SNES systems. However, the first 3D incarnation of the Mario series, *Super Mario 64*, was not as immediately successful, even though the control system was as close to optimal as could be hoped. It was helped somewhat by the sheer eye-candy and novelty value, but for the average player, it was nowhere near as "pick up and play" as the earlier games, partially due to the added complexity of managing the camera as well as Mario.

The notable exception to the simple control systems mentioned previously is the specific sub-genre of fighting games. For these, moves such as walking, kicking, and punching are fairly straightforward to perform. But for the more complex and rewarding combo moves, those that can cause more damage to the opponent (and usually carry a correspondingly higher risk due to taking longer to perform), the player is expected to perform a long string of commands in the correct sequence in order to be able to pull off the advanced move.

At the other end of the spectrum are games in which the player's movements are directly emulated in the game. Without considering VR systems, a mass-market example of this is the arcade game *Dance Dance Revolution*. This is controlled by a set of footpads that the player has to dance upon in attempts to match the flashing icons that appear on the screen. Consequently, the player's avatar is controlled directly by the dancing (or more accurately, stomping) of the player.

Special Design Considerations for Action Games

We've already covered most of the design considerations for action games in this chapter, but there is one important point that we have not yet considered. If we compare a game such as *Defender* with a game such as *Super Mario World* (aside from the cutesy graphics of the latter), when just watching them being played, one would appear to be more difficult than the other.

Defender is a very unforgiving game. It tolerates no mistakes on the part of the player. If the player makes a mistake, then the player loses a life. End of story.

Super Mario World, however, is a lot more tolerant of player mistakes. The difficulty of some of the tougher levels are on a par with those of *Defender*, so it's not just a simple matter of the game being easier to play. No, the difference between these two games is the "perceived difficulty." Determining the perceived difficulty of a game is fundamentally the answer to the following two questions: What is the learning curve for the beginning player? How difficult is it for the player to recover from mistakes?

In *Defender*, the player is dropped into the thick of the action with no gentle introductions, and a mistake costs a life. In *Super Mario World*, the difficulty of the first few levels is gently ramped, and mistakes on the part of the player are tolerated. For example, if a player guides Mario too close to the edge of a platform, he has the chance to correct the error because Mario teeters on the edge for a second before dropping.

The target market for a game often decides which of these two extremes it will follow. *Defender* was an arcade game, designed to generate maximum coin throughput. *Super Mario World* was aimed at young players, and as such was designed to be easily accessible—the clichéd "easy to learn and difficult to master."

Action Game Worksheet

As you design an action game, consider the following questions:

1. Is this game a shooter or a non-shooter? If it is a non-shooter, what actions will the player take to defeat enemies?

2. Is the world (not the display mechanism) essentially 2D or 3D? If the world is 2D, should the display mechanism be 2D also, or would the gameplay benefit from 3D graphics?

3. If the world is 2D, will the whole world be visible on the screen, or will it scroll? If it scrolls, in which direction(s) does it scroll?

4. Does the player need a mini-map to see key offscreen elements of the world before they arrive onscreen? What about an automap for allowing him to record where he has been?

5. What physical challenges will the game incorporate, and under what circumstances? Speed and reaction time? Accurate steering and aiming? Timing? Combo moves?

6. Will enemies appear in waves? Will there be monster generators or wildcard enemies to break up the regular progression of the waves?

7. Will the game be broken into levels? What things will make one level different from another (landscape, enemies, speed, perspective, and so on)? Don't forget cosmetic items like music and architecture. Will levels end with a boss?

8. How will the avatar's life be managed: as fixed lives, energy bars, or some combination? Can the player obtain more lives? If so, how?

9. What power-ups will there be, if any? For each one you plan to incorporate, do the following: state what it does, what it looks like, what it sounds like when activated or how or where it is to be found or obtained, how common or rare it is, how long its effect lasts, and how the player will be able to identify it (by sight and the sound it makes).

10. Will the game give the player clues that allow him to anticipate challenges, or must the player depend entirely on trial-and-error to learn his way through it?

11. Does the game involve exploring unknown territory? If so, how linear or non-linear will it be? Traditional arcade and side-scrolling games gave little or no choice; games like *Spyro the Dragon* offer considerable freedom.

continues

continued

12. Is there a save-game or checkpoint mechanism that prevents the player from having to start over from the beginning?

13. Is the player going to collect anything, in either large or small numbers? Can collected items be "exchanged" for anything useful, or is the player awarded anything when particular thresholds are reached?

14. Is there a scoring mechanism? If so, how is it computed? Does it serve any function besides giving the player a record of achievement?

15. What "locked doors" will there be, and what "keys" will open them?

16. Will the game have, or need, a tutorial mode? If not, how steep do you want the learning curve to be?

17. Does the game have a victory condition other than simple survival? What is it?

Putting It Together

Even though many of the examples in this chapter have used "classic" action games for examples—some of them being nearly twenty years old—this is one genre of game in which the core "gameplay" has remained essentially unchanged since the outset. The lessons that can be learned from an old game such as *Pac-Man* or *Gauntlet* are the same as can be learned from a more recent action game example such as *Quake III*. Sure, the rules have changed a bit, the gameplay has become slightly more complex, and the structure of the game has shifted more from "eternal play" as in *Robotron* (where the player is assailed by wave upon wave of enemies) to a more story-oriented approach, such as the *Mario* series (where there is a well-defined beginning, middle, and end). Even with these developments, the core essence of the action game remains unchanged.

In fact, the biggest change in action games during their lifespan so far has been their graphical complexity. Of course, only those designers that have understood the fundamental nature of action games have made the transition successfully, and they have done this in spite of—not because of—the more sophisticated graphical capabilities of the newer platforms.

Chapter 10

Strategy Games

The origin of strategy games is rooted in their close cousins, board games. If there is any format of game that is closest to the original precomputer form (where that existed), it is the strategy game. This chapter is the most PC-centric chapter in the entire book, but for good reason: Most strategy games are released for the PC. Console efforts so far have been few and far between.

The benefits that the computer has brought to the strategy game genre include the capability to impartially manage complex rule-sets that would be next to impossible for a human to manage without bogging down the game to a level at which it is no longer fun to play.

On the computer, the strategy game has since diversified into two main forms: classical turn-based strategy games and real-time strategy games. Chronologically, the real-time strategy game arrived on the scene after the turn-based strategy game. Our discussion considers both of these forms.

The archetypal example of a computer strategy game is the *Civilization* series, originally developed by Sid Meier, before splitting off into the watered-down *Call to Power* offshoots. Fortunately, games such as *Alpha Centauri* and *Civilization III* from Firaxis rescued the franchise from a quiet demise.

Intriguingly, the computer game *Civilization III* has made a rare transition: from a computer game to a board game. *Civilization III: The Board Game* was released in October 2002, featuring three sets of rules (basic, standard, and advanced) and 784 plastic miniature pieces. Not surprisingly, *Civilization III: The Board Game* is significantly more complex than *Advanced Civilization*, the board game that the original *Sid Meier's Civilization* game was based on in the first place. This is good evidence that although translating and enhancing board games to the computer is an excellent method of producing compelling and fun strategy games, the converse is not necessarily true.

However, the comparative simplicity of the rules of computer-based strategy games (compared to other genres) lends itself to a good analysis of the effectiveness of the rules of play. In essence, strategy games are the easiest genre in which to generate a consistent and balanced rule-set. That is not to say that they are easier to design. However, the rules are easier to analyze for balance, mainly due to the discrete turn-based nature of the gameplay that most strategy games exhibit.

As a general rule, pure strategy games tend to be turn-based rather than real-time. Strategic thinking, at least in the arena of gameplay, does not lend itself well to real-time action. The player often prefers to mull over his moves, considering the impact of one choice over another. In board games, this can result in frustrating "analysis paralysis," in which one player spends a large amount of time min-maxing his move and breaks the flow of the game. Fortunately, computers are infinitely patient, so this sort of behavior should be tolerated—although it should not be required by the game design.

An offshoot of the turn-based strategy game concept is the real-time strategy (RTS) genre. Westwood's *Dune II* is considered to be the first true real-time strategy game, although we believe that the game *Battlemaster* (screens from which are shown in Figure 10.1), released in 1990 for the Commodore Amiga and Atari ST computers, marks the true origin of the RTS genre.

Figure 10.1   *Battlemaster.*

RTS games are differentiated from pure strategy games in that time is a constant pressure. There are no "turns" during which the player can ponder his moves—everything happens at once. Consequently, reaction time and quick action are as important as strategic thinking.

Although the RTS game breathed new life into the strategy genre, and although titles such as *Dune II*, *Warcraft*, and *Age of Empires* propelled it into mass-market acceptance, there has been little innovation to maintain this momentum over the past few years.

Aside from growing more complex, prettier, and larger over the years, the fundamental design of the RTS has remained virtually unchanged since the beginning.

The Common Elements of Strategy Games

Strategy games, whether turn-based or real-time, all feature a core management mechanic. The primary factors that influence whether a strategy game is compelling are listed here:

➤ **The theme.** For example, not many people will be interested in managing a colony of nematodes. Strategy games tend to have themes with sweeping importance, such as conquest (*Age of Kings*), exploration (*Sid Meier's Colonization*), or trade (the *Tycoon* series of games).

➤ **The presentation layer.** By nature, strategy games often have extremely complicated underlying mechanics. Consequently, the design of the player interface to the game is critical. The interface can organize and simplify this complexity for a player or, if not handled well, can make the game overwhelming and confusing.

➤ **The perspective.** Strategy games have traditionally used only a few perspectives for the player to experience the game world. Most strategy games tend toward grand-scale manipulation of the game world, but a few require the player to control a small group or a single avatar. The games that implement the latter option tend to place a greater emphasis on arcade action and real-time activities.

Themes

Strategy game themes are often derived from one or more of the following basic activities, which lend themselves well to implementation on a range of scales: conquest, exploration, and trade. More often than not, a strategy game blends these three activities. The extent to which any particular activity is dominant over the other determines the overall flavor of the game. However, the three activities are usually mutually interdependent.

For example, *StarCraft* uses conquest as its primary mechanism. Exploration and trade do feature in the game, but only as an enabler for the player to conquer more effectively. The player must explore the area to be conquered and set up resource-processing plants to allow resources to be traded for weapons and units.

Sid Meier's Colonization is primarily about exploration; the basic goal of the player is to explore the new world. Secondary aims are to settle colonies and subsequently defend those colonies from attacks by the displaced natives and the other colonizing nationalities. In this game, the three primary activities of conquest, exploration, and trade are quite evenly distributed. However, the enabler for conquest and trade is exploration. You can't trade or conquer before you've explored who to conquer or trade with.

Hasbro's *Monopoly Tycoon* focuses on trade as the game's main activities. Players are required to trade to increase their value, while simultaneously preventing their opponents from increasing their value. Exploration is not really used in *Monopoly*, but it could be argued that the competitive nature of the game implies that conquest is a small part of it: You can win only by defeating your opponents.

As we've mentioned, the roots of the strategy game can easily be traced back to the board game. In fact, board games make an excellent starting point to discuss the features of computer strategy games—their rule-sets are simple enough to grasp in entirety, and observations on the effectiveness of these rule-sets scale well to apply equally effectively to the more complex computer strategy game. Consequently, we examine each of these three core activities in more detail, using board games as examples.

Conquest

Conquest is the most immediately engaging activity in strategy games. On many levels, it directly appeals to the (mostly male) players' psyches and allows the player to command great armies, lead crack squads into dangerous territory, or become the evil dictator that they always dreamed of being. Consequently, due to the mainly male player demographic, the majority of computer strategy games released to this point have been heavily based around conquest.

Conquest—at least, in the physical sense—is facilitated by allowing the player to engage in conflict with one or more foes. The mechanisms for regulating and resolving conflict between entities in strategy games have been well-studied and understood. In fact, Game Theory, a respected scientific field, is devoted entirely to understanding and resolving the outcome of conflict under known conditions.

The essence of conflict is a contest between two or more opponents, each with an inherent set of attributes that are used to determine the outcome. Often, to achieve game balance, these conflict relationships are resolved with the use of an SPS (Scissors-Paper-Stone) mechanism, with an early example coming from *The Ancient Art of War*: knights beat barbarians, barbarians beat archers, archers beat knights. This approach is simple and—if implemented well—guarantees a fair relationship between all the conflicting entities. The use of the SPS mechanism is also a telling reminder of the board-game origin of the modern computer strategy game, although the computer allows for much more complex relationships, including compound relationships. Computers are ideal for handling this sort of complexity automatically—board games that attempt to implement this level of detail in their rules seem to get bogged down in a morass of rules. Of course, some people like tabletop war-games that last for weeks on end—but they are in the minority. Much of this material was covered in Chapter 8, "The Internal Economy of Games and Game Balancing," but we'll be extending that discussion here to cover the specifics of conflict in strategy games.

Consider an imaginary contest between two players, each with a squad of men, as shown in Figure 10.2. The red player has a squad of archers, and the blue player has a squad of horsemen. Typically, in a one-on-one battle between the two squads, the blue player will be victorious. That is because the horsemen can ride down the archers en masse before they can cause too much damage. Archers are less effective at close range;

consequently, as long as the blue player can get through the initial barrage of arrows, he is assured victory. In terms of unit equality, we can say that one horseman will strongly tend to beat one archer. Given no other variation is parameters, this rule is inviolate: Horsemen beat archers.

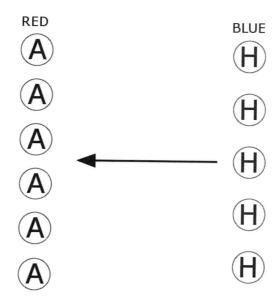

Figure 10.2 Red versus blue: Blue is victorious!

The red player is obviously not impressed by the outcome of this skirmish and decides to replace his archers with peasants. The peasants line up in formation, as shown in Figure 10.3, and are soundly beaten by the horsemen, who can deal out damage far more efficiently than the peasants. The result is the same: Blue wins. From this, we can say with certainty that, given no other variation in parameters, horsemen beat peasants.

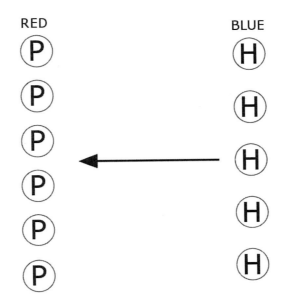

RED   BLUE

Figure 10.3   Red versus blue: Blue is victorious again!

However, let's assume that the red player replaces two thirds of his archers with peasants. He places his peasants in a row facing the horsemen, and his archers remain at a
safe distance behind the peasants, as shown in Figure 10.4. Now, to reach the archers,
the blue player's horseman must first defeat the peasants. While they are doing so, the
archers are free to rain arrows on the horsemen, causing much more damage than
the archers from the previous encounter. The delay caused by the peasants allows the
archers to pick off the horsemen. The net result: Red victory. This is an example of
compound SPS effects—in other words, the whole is greater than the sum. Archers
alone get slaughtered by the heavily armed and faster horsemen, as do peasants. When
used together, their combined strength and weakness overlap to create more than a
match for the beleaguered horsemen.

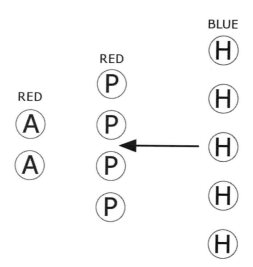

Figure 10.4   Red versus blue: Red is victorious!

This is an obviously simplified example, but the results scale up from the squad level to the scale of grand armies—the same rules apply. Of course, this result brings some additional complications to the SPS model. With combination effects such as this, you now have to consider placement and other factors—consider the result if the red player had switched the positions of the archers and peasants, as shown in Figure 10.5. Then the compound effect would have been wasted—instead of each type of unit covering for the others weakness, the converse would be true.

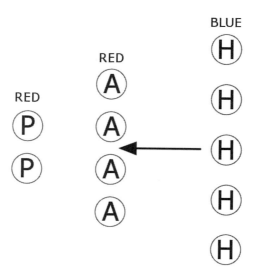

Figure 10.5   Red versus blue: Red's big mistake!

A detailed discussion of the relative merits of formations is beyond the scope of this book, but it is interesting to realize that explicit formation rules do not need to be explicitly implemented in the game design. In fact, outside of a few remote situations, you should never explicitly design such a high-level set of rules into your game. Concentrate on the lower-level individual unit parameters, and the higher-level features such as formation effectiveness will emerge from those.

In the four red versus blue examples we have just discussed, you will notice that there is no need for the conflict-resolution rules to be explicitly built in. Instead, the following set of individual unit rules will produce the desired results:

➤ Archers are lightly armored and move at a reasonably quick rate. They need a minimum combat distance of 10 yards, and they deal average damage per second.

➤ Horsemen are heavily armored and move quickly. They can engage only in close combat, and they deal above average damage per second.

➤ Peasants are medium armored and move slowly. They can engage only in close combat, and they deal average damage per second.

Assume that a unit dealing *above average damage* causes only slightly greater damage than a unit dealing *average damage*. A factor of 1.5 differentiating the two damage levels would be suitable. Any greater than that, and there is a fair chance that the defending peasants in Figure 10.4 would be finished off quickly enough to allow the horsemen through to defeat the archers.

The nature of the parameters used to define the abilities very much depends on the nature of the units and the environment they are in. For example, the turning arc of an individual foot soldier is not really an important consideration and can be safely ignored. However, in Taldren's *Starfleet Command III*, shown in Figure 10.6, the turning arc of a starship is an extremely important factor—you cannot fire on an opponent if your available weapon is facing the wrong way. This can make the difference between victory and defeat if your starship cannot turn quickly enough to return fire. Of course, this could have made for an extremely frustrating and arbitrary game if the designers had not had the foresight to build in an exception clause: The player has the option of choosing to perform a high-risk "rapid turn" (which brings to mind images of shaking cameras and aging actors throwing themselves around a set in synchronization), the success of which depends on the skill of the helmsman and the amount of time since that particular maneuver was last performed.

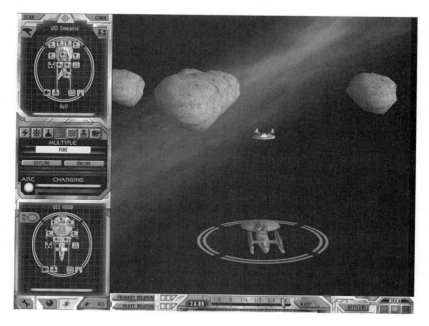

Figure 10.6 Taldren's *Starfleet Command III*.

Conflict does not necessarily have to involve physical combat. Whereas RTS games and "simpler" strategy games tend to focus on the combat aspects, the more advanced and progressive games tend to keep combat as a "last resort" option, more closely mirroring reality. For example, *Civilization III* uses diplomacy as another method of introducing conflict to the game. In real life, diplomacy is considered to be the "polite face" of war; in *Civilization III*, it is no different. The response of the enemy leaders to your diplomatic overtures depends in large part on whether you have the force to back up your tough words. Of course, diplomacy isn't all about trash-talk and "who-has-the-biggest-missile" contests—it also allows for the formation of diplomatic alliances and missions of peace. Somehow, though (and maybe it's just the way *we* play the game), the fine words of friendship are soon forgotten once the alliance has outlived its usefulness.

The use of diplomacy is more suited to a slower-paced strategy game—designed to be played over a long period of (game) time. The extra nuance and depth that it can add to an otherwise bog-standard strategy game is well worth the extra time and effort spent designing and implementing a worthwhile diplomacy system. Diplomacy gives the player an extra degree of freedom, and this allows for the creation of more devious and interesting game plans than would be possible otherwise. Diplomacy, in this case, is a catch-all term we are using to also include actions such as espionage and spying.

Exploration

Games that focus on exploration often use the conquest activity in almost equal parts. Consider *XCOM: Enemy Unknown*, which depicted the secretive invasion of Earth by aliens. In this way, it was both familiar *and* unfamiliar. Players were aware of the map of the Earth, but the location of hidden alien bases and UFO landing sites was a mystery until the player sent out a squad of XCOM soldiers to investigate the site.

Like conflict, exploration isn't just a physical phenomenon. *XCOM* is a particularly good example of this. First, investigating alien bases and landing sites requires physical exploration—the entire area is shrouded in darkness, revealed only when the player's soldiers gain line of sight (LOS) on an area. This approach to implementing exploration is used in most strategy games (known as "the fog of war"), with minor variations here and there, as shown in Figure 10.7. The physical exploration of the area reveals aliens scouting the area, who do not hesitate to fire on the soldiers using their superior weaponry. In Figure 10.7, the bright area shown is the currently visible area, the dimmed area is the explored but not currently visible region, and the black area is land that remains unexplored.

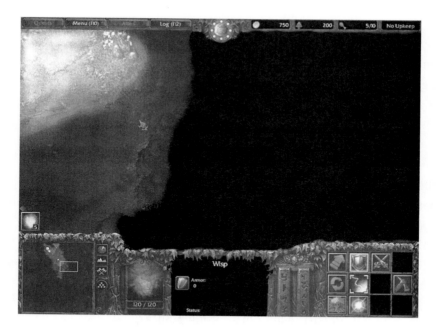

Figure 10.7 The fog of war (from *Warcraft III*).

If the soldiers defeat the aliens at a site cleanly enough to be able to recover some of their advanced technology, the second form of exploration comes into effect. The XCOM squad takes the technology back to the base, and the player can assign researchers to unlock the secrets of the alien technology. When they have discovered how the alien technology functions, the XCOM experts can duplicate it, giving the player a better chance against the stronger aliens with even better technology.

Again, this is a common mechanism for allowing the exploration of nonphysical frontiers—in this case, the frontiers of science. Like the fog of war, this mechanism has also been around long enough to acquire its own name: the "tech-tree." An example of this, from the game *Natural Selection* (www.naturalselection.org), is shown in Figure 10.8.

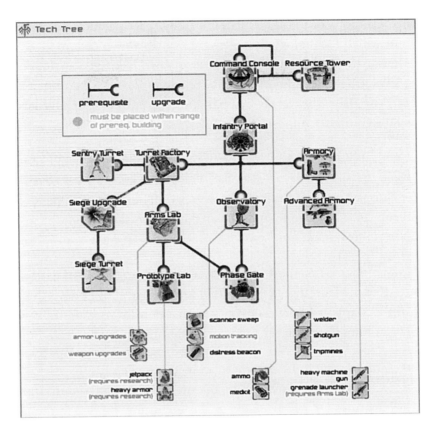

Figure 10.8   A tech-tree from *Natural Selection*.

XCOM: Enemy Unknown was by no means the first computer strategy game to implement a tech-tree, and it has been used in virtually every computer strategy game ever since. Usually, when a particular mechanism has been used this much, it becomes stale through overuse. Fortunately, though, in the case of the tech-tree, it is such a general concept that it rarely seems stale. Of course, it's also true that no one has come up with a better idea yet.

The tech-tree serves other purposes in a game as well. Mainly, it serves as a means of limiting and rationing the spread of technology. This can be used to pace the game effectively so that the progression from (for example) stone age to iron age to machine age can be managed in a somewhat realistic fashion.

Of course, this technique can also be misused. In most RTS games, the single-player campaigns limit which technology upgrades are available on a certain level. This is a rather heavy-handed way of ensuring that the campaign balance is maintained and that the difficulty level progresses smoothly. This approach prevents the more experienced player from blitzing the earlier levels by upgrading his units to a greater level than the (usually scripted) computer opposition.

The problem with this approach is that the implementation of an artificial upgrade barrier really jars the suspension of disbelief. The player ends up wondering why she could not upgrade her units to the next level, especially when it was possible to do so on the previous level. There are methods available to alleviate this problem, although none of them is an ideal solution.

The first and most obvious method is to maintain consistency. When a player has gained the knowledge of an upgrade, then that knowledge should never be taken away temporarily (for example, with levels of an RTS that disallow certain units without a good reason, even though the player previously was able to create those units).

The second method by which the designer can justify preventing access to certain units is to provide an excuse. For example, the pre-mission blurb could state, "Advanced cybermarines are not available in this environment, due to the risk of the increased power consumption of their enhanced exoskeleton armor causing a chain reaction in the methanogenic gas atmosphere," or "Flying units are disallowed in this mission due to the risk of being detected by the enemy's early warning system." What works for *Star Trek* script writers will also work for you as a designer.

The third—and, in our opinion, best—method is not to disallow any previously accessible upgrades. Instead, vary the shadow costs of the units that you want to prevent the use of on a level-by-level basis. For example, if the advanced cybermarine requires a larger quantity of a certain resource, then make that resource extremely scarce. Better still, make it a choice between a certain unit or structure that is *required* to achieve victory. Be upfront about this: State it in the mission objectives. Then, if the player wastes all his resources on building cybermarines instead of achieving the mission, he will have only himself to blame. Another way that the shadow costs can be varied for a particular unit (or class of units) is to make sure that the enemy is extremely proficient in taking out that kind of unit. For example, if you want to disallow flying units, then arm the computer opponent with extremely effective antiaircraft weaponry; above all, make it clear to the player that this is why his strategy is failing. (We find that opponent taunts are a wonderfully sarcastic way to achieve this.)

Many other variations of this method can be used, and they are all preferable to the first two methods. The key benefit of this third method is that it does not directly *prevent* the player from deploying a certain kind of unit—it just makes sure that it is not wise to do so under certain circumstances. This is a restriction that the player can actually appreciate and accept as part of the game, rather than something that appears to be an arbitrary decision by the game designer to hack a mission into place.

Trade

The whole conflict/trade/exploration (physical and tech-tree–based) concept is the basic overarching play mechanic of strategy games—particularly turn-based games. In real-time games, the higher-level aspects of conflict are toned down to a more visceral level and the importance of trade is greatly diminished.

Usually in RTS, trade is handled simply: Resources such as gold or oil are mined using worker units and are directly exchanged for more units. In this way, an extremely simplistic wartime economy is set up. The important thing to realize is that the economics of a strategy game do not need to be realistic—they must be merely consistent with the world in which it is based. For example, to be completely realistic, the troops in *Warcraft* would require supply lines to maintain them. However, this is not feasible because it would add unnecessary complexity to the game. Instead, resources are decentralized and can be used from anywhere on the map: Food produced on farms is magically eaten by units, even if they are on the other side of the world.

This decentralization of resources can cause certain balance problems in games if they are not carefully handled. For example, one particular weakness of this genre of game (which we first spotted in *Age of Empires*) is the "amoeba problem."

In *Age of Empires*, it is possible to send a lone peasant into an inaccessible area and build a structure, such as a barracks. Assuming that it is not spotted, this structure can immediately start producing troops right on the enemy doorstep, with no regard for supply lines or resource distribution. Clearly, this amoebic invasion is unrealistic and effectively weakens the game. Players of *Age of Empires* and other similar games generally have certain expectations of adherence to reality, and this exceeds those expectations.

Unfortunately, forcing players of an RTS to deal with supply-line issues is not a good solution. In his regular design column for U.K.–based *Develop* magazine, Dave Morris postulated a potential solution for this: Reward the player for maintaining the supply line (by enabling units to heal/self-repair in the field), but don't explicitly punish the player for not maintaining the supply line. It's difficult enough having to handle the battle, without having to handle the supply as well. A solution for this (which has been at least partially implemented in one RTS to date) is to use influence maps to indicate the areas to which resources are distributed. Two out of the three races in *StarCraft* use a limited form of influence map to indicate where their influence has spread. The Protoss power beacons (used to provide power to the Protoss structures) have a limited radius of power distribution, and the Zerg Creep provides a nutrient-rich building surface for the Zerg to grow their organic structures. Interestingly, the human player has no such restrictions.

Slower-paced strategy games allow the player to focus a lot more on trade and other aspects of resource distribution, and allow this to become a much more integral part of the game. For example, consider the territory map shown in Figure 10.9.

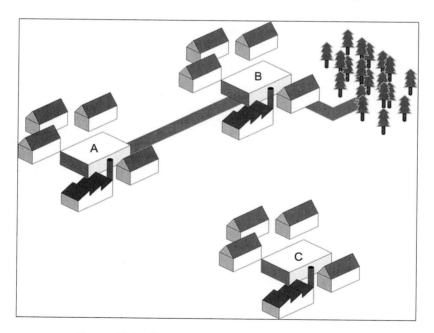

Figure 10.9 Resource distribution across a territory.

Town B has access to a forest—it has a road (supply line) leading directly to the forest, providing a ready source of lumber. This allows Town B to build wood-based units, such as catapults. Town A is linked to Town B via a road. This means that there is a readily available supply route between Town A and Town B. Hence, Town A has exactly the same production capabilities as Town B. Anything that is available to Town A is also available to Town B, and vice versa. Town C is a newly built town. No roads have been built to Town C, so it will not have access to the resources of Towns A and B until a linking road is built.

This is the approach taken by *Civilization III*. Of course, it's still not an entirely accurate solution—materials are assumed to travel instantaneously along the roads. (It's interesting to note, though, that previous iterations of the *Civilization* series *did* implement trade caravans, but *Civilization III* abstracted these to improve gameplay.)

Not only do supply lines make gameplay that much more involving—it's not just a case of cranking out units and killing the world—but they also add a dimension to the range of possible attacks that a player can perform on an enemy. If you want to sack an enemy city, it makes sense to cut off the supply lines to the rest of the enemy empire (by destroying the road), thus preventing the soon-to-be attacked city from building the more advanced units to defend itself. In *Civilization III*, destroying the road also serves another purpose: It slows down the passage of reinforcement units from other cities and thus increases the chances of a successful siege.

The depth of your economy depends on the pace of the game. However you choose to implement your economy, you should realize that the economy is the cornerstone of your game—even if it appears to be just a minor part of your design, the economy provides you with the easiest and most flexible range of methods for altering the game balance, by altering the costs (both direct and shadow) of performing operations within the game world.

Remember, though, that when it comes to the true costs of operations, the raw unit of the economy is a function of *effort* and *effectiveness*. Effort is the amount of raw material (including time) required of the player to produce a unit; effectiveness is the usefulness of that unit relative to all other units available in the game.

Setting

The choice of setting for your strategy game, although not as important as the underlying gameplay mechanisms behind it, is still a vital consideration. If the same underlying gameplay is dressed up with a different setting, it can feel like a totally different game. The core mechanics of a strategy game are the closest thing we have to a universal game-construction kit. You can transplant them into many different settings and get a different game.

The choice of setting is highly dependent on your target market. Thus far, the three most common settings for strategy games have been historical, sci-fi, and contemporary (the latter particularly in the case of business-based strategy games).

For games with a more militaristic setting, the present day is not necessarily the best choice, unless you're willing to court controversy and risk negative public opinion. Although this could gain your game some degree of notoriety, unless the game itself is a superlative addition to the gaming world (think *Grand Theft Auto III*), the disadvantages of such exposure will greatly outweigh any advantages—especially when it comes to your *next* game.

Sci-fi settings are a good choice, but unless you have a compelling world to present, you run the risk of falling flat. The danger with sci-fi is that it is so easy to add weird and fantastical components without stopping to think whether you should add them. This is the Star Trek syndrome, and we hate to think of the difficulties presented to game designers who have to design for the Star Trek universe.

If you ever watch the *Star Trek: The Next Generation* series, you will understand what we mean: Captain Picard and crew always have a solution for a problem, no matter what the odds are. If they're not inverting the phase inducers, they're inducing the phase inverters to beat some otherwise insurmountable problem. The problem with technology is that it too easy to see it as a panacea—and that can cause consistency dilemmas. If a self-consistent futuristic technology is to allow one thing, such as autoregenerating force weapons, then why wouldn't the technology be adaptable to provide a force shield to protect a unit from harm indefinitely?

Historical settings offer rich pickings for strategy game design. Consequently, many strategy games are set in the past—either portrayed accurately or set in the realms of mythology. The danger here is in mediocrity through familiarity. So many games have been set in the past that we are running out of room. There are not so many more areas of history left that resonate with the modern game player. However, we believe there is still room for original approaches within this area. For example, gangster games, such as Eidos' *Gangsters* and *Gangsters II*, were (at the time) fresh takes on 20th-century history.

Interaction Model

For strategy games, the interaction model for the player tends to be on the large scale. Rarely will you find a strategy game with a single avatar, although the PC version of *Battlezone* (not to be confused with the original coin-op) is a notable exception. Generally, the player is given a godlike view of the game world, indirectly controlling the units under his command. The true interaction model, in this instance, is related to the scale of the world. How many units does the player indirectly control? Is it a small squad, or is it a large army?

The feel of a small squad is much more personal and intimate than a large army. The personalities of the units can be explored more, and the player tends to care more about the individual fates of his units. Also, with smaller groups, individual character progression (in terms of improvements in skill and ability) can be dealt with more thoroughly. The *XCOM* series of games had particular strengths in the area—the player controlled several small squads of soldiers. This number (about 20 on average) was small enough for the player to be able to keep a handle on each individual member. Incidentally, in these games, the player could also build up a team of noncombat players because the scientists that research the alien technology are all recruited individually by the player.

For larger-scale games, it would be too hard for the player to keep track of every single unit in the army. Some games do attempt to do so, and usually this is in one of two ways. The first of these methods is to dramatically simplify unit progression (such as Recruit, Veteran, and Elite, as in *Civilization III*) so that it can be fairly easily understood. The other approach, which is taken by *Warcraft III*, is to nominate certain units as Hero units. These units are easily distinguished from normal units and are effectively like a squad within an army. The player can easily focus his attention on the small number of heroes relative to the total number of units in his army.

Yet another interaction model that is prevalent in strategy games is the abstraction model. In this form, there is no physical representation of the player—or the player's forces—in the game world. Instead, the player deals with the data and statistics both directly and indirectly. This last model is more often seen with business-based strategy games such as *RollerCoaster Tycoon*. In this game, the player has no avatar. She deals directly with the game world and can see the results of her actions both by examining the visual representation of her theme park and by reading the statistics and reports provided. *RollerCoaster Tycoon* is also discussed in Chapter 14, "Construction and Management Simulations." *RollerCoaster Tycoon* is barely different from *Age of Empires* (as one example) in that respect. In both games, you build buildings and tell your units what to do. In *RollerCoaster Tycoon*, your units are simply repairmen, janitors, and other service people. In both games, you have no single avatar, but you view the whole world.

Perspective

Almost without exception, up until about the year 2000, the primary perspectives used for strategy games were either 2D top-down or, more recently, 3D isometric views, usually tile-based. With the advent of powerful 3D graphics cards, a few strategy games appeared in full 3D, but usually these were gimmicks. Mostly, the use of 3D is limited to isometric—the 3D hardware is used just to give it a little extra flair.

Even with the most powerful graphics card, the most important part of a strategy game is the ability for the player to get the big picture. The player cannot strategize effectively if he is forced to focus on the view from one avatar's perspective—as in Activision's *Battlezone*. That's why real-life generals stand in little tents pushing toy soldiers around on 2D maps.

Even the use of tile-based game worlds is almost always used within the strategy genre because it lends itself well to tactical thinking. (It also lends itself well to programming, but that's beyond the scope of this book.) If a player can think in terms of consistent regions as having particular properties, that allows her to form her internal mental model of the game world that much easier. By simplifying this, we remove one more obstacle separating the game and the player.

User Interface

The user interface to a strategy game (as with many other game genres) can make or break it. The difficulty in the case of a strategy game is that often the game must seamlessly present the player with different scales of information. This is a difficult task to achieve without breaking the flow of the game.

Most strategy games take an approach based on a familiar paradigm. They present the data in windows, much in the same manner as a windowed operating system. Usually this is not a fully featured window system. Hence, it can be a little confusing to the novice player, who might not initially understand why he cannot perform the same actions with the game windows as he is allowed to with his operating system windows.

This problem could be side-stepped by using the windows provided by the operating system to present the game, but, understandably, no designer wants her game to look like just another business or productivity application. It certainly does nothing for immersion.

So, assuming that you take a windowed approach, try to ensure that, within reason, it behaves as the player would expect. Make buttons clear, concise, and recognizable. If possible, provide context-sensitive commands—that is, commands that appear only when appropriate. Another good thing to consider is the possibility of providing separate levels of command—a beginners mode and an advanced mode—so that the player can issue command with a finer grain as she becomes more experienced. Ensure that commands are well separated by area of functionality. *SimCity 4* does a fantastic job with the user interface. All of the commands are separated by functionality into an intuitive nested sequence of menus. At the top level, the player can choose between mayor mode and god mode. Mayor mode provides standard commands (segregated into functional areas, such as roads, power, water, civic buildings, and land zoning) that pertain to the building of the city. God mode provides another unrelated set of commands that allow the player to unleash all sorts of fantastical and supernatural events upon her unsuspecting sims. Technically, *SimCity 4* is a construction and management simulation, but for the purposes of our discussion here, the interface shares a lot in common with strategy games and is valid for this example.

Above all, remember to cater to both experienced and inexperienced players. Inexperienced players will want clear and easy ways to find commands, while more advanced players will merely want quick access. For the advanced players, provide keyboard shortcuts for *every* command in the game.

Designing Opponents

Designing opponents in strategy games is a subject of much research and investigation. Various approaches have been tried, including standard hierarchical Finite State Machines (hFSMs), neural nets, and genetic algorithms.

The problem with these latter two is that it is difficult to guarantee a consistent result, and it is even more difficult to diagnose why a particular result occurred. In the tight time constraints of most game-development cycles, no one really has the time to determine why an essentially opaque AI system isn't working properly.

The system that has had the most success so far is the goal-oriented hFSM system. With this approach, the AI chooses a top-level goal, such as "Take and hold this hill" or "Increase customer satisfaction," and delegates the tasks required to achieve the overall goal to subordinate hFSMs, which further delegate down to the individual unit level. It's similar to an army or any other hierarchical power structure, such as a corporation. The boss states the high-level goal and hands it down to his divisional managers. These managers translate the high-level goal into something meaningful for their division and then hand it down to their supervisors. The supervisors further transform these subgoals into meaningful tasks for their staff and partition out the work. From there, the staff members are free to interpret their tasks and to accomplish them as they see fit (within reason).

This approach has several elegant and pleasing features, the most notable of which is a controlled use of emergence. This approach also lends itself well to design. It is conceivable to design the rough pattern of an AI opponent on paper in this fashion. Of course, unless you are extremely lucky or unbelievably talented, it will still require much tweaking after it is implemented, but it should be possible for you, the designer, to at least communicate your overall goals for the AI to the developers. For more fundamental information on balance and tuning, refer back to Chapter 8.

Strategy Game Worksheet

When beginning the design of a strategy game, consider the following questions:

1. Is the game turn-based or real-time? The answer to this question will have tremendous consequences for the nature and feel of the gameplay.

2. Is the game world 2D (as in checkers), 2.5D (as in *Starcraft*), or fully 3D (as in *Populous: The Beginning*)? Will the game offer a perspective other than the usual aerial one?

3. Which of the classic themes (conquest, exploration, trade) will the game include? Remember that it can include any or all, and that "conquest" does not necessarily mean "combat."

4. Some games, like Go, are about control of territory rather than destruction of units per se. If this is true of your game, how is territory seized and how is it retained (or retaken)? What methods are used to indicate to the player who owns a particular region?

5. If the game involves units in combat, what are the units and what are their key characteristics (strength, speed, range, reloading time) and limitations? Is there a scissors-paper-stone model to balance them; if not, what discourages the player from always choosing the "most-effective" unit?

6. Is the player given a fixed number of units at the beginning, as with most strategy board games like chess, or is there a production mechanism? If there is a production mechanism, what are the production times and costs of each unit, and what (if anything) is consumed by production? If something is consumed by production, where does it come from in the first place?

7. Real-time strategy games are prone to certain dominant strategies: the "tank rush" of *Command & Conquer* and the race for resources in two-player *Dungeon Keeper*. In both cases, these blunt approaches tend to overwhelm more subtle strategic details. Can you devise means of predicting and avoiding them?

8. Does the game include a technology tree? If so, what is it and what causes the player to move along it (time, expenditure, collection of points, and so on)? What does it add to the player's experience of the game?

9. Does the game include logistics (maintenance of supply lines)? What supplies must be provided, and what happens if supply lines are broken?

10. What is the game's setting, if any? If the units are unfamiliar to the player, what visual cues or other cues will you use to indicate the difference between, for example, a dragoon, a cuirassier, and a grenadier?

continues

continued

11. Is the game a large-scale one, with hundreds or thousands of units, or a small-scale one with tens of units? How will this affect the player's perception of them? What user interface features will be needed to manage them?

12. How much can the player see? Will the game offer perfect information like chess, an exploration feature in which the landscape is unknown until explored, or a "fog of war" feature in which regions unobserved by a unit cannot be seen?

13. If you can get hold of a copy, take a look at the level editor supplied with *Warcraft III*. Which of the level-building features (triggers, timed events, and so on) would you like to include in your game?

14. Strategy games require particularly powerful AI, especially if the game is supposed to play in general circumstances and not just pre-built and pre-balanced levels. Given the rules of the game, what goals should the AI work toward, and how should they choose the actions to achieve those goals?

Putting It Together

Covering all aspects of the whole genre of strategy games in a single chapter is an impossible task. Thus, here we have focused on the core mechanic behind all strategy games: the triumvirate of conflict, exploration, and trade. An excellent example is *The Settlers of Catan*, shown in Figure 10.10.

The rules of this board game are exceptionally concise and very well balanced. Trade, conflict, and exploration are all included in equal measure. Examination and understanding of these rules—how and why they work so well—will form an excellent basis for the design of your own strategy game, no matter what format or genre.

At any rate, *The Settlers of Catan* should be considered required coursework for anyone planning to design a strategy game.

Figure 10.10   *The Settlers of Catan.*

The three elements of trade, conflict, and exploration are the foundation of the strategy game, the lowest level upon which the rest of the game is based. If you plan to design a strategy game, a good way to start is to examine the mechanics of a good board game. Board games are simple enough for a single person to grasp the entire rule-set and, consequently, lend themselves well to analysis.

Chapter 11

Role-Playing Games

Computer role-playing games (CRPGs), like their cousin, the strategy game, are also another genre derived from pen-and-paper games. Role-playing games comprise an interestingly diverse genre, ranging from simple arcade-style games, such as the *Diablo* series, to ponderous graphical adventure style games, such as *Anachronox*. The two things that almost all role-playing games have in common are as follows:

➤ Configurable player-characters that improve with experience

➤ Strong storylines

For example, it could be argued that the arcade game *Gauntlet* and the role-playing game *Diablo* would be markedly more similar if *Diablo* did not include the capability to configure the player's character. Similarly, *Anachronox* would be considered an arcade-adventure if the main character's abilities were static throughout the game. Consequently, this chapter will focus on discussing the elements of role-playing games that distinguish them from other genres.

For some players, the single most important part of the game (at least thus far in the development of CRPGs) is the story. In *Swords and Circuitry* (Premier Press), Neal and Jana Hallford describe several types of computer role-player. Each of these player types looks for something different out of their role-playing experience. Hallford names the "story-chaser" as one of the primary player types. There are several other player types mentioned in *Swords and Circuitry*, but the area of CRPGs where the most potential for questions remains is the domain of the story-chaser. The story-chaser is primarily interested in progressing the story. For her, the game is merely a vehicle for the story, and every action and interaction is intended to progress the story line. The player steps into the story, and becomes a very real part of it. Usually, this involves the player becoming the central character in the story, with all the story events revolving around her.

This is where the role-playing part of the game comes in. The player has to be able to empathize with her character in order to feel as if she *is* that character, rather than an all-seeing goddess directing the hapless avatar according to her whims. That is, the player shouldn't feel as if she's playing *The Sims*.

Another type of player mentioned in *Swords and Circuitry* is the character-advancement fanatic. This class of player isn't so much interested in the story, except where it is applicable to developing the player's avatar. We will also be discussing some issues pertaining to this player type in this chapter.

Covering the entirety of role-playing games in a single chapter of a book such as this would be a futile task, especially when the job is handled much better elsewhere, such as the aforementioned *Swords and Circuitry*. Therefore, in a similar vein to the other genre-specific chapters in this book, we will focus on what we view to be the most underserved areas of CRPG design.

The Common Elements of Role-Playing Games

Because of the unique nature of CRPGs, there are two main elements that are key to creating a successful game. The first, and most important, of these features is the story. The second feature is the character development arc.

Of course, there are also secondary features that are implied by the inclusion of these primary features. For example, adventuring and exploring are a big part of most CRPGs, as is combat. However, in our opinion, these are secondary features simply because they are a means to an end: In order for the story to progress and the characters to develop, they have to have something to do. Hence, adventure, exploration, and combat are the mechanisms by which the two primary elements are expressed. This is the state of the art now. In the future, we may get true AI with dynamic story generators and the like. But for the time being, we, as game designers, will just have to wing it with the smoke and mirrors of scripted stories.

CRPGs are, generally, based strongly around a story. There are certain exceptions to this. For example, the *Rogue*-like games—such as *Nethack*, shown in Figure 11.1—are based primarily around character development. In the case of *Nethack*, the story, such as it is, is randomly generated at the beginning of the game, and is solely used as an excuse to persuade the player to explore 20+ layers of dungeon.

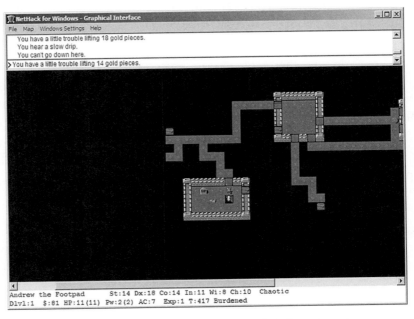

Figure 11.1   *Nethack* (Windows user interface shown).

Although the story may be suspect, the character development and adventuring, exploration, and combat elements of the game are not. *Nethack* offers an amazingly rich player experience, easily rivaling most of today's CRPGs. *Nethack*'s basic game mechanic has been applied successfully to other products. For example, the original *Diablo* from Blizzard owed more than a little of its success to the *Nethack* design. In effect, *Diablo* was a much simplified and extremely pretty version of *Nethack*.

Themes

The theme of a role-playing game can usually be boiled down to one simple statement: "Only *YOU* can save the world!"

Generally, the whole raison-d'être behind a CRPG is to allow the player to experience a pivotal role in world-shattering events that he would ordinarily never see. Of course, usually the exposition of these events is not so blatant as the statement in the previous paragraph—at least not outside the realms of satire.

However, we find it slightly disturbing that in almost all the CRPGs that we have examined, the ultimate theme has been, "Only *YOU* can save the universe/world/city/ tribe/whatever." In fact, we can only think of one recent game where the aim has not been to save the world, and that is *Planescape: Torment*.

Surely there are some other themes out there. There must be plenty of worthwhile quests that don't culminate in the hero saving the world. In fact, why is it necessary for the hero to save anything? This is why *Planescape: Torment* was a breath of fresh air for the CRPG genre. Unfortunately, this doesn't seem to have been taken up by the rest of the CRPG industry. Even Bioware, the developers of *Planescape: Torment*, resorted to the tried-and-trusted "save the world"-type storyline.

Here are some alternatives to the "save the world" storyline:

> ➤ Find and punish the person responsible for a loved one's murder (*Baldur's Gate*).
>
> ➤ Learn the secret behind your hidden parentage (*Star Wars*).
>
> ➤ Rescue the kidnapped princess (*Mario*).
>
> ➤ Find and reassemble the long-lost pieces of the magic thingy (*Nox*).
>
> ➤ Destroy the dangerous object (*Lord of the Rings*).
>
> ➤ Kill the marauding monster (*Beowulf*).
>
> ➤ Transport the valuable thingy past the people trying to seize it (*Mad Max*).
>
> ➤ Try and get back home (*Nox*).

Note that although many of the preceding examples did end up with the main character saving the world, it was not (in most cases) the main thrust of the story—more an accidental side effect.

When you design your role-playing game, try not to use the "save the world" storyline. However, if you do decide to stick with it, at the very least don't make it obvious to the player—at least, not at first. Of course, asking you to eschew the tried and trusted (and easy to sell) classic storyline is probably a bit too much to ask, really, but at least consider the possibility that "saving the world" doesn't have to be the ultimate goal of your game. Consider the success that *Planescape: Torment* achieved, critically if not commercially.

Setting

To the casual observer, CRPGs would seem to have two main settings: Tolkien-esque fantasy or sci-fi. This is not far from the truth. However, this is not necessarily as much as a disadvantage as it first appears. The fields of fantasy and sci-fi, respectively, are extremely popular genres. Witness the number of successful sci-fi and fantasy films. *Star Wars* remains a classic space opera. *Lord of the Rings* became an instant classic both in book form and in the cinema. One of the reasons for the success of these (and many other works) is the enduring appeal of fantasy and sci-fi. As kids, we all dreamt of being in a fantastic world peopled by magical creatures. Our folklore and legend often speaks of supernatural creatures and the magic of faeries. Consequently, it's a natural assumption that our tendencies toward role-playing would also involve the fantastic and unreal.

Far from being a straitjacket, the reliance of CRPGs on sci-fi and fantasy settings seems to be a logical choice based on both the nature of the game and the nature of the target audience for those games. We have often wondered about the feasibility of a role-playing game set in the modern-day real world. Without setting it in a fantastic environment, such as the world of 007, it would be difficult to generate player interest in a game that promises a role-playing experience similar to their own life. Generally, games-playing—particularly computer games-playing—is a form of escapism. The player wants to avoid the drudgery of everyday life and enjoy herself in another place entirely. In the case of CRPGs, why would a player choose a role in which she found herself emulating her own real life?

Consequently, CRPGs attempt to take the player as far away from real life as possible, while still maintaining a consistent world. The easiest—and most logical—means to do this is to set the game in the future or in a mythical setting.

This is not to say that you must choose only a sci-fi or fantasy setting for your CRPG. For example, there are plenty of real-world activities that only a few individuals get to experience. One can easily imagine a CRPG based around the progression from rookie to veteran of an L.A. street cop (Sierra's *Police Quest* series do not count—they were pure adventure games). There are plenty of other similar professions that could (and should) be effectively given the CRPG treatment. However, the overwhelming majority of CRPGs are firmly entrenched in either the sci-fi or fantasy camp.

Commonly, CRPGs pride themselves on the inordinate length of time required to complete them. It's not uncommon to see advertisements for CRPGs boasting "over 120 hours of gameplay." That's all well and good, but how many people—outside of a relatively small hardcore contingent—have both the time and the disposable income to invest in such a marathon game-playing session? Of course, usually the game experience is broken down into a number of serialized episodes (see Chapter 4, "Storytelling and Narrative") in order to make the game more manageable; but even with this concession, there are few players who are prepared to commit that much time to what is essentially a frivolous activity.

Notwithstanding the inherent problems with games of this length, we must also consider the difficulty of creating a story compelling enough to keep the player intrigued for this length of time. The most important part of the story is the opening. If you manage to hook the player with a good opening, then the chances are you've got her for the rest of the game. If your opening is not engaging, then it doesn't matter how compelling the rest of the story is—you will have lost a large percentage of your audience.

So, given that CRPGs seem to be fixated around the aim of saving the world, the opening to the story is even more crucial. The player is likely to be starting the game with the preconception that his quest is to save the world, so why bother telling him? Lead him astray and confound his expectations. Above all, don't tell him straight out that his quest is to save the world! Numerous alternative introductions to a game's story are more effective, as we'll see in the examples that follow.

Opening a story is one of the trickiest parts of the entire process of story-writing. The balance between exposition and mystery has to be just right in order to induce the largest percentage of players to probe further. Too much mystery, and the player will have no reason to investigate further. He won't know what he's supposed to be doing, or why. And generally, he will have no impetus or desire to find out.

It's a similar situation if your story has too much initial exposition, or worse, badly delivered exposition. Telling the player too much about his initial situation can cause an initial reaction of "So what?". Let's examine some examples of opening stories in CRPGs, and analyze them based on these criteria.

Nox

His name is Jack, an auto mechanic who lives in a trailer park in south central Florida. An unlikely hero, but that's what he becomes when a cosmic accident plucks him out of his easy chair and drops him on Nox, a world of magic, monsters, and an evil sorceress named Hecubah. All he wants is to go home, but to get back to Earth, he'll have to save the planet he landed on.

The opening movie for this game shows the sorceress, Hecubah, performing a ritual to retrieve a magical orb. As she does this, we can see that the orb is currently situated on top of a malfunctioning television belonging to the hero, Jack. As he hits the television, the orb starts to glow. Jack picks it up and is sucked into Hecubah's world, Nox, landing on a flying ship piloted by a mysterious Captain.

Humor is used well here. First, there is the clear contrast between Hecubah and the trailer-trash existence of Jack; second, during Hecubah's ritual, one of the candles goes out. She relights the candle, muttering to herself that she will kill all the candle-makers when she rules the world, and then recites the spell to herself in a normal voice, in order to work out how far she had gotten. The contrast between the overly dramatic spell ritual, and her matter-of-fact megalomaniacal comments are a good source of humor.

The story begins with our hero stranded in a strange world, wanting to return home. And initially, this is all the player knows. As we progress into the first few minutes of the game, we begin to discover the scope of the tasks required to allow Jack to return home. The emphasis here is not that Jack "must save the world," merely that "saving the world" is the only chance he has of getting home. Home is a concept that we are all familiar with, so this problem resonates well with the player. It's easy to empathize with Jack, and empathy is a good player hook. The player can relate to Jack—he is not some muscle-bound superhero or supreme wizard. He is just a normal guy who wants to get home.

Anachronox

> The first artifacts were found about three hundred years ago. Left by some long-dead alien race, strange mysterious devices were found all over the galaxy. Dubbed "MysTech" (short for Mysterium Technology), some of these ancient machines healed, some were weapons, and some have never been fully understood.
>
> …
>
> Sylvester "Sly" Boots sat in Rowdy's, a seedy bar on the seediest street in a section of Anachronox called the Bricks. After surviving an attack of a group of henchmen, a hairy old man admired Boots' handiwork and asked for his help. Soon Sly was joined by his lackey robot, an old flame turned mercenary, his holographic secretary, and a renegade scientist on a journey across space, across the dimensions, and beyond. Someone is causing the universe to folding in on itself, destroying all existence as we know it! And this group of people are the only ones that believe it is happening, and the only ones that can do something about it….

The opening story for *Anachronox* gives a little background on the world that the player finds himself in. It portrays human civilization as having advanced too far, too fast, by making use of advanced technology left by a long dead race. Now, the dregs of humanity are scattered across the universe. Sylvester "Sly" Boots is one of these dregs. After being thrown through his office window for outstanding debts to the local crime-lord, he desperately needs a source of money.

This is how the game opens. There are no grandiose quests to undertake, and the player is not told that he has to "save the world." Instead, the player's task is to find a job for the hero, so he can make some money. Assuming that the background story, involving MysTech and the bizarre world in which Sly is living, intrigues the player sufficiently, then this is a good hook. Like Jack from *Nox*, Sly is a just a normal guy who has had a bit of bad luck. Again, this kind of character is easy for a player to empathize with. His obvious imperfections mirror our own, allowing the player to relate to the character more easily.

Arcanum: Of Steamworks and Magick Obscura

> The steam-powered airship you are traveling on suddenly comes under attack from two mysterious airplanes. Stumbling through the wreckage at the crash site, you come across a dying gnome. He gives you a ring and implores you to "find the boy" and "save the world."

Although *Arcanum* is a fairly good example of a CRPG, the opening story breaks all the rules of engagement that we have discussed so far. The player is given no real impetus to perform the gnome's wishes, and after all, why should he? What if he does not want to role-play a world savior from the get-go? This opening stretches credibility, because it is unlikely that such a situation would occur.

Of course, this is a subjective view, but in our opinion, it would probably have been better to ease the player into the story with a little more subtlety. There is nothing inherently wrong with requiring the player to use a magic ring to save the world, but there is no reason why the game should reveal this to the player immediately. A little mystery and intrigue would go a long way in making the opening to this game more appealing. It may have been a better opening if instead of immediately revealing the overall quest to the player, it had been unfolded in a more piecemeal form. For example, the dying gnome could have asked for help to find "his boy," implying that his son was missing in the crash. This would have led the player to search for a young boy in the wreckage site. The player may then have found the (wrong) boy and returned to the gnome, who had by this time expired. This now leaves the player with an interesting dilemma: what to do with the boy he has rescued, who is now crying for his mommy and wants to go home.

Consider an analogous situation: Which of these two examples would be the better opener for a game?

1. You enter the inn after a tiring day's travel. Immediately, an old man runs up to you. "You have to help us! It's nearly sunset and the vampire in the castle will kill my granddaughter tonight."

2. You enter the inn after a tiring day's travel. The room silences as you enter, and all eyes turn toward you. You approach the bar, and the inn's customers return to nursing their drinks, resuming their muted conversation. In a dark

corner, you notice an old man clawing and tugging and the robes of an affluent-looking merchant. You can overhear the merchant saying, "You sold it fair and square. If you don't have the money, you can't have it back. Get him away from me, Silas!" The merchant's companion shoves the old man away and stands over him menacingly.

The old man collapses in a heap in the corner and sobs to himself.

If you approach the old man, he avoids you. Asking the other bar customers what the problem is gets you nothing but icy stares or uncouth insults. Finally you ask the barman what's going on. "I ain't talkin' about it. It's bad luck, see? Just don't go out that door after dark if you wanna stay safe. I've got a nice room I can offer you for just 80 ducats.... Yeah, it may be expensive, but it's that or the outside, and you don't want that."

You approach the old man with and ask him what is wrong. He seems nervous, his eyes staring wildly. "Could you spare 20 ducats to keep an old man alive? I sold my cross, I'm stupid, I wasn't thinking. I don't want *him* to get me. Please, sire? Save an old man!"

At this point, the player can probably figure out that there is something strange going on. Especially if they have knowledge from elsewhere in a game that the prices are greatly inflated for the room and the cross. Buying the cross for the man will cause him to become more friendly and talkative, and he'll start to tell the player snippets about the "thing on the hill." At this point, the player will be able to talk to some more of the customers. (After they see the player buy and handle the cross, they'll know that the player is not a vampire.) However, they won't talk openly due to fear and superstition, but the player will get hints that there is a vampire in the castle on the hill, and that he takes a young girl from the town once a month. The customers may also hint that there are untold riches and treasures secreted in the vampire's castle (and it may or may not be true—they may just be trying to entice the player to kill the vampire).

In terms of the quest, there is little or no difference between the two methods of exposition. However, the latter example is more believable and certainly more engaging than the former full disclosure. It's okay to make the player work a little to find out what is going on. If done well, it only serves to draw the player further into the game world.

Planescape: Torment

You awaken, frigid and confused. Scanning the room, all you see are stone tables like the one you are lying on and a sign that reads "The Mortuary". You aren't dead, so why are you here and, more importantly, who are you? Your thoughts are interrupted when a floating skull approaches you and starts talking! He informs you that you had just died again. What does he mean, again?

Planescape: Torment is fairly unique in the realm of CRPGs because of its focus on the main character. The opening of the game is a complete mystery to the player. After a short cut-scene showing snippets of a woman and some strange supernatural entities, the player wakes up to find himself lying on a mortuary slab, accompanied by a weird talking skull.

This opening is a particularly good example of minimizing exposition and maximizing mystery. From the opening, the player can surmise that his avatar once had a normal life, with a love, and that something strange has happened to cause him to become a cursed immortal. This is an interesting dichotomy because of the inherent human fascination with mortality. Who wouldn't want to be an immortal, no matter what the price? This is the question that this game poses. During the game, the player discovers that sometimes the price of immortality is too much to pay, and the overall goal of the game is to undo the damage that caused the avatar to become immortal in the first place, thus allowing the avatar to finally die.

Fallout

Our existence: a subterranean fallout shelter modified to house 1000 people indefinitely after a nuclear holocaust. It's been nearly 80 years, and we still don't have any idea what's out there. Sure we've sent out volunteer scouts, but none of them returned....

Now our water recycler has failed. Rationing has begun, but someone needs to leave the vault to get a replacement microchip for the water recycler and look for other survivors.

We drew straws. You drew the short one....

At the beginning of this game, the player finds his avatar locked outside of his vault, Vault 13. The immediate priority is survival. It's dangerous outside the vault, and there is no hope (or reason) to attempt to return without the water chip. Fortunately for the player, it looks like the water chip will be easy to obtain. Vault 15 is only a day or two away, and provided that he can survive that long, it should be a reasonably easy matter to obtain a new chip.

The approach that is taken by the *Fallout* story is to allow the player to continue on what seems like a simple quest, and then to throw in complications at the last minute: The water chip cannot be obtained from Vault 15. It stands in ruins, and the control room lies under tons of rock. This "false ending" approach is used more than once in *Fallout*. When the avatar does finally get hold of another water chip and returns to the vault, he comes to the realization that Vault 15 was attacked—and that due to his actions, he has now revealed the location of his home vault to the same elements that attacked Vault 15. The adventure continues, and the avatar is now tasked with destroying the forces that threaten his home vault.

The opening to this game is again intriguing. The theme of returning home is a common one used in CRPGs to involve the player, and it is used here to good effect. The final twist at the end of the game, once the player has achieved all of his goals, is that he has been changed so much by his experiences in the outside world, he cannot return to his home vault. This bittersweet irony is a very good example of excellent story-telling in a role-playing game.

Interaction Model

The interaction model for CRPGs is comprised of three main segments: character management, navigation and control, and inventory.

Each of these segments represents an important interface to the game. Although they are generally handled separately, they must integrate seamlessly in order to maintain the players' immersion into the game.

Character Management

The player needs the ability to manage her characters. Most CRPGs use a system based on an old paper RPG to handle their game mechanic, and so it is during character generation and maintenance that the "bare bones" of the system are so often visible.

Character attributes are usually generated in terms of die rolls and displayed in a numeric form. Often, if the player does not like what is rolled, there is a button provided for re-rolling the dice. Although it does vary from game to game, there is a stock set of attributes that most games use: Strength, Dexterity, Wisdom, Stamina, Intelligence, and Charisma. These are based on the original *AD&D* (*Advanced Dungeons and Dragons*) character statistics. All the basic character development decisions, and some in-game decisions, are based on tests against some combination of these. These tests are usually done via simulated die roll. For example consider the following hypothetical situation: Jonny Rock, the warrior, wants to smash down a door. He has a strength of 17, and the GM rules that he must roll three D6 (six-sided dice). If he rolls higher than his strength, he fails to break the door. If he rolls lower than his strength, then the door splinters to pieces.

Sometimes—for example, in the case of the *Fallout* series—secondary attributes are calculated from the primary set. For *Fallout 2*, the primary set of attributes includes Strength, Perception, Endurance, Charisma, Agility, Intelligence, and Luck. The secondary set of attributes include Hit points (calculated from strength and endurance), Armor Class (based on agility), and several other derivations. *Fallout* is a particularly good example of a well thought-out base rule-set. In addition to skills being limited only by the abilities of the character, it also has an intriguing set of "traits" available—extra abilities that can be developed, but that usually come with a disadvantage as well as an advantage.

The use of attribute sets such as these clearly has roots in pen-and-paper role-playing games. This is a sensible foundation for a CRPG, but in many cases it is not done justice. One of the major design influences on pen-and-paper RPG rules was that they had to be simple enough for a human game master to understand and apply quickly. Computers suffer from no such restriction, yet we still see CRPGs slavishly following the pen-and-paper rules to the letter, even to the point of destroying the atmosphere. Even acclaimed games such as *Baldur's Gate* have been known to flash the words "Saving Roll" onscreen if your character had a lucky escape in combat. The player does not need this information—she does not need to be reminded that she is playing a computer game based on *AD&D* rules. That's irrelevant information that serves no purpose in the game. Of course, the player should have access to the basic information, such as their attributes and skills, but exposing the inner mechanics of the game system in this way is unnecessary and counterproductive.

We see no reason why the player should be directly exposed to the die rolls that govern the underlying system. The *Fallout* series uses a percentage-based system, which is kept out of the player's way fairly well. Generally, the player does not need to be told that she failed her saving roll by 3%. That reminds the player that she is only playing a statistics game. However, the player does need to know why she failed and how badly she failed; otherwise, she will not know whether her character just cannot perform that particular act, or whether the character didn't quite get it that time, but maybe will the next time. After all, the player is one step removed from the character, and cannot know what the character would know. Chances are, a character would be aware of whether the task is hopeless, or whether it's just a particularly difficult one that will take a while. Character-based feedback is a good way to indicate this: "Darn! I really screwed that one up!" or "Whew! Nearly had it there," for example.

Of course, there are players—those who are primarily focused on character advancement—who *want* and *need* to see all the numeric data, as opposed to the story-chasers who find that all the numeric data spoils the fantasy. Both types of player like CRPGs, but for different reasons, and it's tricky to serve both groups. The ideal solution would be a game that played both ways—one mode that showed the "arithmetical guts" of the game, and one that reduced the numbers to a minimum and converted them to power bars and other display mechanisms, as discussed previously.

CRPGs are also unique in that they allow the player's avatar to learn new skills, and continue to develop them as they play. One of our pet peeves about the skill system comes into effect when it is coupled with the class system. In case you are unfamiliar with the class system, this is an arbitrary set of restrictions that prevent characters of a certain class from learning particular skills. Sometimes there is a justifiable reason for this, and sometimes there is not. Either way, it seems like a particularly heavy-handed way of enforcing a degree of balance in the game. Worse still, some of these restrictions seem to be arbitrary. For example, in the *AD&D* third edition rules, clerics cannot use bladed or piercing weapons. Therefore, if the cleric was in a threatening situation where the only weapon available was a knife and magic was not an option, he would be defenseless. In reality, of course, we would expect to be able to pick up the knife and start slashing.

Not all role-playing games restrict the player to a class-based system of skills. A better method is to allow the player to attempt to learn as many skills as she wants and be restricted only by the time available to her, and her avatar's aptitude in that skill as based on her primary attributes. In these cases, it still makes sense for a character to specialize, especially if like skills are interrelated and unpracticed skills gradually decline. For example, learning the skill of "basic mechanics" would provide a solid basis for developing the "lock-picking" skill, whereas learning "basic gardening" would not.

In this way, a player doesn't run into arbitrary restrictions, and can choose whether to turn her character into a narrow-but-deep specialist, or a wide-but-shallow jack-of-all-trades. The most important thing to realize here is that it is not for the game designer to arbitrarily restrict those choices. Of course, some restrictions do make sense. For example, a lawful, good paladin should be restricted from performing evil acts. But again, this should not be an arbitrary "thou-shalt-not" restriction. Instead, there should be dire consequences for performing these actions, such as a loss of patronage and protection from the paladin's god, or worse. In other words, the player should still have the choice to act out of character, if he is willing to face the dire consequences.

Another problem with the skills system as currently used in CRPGs is that, in most cases, it has not been adapted well to the computer, and still has its roots firmly in the turn-based nature of the original pen-and-paper rules. For example, if we consider a character that has a 10% chance of picking a lock, then we can conceive of a situation where the player is repeatedly clicking on the "Pick Lock" button until he succeeds. This is dull and unnecessary, especially on a computer.

A better method would be to display a progress bar. The speed with which the task progresses depends on the character's skill in that area—that is, it progresses quickly if the character has a high skill level, slowly for a low skill level, or not at all if the task is too hard. If the player needed to interrupt the task because it was taking too long, then he should be able to. For example, the progress bar could flash red if there is a chance of being interrupted, such as if a character is within range of the player's avatar and stands a chance of detecting the activity. Give the character a small amount of time—based on their dexterity and intelligence—of stopping before the check, or no chance of avoiding the check if their combined dexterity and intelligence is too low. This approach would be more immersive, and would heighten the tension and immediacy of the game.

Navigation and Control

The range of actions that a player can take in a CRPG is usually much greater than any other form of game. Consequently, there is a corresponding increase in the complexity of the interface. For PC titles, this is handled by a combined mouse/iconic interface (for the most part—some titles resort to keyboard only), and similarly console titles tend to duplicate the functionality of a mouse using analog controllers. See Chapter 6, "Creating the User Experience," for more information on user interface design. Much of the advice in that chapter is directly applicable to CRPGs.

Inventory

The inventory system for CRPGs has been a perennial sticking point for most gamers. It seems that the perfect inventory system has not yet been designed.

The difficulty with designing a good inventory system is in handling the complexity of everyday objects in a manageable fashion. Certain assumptions have to be made. Of course, it is theoretically possible to simulate physically accurate representations of packing objects into a limited space, but that would be overkill, and possibly difficult to administer.

The classic solution chosen for inventory management is to divide the player's carrying capacity into an array of boxes. Each box can carry one type of item, and assuming an item is small enough, several items of the same type will be stored in the same box, up to some maximum limit. An example here would be gold. If every pile of gold a character picked up in *Diablo II* went into a separate box, then there would soon be no room left in the inventory for other items.

Usually item weight is used as a secondary constraint. It does not matter how many boxes the player has free; his character can only carry so many "magical lead weights of righteous indignation."

The reason that the inventory is so important is that the player usually spends a disproportionate amount of time micromanaging the contents. Often, this micro-management breaks a cardinal rule of human-computer interaction: Don't force the player to perform a menial task best handled by the computer. For example, consider the situation in Figure 11.2. The player has found a staff, and cannot put it in his inventory because he doesn't have enough free boxes in the right configuration. The staff takes up 1×4 boxes, and the biggest space he has available is 1×3. If he moves the apple in the top space, however, he will have a space of 1×4 and will be able to store the staff. The question is, is that fun for the player? Probably not, and it should be handled automatically. To make matters worse, consider the alternative situation where only a 4×1 (horizontal) space is available. Why can't the staff simply rotate by 90 degrees and fit in the 4×1 gap at the bottom? Most CRPGs that we have played cannot handle that simple concept. Thus, the importance of the inventory interface is paradoxical. It *is* important, but it *shouldn't* be. It should be the least intrusive part of the game interface.

Even more fundamentally, this inventory abstraction is 2D. That's not to say that 3D would be better, but the major disadvantage with it being 2D is that the model strictly enforces placement rules as if the object storage area really was a 2D construct. It's almost as if the designers of CRPGs have entirely forgotten that storage packs really do have a volume.

Figure 11.2   An inventory problem.

Worse still is the hypothetical situation shown in Figure 11.3. We're not aware of any games that do this, but it does show the arbitrary absurdity of this fundamental problem with inventory management in most CRPGs. In the figure, the player has a 5×1 staff to fit in a 4×4 inventory. There are 16 spaces available in the inventory, but the player still has no way to fit the staff in. In reality, of course we could cram the staff in—even if it stuck out of the top of our pack.

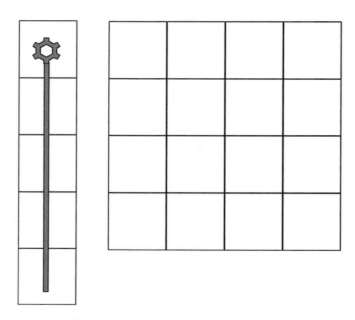

Figure 11.3 Another inventory problem.

This section highlights various problems with the currently accepted abstraction of inventories used in most CRPGs. It's not as if there is anything fundamentally wrong that cannot be fixed; it's just that most inventories don't go far enough and force unnatural restrictions on what the player could reasonably expect to carry (for example, in *Nox* there is a hard limit on how many items of a certain type you can carry—even if you have space for more). The other main problem with the inventory convention is that it forces the player to do a lot of micromanagement that is otherwise unnecessary and is certainly not fun. Players want to role-play, not pack for a vacation.

Perspective

Originally, CRPGs were essentially top-down affairs, as shown earlier in Figure 11.2. The gradual improvements of graphics technology (aside from a few anomalous entries such as *Ultima Underworld II*, shown in Figure 11.4) meant that many CRPGs are now presented in isometric 3D, as shown in Figure 11.5.

Figure 11.4   *Ultima Underworld II.*

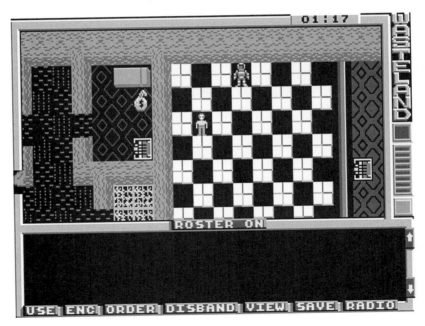

Figure 11.5   *Wasteland.*

Since the advent of hardware-assisted 3D technology, there have been many more instances of 3D-accelerated CRPGs. Some of these have been fully first-person 3D, such as *Elder Scrolls III: Morrowind* (although it does also provide a third-person view, shown in Figure 11.6). More CRPGs, however, have stuck to the classic third-person isometric approach, such as *Baldur's Gate: Dark Alliance* on the PS2, or *Neverwinter Nights* (shown in Figure 11.7).

Figure 11.6 *Elder Scrolls III: Morrowind.*

Figure 11.7   *Neverwinter Nights.*

CRPG Worksheet

When beginning the design of a CRPG, consider the following questions:

1. Which type of game are you going to create? Is it going to be heavy on story (as in *Planescape:Torment*), or will character advancement and combat be the main thrust (as in *Nethack*)?

2. If it is story based, then how are you going to structure the quests? One big overarching quest with mini side-quests, or a more free-form approach? This will have an impact on the difficulty of production and the feel of the game.

3. What is the setting for your game? Are you going for the standard sci-fi/fantasy fare, or are you using something else? Are you using a licensed work? Are you convinced that what you have is different, yet recognizable enough to be compelling?

4. How will your world function? What are the underlying rules for the way the world works? Are they self-consistent and logical? Are they based on a pre-existing system (as in *Baldur's Gate*)?

continues

continued

5. Is the player going to be given a group of avatars, or will he be responsible for a single avatar? Will his character be configurable (as in *Arcanum*), or will he be forced to take a pre-defined role (as in *Anachronox*)?

6. What will be the primary focus of your game? Will it be uncovering the story, improving the player's character, or combat and exploration? The majority of games attempt to cover all these bases equally, but some exceptional ones have focused more on one aspect, such as *Anachronox* and *Diablo II*. This affects the pace of your game.

7. Considering interactivity with non-player characters: Is your game intended to be short, but deep (as in *Fallout*) or sprawling, but shallow (as in *Diablo II*)? This has an impact on whether your player considers herself to be immersed in a world, or playing a story.

8. What will be the perspective used in your game? Will you use standard isometric 3D (as in *Fallout*) or will you use a fully 3D engine (as in *Elder Scrolls III: Morrowind*)? Will you use something else entirely?

9. Is your game going to include a magic system? How is this magic system going to be constructed? Will it be based on pre-existing concepts, familiar regimes (such as Law/Chaos/Good/Evil), or something completely new? Will it be internally self-consistent or not? How will it be balanced with nonmagic forces within the game?

10. How will you handle inventory management within the game?

11. And finally, will your player's character end up saving the world? Are you sure you want to do that? Can you think of anything slightly more original (as in *Planescape: Torment*)?

Putting It Together

The design of a CRPG is not a small undertaking. Aside from the fact that putting together a complex and believable world is an extremely difficult task, the amount of effort that goes into the design is extremely high when compared to other types of games.

A recent trend with CRPGs, evidenced by *Neverwinter Nights*, *Elder Scrolls III: Morrowind*, and *Arcanum: Of Steamworks and Magic Obscura*, is the provision of an editor with the game to allow the more involved players to create their own scripted adventures in the game world.

This is a trend to be encouraged, because it extends the longevity of the game, which in turn increases sales. *Neverwinter Nights* has taken this to the extreme, and allows players to actively run the game, editing an adventure in real-time as other players journey through it.

While this is currently the pinnacle of CRPG design, there is still a long way to go. There is, in our opinion, an overly heavy reliance on the old pen-and-paper rules. Although they are useful as a basis, there are better solutions available for CRPGs. It does nothing for casual players to see "+20 Pushback" appear onscreen during combat. It only reminds them that they are just playing a game.

Another, more fundamental problem, only partially solved by the active GMing allowed by *Neverwinter Nights*, is the scripted nature of gameplay. It isn't *true* role-playing. The player isn't allowed to do absolutely anything, as they would be in the pen-and-paper game. This latter problem isn't something that will be solved anytime soon; suffice it to say that until we have true AI and dynamic content generation technologies available to us, all CRPGs are really only fixed-story games. As a designer of CRPGs, it's your job to arrange the smoke and mirrors successfully so that players feel that they are in a living, breathing world with the freedom to do what they want.

The true CRPG would allow the player to do absolutely anything, anytime, anyplace, but we're years, possibly decades, away from that level of technology.

Chapter 12

Sports Games

Sports games set an unusual challenge for the game designer. Unlike most other games, which take place in a world the player knows little about, sports games emulate a world the player knows a lot about: sporting events as they are in real life. No one has ever really led an army of elves into combat, and only a small number of people know how it feels to fly an F-16 fighter jet, but a great many people know what professional football looks like and how the game is played. Sports games belong to a small number of genres that permit a direct comparison with the real world.

Not all sports games are ultrarealistic, of course. Some, such as Electronic Arts' old Genesis game *Mutant League Football*, are fantasy games, even if they are based on real sports. Others, such as Midway's arcade game *NFL Blitz*, simplify a sport and deliberately make it more extreme for dramatic purposes. Most of these kinds of games are designed to appeal to kids, who might not know much about the real sport. But for aficionados, the game must be a reasonably accurate depiction of the real thing, and they will see any deviation as a flaw.

This chapter discusses athletic sports, as opposed to sports such as motor racing. Although racing games are often sold in the sports category, from a design standpoint, they really belong in Chapter 13, "Vehicle Simulations."

> ### A Note on Terminology
>
> Because sports games simulate other games, as opposed to a war, a race, or an economic competition of some kind, the words *player* and *game* are ambiguous. Does *player* refer to the person playing the computer game or one of the athletes playing the game on the field? In this chapter, we use the following convention: *Player* refers to the person playing the computer game, as it does throughout the rest of the book. We call the people *in* the game *athletes*. *Game* refers to the computer game. When we refer to one particular contest, we call it a *match*. The type of match that the athletes are playing (basketball or soccer, for example) is called the *sport*.
>
> A great many sports involve a playing area with a goal at either end and athletes trying to manipulate some object into the goal. Basketball, ice hockey, water polo, and soccer are all examples. We refer to these collectively as *soccerlike games*.

The Common Elements of Sports Games

Using the elements of a game that were established in Chapter 2, "Game Concepts," we can observe the following characteristics of serious sports games.

Rules

The rules of a sports game are, for the most part, the rules of the sport that is being simulated. You might find that you need to relax these rules in some areas, particularly with respect to faults, fouls, or judgment errors that the player might make. Because the player is using a handheld device to manipulate an athlete onscreen instead of playing on the field himself, it's much more difficult to judge when his avatar is about to bump into someone, cross into a forbidden zone, and so on. A few games allow the player to set the level of "refereeing" to forgiving or strict, depending on which way he likes to play.

You'll also have to address an important question about errors that are not the player's fault. In American football, a certain number of penalties are called each match for "holding," grabbing hold of another athlete instead of merely pushing him. This is an aspect of the sport that a computerized version could avoid entirely: It could simply make it impossible to hold someone. Of course, a match in which no holding penalties ever occurred would feel unrealistic. On the other hand, a match in which holding penalties occurred at random might be frustrating for the player. This is another issue that can be controlled by the refereeing variable described earlier.

Competition Modes

Sports games are just about the only games that allow all possible modes of competition, depending on the sport: single-player, competitive, cooperative, and in teams, if the platform supports enough input devices. People love to play sports games competitively, and if several people play together, they like to do it in teams as well. Sports games are far more successful on console machines than they are on PCs because console machines allow so many people to play at once and are attached to a TV (usually with a 19-inch screen or better) instead of a monitor, so all the players can see clearly. Because many real sports are played by teams of people, they naturally offer opportunities for multi-player action.

One other competition mode you should consider including is one with no players at all: the computer versus itself. Few other games besides chess games ever implement this mode; after all, people play computer games to interact, not to watch. However, with sports games, people do occasionally like to let the game play itself and watch the results, just as if they were watching a real match on TV. Another good reason for doing this is to allow the computer to play simulated matches that the player doesn't want to play. This is explained in the section, "Simulating Matches Automatically," later in this chapter.

Victory and Loss Conditions

The victory and loss conditions for a match are the same as in the real sport. However, many sports played in leagues or by seasons can be simulated in a variety of game modes:

> ➤ **Season mode.** The player selects a single team (or athlete, for individual sports such as skiing) from all those available and plays a series of matches throughout a season, trying to make it into the championships. The schedule of play for the season and the rules for moving into and up the championship bracket are adopted from the real sport. Some season modes allow a player to play not just one team's matches, but every single match played throughout an entire season.

➤ **Exhibition mode.** In this mode, the players play one single match, but it has no long-term consequences, just like exhibition matches played by real teams. Whoever wins the match, wins the game.

➤ **Sudden death.** As a variant of exhibition mode, players play a match only until the first score is made. Whoever makes the first score wins the match. This is handy for very quick games, although it means that luck plays a much greater role in determining the outcome.

➤ **Round robin.** Players in a group each take a team and play each other's team a fixed number of times, sometimes just once. Whoever has won the most matches at the end is the winner.

➤ **Tournament mode.** In this single-elimination tournament, any player who loses any match is dropped, and the winner goes on to play the winner of another match. This requires that the number of players be a power of two.

➤ **Franchise mode.** The player controls a team over the course of several seasons, trying to build its strength through the years. This mode is often found in games that include mechanisms for hiring athletes and trading them among teams. For games such as tennis, in which most athletes play alone, the equivalent mode is called *career mode*—that is, the player controls the athlete over the course of several years of his or her career.

Setting

The game's setting is the normal venue for the sport, usually a stadium or an arena. It adds a great deal of verisimilitude to present these accurately. Players enjoy being able to recognize the architectural details of their favorite stadiums. The shape of the actual playing areas in American football and basketball is fixed, but different baseball fields are famous for having different effects on gameplay. Some sports, such as skiing and bobsledding, have venues that vary enormously and require a great deal of practice to learn.

Outdoor fields are also subject to changes in the weather, which can significantly affect the game. Rain hampers traction on a grass field, and snow makes it worse still. Players have to run more slowly and carefully. Wind affects the flight of balls and the accuracy with which they can be thrown. These factors all add enjoyable variety to a game.

The crowd also contributes significantly to the setting. Although you won't want to devote a lot of graphical resources to spectators, the sounds they make add greatly to the atmosphere. The volume should go up at tense moments. If there are any commonly used chants at different times, the players should hear them; there should be cheering after a score by the home team and a sudden silence after a score by the visitors. Horns, whistles, and vendors calling out "Ice-cold beer here!" are all part of the experience.

Interaction Model

The interaction model in sports games varies considerably depending on the sport, but in most cases, the player is controlling an avatar who is one of the athletes in the match. In one-on-one sports such as tennis, this is straightforward, but in team sports, the player's control usually switches automatically from one athlete to another as the focus of play changes. In basketball games, for example, control normally switches to the athlete who has the ball. If the player's team is on defense, most games let the player choose which athlete to control and to switch quickly from one to another as conditions change. This often requires significant changes to the user interface as play progresses.

Perspective

In one-on-one sports games, the perspective is seldom difficult to manage. Choose a spot where you have a clear view of the athletes and where their movements and activities will map neatly onto the machine's input devices. As a general rule, you shouldn't do sports games in the first person. A lot of the fun of watching a sport is in seeing the athletes exercise their skills, and in first person, you can't see your avatar doing that. For example, you could make a tennis game in the first person, but you wouldn't get to see your athlete playing tennis, and you might not even get to see your racket hit the ball. An overhead perspective, with your tennis player at the bottom of the screen and your opponent at the top, presents a much more natural view and lets you see both athletes running, jumping, serving, and so on.

Team games are more tricky, particularly when the focus of attention moves from place to place. With most soccerlike games, an end view or a side view, from a somewhat elevated position, works best. American football, however, is almost unplayable from a side view because too many athletes are behind other athletes and you can't see gaps in the line.

User Interface Design

In most other genres, the user interface changes infrequently and only in response to explicit actions by the player. Sports games are unusual in this regard; the user interface changes on a second-by-second basis, depending on conditions in the match itself. American football is a particularly complex example. On each play, the player on offense selects the formation and play to be run, then calls signals and makes adjustments at the line of scrimmage, and then takes the snap and either hands off the ball, passes it, or runs with it himself. If he passes it, control switches to the athlete for whom the pass is intended, and a whole series of new options for running, jumping, diving, and dodging defenders comes into play. Each of these different states requires that certain moves or choices be assigned to buttons on the controller, and these assignments change rapidly as play progresses.

The hardest thing about sports game user interface design is that you have to map athletic activities—complex motions of the whole human body—onto a game machine's input device, typically a handheld controller with binary buttons. Think about what kinds of things the player will want to do at each stage of the game and how best to make them available. Whenever possible, make sure that similar actions in different modes are assigned to similar buttons; for example, if you have a "jump" action in both offensive and defensive modes, assign it to the same button in both cases.

In team games, the player will normally be controlling one athlete at a time. This is usually indicated by displaying a circle or star under the athlete's feet. A good many games also draw symbols on the field to help the player overcome the lack of depth perception—the spot where a flying ball is due to land, for example.

When the player is on defense, include a button to automatically change control to the most appropriate defending athlete (in soccerlike games, this is usually the one nearest to the ball). Another useful pair of buttons allows the player to cycle control forward and backward through all the athletes on the team.

Most sports games avoid pull-down menus and anything else that resembles a computer's desktop, so as not to interfere with the fantasy. Pop-up windows and semitransparent overlays are common, particularly if they can be styled to look like the graphics seen on TV. These are subject to style variations from year to year. We suggest that you watch matches on TV for examples of how the overlay graphics are handled.

Unless you're simulating archery or bowling, don't forget that a sports game is essentially an action game. No matter how complex the sport is, the user interface must be as smooth and intuitive as you can make it.

Player Roles

The player's role is most commonly that of an athlete, but not one particular athlete. In a team sport, the player's focus of control usually follows the action rather than being tied to a single individual. Thus, the player's role shifts rapidly, especially if some athletes play specialized positions such as catcher or goalie.

Another common role is that of coach, again seen chiefly in team sports. The coach selects the starting players for the team, sets offensive and defensive strategies, and makes player substitutions during the match. The player usually switches to the coach role during timeouts or other pauses in the action.

Finally, there's the role of general manager of the team. The general manager is responsible for hiring and firing decisions and trying to recruit the best players within the limitations of the budget. See Figure 12.1 for an example. A few sports games are about *only* this aspect of the sport and don't include live simulations of the sport itself. These are occasionally called *manager* games and are particularly popular in Europe.

Figure 12.1   EA's *Madden NFL 2002* athlete-trading screen, a management function.

Structure

The structure of a sports game is typically simple. Its main play mode is *match play*, simulating the sport itself as it is played. You can usually pause the game and bring up a pause menu. While the game is paused, you can substitute athletes, change the camera view, adjust the AI if it can be adjusted, and perform other sorts of coaching tasks. You can also save the game for later or abandon it.

Outside of match play, most of the game's modes relate to other aspects of the sport: studying the athletes' ratings and performance statistics, hiring and trading them, establishing a depth chart, and following the sport's playing schedule on a calendar. The screen layouts tend to reflect the bookkeeping nature of these activities, often resembling tables or graphs.

Special Design Issues for Sports Games

Sports games face a number of design issues that are either rare or irrelevant in other kinds of games.

Physics for Sports Games

During play, your game will be running a physics engine that determines the behavior of moving bodies in the match. The physical behavior of an inanimate object such as a baseball is comparatively easy to implement. The physical behavior of humans, however, is much more complicated. Early sports games tended to treat a running athlete rather like a rocket: She had a velocity vector that gave the speed and direction of her movement, and an acceleration vector that gave the force and direction with which she was pushing. Modern sports games have much richer simulations with a great many variables, taking into account such things as the friction coefficient of the playing surface—for example, rain and snow make fields slippery and reduce traction.

Designing the physics simulation for a sports game is a highly technical problem and is beyond the scope of this book. However, we offer one caveat: Because a sports game is a simulation of the real world, it is a common error to think that the physics in a sports game should be as realistic as possible. They shouldn't be, for two reasons:

> ➤ First, the player is not actually running around on the playing field herself; she is sitting in a chair, watching a screen, and controlling an athlete through a hand-held controller. She has neither the immediate experience of being on the field nor the precise control over her movements that a real athlete does.

> ➤ Second, the player is not a professional athlete. There is a good reason why only a small number of people are capable of hitting a baseball pitched at 95 miles per hour. The length of time that the ball is within reach of the bat is about 0.04 seconds. It's simply not realistic to expect that an ordinary person, looking at a video screen without the benefit of depth perception, could react that fast.

For both of these reasons, it's necessary to fudge the physics to make the game playable. We slow the pitch so that the batter has a reasonable chance of hitting it, and we artificially adjust the position of the bat so that it intersects the path of the ball. It doesn't matter whether the physics perfectly copy the real world as much as whether they seem to be producing a reasonable simulation of the sport as it is played by professionals. Even in a highly realistic game, your objective is to provide an enjoyable experience, not a mathematical simulation of nature.

Rating the Athletes

One of the biggest tasks you have in designing a sports game is developing a rating system for the skills and athletic abilities of all the athletes in the game. The rating system provides the raw data that the physics engine needs to simulate the behavior of the athletes accurately. As your programming team develops the physics engine and game AI, you should work with them to determine what ratings are needed. Researching the athletes' performance and setting the ratings for them is a task that can take many months, and you will probably want to delegate it to junior designers or assistant producers.

In most team games, the athletes have one set of ratings common to all of them, plus specialized ratings that apply only to athletes playing a particular position.

Common Ratings

These are examples of the kinds of ratings that might be common to all the athletes in a game:

➤ **Speed.** The athlete's maximum moving (running or skating or swimming) speed under ideal conditions.

➤ **Agility.** A measure of the athlete's ability to change directions while moving.

➤ **Weight.** Simply the athlete's weight, which affects the force he transmits in a collision and the inertia he has when struck by someone else.

➤ **Acceleration.** The rate at which the athlete can reach top speed.

➤ **Jumping.** The height to which the athlete can jump.

➤ **Endurance.** The rate at which the athlete gets tired during the course of the game.

➤ **Injury resistance.** The probability that an athlete will be injured.

Specialized Ratings

These ratings apply to a specific position—in this case, the quarterback in American football:

➤ **Passing strength.** The distance that the quarterback can throw the ball.

➤ **Passing accuracy.** The precision with which the quarterback can throw the ball.

➤ **Dexterity.** The quarterback's general dexterity in handling the ball. This affects his chances of dropping the snap or fumbling a handoff.

➤ **Awareness.** The quarterback's ability to sense that he's about to be tackled and to try to get out of the way.

Athlete AI Design

The AI in most computer games is rather crude. In action games and first-person shooters, the player's AI-driven opponents typically have a small number of behaviors triggered by specific events (appearance of the player on the scene, being shot at, and so on). When they're together in a group, they very seldom act in concert or assign special roles to particular individuals, nor do they help each other. It's every monster for itself. When there are no stimuli, they go into a simple idle loop, walking aimlessly around or standing still.

These kinds of actions aren't acceptable in a sports game. People don't mind if a monster in a first-person shooter wanders randomly around, but the athletes in a sports game must behave like humans, and that means deliberate, intelligent action. Particularly in team games, each athlete is working with the others on the team to accomplish particular goals. The position the athlete plays dictates behavior to some extent, but within those boundaries, the athlete still has to respond intelligently to a number of possible events. In a relatively simple sport such as tennis, there might not be many of these events, but in a highly complex sport such as American football, with 22 players on the field at a time, there can be hundreds.

Defining the State Space

The best way to design sports-game AI is to map out a game's states as a giant flow-chart. There could be far more states than you realize at first. *Corner kick* in soccer is not just one state, but several. There is the period before the ball is kicked, after it has been kicked but has not yet touched another athlete, after it has been touched by another athlete, and so on. See Figure 12.2 for a partial example.

Consult the official rules of the sport as you construct the flowchart: They will often describe states in detail, with special rules applying to each. However, the rules alone are not enough; they describe game states for the purposes of listing legal and illegal actions, but not for tactics or strategy. Whenever something changes that requires the athletes to adopt a different tactic, the game has moved into a different state.

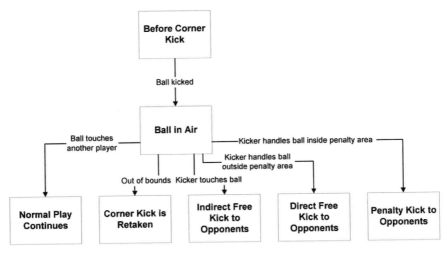

Figure 12.2   A flowchart detailing part of the "corner kick" situation in soccer.

Setting Collective and Individual Goals

After you define the game states, you can start thinking about what the team should do in that state—where each athlete should be trying to go and what he should be trying to do to support the team's collective goal at that moment. In some cases, these activities are defined with reference to a specific individual on the opposing team, trying to prevent him from doing his job. The software must have a way of matching up athletes with their opponents, just as the real athletes do.

When you have defined what the team should be trying to accomplish in a particular state and have assigned each athlete a role, you then must define exactly how the athlete is to perform that role: what direction he moves, what other movements he makes, which animations should be displayed, and so on. If the role is a defensive or supportive one, such as covering an opposing athlete, the individual AI for it might still be fairly complex. For example, a soccer player dribbling the ball might make a feint, trying to fool his opponent into thinking he's passing the ball. The software knows perfectly well that this is a feint, but sometimes the defender should be fooled and sometimes he shouldn't, depending on his awareness rating and, in either case, how he responds.

An athlete with nothing to do shouldn't just stand still. Most sports games include *fidgets*, short animations in which the athlete shifts his weight, stretches his arms, or makes some other neutral action every few seconds. Even if play is underway but the athlete is not closely involved—the third baseman on a fly ball to right field, for example—he at least should turn and watch the action.

Injuries

Injuries are a sad but common side effect of sports, and serious simulations take them into account. Because they occur somewhat randomly, they're outside the player's control and can be frustrating. Most sports games allow the players to turn off injuries if they don't like the effect that they have on the game.

Although it's possible for an athlete to injure herself simply by running or jumping, this doesn't provide the player with any visible explanation for why the injury occurred. A lot of sports games therefore limit injuries to cases in which there has been a collision of some kind, usually between two athletes. To determine whether an injury has occurred, you should include such factors as the relative speed of the two athletes, their weights, their respective susceptibilities to injury, and a random factor. The heavier an athlete is, the more force she imparts in a collision, and it is the force that does the damage to the other athlete.

Some positions, such as the pitcher in baseball, are simply so stressful that they can result in injuries without a collision, especially the longer the pitcher stays in the game. You can compute the probability of an injury on every pitch and raise it slightly with each one.

You can also decide which part of the body sustained the injury and the length of time for which it will disable the athlete. Study reports of injuries and recovery times for the sport you are simulating. If your game tracks athletes over a period of time, you will have to consider the cumulative effect of injury and recovery time on their careers.

Arcade Mode Versus Simulation Mode

Arcade mode versus simulation mode is a realism switch that lets the player adjust the behavior of the game to suit his tastes. Arcade mode makes the game more exciting at the expense of realism; simulation mode makes it a more accurate simulation of the real sport at some expense in fun. For example, in baseball, an athlete is doing well if he has a .333 batting average—that is, gets a hit only one time in three. Some players might find that a little dull. Switching the game to arcade mode could let the player get a hit 50 percent of the time or even more. It skews the play toward lots of action and relatively few strikeouts or walks. In American football, you could artificially increase the number of completed passes by improving the quarterback's throwing accuracy and the receiver's catching skills.

To implement arcade mode, you'll have to decide what sort of changes to the real game would make it more exciting. If you want your game to have both arcade and simulation modes, we recommend that you start with the serious simulation first and then design the "fudges" that make it arcadelike. Serious simulations are much more difficult to tune, and it's important to get them right first. If you start with an arcade-like design and then try to make it serious, you might never get it right.

Simulating Matches Automatically

Sports games that can play an entire season for a whole league of teams often provide a means of simulating matches automatically, without the player having to play them. For example, each team in professional baseball plays 162 matches in a season. With 30 teams and 2 teams in each match, this is a total of 2,430 matches—only the most rabid fan would want to play them all personally. To generate results for matches that the player doesn't play, you need a way of simulating a match. Of course, you'll want the resulting scores to accurately reflect the relative strengths of the teams: A bad team should be able to beat a good team occasionally, but not often.

Computer Versus Computer

The simplest way to simulate matches automatically is to let the computer play out the match in computer versus computer mode, as described in the section, "Competition Modes," earlier in this chapter, and record the results. If the game's simulation model is good, it should produce scores that reflect the real abilities of the competitors. Unfortunately, this is a slow way to do it. If the player wants to generate results for a match that she doesn't really care about, she probably wants it done quickly.

Simulation Without Graphics

One solution is to simulate the whole match exactly as in computer versus computer mode, but to turn off the graphics so that nothing is displayed. Because displaying the graphics often takes up the majority of the computer's time, an entire match can be simulated in a few seconds. Electronic Arts' *Earl Weaver Baseball* game did this successfully. It makes the programming more complicated, however, because throughout the whole program, there have to be checks to see if the game is in simulation mode or display mode. When you do this, test the game to be sure that the results without graphics are the same as those with graphics.

Faking It

The alternative many games adopt is to fake it—in effect, to roll dice to generate game scores. The dice are loaded somewhat so that good teams get high scores and bad teams get low ones, and whichever team rolls the highest score wins the match. You will need to devise a suitable algorithm for generating point values: In games such as American football and rugby, in which different numbers of points are awarded for different kinds of scores (touchdown, field goal, and so on), certain score values are much more common than others. It's extremely rare, for example, for a team to end an American football game with a score of 2. You'll also need to make sure that your algorithm creates a reasonable random distribution; no professional soccer game should ever end with a score over about 15.

One disadvantage of this dice-rolling technique is that it doesn't generate any other statistics besides the scores themselves. In a particularly statistics-rich sport such as baseball, if you don't generate performance data for each individual player, some fans will consider your game to be a lightweight, not a serious, simulation. It's up to you to decide just how important that market is to you and how much effort you're prepared to exert to meet their expectations.

Licenses, Trademarks, and Publicity Rights

Many years ago, small developers could make and sell computer games using names such as "NFL" and get away with it, because the National Football League never knew it was happening. You can't do this now. Interactive entertainment is big business, and you have to be scrupulously careful to avoid violating trademarks or personal publicity rights.

Team and League Trademarks

The exact details vary from league to league and country to country, but generally in America, the name, logo, uniform design, and other indicia of all the teams in a league, plus the name and logo of the league itself, are licensed for use by the league. You, or your publisher, will have to negotiate an agreement with the league to use these symbols in your game. Before Electronic Arts signed an agreement with the NFL, early versions of *John Madden Football* referred to teams only by their town names (such as San Francisco or Chicago) rather than by their team names (the 49ers and the Bears) and did not show any logos. The colors of the uniforms were similar but not exactly the same. You can pull this trick, too, if you dare, but you're risking a lawsuit if you get too close.

Individual sports, such as gymnastics or figure skating, are often governed by a variety of bodies in different countries around the world. The names and indicia of particular events, such as the Kentucky Derby, are owned by the organizations that produce them—in this case, the Churchill Downs racetrack. In recent years, these groups have begun to exploit their intellectual property rights in a variety of ways, so they tend to come down hard on anything that seems to be an infringement. Don't assume that just because an event has been around for decades, you can freely use its name.

Personal Publicity Rights

You cannot use the name or photograph of a real athlete without permission. An athlete's name and likeness are part of his personal publicity rights, and, of course, famous athletes sell the rights to use their names for millions of dollars when they endorse a particular product as an individual. You might need to negotiate with an organization that licenses the rights to use all the players' names collectively. This might be the league, in some cases; in others, however, including the NFL and Major League Baseball, you have to contact the athletes' unions. And unless you have the endorsement of a specific athlete, you must make sure that your game displays all athletes in approximately the same way, or endorsement could be implied. You can't make it look as if an athlete has endorsed your game when that's not the case.

Photographs present further difficulties. You must obtain a license from the person *in* the photograph and also from the person who *took* the photograph: the photograph's copyright holder. Again, some governing bodies have special clearinghouses for these kinds of things: NFL Photos is a special department of the NFL that licenses still photos for all the photographers who are accredited to take pictures at NFL matches. The license, however, does not grant you the personal publicity rights of the athlete in the picture; you have to obtain those separately. You can also license photos from the trading card companies, as well as from journalistic bodies such as the Associated Press, and from private photo libraries.

In short, the whole issue of rights in sports games is a legal minefield. Nowadays, even the stadiums might claim special rights, and many stadium owners auction the name of the stadium to the highest bidder, as with 3Com Park in San Francisco. As a designer, you probably won't have to deal with obtaining all these licenses yourself, but you should know that it's not safe to specify simply that a game will use all the team and player names and photos. Obtaining them and the right to use them is a very costly and time-consuming business. It's best to design the game in such a way that it doesn't depend on having these things, unless you're certain that they will be available.

Audio Commentary

Most sports games try to reproduce the experience of watching the sport on television. An important part of that experience is hearing the announcers' commentary, or play-by-play. Most TV and radio sports broadcasts include at least two people, the *play-by-play man* and the *color commentator*. The play-by-play man describes the play on a moment-by-moment basis. The color commentator, usually a retired coach or player, offers insights about strategy and tactics, as well as background material on the teams or individual players. A third voice that you occasionally hear is that of the stadium announcer over the public address system. His remarks tend to be quite formulaic, although they do occasionally include requests to move misparked cars, retrieve found children, and so on.

Defining the Events to Describe

A good way to size up the job of duplicating the audio experience is to record a TV broadcast of a real match and then transcribe everything that is said and by whom. Do this for two or three matches, and you will begin to notice patterns in the play-by-play: The announcers tend to announce the score at particular times, they use certain repetitive language, and so on. As you watch the match on videotape, take note of the different kinds of events that occur and the different remarks they elicit from the commentators. The color commentator's events aren't the same as the play-by-play man's. The color commentator speaks at more dramatic moments, or when an athlete has done something particularly spectacular (or particularly bad). For example, in tennis, you might have a color comment like, "She's having a terrible time with those double faults" when an athlete commits four double faults in a single game. Be sure you play it only once, however—not on every subsequent double fault.

When you have a set of match events that you want to create commentary for, sit down with the programmers and discuss them to make sure they are detectable. Some, such as a strikeout in baseball, will be uncomplicated, but a lot of them will be judgment calls. For example, a dropped pass in football that the player really *should* have caught is not so easily detectable; you can detect the dropped pass, but what determines whether he should have caught it? It must be calculated from such things as the receiver's dexterity rating and the accuracy with which the pass was thrown in the first place—provided that it wasn't tipped away by a defender. It's always best to err on the side of caution in these cases: Don't design judgment calls that the player is likely to disagree with, or he'll think your game is stupid. As the saying goes, "It's better to remain silent and be thought a fool than open one's mouth and remove all doubt."

Don't forget the introductory and wrap-up material at the beginning and end of the match—for example, "Welcome to Mile High Stadium for today's game between the New England Patriots and the Denver Broncos. It's a cold and windy day."

Writing the Script

When you have established the events that need audio commentary, you can start to write the audio recording script that will implement it. For each event, you will typically want to record four or five variant comments so that the players don't hear the same thing every time the event occurs. Obviously, the more comments you can write per event, the better your game will sound. The number of comments is really limited only by the available space on the distribution medium and the number of things you can reasonably think of to say about a given event.

As you write the script, you will discover places where a name or number will need to be included, usually the names of athletes or teams or the current score. If the sport is one with a large number of athletes, you cannot afford to record the sentence with every possible athlete's name in it. Instead, you will need to record the sentence as a whole using a sample name and edit the resulting audio file into clips, one part before the name and one part after. Your programmers must devise a method of streaming the sound clips, inserting the correct name in the right place in such a way that they sound seamless. When you record the sentence, use a sample name that begins and ends with a *T* or a *K* sound so that it doesn't slur into the rest of the sentence and so that it can be cut cleanly. For example, "Merrick steps up to the free throw line" enables the engineer to cut between *Merrick* and *steps*, whereas "Rogers steps up to the free throw line" would produce a slur from *Rogers* into *steps*.

Whenever possible, you should try to write the script in such a way that names are at either the beginning or the end of a sentence. You can then have your voice talent record the names of all the athletes who appear in the game. Each name will need to be recorded twice, once using the voice inflection for the beginning of a sentence, and once at the end. Don't try to record the names by themselves; record a complete sentence and then throw away all but the name, for example, "Thomas takes it" and "I'll pick Thomas." Again, using the *T* and *K* sounds adjacent to the name allows a clean cut in the audio.

Case Study: *Madden NFL Football*

Madden NFL Football is one of the longest-established and best-selling game franchises in the history of our industry. From its earliest beginnings on the Apple II, it has grown into a financial powerhouse that produces a new edition on several different platforms every year and makes millions of dollars for its publisher, Electronic Arts. Versions of *Madden* have appeared for personal computers and every major console machine ever produced.

Madden is not redesigned every year, nor is its code rewritten. Its artwork and video sequences are updated, and it gets new features each year, but it undergoes a complete overhaul only every four or five years—often when a new generation of game console appears. The majority of the design work each year consists of tuning and improving the gameplay and adding more features. These features expand the "football experience" to include aspects of the sport that go beyond playing a single match against another team. Among them are the following:

- Ability to hire and trade players among teams, subject to the limitations of the salary cap established by the NFL.
- Participation in the NFL draft.
- Detailed performance statistics on players.
- Season, tournament, and practice modes.
- Franchise mode, letting players take a team through several seasons in an effort to build a dynasty.
- A play editor, allowing players to customize their playbooks.
- Madden University, which includes detailed tutorials about offensive and defensive strategies, commentaries on the strengths and weaknesses of each team, and historical background.
- Adjustable AI, enabling players to set the coaching stances of computer-controlled teams to aggressive, neutral, or conservative.
- Arcade mode, a simplified and exaggerated form of the game.

As you can see, even though the sport itself changes little from year to year, new features and details can always be added to a sports game.

By far, the largest single task in developing *Madden* every year is research: rating the skills of the real players who appear in the game, keeping track of which team they're playing for, finding photographs of them, and so on. In addition to researching the players, the production team must research the coaches—trying to find out what kinds of plays they like to run, whether they're aggressive or conservative, and so on. The team's playbooks must be updated every year to reflect changes in coaching practice, and the new plays must be tested to make sure that they're effective but not unstoppable.

continues

continued

> In short, *Madden* is a highly successful sports game that offers its players a wide range of playing styles, from the quick and easy arcade game to the detailed minutiae of designing plays and adjusting rosters. As a game that tries to "do it all," it's well worth studying.

Other Peculiarities

The following sections detail a few other issues peculiar to sports games.

Invented Sports

From time to time, someone tries to create a sports video game of a completely invented sport, as opposed to a take-off of an existing one. Empire Interactive's *Speedball 2100* was one such game. Experience shows, however, that this is a risky enterprise. Hardcore sports gamers are seldom interested in completely new sports; they'd rather play a game that simulates a sport that they're already familiar with. Other types of gamers aren't that interested in sports games anyway and aren't very likely to want to play a one-off sports game unless it appeals to them for some other reason. If you're thinking of inventing a new sport specifically for a video game, we advise you to design it *as* a video game, without concerning yourself with what it might be like in the real world. This is how *Speedball* was designed; although it was theoretically a sport, it included powerups and other arcade-game elements to make it more interesting.

As we said earlier, one of the trickiest aspects of sports game design is mapping real-world activities to a limited input device. Players are willing to tolerate some awkwardness in the user interface when it's a real sport because they understand the problems. With an invented sport, they're unlikely to be so generous. When designing a completely new sport, you might consider working backward from the controller to the sport itself, designing around the limitations of your hardware.

Instant Replay

Instant replay is now an essential part of watching sports on television, so naturally video game players want it as well. It's not difficult to design, although it might be difficult to implement. Your game will need to keep track of the exact position and animation step of every player and other key objects on the field in each game frame. When the player requests an instant replay (usually through a pause menu), the game can play them back. Of course there is a limit to how much of this information you can keep around, and some natural boundary is likely to suggest itself—in baseball, the time since the most recent pitch; in American football, the time since the ball was snapped. In continuously flowing games such as basketball, you might have to establish an artificial time limit.

The best instant-replay mechanisms allow all the following features for maximum flexibility:

> ► Play, stop, fast-forward, rewind, and single-frame advance and reverse operations, to allow the player to see exactly what happened at every instant.

> ► The ability to move the camera in all three dimensions.

> ► The ability to pitch the camera up and down, and turn (panning) it left and right.

> ► The ability to lock the camera to a given athlete or the ball, to follow something wherever it goes. This is usually done by showing a symbol on the ground that represents the camera's focus of attention. If the symbol is directly under an athlete's feet when the player stops moving the camera, the camera locks onto that athlete.

Instant replay lets the players see the action from perspectives that they can't use when actually playing the game. For the game's publisher and developer, it's an invaluable tool for grabbing dramatic screen shots or gameplay footage for sales and demonstrations. You should consider it an essential feature of any sports game that you design.

Camera Difficulties in Games with Widely Separated Action

In most sports, the focus of the action is in one location. In a race, it's on the leaders. In any soccerlike sport (soccer, hockey, basketball, water polo, and so on), it's on the object that's supposed to go into the goal; similarly, in any tennislike sport, it's on the ball. Baseball and cricket are unusual in that the action takes place in two places at once: where the ball is and also where the runners are. In baseball, this can be as much as 400 feet away. You can't show both the runners and the ball without zooming out to a blimp view so high up that nobody can see anything clearly.

To solve this, most baseball video games implement a picture-in-picture solution: The camera follows the ball, but a small diagram of the baseball diamond in one corner of the screen shows the positions of the runners, often as no more than colored dots (see Figure 12.3). When a runner reaches a base, his dot changes color to indicate that he is safe. The player controlling the fielders watches the main screen, and the one controlling the runners watches the diagram (keeping one eye on the main screen to see if the ball is coming). Because cricket has only two stumps instead of four bases, this arrangement is even easier.

Figure 12.3   3DO's *High Heat Baseball*. Note the inset showing player positions. The round dots adjacent to the bases are runners taking their leads.

Home-Field Advantage

Considerable debate has raged over the years about whether to build a home-field advantage into sports games. Although the home-field advantage is statistically significant in a number of sports, we recommend against it. Players like to feel that they are playing a fair game, and if they know that the odds are artificially stacked against them whenever they play an "away" game, they will resent it. It's also unclear exactly how the home-field advantage should be implemented. The phenomenon is normally observed from win-loss statistics, but, of course, the computer can't simply turn a loss into a win. It could shave off a percentage of goal-scoring attempts, but even this is likely to have odd side effects. If a scoring attempt that clearly should have succeeded fails for no visible reason, the players are bound to notice it.

Sports Game Worksheet

In designing a sports game, consider the following questions as a starting point:

1. What sport am I simulating? Is it a real sport or a made-up one? If it's real, do I want to get a license from a governing body?

2. What are the rules of my sport? If it's a real sport, can I really implement them all, or will it have to be a subset?

3. What competition modes am I going to offer—single-player, competitive, cooperative, teams? Which ones make sense for my sport, and which don't?

4. In addition to playing a single match, what other game modes will I offer? Season, tournament, franchise, career?

5. What is the best perspective for playing my sport? Directly overhead, from the sidelines, from some other angle? What intelligence needs to be built into the camera to make the game easy to play? How will I handle displaying actions at widely separated points?

6. How do I map the actions of an athlete, or an entire team of athletes, to the controls available to the player? Will the functions of the buttons need to change during the course of play? When and why? What additional markings should I draw on the field of play to compensate for the player's lack of depth perception? What pop-up windows over the play will the player need, and how do I prevent those from obscuring the action? When play is not in progress, how does the rest of the user interface look and work?

7. What roles will the player play in the sport? Athlete, coach, general manager? When does the player switch from one to another and why?

8. What's the general structure of the game? What screens do I need, and how do they lead from one to another? Can the player trade athletes among teams in the middle of the season, for example?

9. What changes will I need to make to the physics of the sport to make it playable by ordinary mortals?

10. What characteristics describe an athlete's abilities? How will they affect the way her behavior looks on the screen? Will some athletes have ratings peculiar to the positions they play?

continues

continued

11. What states can the game be in, even in times between active play? How does an athlete behave in each state? What are her goals in each state, and in team play, what is the collective goal of the team in each state? How does the individual athlete's behavior contribute to meeting the team's goal?
12. Am I going to offer automatic simulation of matches? How will that be done?
13. What will the audio commentary be like? What events will it cover?
14. How does instant replay work?

Putting It Together

A good sports game design requires compromises. We do not yet have the computing power to simulate a real sport in all of its complexity and detail on a home computer or video game console—and even if we did, we still don't have input and output devices that allow a player to feel as if he's really down on the field. Someday, when virtual reality is perfected and home computers are as powerful as today's supercomputers, we might be able to do this. In the meantime, it's the job of the sports game designer to fit the sport to the machine. Sports game design doesn't require nearly as much raw creativity as designing an adventure game or a role-playing game. It's a more subtle process that entails endless tuning and tweaking to find the right balance between realism and playability. When you get it right, you have a product that can sell for years and years.

Chapter 13

Vehicle Simulations

Vehicle simulations try to create the feeling of driving or flying a vehicle, real or imaginary. In simulations of real vehicles, one of the chief goals is verisimilitude, an (apparently!) close relationship to reality. You can expect your players to know a lot about these machines and to want an experience that is at least visually similar to that of really controlling one. The machine's gross performance characteristics (speed and maneuverability) should also be similar to reality, although its finer details probably can't be, for reasons we'll discuss in this chapter.

If you're designing an imaginary vehicle, you're free to create any kind of driving experience that you like without being restricted by such things as gravity, G-forces, fuel capacity, and so on. Your game really needs to just create the feeling of movement; what limitations you place on that movement are up to you. In this chapter, we concentrate, for the most part, on simulating real vehicles because that's the bigger challenge. Also, because the vast majority of vehicle simulators are flight simulators and driving (usually car-racing) simulators, we devote most of our attention to those. A short section devoted to ships, tanks, and spacecraft is included at the end.

The Common Elements of Vehicle Simulations

People play with flight simulators for one of two reasons. Either they want to experience the joy of flight in a variety of different aircraft, to see how the planes or helicopters look and perform, or they want to fight in aerial combat. In effect, they want to fly aircraft in either civilian or military roles, and that's how we refer to these roles here.

Just as flight simulators tend to fall into military or civilian categories, driving simulators tend to fall into *organized racing* and *imaginary racing* categories. Organized racing simulators try to reproduce the experience of driving a racing car or motorcycle in an existing racing class: Indycar, NASCAR, Formula 1, and so on. Like sports games, they require a license to use the official name and indicia of the racing organization. Imaginary racing games are just that: games about racing in imaginary situations, driving madly through cities or the countryside or even fantasy environments.

The vehicle-simulation market is sharply divided between the purists and the casual players. The purists demand highly accurate simulations of real vehicles with all their quirks and limitations. If a purist forgets to retract the flaps after takeoff, he wants those flaps to be damaged by excessive airspeed and to be stuck in the down position, with appropriate consequences for the plane's handling characteristics. The casual players don't care about the details as long as they can fly or drive around fast and (depending on the game) shoot at things.

An Extreme Case

The takeoff sequence in the game *Megafortress* had to be the longest for any consumer-level flight simulator ever made. The game simulated a hypothetical stealth-modified B-52 bomber. This is what you had to do to get the plane off the ground (fortunately, it was already lined up on the runway):

1. Switch on battery power.
2. Switch on interior lights.
3. Switch on power to all eight engines.
4. Fire starter cartridges for all eight engines.
5. Switch off battery power after the engines are running.
6. Switch on navigation lights.
7. Switch on landing lights.

8. Pressurize the plane to noncombat levels.

9. Tune radio to correct frequency (this also served as the game's copy protection).

10. Lower flaps.

11. Release brakes.

12. Throttle up all eight engines (fortunately, this could be done simultaneously).

13. Pull back on stick. (Plane takes off.)

14. Raise landing gear.

15. Raise flaps.

This sequence involved moving back and forth from the pilot's seat to the co-pilot's seat a couple of times, too. Soon after you got into the air, you had to switch all the lights back off to avoid detection by enemy aircraft. If you forgot to pressurize the plane, the crew would complain of being cold. When you entered into combat, you were supposed to lower the air pressure to avoid a violent decompression if the plane was hit.

Megafortress was a techno-geek's dream. It was not, however, a big financial success as flight simulators go.

The Rules

Some vehicle simulations aren't games at all, in the sense of being a contest or a competition. Their only goal is to let the player experience controlling the vehicle, so they don't have any rules other than the laws of physics. Most vehicle simulations, however, are set in a competitive context, either a race or a battle of some kind.

One factor to consider is how you want to handle damage. Lightweight racing sims don't simulate any damage at all; if the car hits something, it simply bounces off, which tends to slow it down. This allows the driver to be much more careless. She can afford to hit a few things and still win the race—at least in the earlier, easier stages of the game. Other games model damage as a single variable, such as hit points in a role-playing game. When damage reaches a certain level, the vehicle simply stops running (which, in the case of an airplane, means that it crashes or explodes).

Accurate modeling of damage requires dividing the vehicle into areas, determining which area has been damaged by a collision (or, in a military simulator, by enemy fire), and deciding how that damage affects the performance of the vehicle. For instance, a race car with minor damage to the airfoils or body can continue, although with a performance penalty, but a blown tire will force it to halt. With airplanes, the consequences can be dramatically different depending on what has been hit. A plane is still flyable if its tail has been destroyed, but it will be unstable and extremely difficult to handle.

Competition Modes

In military flight simulators, the competition modes are similar to those of first-person shooters: solitaire against artificial opponents, multi-player death matches (every player for himself), and team-based play. Civilian flight simulators usually have only a solitaire mode, although they can also allow races and follow-my-lead competitions. Driving simulators are generally solitaire games or multi-player races, and are seldom team-based.

Both military flight simulators and organized race-driving simulators often include a career mode, in which you create a pilot or driver and follow his career (trying not to get him killed, of course), racking up victories and collecting performance statistics. They also include campaign modes, in which a race driver tries to win in a real racing circuit, collecting points according to the official rules of the circuit.

In military flight simulators, the campaign mode can work in various ways. In one approach, the game offers a series of missions one at a time in which the player must achieve a specified victory condition before going on to the next mission; completing all the missions constitutes winning the campaign. In another approach, the player can play all the missions in order, whether she meets the mission objectives or not. However, if she plays through all of them without achieving enough mission objectives, she loses the campaign. This more closely approximates what happens in a real war. The better you fight on any given occasion, the more chance you have of winning the war in the long run, but you can still afford to lose the occasional battle. But as the designer, you have to provide clear feedback to the player about how she's doing as she goes along.

Gameplay and Victory Conditions

The primary challenge in any vehicle simulator is in controlling the vehicle: learning to speed it up, slow it down, and steer it to where you want it to go without crashing it into something. In the case of flight simulators, you can make this challenge simple, requiring the player to know almost nothing about aerodynamics, or extremely difficult, modeling the behavior of an airplane accurately. Unlike a car, airplanes respond rather slowly to their controls, often beginning to execute a maneuver several seconds after the player has first moved the yoke or joystick. Because players are more used to driving a car, they will tend to overcontrol the plane: Finding that it doesn't respond immediately, they'll push the stick farther and then wildly overcompensate in the opposite direction when the plane finally does much more than they intended in the first place. If you want to present a realistic challenge, you can model this problem accurately.

In driving simulators, the chief challenge is staying on the road without crashing. Without being able to feel the G-forces on his body, the player has to depend on other cues to determine how fast he is going and how hard he is braking.

Military Flight Sims

In military flight simulators, the player must not only fly the aircraft, but also achieve the mission's objectives, usually attacking enemy aircraft and ground installations. Modern air-to-air combat, conducted with long-range guided missiles and often directed by Airborne Warning and Control System (AWACS) planes, is something of a chess game—a rather cerebral exercise. Hence the continuing popularity of World War I and II flight simulators and fictional ones such as *Crimson Skies* (see Figure 13.1). These let the players dogfight: twisting and turning through the sky, hiding behind clouds, diving out of the sun, and blasting away with bullets at short range. It's a much more action-packed experience.

Figure 13.1 A pilot's view in *Crimson Skies.* Note the very simple instrument panel.

The gameplay in military flight simulators is defined by the role of the aircraft being simulated. Fighter planes are designed primarily to attack enemy aircraft and to protect friendly aircraft and ground units from air attacks. Attack planes are designed to attack moving ground targets; bombers are designed to attack stationary ones. Most military flight simulators offer a series of missions, often with primary and secondary objectives; achieving them constitutes victory. The objectives are usually to shoot down enemy fighters or to destroy ground targets, all without being shot down yourself, of course. Being killed or having your plane shot down constitutes a loss. You can also rate the success of a mission according to the number of objectives achieved, the length of time it took, and the amount of damage sustained by the aircraft, assigning extra points for a swift and safe return.

Civilian Flight Sims

Civilian flight simulators such as the venerable but excellent *Microsoft Flight Simulator* (see Figure 13.2) seldom have any victory conditions, unless they implement racing or specific challenges, such as tests of speed and accuracy. Many of them are not really games in the competitive sense at all; their goal is to let the player fly and try different things with the aircraft rather than to present him with a specific mission to accomplish. However, civilian flight sims can present a wide variety of challenges: flying at night; flying in rain, fog, or strong winds; and using visual flight rules or instrument flight rules. Landing smoothly and safely, particularly in adverse weather conditions, is always the most dangerous moment in a flight and usually represents the toughest challenge that a civilian flight simulator has to offer. Most of them provide an *autoland* function that simply returns the plane to the ground without the player having to land it

Figure 13.2   An instrument panel in *Microsoft Flight Simulator 2002*.
This is a game for serious pilots.

Racing Sims

Organized racing simulations, like sports games, take their gameplay from the real thing. The challenge is primarily to win races without crashing. Some games also include an economic element: The player wins prize money for doing well in a race, and the prize money enables her to buy better equipment. This produces positive feedback that must be counteracted to balance the game; as the player improves, her artificial opponents must also improve to offer her a worthy challenge.

Setting

The settings of flight simulators consist of the plane itself and the ground that it flies above. With a few exceptions, such as *Microsoft Combat Flight Simulator*, most flight sims don't offer interesting terrain. If your flight simulator has a historical setting, you can do a lot on the ancillary screens to set the mood. Electronic Arts' World War II flight simulator, *Jane's World War II Fighters*, shows a hanger full of period aircraft and other gear, and it even plays Glenn Miller tunes in the background. Unfortunately, in the pursuit of historical accuracy, Electronic Arts set all its combat missions above the Ardennes mountains in the wintertime: a bleak, snowy landscape covered with leafless trees. The technical quality of the graphics was superb; it's too bad they weren't depicting something more interesting. Its competitor, *Microsoft Combat Flight Simulator*, was less historically accurate but more fun to fly around because you could buzz the Eiffel Tower or London's Houses of Parliament.

Driving simulators are set on either racetracks or roads, except for a few off-road simulators. Off-road driving offers the fun of bouncing all over interesting terrain without having to steer carefully. Narrow, twisting mountain roads are a popular choice for road-based games because they offer both an interesting challenge and pretty scenery.

Weather is a critical factor to consider in designing the settings of both flight and driving simulators. Can the player drive or fly at night? In rain? In fog? Rain plays an important strategic role in automobile racing because the drivers need to make a pit stop to switch to rain tires, which hold the road better. The pit stop takes time, but if they don't do it, they run an increased risk of crashing.

Because flight and driving simulators rarely show other people, their worlds can seem eerily devoid of life. Cities are depicted as collections of buildings with no pedestrians and (in flight simulators) no vehicles. Airports have only one plane, the player's, and no ground staff. Simulator designers often feel that because these things aren't critical to the gameplay, they're a waste of time to implement. Still, they add considerably to the sense of immersion.

Interaction Model

The interaction model in a flight simulator is quite straightforward: The player's plane is his avatar. The plane's controls are mapped onto the computer's input devices, and the player's view is normally that of the pilot, forward through the cockpit windows.

Perspective

As with sports games, flight and driving simulations frequently offer a variety of camera perspectives. Although the game is not playable from all of them, they can be used for taking dramatic screenshots or instant replays of action.

Views Common to Driving and Flight Simulators

Both driving and flight simulators implement certain standard views:

➤ **Pilot's/driver's view.** This is the "normal" view that most simulators offer by default. The player sees what the pilot or driver would see from that position in the cockpit or driver's seat. The vehicle's instruments take up the lower half of the screen, and the view out of the windshield is shown in the upper half, often partially obscured by parts of the canopy or the nose of the car or plane. Most sims offer separate "look left," "look right," and "look backward" views, as well as a mode in which the player can swivel the view smoothly through 360° as well as up, to see what's overhead, and down, to see instruments located below the pilot's normal line of sight.

➤ **Cockpit-removed view.** This is an unrealistic but dramatic perspective in which the pilot or driver's view out of the front of the vehicle is shown full-screen rather than being partially obscured by the cockpit. Critical instruments are shown as semitransparent overlays in the corners of the screen, so as not to interfere with the view too much. Even these can be removed, providing an unobscured view of the world outside, with no visible indication that the player is in a vehicle at all.

➤ **Chase view.** This is an exterior view of the player's vehicle, as if from another one following closely behind and mimicking its movements. In flight simulators, the plane always seems to be level and the world turns around it. For example, if the player banks her plane, the horizon tilts while the player's plane appears to be level in the middle of the screen. In driving simulators, the chase view is usually somewhat elevated so the car does not obscure the player's view of the road in front.

➤ **Rear, side, and front views.** These are exterior views of the player's vehicle from all four sides. If the player's plane banks, the view does not bank; the ground remains below.

➤ **Free-roaming camera.** Used only in an instant-replay mode, this enables the camera to be moved anywhere in the world and tilted or rotated to look in any direction. This view is useful for players trying to analyze exactly what happened in a particular encounter.

Views Unique to Flight Simulators

The following views are found only in flight simulators—and military ones, at that:

➤ **Ground target view.** This is a view of a target on the ground that is currently selected for attack. The camera is positioned at a nearby ground location, facing the target, and does not move. This view lets the player watch incoming missiles or bombs arrive and see if they hit the target accurately.

➤ **Bomb or missile view.** This is the point of view from a recently released bomb or missile, as if it had a camera in its nose (many modern weapons do). This allows a particularly dramatic perspective as the weapon approaches its target. This view usually disappears after the weapon detonates, and the perspective returns to the default view.

Views Unique to Driving Simulators

The following views occur only in driving simulators. Obviously, the cars are not drivable from these perspectives, but they are great for instant replays.

➤ **Trackside view.** Many racetracks have cameras located at fixed points around the track. The camera can be either locked to a specific viewpoint or made to track the player's car as it moves past. It's also common to have a routine that switches from one trackside camera to another to follow the leaders as they go around. This gives a good simulation of watching television coverage of a race (see Figure 13.3).

➤ **Grandstand view.** This is the traditional spectator's view of the finish line.

➤ **Blimp view.** This is a high aerial view looking straight down onto the racetrack or course, letting you see all the cars at once.

Figure 13.3   A typical trackside view in *NASCAR Racing 4*.

User Interface Design

The biggest challenge in designing the user interface of a vehicle simulator is in mapping the vehicle's real controls to those available on the target machine. For serious simulations, analog controls are essential; the binary D-pads of older handheld controllers don't allow the kind of precision needed for accurate steering. It used to be that serious simulations simply weren't possible on console machines, but now that most console machines offer analog joysticks, mapping the controls of a race car to those of a home console machine isn't quite as much of a problem.

Force-feedback joysticks, throttles, control yokes, steering wheels, and pedals (rudder for planes, and gas and brake for cars) all help immensely, and serious players will have them. You can greatly improve the quality of the simulation experience for such players by supporting them. However, don't design—and, more important, don't tune—your game with a presumption that your players will have this kind of hardware. It should be an enjoyable experience even with only a standard console controller or a mouse and keyboard. If it's not, you've severely limited your audience and your game is bound to be slammed in reviews.

Military flight simulators always require some simplification from the real thing; you will have to decide how much. Real military aircraft are flown only by special people who have had months or years of training, much of it spent sitting in classrooms. Because we want our players to be able to fly the planes within a few minutes of installing the software, we have to make considerable compromises in the realism of the game. You will almost certainly want to reduce the number of instruments in the cockpit and the number of functions that some of them perform.

One common simplification that almost all flight simulators make is to produce automatically coordinated flight. Ordinarily, the pilot of an airplane must coordinate the movements of the ailerons and rudder when turning, to prevent the plane from skidding sideways in the air, in the same way that a car skids sideways on wet pavement if it takes a turn too fast. Because the plane has no tires gripping pavement to control the direction it is facing, this can happen easily. However, most players have only one control mechanism, the joystick. To simplify flight, the left-right motion of the joystick controls both the rudder and the ailerons simultaneously, producing automatically coordinated flight.

Another common simplification for flight simulators is made in the navigation. Modern planes have global positioning systems, but World War I and II pilots still needed to know proper navigation, plotting their courses by the stars at night and by landmarks or dead reckoning during the daytime. Because this isn't the most exciting thing about flying, just give the player a map.

The Player's Role

The player's role in a flight simulator seems as if it should be quite straightforward: It's that of a pilot. In single-seat aircraft, that's all that is required. However, if you're going to simulate larger aircraft, such as bombers or two-seat fighters, you'll have to decide how you want to handle the varying roles available. In LucasArts' excellent World War II simulator *Their Finest Hour,* the player could play any of the waist and tail gun positions of the Junkers JU-88 bomber while leaving the plane on autopilot, or he could set the guns to fire automatically at any target that came into view. To drop the bombs, however, he had to take over the bombardier's position personally. Three-Sixty Pacific's game *Megafortress* required the player to manage no fewer than five different stations: pilot, co-pilot, navigator, electronic warfare specialist, and offensive weapons officer. Each had its own instrument panel and responsibilities, and the player had to move constantly from one to another to check on conditions and respond to emergencies. At times when the player was away from the pilot's seat, the plane flew on autopilot toward the next waypoint.

In racing-oriented driving games, the player's role is that of a racing driver most of the time, but the more serious simulations, such as *Indycar Racing*, also allow the player to be a mechanic, modifying the angle of the airfoils, changing tires to compensate for weather conditions, and so on.

Other Vehicles

Flight and driving simulators are by far the most popular kinds, but there are other sorts of vehicle simulators as well, usually in niche categories.

Boats and Ships

Most boat simulations are of powerboats or jet skis, offering the same kinds of speed thrills that driving simulators do (see Figure 13.4). The handling characteristics of powerboats are different from cars; because they're in a fluid medium, they don't "hold the road" the way a car's tires do, so they can't turn as sharply as a car can. Powerboat simulations are usually races over a twisting course marked off by buoys. Jet ski or fantasy water vehicle simulations often have outrageous jumps and other challenges as well.

Figure 13.4 *Power Boat Racing*, in a third-person perspective. Note the semitransparent map overlay and instrument panel.

There have been a few simulators of warships over the years, often fairly small craft with high speed and maneuverability, such as the PT boat of World War II fame. Larger vessels such as battleships and aircraft carriers move more slowly and deliberately, and, therefore, tend to be simulated not as individual vehicles, but as part of naval warfare simulations involving whole fleets, such as *Harpoon*.

Submarine simulations such as *688 Attack Sub* are fairly popular because of the specialized nature of their situation and because they can move in three dimensions. They normally concentrate on rather old-fashioned submarine activities, such as looking through the periscope and firing torpedoes at surface ships. These are the sorts of things we associate with submarines from watching old war movies, and, of course, they're the most visually dramatic. Few games simulate the modern role of submarines, hunting and hiding from one another in total darkness, because it's too cerebral of an activity.

Sailing ship simulations are another rarity. Although sailing a ship is a complex and interesting challenge, such games appeal only to a specialized market. Most people prefer simulations in which you can point the vehicle in the direction you want to go and push the gas pedal to get you there. Few ship simulations model the ocean in all its complexity, with shoals and currents, tides and storms. Rather, they tend to treat it the way driving simulations treat the ground: simply as an area over which ships move. Pirate games such as *Sea Dogs II* (see Figure 13.5) and *Pirates: Legend of Black Kat* are usually arcade or role-playing games rather than sailing simulations.

Figure 13.5   *Sea Dogs II.*

Tanks and Mechs

Tank simulations seldom implement the complexity of tank battles as they really happened in World War II, the Arab-Israeli wars, or the Gulf War. Real tanks don't move all that fast, have limited visibility, and carry only a few types of weapons, so they don't appeal much to the casual gamer. Like combat flight simulators, tank simulators are usually about a lone tank operating against other tanks and a variety of other enemies.

From a gameplay standpoint, the most interesting characteristic of a tank is its rotating turret, which enables it to shoot in directions other than the one in which it is facing. (Notice the example in Figure 13.6.) It can be difficult to design a good user interface for this. You will need to provide a mechanism for rotating the turret that is separate from the mechanism that steers the tank, and a separate view window for aiming and firing the gun. Real tanks have a commander and a gun crew as well as a driver, but as with bombers and other multi-seat aircraft, you will have to find a way to let a single player control everything.

Figure 13.6 A tank in *Panzer Elite*. The turret is facing in a different direction from the tracks.

A more popular alternative is the *mech*, a science-fiction cousin to the tank that is usually depicted as a large armed and armored walking machine (see Figure 13.7). Because mechs aren't restricted by reality, they can carry all sorts of imaginary weapons and hardware, and they can be optimized for single-player play.

Figure 13.7 *MechWarrior 4: Mercenaries.*

Spacecraft

There are almost no simulations of real spacecraft except for quasi-educational ones about the space shuttles because real spacecraft behave far too slowly and deliberately to make for an interesting game. The majority of spacecraft simulations, therefore, are science fiction, and they typically consist of either fighter planes in space, such as the *Wing Commander* series, or capital ship simulations, such as the many *Star Trek* games. The fighter types are simple action games with only a few variables to manage: Fuel, ammunition, damage, and shields are about it. Capital ship simulations are more strategic, giving the player control of a wide range of weapons and other equipment.

Special Design Considerations for Vehicle Simulations

Some design issues are particular to vehicle simulations and are described in the following sections.

Creating the Sense of Speed

In a flight simulation, there's little need for a sense of speed because simply flying fast is rarely the point. Most players either are trying to fly accurately and aerobatically or are engaging in aerial combat. Although speed is an important factor in the game, conveying that sense to the player isn't critical to the experience.

In driving simulations, however, the sense of speed is all-important. Here are some ways to create it:

> ➤ **Give the player a speedometer.** This is the most obvious way to inform a player of his speed, but it creates a purely logical awareness, not a visceral one. It might also help to give him a tachometer so he can see that the engine is near its maximum potential.

> ➤ **Vary the driving surface.** Don't present a smooth ribbon of black, but make the road a series of continuously changing dark grays. (Look back at Figure 13.3, *NASCAR 4*, to see this done well.) The rate at which these move toward the car will help to create the feeling of speed. Don't just use a set of random dots, though, or

at high speed they will just look like a static, flickering surface. It's better to implement them as a series of narrow strips parallel to the road's edges. Also, on roads (as opposed to racetracks), be sure to implement the dotted white line down the center. The sight of the lines flicking by gives a continuous visual cue to the speed, as well as a good way to tell when the vehicle is speeding up or slowing down.

➤ **Include roadside objects.** A continuous fence, guardrail, or strip of grass doesn't do much to give the player a feeling of motion. Make sure there are lots of trees, road signs, and bridges. Anything that is vertical beside the road, or that passes over or under the car, will help to create the impression.

➤ **Use sounds.** The sound of the engine is the most obvious auditory cue, but there's also road noise (the sound the tires make on the pavement), wind noise, and tires squealing as they round corners. Another excellent cue is a Doppler shift as the car passes, or is passed by, some noise-making object.

G-Forces

The driver of any vehicle feels a variety of forces affecting her body: acceleration, deceleration, and centrifugal force. She can feel these forces as pressure driving her body in one direction or another, usually into the seat or against the belts holding her in. The forces give a lot of valuable feedback about the behavior of the vehicle. Unfortunately, in a simulator, we can't provide any of those feelings to the player, so we have to substitute other indicators. With driving simulators, it doesn't matter that much because automobiles seldom generate significant G-forces, and the player has plenty of other visual cues, as described in the previous section.

Military aircraft can generate powerful G-forces, but because the player spends most of her time looking at the sky, there's nothing to indicate them. The engines of modern fighter planes are powerful enough to tear the plane apart if it is mishandled, and if you're doing a realistic simulation, you might want to include this deadly little detail. If so, you should include a G-force meter showing the amount of stress being applied to the plane (and pilot). Most aircraft are designed to sustain strong downward G-forces, but not upward ones. In addition, pilots undergoing strong downward G-forces can black out momentarily as all the blood drains out of their heads. They can also suffer an experience called *redout* if they encounter a strong upward G-force, as too much blood flows into their heads. Many games simulate these conditions by fading the screen to black or to red, which, in addition to preventing the player from seeing anything, gives a clear indication that something is wrong.

Designing Opponents

The easiest way to design a variety of opponents in a vehicle simulation is simply to vary the performance characteristics of their vehicles. One plane climbs slightly faster than another; one can turn more sharply. The player will experience different challenges in dealing with each one based on their design parameters. However, this kind of variety is static and, after the player has figured it out, is easily beaten. As soon as he discovers that a Supermarine Spitfire can consistently outrun a Messerschmitt BF 109 in level flight, it offers an obvious strategy for Spitfire pilots: "boom and zoom" (hitting and running away).

To create further variety in the behavior of individual opponents, the AI for those opponents should be designed around getting perfect performance from the vehicle and then creating variations from perfection. For example, it's possible to create a "perfect" AI driver in a racing simulation. He always follows the most efficient line around the track, he always shifts gears at precisely the correct moment, and he knows the ideal speed at which to take each corner without spinning out. If such a driver has a better car than the player's, he will be unbeatable. The trick, then, is to modify the AI driver's judgment so that it isn't perfect—so that he doesn't always shift at exactly the right time or follow the most efficient line. It is the combination of factors, both vehicle characteristics and variable driver skill, that provides the variety among opponents in vehicle simulators.

As you study the business of flying or driving, you will discover other tricks to incorporate into the AI: drafting behind other cars, for example, and diving out of the sun to surprise the enemy in a dogfight.

Intellectual Property Rights

As a general rule, you can model and simulate military equipment without obtaining permission from their manufacturers. Because such machines are not sold to the general public, nor are generally exploited in any other way, their appearance is in the public domain. Automobiles are another story, however. If you are going to simulate an existing car and use its real name and logo, you must have a license from the manufacturer. The manufacturer might not be willing to let you show the car crumpled and burning by the side of the road, either. This accounts for the large number of vehicle simulations in which the cars can flip over in an accident but never get damaged—they flip back upright a second or two later, as in *Beetle Adventure Racing*. Or, you can do as *Interstate '76* did and model cars that look rather like existing vehicles and have similar names, but don't actually use the manufacturer's indicia.

Vehicle Simulation Worksheet

When beginning the design of a vehicle simulation, consider the following questions:

1. What vehicle are we going to simulate? Is it an existing car, plane, boat, tank, and so on, or is it a fantasy-vehicle?
2. If it is an existing vehicle, are we aiming for the purist player who knows all its technical specifications, or for the casual player who simply wants to enjoy using it? How detailed is the physics model going to be?
3. How will the game handle damage to the vehicle? Can it be visually shown to be damaged? (Licenses for real vehicles sometimes forbid this.) Will damage be treated globally, like hit-points, or locally for individual parts of the machine?
4. What are the competition modes and victory conditions in the game? If this is a military vehicle, what sort of missions are available for it? If it is a civilian one, what kinds of things can it do besides simply racing (if anything)?
5. What settings are available for the vehicle to travel through? Even a flight simulator needs ground to look at below.
6. What camera views are appropriate for this vehicle? If it is a military vehicle, are there special camera views that assist in fighting? Can the player record and even edit instant replays so as to re-live and show off his triumphs?
7. How will we map the many controls of a plane or even a car onto the input devices available to the player? What aspects of the vehicle's controls will need to be simplified? Which can afford to have simple on-off buttons and which require analog controls?
8. If a vehicle is capable of steering in a different direction from that in which it shoots, how can the player control both at once conveniently?
9. What navigational facilities is the player going to need to know where he is (radar screen, overlay map, separate map mode that pauses the game, and so on)?

10. What artificial intelligence is needed to create decent opponents in the game's competitive modes? What sorts of things will the artificial opponents need to manage? Will they be smart enough to take advantage of superior speed, acceleration, cornering ability, braking ability?

11. Do we want to create a sense of speed for the player? If so, how will we create it? (Remember, you can use both visual and audible cues.)

Putting It Together

Designing a vehicle simulation is primarily a question of research and compromise. Unless your game is a lightweight simulation such as *Super Mario Kart*, vehicle simulation is the most technologically oriented of games. Much of the entertainment value comes from the feeling of controlling a real machine instead of meeting strategic challenges or taking part in a story. To provide that value, you will need to research your vehicles thoroughly. If you're designing a military vehicle, you can probably find much of what you need from the Jane's Information Group, publishers of such volumes as *Jane's All the World's Aircraft*, and, of course, from the vehicle's manufacturer. For automobiles, the various enthusiast magazines offer all the data you could want.

The compromises occur when you start trying to control a simulated vehicle with a computer or console machine's I/O devices, especially a large, complicated vehicle such as a B-52 bomber. The kinds of compromises you make, and the places they take you, will depend mostly on whether your target audience is the purist or the casual player.

Chapter 14

Construction and Management Simulations

Construction and management simulations are games about processes. The player's goal is not to defeat an enemy, but to build something within the context of an ongoing process. The better the player understands and controls the process, the more success he will have at building.

The first really successful computerized construction and management simulation (which we refer to as a CMS from now on) was *Sim City*. We'll look at it in some detail later in the chapter. *Sim City* proved that computer games don't need high-speed action or violence to be a success; it succeeded in part because it *didn't* have those things and appealed to a broad audience.

At the end of this chapter, we also have a section called "Pure Business Simulations," devoted to games in which the player doesn't really "construct" anything, and another section called "Hybrid Games," about games that are a hybrid of CMS and war games, such as *Age of Empires*. Military strategy is addressed in Chapter 10, "Strategy Games," but some of these hybrid games include interesting economic elements as well; we'll refer to them throughout this chapter, where appropriate.

The Common Elements of CMSs

Most CMSs give the player the chance to build and manage some entity—a city, a building, an anthill, or whatever—using two general sets of tools: one for building and one for managing. Building is easy, but managing is tricky indeed; we discuss that aspect of the simulation first.

Rules

The rules of a CMS define its internal economy and the ways in which the player can influence that economy. Creating and balancing an economy is one of the most complex and difficult jobs a game designer can do, and you can be sure that no matter how carefully you have worked it out, there will be consequences and relationships that you never considered. This is sometimes called *emergent behavior*, and whether it's desirable or not is up to you. Only playtesting and tuning will get the game right in the end.

Resources

An *economy* is a system in which resources are produced, consumed, and exchanged. In many CMSs, the primary resource is money. The characteristics of the resources affect the way a game is played. For example, resources can be tangible, requiring storage space that must be constructed and paid for, or intangible, occupying no physical space and costing nothing to move from place to place. Money is usually treated as an intangible resource, but food and building materials are generally treated as tangible entities. There are occasional exceptions: *Dungeon Keeper* (another hybrid game) treated gold as a tangible resource that had to be mined and transported back to a treasury, and the player had to expand the treasury when it got full.

A number of games treat resources in a mixed fashion, sometimes tangible and sometimes intangible. Both *Dungeon Keeper* and *Age of Empires* required that resources be transported from their production points to a storage facility; during this period, the resource was vulnerable to destruction or seizure by an enemy. However, in *Age of Empires*, when a resource was stored, it could not be seized or destroyed even if the enemy demolished the storage pit. In effect, resources became intangible when they were stored.

Similarly, most CMSs don't require a resource to be physically transported to be spent or consumed; the commodity simply vanishes from its warehouse. When constructing a building in *Age of Empires*, the player doesn't need to transport the stone from the storage pit to the construction site. This takes an extra management burden off the player.

One game that treats all resources as tangible, including money, is *The Settlers* from Blue Byte Software. In *The Settlers*, every kind of resource (and there are many) must be transported from where it is produced, either to storage areas or directly to places where it is consumed. Grain, for example, must be carried from the grain farm to the windmill for grinding, the flour must be carried from the windmill to the bakery, and the bread must be carried from the bakery to the mines, where the miners eat it.

Sources

Every resource, intangible or tangible, must have one or more sources—that is, ways in which they come into the game. In *Monopoly*, for example, money comes into the game from the bank. All the players start with a certain amount of money, and they get more each time they pass Go. They can also mortgage their properties for money, and they might get more money from the bank through the actions of the Chance and Community Chest cards.

Unlike *Monopoly*, which is turn-based, CMSs usually have a *production rate* for each resource. This production rate can be fixed or variable, and rates can be different at different sources—that is, some sources might produce the resource faster than others.

Finally, regardless of production rate, sources can be *limited* or *unlimited*. A particular source might contain a limited amount of a resource and might cease production when it is depleted. If the entire game contains only a limited amount (that is, all possible sources contain limited amounts), the game can be said to be *closed-ended*. The game must eventually end or fail when the essential resource is gone. On the other hand, if the amount of the resource is unlimited, the game is *open-ended*—it can continue indefinitely. *Dungeon Keeper* again provides examples of both. Gold mines in *Dungeon Keeper* produced only a certain amount of gold. Because various activities consumed gold, eventually the dungeon must run out of money. Some dungeons, however, contained gem mines as well as gold mines (a misnomer because what they actually produced was also gold). The difference was that a gem mine could never be exhausted. It continued to produce gold indefinitely.

Drains

A *drain* is an activity that consumes resources. The two most common drains in CMSs are *construction*, building or buying new things to serve some purpose, and *maintenance*, ongoing spending required to prevent loss or decay. Construction happens only when the player wants it. Maintenance can be player-controlled, but it is often an automatic function that occurs whether the player wants it to or not.

Because resources are valuable, the player wants to know why a resource is disappearing from the world and what she is "getting" to compensate for its loss. In *Monopoly*, players get money from the bank by passing Go—in effect, for no reason at all—but whenever a player has to give money back to the bank, a reason is given: The player has been fined, has to pay certain expenses, and so on.

Maintenance seems like a sort of meaningless cost. It bothers some players, who would rather buy something once and never have to worry about it again. If you characterize it as a "rental" rather than a purchase, it makes more sense to them. Paying employees is a good example of a maintenance cost. You can't own employees; you can only pay their wages on an ongoing basis.

Converters

A *converter* is a location or activity that turns one or more resources into another. In effect, it drains one resource while serving as the source for another at the same time. *The Settlers* is full of converters (see Figure 14.1). The bakery, for example, turns flour and water into bread. The iron smelter takes iron ore and coal (or charcoal) and produces iron bars. In designing a converter, you must specify the input-to-output ratio between resources consumed and resources produced, as well as its production rate. For example, the windmill in *The Settlers* converts grain into flour at a rate of one to one: One bag of grain produces one bag of flour; none is wasted. This takes 15 or 20 seconds to do. The iron smelter turns one load of ore into one iron bar, consuming one load of coal in the process. However, if it is using charcoal instead of coal, it requires three loads of charcoal for each iron bar because charcoal is less efficient than coal. (That's the given reason, anyway; the real game-design reason is that charcoal is an unlimited resource because it comes from wood, which is renewable, whereas coal has to be mined and eventually runs out. To discourage players from simply using charcoal for everything, the designers made it a less efficient mechanism.)

Figure 14.1   *The Settlers III*. The iron smelter is in the center. The coal and iron ore mines are immediately below.

Deadlocks

A *deadlock* is a condition that occurs when you need a resource to construct a production mechanism to produce more of the same resource, or when two processes are each waiting for the other to complete. The chicken-and-egg problem is a classic deadlock. To use an example from a real game, in *The Settlers*, a player must have stone to build a stonecutter's hut, which then produces more stone. Ordinarily, the game starts with some stone already in storage, so if the player builds a stonecutter's hut right away, it will produce the stone needed for other activities. However, if the player uses up all her stored stone constructing other buildings, she might not have enough to build a stonecutter's hut, and she will be in a deadlock. Fortunately, *The Settlers* gives players a way to break the deadlock: They can demolish another building and get back enough stone to build a stonecutter's hut after all.

In designing a CMS, you need to watch out for deadlocks, which can occur whenever there's a loop in the production process. To avoid deadlocks, either avoid such loops or provide an alternative source for one of the resources, even if its value is minimal. This

is the point of collecting $200 when you pass Go in *Monopoly*. If you have no proper-
ties, you can't earn money by collecting rent, but if you can't collect rent, you can't buy
properties. *Monopoly* solves this by giving the players money to start with and by giving them $200 every time they pass Go. As the game progresses, that $200 becomes
less significant, but it is enough to break a deadlock.

Static and Dynamic Equilibrium

It's possible to design a system in such a way that, left alone, it returns to a state of
equilibrium. Static equilibrium is a state in which everything remains constantly the
same: Resources are flowing steadily around without any significant change anywhere.
Dynamic equilibrium occurs when the system fluctuates through a cycle. It's constantly
changing, but it eventually returns to a starting point and begins again.

Here's an example of static equilibrium. Suppose you have a miller grinding wheat to
make flour, and a baker baking bread from the flour. If the bakery consumes the flour
at exactly the same rate at which the mill produces it, then the amount of flour in the
world at any one time will remain static. If we then perturb the system by stopping
the bakery for a while, the flour will build up. When the bakery restarts, the amount
of flour available will be static at the new level. The system returns to equilibrium
because the key factors—the production and consumption rates of the mill and the
bakery—are the same (see Figure 14.2).

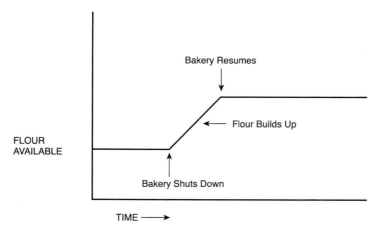

Figure 14.2 An example of static equilibrium.

Now let's suppose that there's only one person who has to do both jobs herself. She mills for a while, then she bakes for a while, then she mills again, and so on. This is an example of dynamic equilibrium: Things are changing all the time, but they always return to the same state after a while because the process is cyclic. If we tell the woman to stop baking and only mill for a while, and then resume baking again later, again the flour builds up. When she resumes baking, the system settles into a new state of dynamic equilibrium (see Figure 14.3).

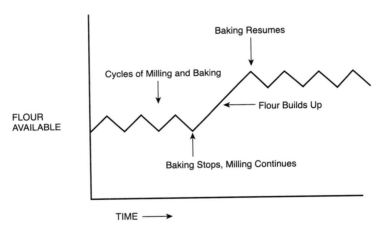

Figure 14.3 A new state of dynamic equilibrium.

When a CMS settles into a static equilibrium, players can easily judge the effect of their actions on the system by making one small change and watching the results. This makes the game easy to learn and play. Dynamic equilibrium is more difficult for players to handle. With the system in constant flux, it's hard to tell whether what they're seeing is the result of a natural process or something they've done. We have a similar problem making ecological decisions about our planet. For many years, people believed that the environment should be in a state of static equilibrium: that there should always be exactly enough plants for the herbivores and exactly enough herbivores for the carnivores, and any deviation from this was caused by environmental mismanagement. More recently, we've come to realize that there are natural fluctuations in the sizes of animal populations and that big changes are not necessarily the result of human actions; they can occur in the ordinary course of events. This makes environmental management all the more difficult.

If your system does settle into a state of equilibrium, static or dynamic, it takes the pressure off the player to do anything. She can simply watch it go for a while and make adjustments when she feels like it. Some CMSs do work that way, but most give the player more of a challenge. Rather than settling into equilibrium, there is an imbalance somewhere. Entropy in the system causes it to "run down" unless the player takes action to keep it going. To use our milling/baking metaphor, perhaps the player has to personally keep the mill supplied with wheat. If the player doesn't keep an eye on the wheat supply, both milling and baking come to a halt.

Whether your system settles into equilibrium or runs down without player action, one thing is certain: The player should always have to do something to obtain growth—he should have to press on the gas pedal of your game, as it were. If the system can grow of its own accord, there's no reason for the player to interfere. This is the player's essential challenge: figuring out how to produce growth using the many levers and knobs that you have given him. In effect, the player is himself an element of the simulation, and growth should be dependent on his active participation.

Disasters

Random disasters are another way to force the player to act. *Sim City* tends to settle into a very slow decline if left alone, chiefly because the roads become worn out. To put more pressure on the player, fires, tornadoes and monster invasions crop up periodically, doing considerable damage. If the player does not take action to repair the damage, the city eventually dwindles down to nothing as a result of repeated disasters.

Case Study: *Sim City*

Although it isn't the oldest CMS, the spiritual father of them all is *Sim City*, published by Maxis (now a part of Electronic Arts). *Sim City* was originally designed for the Commodore 64, although it was most successful on the IBM PC, and the first version of the game is now playable for free on the Web. (Visit `http://simcity.ea.com/play/simcity_classic.php` if you're interested.) It was followed by a host of other games in the same mold: *SimAnt*, *SimTower*, *SimFarm*, and so on, which met with varying success.

The object of *Sim City* is to build a city and attract people (called *sims*) to live and work there. The basic economic unit is money, which the player can spend in various ways to improve the city. The player's primary job is to zone tracts of land into one of three types: residential, commercial, or industrial. As people move into the city, these areas begin to be occupied and to produce tax revenue, thereby replenishing the city's coffers. This produces a straightforward positive feedback loop: Zoning costs money, but occupied zones produce more money, thereby enabling the player to do more zoning.

The positive feedback is kept in check by other demands on the city's purse. Sims will not move into any zoned region; it has to have other benefits as well. Every zoned region requires electricity, and the player has to buy power plants and electrical lines to provide it. The sims also need a way to travel from the residential to the industrial zones to work and to the commercial zones to shop. This requires a road and a rail network, which also cost money. If the roads are inadequate to meet the traffic, or if the sims have to travel too far to work, they will begin to move out of the city, with a resulting loss of tax revenue. Finally, when the city reaches certain population thresholds, the sims begin to demand expensive amenities: a sports stadium, an airport, and so on. Again, if these are not provided, the sims begin to leave.

In addition to the electricity, roads, and civic amenities, there are other cost centers. Fires break out from time to time; if left unchecked, they destroy the buildings and leave the land unzoned. To combat this, the player has to build and maintain fire stations. Industrial areas are a source of crime, which depresses property values and reduces tax revenues. Crime can be suppressed by building police stations, at yet more cost. Industrial areas and roads also cause air pollution, which further depresses the value of nearby residential property. There is no way to reduce air pollution; you simply have to keep industrial and residential areas separate.

The vital calculations in the game are the ones that determine whether people move into the city or move out, and how valuable a given zone is. The more valuable a zone is, the higher its population density becomes and the more tax revenues it produces. The player can build parks and situate residential zones near woods and rivers to increase their attractiveness.

Although *Sim City* is now an old game, it serves as an excellent model to study (see Figure 14.4). Because it was designed for low-performance machines, it couldn't be too complex, and its internal economy is reasonably easy to understand.

continues

continued

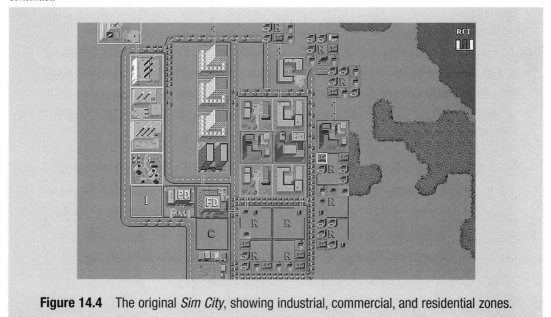

Figure 14.4   The original *Sim City*, showing industrial, commercial, and residential zones.

Setting

It's easy enough to say that CMSs are about a process, but the process has to be meaningfully displayed on a computer screen, and it must fire the player's imagination. Most CMSs take place in the context of a physical space, usually a two-dimensional world in which buildings or other objects can be constructed. *Caesar* is about building an ancient Roman town, so the setting is a landscape near a river. *Civilization* is about exploring a world while at the same time advancing a civilization both culturally and technologically, so its setting is an entire continent, or several of them.

A few pure business simulations don't take place in a physical setting, and they're discussed at the end of the chapter.

Gameplay

The challenges in a CMS are largely economic. The player must understand how the internal economy of the game works and how to manipulate it to produce economic growth. Growth provides the resources required for the construction that is usually the overall goal of the game.

Indirect Control

A war game is a game of direct control. The players tell their troops exactly where to go and what to do, and they do it. The simulated soldiers have little or no autonomous behavior or artificial intelligence. If told to stand and wait someplace, they'll wait there forever.

The majority of CMSs, on the other hand, are games of indirect control. The game simulates a process, and the player can alter that process only in limited ways. The process must be manipulated indirectly, and the player has to learn how the controls affect its inner workings. If there are simulated individuals in the game (see the "Simulating Individuals" section later in this chapter), for the most part, they can be controlled only indirectly. They have a behavior model that governs what they do, and it responds to stimuli, but they can't be given direct orders.

However, the dividing line between direct and indirect control is a fuzzy one. Certain player activities, such as choosing the location of new construction, will be direct. Others, such as trying to boost sales by reducing prices, will be indirect. Reducing prices is direct, but the (hoped for) consequent rise in sales is indirect.

Construction

Construction itself isn't the challenge in a CMS; the challenge is in obtaining the resources needed for the construction. Construction is the part of the game that lets the player exercise her imagination and create something unique and personal. Accordingly, you, as the designer, need to find a way to make this easy and enjoyable.

Construction mechanisms in CMSs tend to be one of two types: *buy* or *design-and-build*. When the player buys an object (a segment of wall, say), the resources to build it are deducted from stockpiles, and the object immediately appears in a designated location. This lets her build rapidly, adding pieces like using Lego bricks. You should use this mechanism if construction is the primary activity in your game. If so, it needs to be easy and continuous, not something the player has to wait for. This is how *Sim City* worked: Zoning property and constructing civic amenities such as police stations and airports happened instantly because it was the primary activity in the game.

The design-and-build mechanism is more often seen in games in which the player does a little construction, then some management, then more construction, and so on. In design-and-build, the player marks out an area where new construction will appear.

The game often displays the new building in a ghostly, semitransparent form to indicate that it is under construction. However, it takes time to build. If the game includes simulated people, you might be able to see them at work on it; if those people go away or die for some reason, the building might be left in a partially completed state.

In design-and-build, you don't have to remove all the required resources from storage at once because the construction takes place over time. In *The Settlers,* wood and stone had to be physically transported a little at a time from stockpiles to the construction site. This puts an extra burden on the player to manage his resource flow, but it does give him more control. In contrast, *Age of Empires* deducted the resources necessary for construction immediately when it was designed. They drained out of the game rather than being transported to the site. Although this was unrealistic, it meant that the player could build something only after he definitely had enough resources for it, and he didn't have to worry about moving things around all the time.

Dungeon Keeper was particularly interesting because construction was actually excavation: It took place underground, and the player couldn't see the area he was excavating into. Excavations often led into immovable rock or to existing caves, underground rivers, or pools of lava. It was also irreversible: When an area had been excavated, there was no way to close it up again. This encouraged players to be cautious. Suddenly excavating into an area full of enemy creatures was a major hazard of the game.

Demolition

In addition to letting your players construct things, you might need to give them a way to demolish things. A big part of the fun of a CMS is building your city, theme park, or whatever the way *you* want to build it. If a construction decision is irreversible, it means whatever the player is building can get only bigger, never smaller, and the player cannot change his mind or react to new circumstances. This might be okay for strategy games (many war games, for example, allow you to build factories and defenses but not demolish them), but in CMSs, it prevents the player from exercising his full creative freedom; hence, the need for a demolition feature.

You should consider whether you want demolition to cost something, cost nothing, or actually earn money. If it costs money to demolish something, you are, in effect, penalizing the player for changing his mind and perhaps encouraging him to plan more carefully in the future. He has lost not only his initial construction cost for the item, but the demolition costs as well. If it costs nothing, the player has lost only his construction costs. If he actually gets something back, it's usually called "selling" the item rather than demolishing it, and it further reduces the price the player pays for changing his mind. If he can sell it back for exactly as much as he paid, there is no net cost at all for building a thing and destroying it later. This is rare in CMSs because it removes some of the challenge. Players can build madly, secure in the knowledge that they can always get their money back by selling.

A player must *never* be able to sell an item back to the computer for more than he paid for it, unless he has expended further resources to upgrade it somehow. If the players can buy from and sell to the computer at will, and there exists *any* mechanism by which they can sell something for more than they paid for it, they will exploit this ruthlessly, piling up huge fortunes by endlessly buying and reselling and ignoring the rest of the game. There are various ways to prevent this. One is to make sure that it is simply impossible to make a profit; all sales must be for less than the original purchase price. If you want players to be able to make a limited profit, you have to place limits on the amount of buying and selling they can do. The computer can refuse to sell items to them after a while or can refuse to buy them back. The computer itself can have a limited amount of money and be unable to buy if it has run out. And in a multi-player game, you can let players buy and sell at a profit to one another, but not to the computer itself. Transactions among the players don't change the total amount of money in the game; it's selling things back to the computer that have the potential for abuse.

Victory Conditions

A good many CMSs have no victory condition; the player simply builds whatever she likes as effectively as she can within the constraints of the system. These games might well have a loss condition, however: total depletion of resources (or, in monetary terms, bankruptcy). This is the loss condition in *Monopoly*, for example. Victory in *Monopoly* consists simply of bankrupting all the other players.

If you do want to define a victory condition, it's best to do it in the context of a scenario of some kind. Give the player a partially constructed city (or whatever) and a set of initial conditions, and then define the victory condition as achieving some other condition. It could be as simple as, "To win, your enterprise must be worth $5 billion," but it can be as complex as you like. You can also start the player in rapidly deteriorating conditions and challenge her to turn them around or simply to survive for a certain length of time.

Competition Modes

CMSs are almost always single-player games. It's possible to make them two-player or even multi-player, but it's not a natural way to play. CMSs encourage planning and thought, not frantic action. If the players are competing for the same resources, it becomes a race to see who can grab the most, ignoring the other aspects of the game. If the players are separate and have symmetric starting and victory conditions, the game tends to be about optimizing efficiency. If the conditions are asymmetric, the game will be difficult to balance.

CMSs let the player be playful, to build and experiment in the world you've given him. That's seldom consistent with competition. One major exception is in hybrid games, those that have a military element as well as construction and management elements. They're discussed in the "Hybrid Games" section later in this chapter.

The Player's Role

When designing any game, the first question you have to ask yourself is, what is the player going to do? The answer to this question usually arises out of a clear statement of the player's role in the game: pilot, general, adventurer, irradiated hedgehog, and so on. In a CMS, however, it's less easy to define the player's role because it seldom corresponds to an actual job in real life. The mayor of a city doesn't really lay out its streets or make zoning decisions personally.

This is one of the few genres in which we don't think you have to define the player's role in familiar terms. You still have to concern yourself with what the player is going to do, of course, but it doesn't matter that much what you call him.

Interaction Model

The player is almost always omniscient in a CMS because she needs to see what is happening all over the game world. It's difficult to control a global process from a local perspective. Most CMSs don't give the player any kind of avatar. Those that do usually make it temporary. If the player is building a city or a space station or some other structure, she could well want to see what it would look like from the perspective of someone inside it. For example, in *Dungeon Keeper*, it is possible for the player to "possess" a creature in her dungeon: to take control of that creature and walk around the dungeon in the first-person perspective (see Figure 14.5), seeing through its eyes. However, this feature is mostly cosmetic. It is occasionally useful in the military aspects of the game, but not at all in the management aspects. In short, we think the "down inside" view is a fun one and the player will enjoy it, but the primary interaction model in a CMS needs to be omnipresent.

Figure 14.5 *Dungeon Keeper 2*, omnipresent view (top) and inside view (bottom).

User Interface

Because CMSs aren't trying to create an illusion of reality in the way that first-person shooters or flight simulators are, their user interfaces can be more "computerlike," using pull-down menus and rows of buttons along the edges of the screen. In a CMS, the emphasis is more on convenience than verisimilitude.

Perspective

The user's perspective in a CMS naturally depends on what's being simulated. Most CMSs simulate a process taking place over a land area—whether it's a city, a farm, or an entire planet. As a result, they tend to use an isometric perspective and enable you to view the world from one of four angles. The isometric perspective requires little CPU time, an advantage even in these days of 3D hardware accelerators, because CMSs do a lot more computation behind the scenes than other kinds of games. Its disadvantage, at least from a development standpoint, is that your art team will have to draw sprites of everything in the game from four different perspectives—and still more if you offer multiple zoom levels. It also doesn't let the player zoom in to any degree he likes. CMSs are sometimes frustrating in that the closest-in zoom level is a little too close, and the next one out is a little too far out.

If your game simulates a process taking place in a three-dimensional space, you might find it useful to divide the space into layers (either physical or conceptual) to make it easier for the player to navigate around and view. It's also helpful to provide a button that returns the camera instantly to a default perspective so that the player can reorient himself if he gets lost.

Analysis Tools

In a CMS, the player is trying to understand and control a mathematical model. To do this, she needs convenient access to key variables within the model. You should display the most important scalar (single-value) variables—for example, the amount of money she has to work with at the moment—on the screen at all times. The display can be in digits, if that's most appropriate, or a bar graph or some other kind of monitoring device, depending on the nature of the simulation.

Often the player needs to know not only the current value of a variable, but also how that variable has changed over time. This lets her track trends and respond to them before trouble occurs. In *Theme Park*, a business simulation about building and managing (surprise!) theme parks, visitors came in, spent a while in the park, and left again. The player could see them wandering around, but it was difficult to get a sense of the park's popularity just by counting heads. One of the information pop-ups available was a graph that showed how the population had changed over the past 1, 3, or 12 game years.

With vector (multivalued) variables, you'll need a different approach. In *Caesar*, for example, every area of the Roman town that the player was trying to build needed a water supply of some sort. The amount of water available was therefore a vector; it had a separate value for each square on the grid. There were a variety of types of water supplies (wells, pipes, fountains, and so on), and each provided water to a given area around it. In the game's default perspective, showing all the buildings of the town, the player could see the structure supplying the water, but it was difficult for her to visualize exactly how far its coverage extended. To get a clearer picture, she could bring up a different view that hid most of the buildings and instead showed only the amount of water available in each area. The different values were indicated as squares in different shades of blue, from light blue, indicating very little water, to dark blue, indicating plenty. If an area had no water supply, there was no blue at all. The water supply buildings themselves were left visible on the map as landmarks.

These sorts of analysis tools are essential to give the player an understanding of what's going on inside the simulation. *Sim City* had several: fire danger, crime, pollution, and so on. They allow the player to quickly locate trouble spots and take remedial action. These kinds of map overlays should not be a snapshot at a moment in time, but should be continuously updated by the simulation. That way, the player can watch them for a while and tell whether particular situations are getting better or worse—and, most important, whether her actions are having the desired effect.

Special Design Considerations for CMSs

The following sections discuss some design considerations particular to construction and management simulations.

Simulating Individuals

Many CMSs simulate the behavior of a group of people (or, in the case of *SimAnt*, ants) within an environment that the player is managing. If it's a very large number of people, as in the original *Sim City*, behavior is usually modeled statistically and separate values are not kept for each person. However, you might want to simulate the actions of unique individuals that the player can see moving around and doing whatever it is that they do in your world. This will make your game a good deal more entertaining because there will be more for the player to see and because he can follow particular individuals around to watch what they do. It appeals to a sort of voyeuristic impulse and makes the consequences of the player's decisions seem more personal. It's particularly affecting when the player can actually see people who are unhappy packing up and leaving.

Modeling particular individuals rather than statistical aggregates adds considerably to your design job. You will need to create a behavioral model, usually including a scalar degree of happiness or unhappiness, and a set of needs that the person desires to have fulfilled. Various behaviors or circumstances can fulfill those needs. In some cases, the individual will be able to take an autonomous action that fulfills the need (driving from home to work fulfills the need to get to work); whereas in others, the player will have to provide something to fulfill the need (building a school provides educational opportunities). If a need goes unfulfilled, either through a problem that arises within the simulation (traffic jams prevent the person getting to work) or the player failing to act (no school has been built), there should be a negative consequence of some kind (the simulated person becomes unhappy).

Modeling individuals relieves you of the job of creating a statistical model because the behavior of the individuals collectively provides the statistics. However, balancing it will be a much more intricate job. You will probably discover emergent behaviors, unanticipated consequences of design decisions. Some of these will be fascinating and almost seem like intelligence, but others will clearly be degenerate: people locked in a tight behavioral loop, for example, only ever doing one or two things because your needs mechanism isn't balanced properly.

Behavioral modeling is too big of a subject for us to address comprehensively here, and we suggest that you consult the bibliography at the end of this book for further reading.

Mind Reading

If the individuals you're simulating are visible on the screen and the player can select one with the mouse, you can offer another useful analysis tool: mind reading. To let the player know what's in that individual's mind, pop up an icon or even a whole dialog box showing his internal state: current goal, degree of happiness, or whatever other data might be useful to the player. This lets the player get a quick, rough sense of how the people are feeling without having to turn to a statistical analysis screen.

Case Study: *Theme Park*, a Disgusting Example of Positive Feedback

In Bullfrog Productions's CMS called *Theme Park*, the player was supposed to build a single theme park, ride by ride, into an empire of theme parks around the world. In addition to buying the rides, which attracted visitors, the player built shops and restaurants to extract money from them and hired maintenance and cleaning staff to keep the rides working and the park clean.

Each visitor to the park had a number of characteristics: how much money he had, how hungry or thirsty he was, and so on. One of these characteristics was "current degree of nausea." If a visitor became nauseated enough, he would vomit, leaving a mess on the ground that had to be cleaned up. Nausea could be caused by three things. Two of these were riding a particularly violent ride and being near an unclean bathroom. The third cause of nausea was—you guessed it—being near someone else's vomit. If the park was crowded and the player hadn't hired enough cleaning staff to keep the bathrooms clean and the vomit cleaned up, the result was chain-reaction vomiting by the visitors. This did nothing for the reputation of the park and tended to hurt future sales, but it did inject a degree of juvenile humor into what was otherwise a fairly straightforward business simulation.

Advisors

Another tool commonly found in CMSs is the *advisor*: a simulated character who pops up and gives the player advice from time to time (see Figure 14.6). Because problems are often localized in one area of the map, the player might be looking at another area when one occurs and not see it until it has grown severe. An advisor can warn of problem conditions wherever they occur. You should also consider including a screen button or menu item that jumps the screen to the most recently reported problem.

In addition to warning of emergencies, an advisor can give the player information about the general state of the game. "The people need more food," he can say, or "Prices are too high." This lets the player know of global problems without having to consult the analysis tools.

To design an advisor, define both the local and the global problems that you think are important to let the player know about; then set the threshold levels at which the advisor will pop up. If the advisor is going to interrupt the player or say something aloud, don't set these thresholds too low, or the constant interruptions will become irritating. You should also make it possible for the player to turn off the advisor or to consult it only when wanted. Playing without the advisor adds an extra challenge to the game.

Figure 14.6 *Theme Park World.* Note the advisor in the lower-right corner.

You can also create an advisor that consists only of an indicator that remains constantly on the screen, displaying the most urgent global need at the moment.

Pure Business Simulations

A game like *Theme Park World* is a business simulation because it's about attracting customers and making profits. It's the building aspect of it that makes it a CMS. But there are also pure business simulations in which you construct only a financial fortune, not a visible world. The game *Hollywood Mogul*, for example, is about the business of making movies, but it consists only of a series of menu screens about hiring stars and making deals. The player never sees a set or a camera. *Mr. Bigshot*, shown in Figure 14.7, is a fairly simple stock market simulation.

Figure 14.7   *Mr. Bigshot.*

Most of the challenges of designing a pure business simulation are the same as for any other management sim: You must devise an economy and mechanisms for manipulating it. The real trick is to find some way of making the subject visually interesting. Spreadsheets and pie charts have limited appeal, so if you're going to do a management simulation without a construction element, you should try to give it some kind of a setting or to find a visual representation of the process that will make it attractive and compelling. *Mr. Bigshot* accomplishes this with lots of animation, voiceover narration, music, and cartoon characters representing the player's opponents; as the player, you feel rather like a contestant on a TV game show.

By contrast, *Capitalism II* (see Figure 14.8) is a huge, sprawling business sim covering all kinds of products and industries. In addition to showing pictures of them and all the raw materials that go into them, the game allows players to construct or purchase buildings in cities, so there's an attractive *Sim City*-like view as well.

Figure 14.8 *Capitalism II.*

Business simulations will never have the pulse-pounding excitement of a first-person shooter, but they can be highly enjoyable games. As the designer, you'll need to work closely with the art director to make the essentially numeric nature of their gameplay more lively.

Hybrid Games

Civilization, Age of Empires, Dungeon Keeper, and *The Settlers* are all good examples of hybrid games: crosses between a CMS and a war game. In addition to their economic challenges, they all feature exploration and military challenges, varying somewhat from one game to another. The military aspect of *The Settlers* is quite simple, as it must be, given that the economic aspect is exceedingly complex. *Age of Empires* emphasizes warfare and military research more and is more of a real-time strategy game than a CMS, especially because natural resources are limited. Its people can be controlled directly, too. *Dungeon Keeper* is initially about constructing a dungeon, but in the later stages of each mission, it's actually about recruiting and training a balanced army, and then taking that army into battle. Control is a curious hybrid of direct and indirect: Creatures have a distinct behavior model, but they will obey orders as long as they're happy. (If they're unhappy, they might disobey or even desert.) However, *Dungeon Keeper* retains its economic challenges throughout: It's one of the very few games in which the soldiers have to be paid, fed, and given a place to sleep.

If you're going to design a hybrid game, we encourage you to design the economic simulation first (unless it's really simple) and then add the other elements afterward. Because the other aspects of the game usually depend on the underlying economy, a mistake in the economic design can easily ruin the rest of the game. For example, a war game that includes an economy for weapons production might lose all its strategic challenge if the player is able to produce weapons too quickly. The player will exploit his economic strength and overwhelm the opposition with sheer numbers rather than strategic skill.

Construction and Management Simulation Worksheet

When beginning the design of a construction and management simulation, consider the following questions:

1. What process is the player going to manage? What actions will the player take in managing that process?
2. What resources exist in this process? For each resource, how is it produced, consumed, stored, transported, and converted into other resources? Is it tangible, intangible, or a hybrid? Is it limited or unlimited? What determines its production and consumption rates?

continues

continued

3. Which resources can the player manipulate and which can she not?

4. Will the process settle into a static or dynamic equilibrium, or will it run down if not tended by the player? Will disasters affect it?

5. What will be player be constructing, and what function does the constructed item have? Will objects be purchased whole or designed and built over time? For each item that the player can construct, what does it cost and how long does it take to build?

6. Can the player demolish or sell things that she builds? Does this cost or earn resources for the player?

7. Will the game have scenarios with victory conditions? What are they like?

8. What is the player's perspective and interaction model with the game? Is there a way to "get inside" the things she builds?

9. What analysis tools are provided to help her understand the workings of the simulation?

10. Is the simulated population modeled as individuals or as a statistical aggregate? If they are individuals, what is their behavior model? Are there multiple types of individuals? Can the player read their minds?

11. Will the game have advisors? What will they advise about?

12. Is this game a pure business simulation? Accounting and finance are often considered rather dull, so what makes this compelling? Does the game have a setting? If not, how can it be made visually interesting?

13. Is the game a hybrid with other sorts of games? What other elements in the game make it a hybrid (strategic problems, action challenges, puzzles, and so on)? How do they affect the way the game is controlled?

Putting It Together

Construction and management simulations seldom have splashy graphics, pounding music, or moments of high drama (except when disaster strikes). Instead, they call for observation, contemplation, and planning. To many gamers, that sounds terribly dull. Yet good CMSs are enormously popular and can make fortunes even without the latest

3D graphics. *RollerCoaster Tycoon* was a perfect example. What appeals about a CMS is not an adrenaline rush, but the fact that the player gets to make something of his own. Working carefully, tending and tweaking, he can build a tiny settlement on the banks of the Tiber into the glorious city that was Rome. Not the original Rome or the game designer's Rome, but *his* Rome—Rome as it would have been if he had been emperor. That's a different kind of achievement from blasting all the aliens in sight or winning a sports championship. The desire to create is at the heart of all CMS players. To design a CMS, first understand that desire.

Chapter 15

Adventure Games

The term *adventure game* is a bit misleading because a lot of games about being adventurous aren't adventure games—and a lot of adventure games aren't about adventures, at least, in the fairy-tale sense of going forth to seek one's fortune. The reason for the odd term is historical. It's really short for *Adventure*-type game, meaning a game similar to the one named *Adventure* (although it was sometimes also called *Colossal Cave*, just to confuse things further).

What Is an Adventure Game?

An adventure game isn't a competition or a simulation. An adventure game doesn't offer a process to be managed or an opponent to be defeated through strategy and tactics. Instead, an adventure game is an interactive story about a character who is controlled by the player. Chapter 4, "Storytelling and Narrative," discussed this idea in theoretical terms. The adventure game is the idea's practical application, although the way in which interactivity and narrative are handled varies considerably from game to game.

All adventure games are conceptual descendants of the original *Adventure*. Although the genre has changed considerably over the years, the games are characterized by certain qualities that they all share: exploration, collection or manipulation of objects, puzzle solving, and a reduced emphasis on combat and action elements. This doesn't mean that there is no conflict in adventure games (although many adventure games have none)—only that combat is not the primary activity.

The Original *Adventure*

Adventure was a text-only game. Its gameplay was simple but—at the time that it was written—completely novel. The player was an explorer, wandering around in an enormous cave filled with treasures and dangers. A variety of obstacles prevented her from getting into the deeper parts of the cave, but by cleverly using the things that she had found, the player could unlock these areas and continue exploring. The object of the game was to gather all the treasures and bring them out of the cave.

Adventure was the first computer game to give the player a real illusion of freedom, and this remains an important quality of adventure games today. Before *Adventure*, computer games tended to ask specific questions and expect specific, often numeric answers ("How much money do you want to spend this year?"), or to present players with a fixed list of options and ask them to choose one. The player could type anything she wanted in *Adventure*, and game would try to respond appropriately. Of course, the game understood only a limited number of words, but because it didn't tell the player what they were, she never knew the full scope of what it would allow her to do.

Adventure also brought personality to computer gaming. Most of the games written at the time spoke to the player in a kind of programmerese. They gave prompts such as "Enter horsepower:" and printed error messages such as "Value too high, re-enter (5-500):". *Adventure* spoke to players as if it were a person rather than a machine, saying "I don't know how to do that" rather than "Invalid command." It could become sarcastic if the player tried to do something ridiculous or impossible, or even be funny occasionally, another rarity among games of its day. Comedy remains a major element of many adventure games because it discourages the player from taking the game too seriously. Breaches in suspension of disbelief don't bother the player as much in a comic setting as they do in a dramatic one because the player is less immersed in the story in the first place.

The Growth of Adventure Games

Adventure games were highly popular in the early days of personal computers. Because they contained no graphics, they were inexpensive to develop and allowed great scope for both the designer's and the player's imaginations. A group of researchers at the MIT Artificial Intelligence Lab, inspired by the original *Adventure*, wrote a much larger adventure game named *Zork* on the mainframe there. Soon afterward, they converted it to run on personal computers and founded a company, Infocom, devoted to developing text adventures. Infocom published games about all kinds of things: fantasy magic, film noir detective stories, exploration of an ancient Egyptian pyramid, and so on.

The original *Adventure* didn't have any plot; it just offered a space to explore and puzzles to solve. With minor exceptions, its world did not change as time passed. But it wasn't long before games began to explore the notion of "interactive fiction," an ongoing story in which the player was an active participant. Some games were sold along with books that players were supposed to read ahead of time. Of all the branches of computer game design, interactive fiction has been the subject of the most academic research because it challenges traditional conceptions of what narrative is and does.

As soon as personal computers began to get graphics capability (the very earliest were text-only), developers began to add graphics to adventure games and the games really took off. LucasArts and Sierra On-Line dominated the genre, and for a while they produced the best-looking, highest-class games on the market: funny, scary, mysterious, and fascinating. Adventure games provided challenges and explored areas that other genres didn't touch. *Myst*, a point-and-click graphic adventure, was for many years the best-selling personal computer game of all time. (It has recently been supplanted by *The Sims*.)

Adventure Games Today

In the past few years, the market for adventure games has grown more slowly than the market for other genres. Adventure games depend less on display technology than fast-paced action games do; as a result, they get less attention from the gaming press, which has led to a misconception that the adventure game genre is "dead." In fact, adventure games are alive and well; they're just less highly publicized than their high-adrenaline cousins.

The invention of 3D hardware accelerators has actually given adventure games a new lease on life. We usually think of dynamic three-dimensional worlds in the contexts in which they first appeared—vehicle simulations and first-person shooters—but 3D hardware has a lot to offer adventure games as well. The first graphical adventure games came with gorgeously painted but static backdrops for every scene. Players could see a lot of things but could touch very few of them. But when every object is rendered in three dimensions and it's possible to move freely among them, the world becomes much more immediate and alive.

The static-backdrop adventure game is still very much with us, but nowadays it is likely to use scenes created with 3D rendering software and raytracing rather than pixel painting. *Myst* was the first commercial game to use 3D rendered backgrounds, which contributed to its success.

Action-Adventures

The arrival of 3D hardware also gave rise to a new sort of game, a combination of action game and adventure game called, unsurprisingly, an *action-adventure*. The action-adventure is faster paced than a pure adventure game, and it includes physical as well as conceptual challenges. *Indiana Jones and the Infernal Machine* is a good example of the type. *The Legend of Zelda: Ocarina of Time* might be considered another, although, with its levels and bosses, it's closer to being a pure action game. Exactly when a game stops being an adventure game and becomes an action game is a matter of interpretation. By some interpretations, the *Tomb Raider* games are action-adventures because they do include puzzles, but the puzzles aren't all that clever, and the action is so continuous that we would classify it as an action game.

Adventure game purists don't care for action-adventures; generally, they dislike any sort of physical challenge or time pressure. If you plan to make your game an action-adventure, you should be aware that although your design might appeal to some action gamers who might not otherwise buy your game, you might also discourage some adventure gamers who would.

The Replayability Question

At first glance, it would seem that the greatest disadvantage of adventure games is their lack of replayability. Because most adventure games consist of puzzles with a single solution, when you know the solution, there's not much challenge in playing it again.

An adventure game that requires 40 hours to finish the first time might take only 4 the second time.

In practice, however, this turns out not to be much of a problem. Research has shown that a great many players never finish their games at all; even if the game offers 30 or 40 hours of gameplay, many players play for only 15 or 20. This suggests that if they can't replay a 40-hour game for another 40 hours, it's unlikely to bother them. Provided that the game is good value for the money the first time around, it doesn't need to be replayable.

The Common Elements of Adventure Games

In most adventure games, the player's avatar is presented with an explorable area containing a variety of puzzles or problems to be solved. Solving these problems opens up new areas for exploration or advances the story line in some way, giving the player new information and new problems to solve. Exploring the environment and manipulating items in it is a key element of most adventure games, although this is not an absolute requirement. It's theoretically possible to develop an adventure game that consists entirely of conversations with nonplayer characters (NPCs), but we haven't yet seen one.

Setting

In some kinds of games, such as chess and *Quake*, the setting is almost irrelevant. Serious players ignore the idea that chess is a medieval war game or that *Quake* is about space marines on an alien planet. They concentrate on the bare essentials of the gameplay: strategy in the former case and blazing action in the latter. If the setting intrudes, it is only a distraction.

In adventure games, this situation is reversed. The setting in an adventure game contributes more to its entertainment value than in any other genre. Whether it's grim and depressing, fantastic and outlandish, or funny and cheerful, the setting creates the world the player is going to explore and to live in, and it is for many players the reason for playing adventure games in the first place.

Emotional Tone

The majority of computer games have little emotional subtlety. Games of pure strategy have no emotional content at all; action games and war games have little more. Nor do they inspire complex emotions in the player. "Yippee!" and "Damn!" are about the limit of it—exhilaration and frustration, respectively. Role-playing games (RPGs), with their deeper stories, offer greater opportunities for emotional expression, but even when their designers take advantage of it, the emotion tends to get lost in a morass of bookkeeping. The players spend so much time buying and selling equipment and trying to optimize their combat effectiveness that the emotional content of the story is obscured.

Adventure games do not have intricate strategy, high-speed action, or management details to entertain the player. The games move more slowly, which gives players the chance to create a world with a distinct emotional tone.

Interaction Model

All adventure games are avatar-based because the player is being represented by some-one who is inside a story. However, the nature of the avatar in adventure games has changed somewhat over the years. Both *Adventure* and *Myst* were careful to avoid ascribing characteristics to the avatar in the game—sex, age, and so on. The avatar wasn't a character with his or her own personal history; it was the player, but because the game didn't know anything about the player, it couldn't depict her or say much about her. A number of later text adventures asked for the player's name and sex when started up, using that information later in the game. They were trying to create the impression that it really was "you" in the game world, and they didn't want to offend players by assuming that they were the wrong sex. In *Myst*, the world was shown from a first-person perspective, and there were no mirrors in which the player could catch sight of herself.

Eventually, however, game designers began to find this model too limiting. They want-ed to develop games in which the avatar was a character with a personality of his own, someone who belonged in the game world rather than being a visitor there. Two good examples of this approach are Sierra On-Line's *Leisure Suit Larry* series and LucasArts's *Monkey Island* series. In these games, the player could see his avatar walking around interacting with the world. Both Larry and Guybrush Threepwood, the hero of the *Monkey Island* games, are comic figures, and the games are played primarily for laughs.

There was initially some concern that male players would be unwilling to play female characters, but Lara Croft has demonstrated emphatically that this is not a problem. Female players quite justifiably get tired of playing male heroes because there are so many of them. We think the decision about whether to make your game's avatar male or female shouldn't be based on marketing considerations, but upon the needs of the story. In many cases, the avatar's sex really isn't important anyway, although it might influence the way other characters in the game react. Try to design an avatar who is interesting and likeable. Because this is someone the player will be seeing all the time, the avatar must be a person the player can identify with and must possess qualities he is likely to admire: bravery, intelligence, decency, and a sense of humor, for example. Chapter 5, "Character Development," discusses these issues in more detail.

Perspective

The preferred camera perspective of graphic adventure games is changing. The context-sensitive approach is traditional, but third- and first-person games are becoming increasingly common. Here we examine their advantages and disadvantages.

Context Sensitive

In the context-sensitive perspective, the game depicts the avatar over a (mostly) static background. When the avatar walks through a door or off the edge of the screen, the background changes to depict his new location. In the early days of graphic adventure games, the camera angles tended to be quite dull, as in Figure 15.1, from *Leisure Suit Larry in the Land of the Lounge Lizards*.

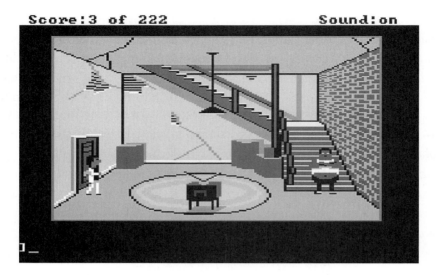

Figure 15.1 A scene in the original *Leisure Suit Larry*.

As display hardware improved, game development began to require more artists and the quality of the artwork improved considerably. The game's art director chose a camera position designed to show off each location to best effect. Compare Figure 15.1 with Figure 15.2 from *Grim Fandango*.

Figure 15.2 A scene in *Grim Fandango*. Note the camera position.

A context-sensitive perspective lets the designer (or art director) play cinematographer, using camera angles, composition, and lighting to enhance the story. Use these techniques with discretion, however. A light touch is best. If you watch movies closely, you'll notice that the majority of shots are pretty straightforward. Movie directors don't use unexpected angles just for the fun of it; they do so to make a deliberate point.

First Person

One of the most famous graphic adventure games of all, *Myst,* used a first-person perspective. The player's avatar was not seen; in fact, like the earliest text adventures, the player didn't really have an avatar in the sense of a character who belonged in the story. Instead, it was the player himself who was in the game world. Unlike first-person shooters, however, *Myst* did not render a three-dimensional game world in real time. The game world consisted of a large number of prerendered still frames, which it showed one at a time as the player walked around. Being prerendered, these stills were finely detailed and highly atmospheric. On the other hand, they couldn't depict continuously moving objects or changes in the sunlight as time passed, and the player couldn't look at things from any angle. The world was rich but static.

A real-time 3D first-person perspective gives the player the best sense of being in the world himself, but it doesn't let the player see his avatar unless the game has a functioning reflective surface in it. It also tends to encourage a more action-oriented approach to playing the game, running around without paying much attention to the surroundings. Finally, 3D hardware is still not advanced enough to render extremely detailed scenes (a room crammed with hundreds of complex objects, for example) in real time.

Third Person

The third-person perspective keeps the player's avatar constantly in view, as in *Indiana Jones and the Infernal Machine* or in action games such as *Mario 64.* This perspective is common for action-adventures in which the player might need to react quickly (see Figure 15.3).

Figure 15.3 *Indiana Jones and the Infernal Machine.* This is the typical action-adventure perspective.

If the third-person perspective always remains behind the avatar's back, however, the view gets rather dull and doesn't let the player really appreciate the environment. And unlike pure action games in which the avatar's actions and motivations are simple, adventure games sometimes need camera perspectives that allow for more subtle situations. In Figure 15.4, from *Gabriel Knight 3*, Gabriel is hiding and watching to see when the maid is going to leave the room.

Figure 15.4   *Gabriel Knight 3* in a context-sensitive camera angle.

The later *Gabriel Knight* games also allowed the player to move the camera around somewhat—as do some of the better action games, such as *Spyro the Dragon* and *Toy Story* (see Figure 15.5). This mimics how a real person can turn his head to look in a given direction without moving his whole body.

Figure 15.5 *Gabriel Knight* as seen from a player-adjusted camera position. The Volkswagen would not be visible if the camera were behind him.

Case Study: *The Secret of Monkey Island*

The Secret of Monkey Island is more than 10 years old now, but it's worth studying because it spawned a highly successful franchise with three more games to date. Although it was ostensibly set on a Caribbean island in the 1700s and was about a young man who wanted to be a pirate, it was full of anachronistic touches and was played for laughs. In that respect, it seemed a lot like certain Disney animated films—*The Jungle Book*, for example—although slightly edgier.

When Ron Gilbert, the designer of *The Secret of Monkey Island*, started work on the game, he had already created an adventure game engine called SCUMM. SCUMM stood for Script Creation Utility for *Maniac Mansion* (an earlier LucasArts adventure game). SCUMM was an important innovation for graphic adventure games: It put the verbs on the screen so players no longer had to guess what their options were, and it did away with typing. More important for the developers, it enabled them to create new adventure games easily, without programming them from scratch each time. Three of the five *Monkey Island* games were made with SCUMM, as well as *Maniac Mansion* itself and several other LucasArts games.

The Secret of Monkey Island included a number of other innovations as well, most notably an insult-driven sword fight. This was a fight between the avatar, Guybrush Threepwood, and a master swordswoman. Rather than making the fight a physical challenge, which would have required a lot of additional programming and would have turned off some players, Gilbert chose to make use of (and make fun of) the way adversaries always insult one another in old swashbuckling movies. When your adversary insults you, you must choose an appropriate comeback quip. If you do, Guybrush advances in the fight; if you choose the wrong one, he is forced to retreat. If you make enough correct quips in a row, Guybrush wins the fight. The insults themselves contain cues as to which reply is correct, so you don't have to find out by trial and error.

It's this kind of humorous lateral thinking that separates great adventure games from merely good ones. The Monkey Island series belongs among the greats.

Player Roles

In most computer games, the player's role is largely defined by the challenges she will be facing, whether it's as an athlete in a sports game, a pilot in a flight simulator, or a martial arts expert in a fighting game. But adventure games can be filled with all kinds of puzzles and problems that are unrelated to the player's stated role. Indiana Jones is supposedly an archaeologist, but we don't see him digging very much. The role arises not out of the challenges (unless you specifically want it to), but out of the story. In an adventure game, the player could still be a pilot, if that's what the story requires, but it doesn't necessarily guarantee that she'll get to fly a plane. And she might be anything else or nothing in particular—just an ordinary person living in an extraordinary situation.

A good many adventure games do connect the player's role with the game's activities, however. Players' roles often involve travel or investigation: explorer, detective, hunter, conquistador, and so on. The player can even be some kind of a scientist, if it's a branch of science that involves travel: geologist or zoologist, for example.

Be sure that the challenges are not too disjoint from the role, however, or it could be frustrating for the player. Heart of China, which was otherwise a straightforward adventure game, included a poorly implemented 3D tank simulator at one point. To continue the game, the player had to use the tank simulator successfully. This was a real problem; adventure game enthusiasts seldom play vehicle simulations, and many could not get past that point. It spoiled the game for them.

Structure

Adventure games typically have only one gameplay mode. Unlike sports games, with all of their team-management functions, or war games, with their battle planning, adventure games don't need a lot of specialized screens. Apart from looking at a map or the inventory or examining objects close up, the player always sees and interacts with the world in the same way, and that doesn't change from one end of the game to the other.

What adventure games *do* have, however, is a story structure: a relationship between different locations in the world and different parts of the story. Over the years, this has evolved. The earliest adventure games, including the original *Adventure*, mostly emphasized exploration rather than allowing the player to participate in a narrative of some kind. The player perceived little sense of time passing—that is, of making progress through a story toward an ending. The game simply gave her a large space and told her to wander around in it. Structurally, it looked rather like the drawing in Figure 15.6.

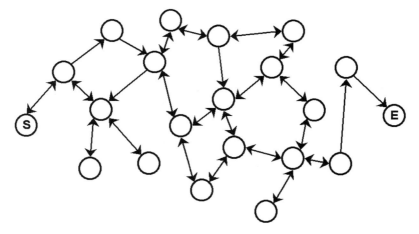

Figure 15.6 The structure of early adventure games. Each circle represents a room. S is the starting room, and E is the end.

As adventure games got larger and began to include a story, designers started to break them up into chapters (see Figure 15.7). The player could wander around all he liked in the area devoted to a given chapter, but when he moved on to the next, the story advanced and there was no way back. If the player needed to take a particular object from one chapter to the next, the story would not let him progress until that object was in his inventory.

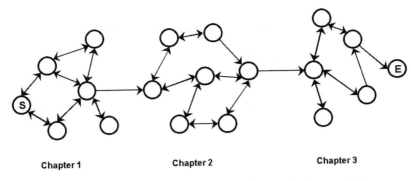

Chapter 1   Chapter 2   Chapter 3

Figure 15.7   The structure of story-driven adventure games.

With the arrival of 3D graphics and the action-adventure, the stories began to be even more linear. Areas occasionally had simple side branches but few complex spaces or loops. The space in an action-adventure is structured more like that of an action game or a first-person shooter (see Figure 15.8).

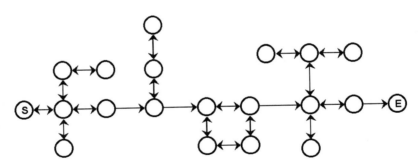

Figure 15.8   The structure of action-adventure games.

Storytelling

This subject is discussed at length in Chapter 4. In this section, we just reiterate a few of the key points and talk about their significance in adventure games. Adventure games rely on storytelling more than any other genre. We can't tell you in this book how to create a good story, but you can learn from innumerable other resources. A great many theories exist, beginning with Aristotle's *Poetics* and continuing to post-modernist literature. If you're trying to make a game that's fun to play and, better yet, sells well, it's probably best to avoid some of the more outré literary theories and stick to what works for the vast majority of books, movies, and television. On the other hand, if you're trying to expand the boundaries of the interactive medium with a never-before-seen work of art, more power to you.

Here are a few pointers about storytelling as it applies to adventure games.

Dramatic Tension

The essence of any story, whether it's interactive or a fixed narrative, is dramatic tension: a situation or problem that is unresolved. This is what holds the reader's attention and keeps her around to see how it comes out. To create dramatic tension, you must begin by presenting the problem. In adventure games, this often happens in a cut scene right at the beginning of the game. The meaning of the scene doesn't always have to be clear; mystery and uncertainty are a common element of dramatic tension. For example, in *The Longest Journey*, we begin by learning that April Ryan, the avatar and heroine of the game, has been having increasingly vivid nightmares whose meaning she does not understand. At the beginning of the game, she has no goal other than to find out why she's having nightmares. Later, more dramatic tension is added as we learn the source of those nightmares and new problems emerge.

The resolution of dramatic tension occurs at a moment usually near the end of the story called the dramatic climax. Short stories frequently have only one source of dramatic tension and one dramatic climax; longer stories can have several in a row, of progressively increasing importance. A really long story can have several major dramatic climaxes at intervals, and what ties them together is a common theme, setting, or characters. Such stories are called *epics* or *cycles*. Richard Wagner's cycle of four operas, *The Ring of the Nibelungs*, is one such. Each opera is a self-contained story with its own dramatic climax, although some characters carry over from one opera to the next, and all of them concern the fate of the same magic ring.

As an adventure game designer, the puzzles create dramatic tension for you. However, they alone are not enough. They are small, individual problems. There must also be a larger problem that is the reason the player is playing the game in the first place.

The Heroic Quest

The majority of adventure games are heroic quests of some kind, a mission by a single individual to accomplish some great (or, in the case of *Leisure Suit Larry*, not-so-great) feat. Although it's possible to write an adventure game that is a detailed character study, no one has done so as a commercial product, and the emphasis on a single person doesn't lend itself to a sweeping epic with a cast of thousands. It's also possible to create a game about a small group of people, but giving the player a group to manage interferes with her identification with one of them as her avatar. Games about groups are easier managed as RPGs because of the natural "party" structure of the quests. An adventure game is more like a novel written in the first person.

Among the characteristics of the heroic quest is that it is always a movement from the familiar to the unfamiliar and from a time of low danger to a time of great danger. For example, if you have a big dramatic climax, it should be the last really major one in the game because anything that follows it is likely to feel irrelevant. This is why the boss enemies appear at the ends of levels in action games. If you defeat the Lord of Terror, it feels anticlimactic and rather unfair to have to fight his second-in-command afterward.

Occasionally exceptions to this structure arise, such as in stories in which the hero is abducted at the beginning, escapes, and is trying to return to his home. However, in these stories, it doesn't get easier and easier until he just strolls in happily. He often returns home to find that things have changed for the worse and must be corrected, or that he must leave again to hunt down his abductor.

Of course, none of this means that there can't ever be periods of quiet; in fact, there should be. In both of J.R.R. Tolkien's most famous books, *The Hobbit* and *The Lord of the Rings*, periods of great danger are interspersed with periods of safety and rest for the heroes, during which they can regain their strength. A long story that consists of nothing but action will feel unrealistic and silly after a while.

The works of Joseph Campbell and Christopher Vogler discuss the heroic quest at length, and we encourage you to read them for inspiration (see Appendix B, "Bibliography," for details).

The Problem of Death

For many years, game designers have debated the question of whether adventure games should allow the avatar to do something that kills him. Some adventure games have proudly noted on their boxes that you can't ever die; others have warnings in the manual that you might encounter dangerous situations. In some respects, this seems like a strange thing to worry about. After all, avatars routinely die in action games and get shot down in flight simulators, so why shouldn't they be able to die in adventure games?

The reason has to do with the nature of the gameplay. In a first-person shooter or a military flight simulator, it's obvious that the avatar is in mortal peril all the time. In fact, in most genres of games, it's win or lose, kill or be killed, and the enemies are clearly marked. Adventure games are different because they seldom have an explicitly declared enemy and the player is encouraged to go everywhere and touch everything. If you tell the player to explore the world and then you fill it with deathtraps, he's in for a frustrating time. Nowadays, most adventure games adopt a "fair warning" approach, making it clear when something is dangerous and (usually) offering a way of neutralizing or circumventing the danger. If you put a dragon in a cave, it's a nice touch to litter the entrance with the bones of earlier adventurers. That ought to get the point across.

Most adventure games have a save-game feature, so death isn't necessarily catastrophic; on the other hand, stopping to save the game does tend to hurt suspension of disbelief. Adventure games shouldn't be so dangerous that the player has to save all the time because it ruins the storytelling. If you are going to include death in your game, we encourage you to autosave the game at intervals so that the player can restore it even if he hasn't explicitly saved it. You don't have to let the player know that you're doing it. Again, it helps to preserve the suspension of disbelief if you don't.

Challenges

The majority of challenges in an adventure game are conceptual: puzzles that require lateral thinking to solve. There are many types of puzzles; we list a few here to get you started:

➤ **Finding keys to locked doors.** By *doors* and *keys,* we mean any obstruction that prevents progress and any object that removes the obstruction. Many adventure game puzzles are of this type. The challenge as a designer is to give players enough variety that they don't all seem the same.

➤ **Figuring out mysterious machines.** This is, in effect, a combination lock instead of a lock with a key. The player has to manipulate a variety of knobs to make a variety of indicators show the correct reading. Try to make their presence reasonably plausible—too many adventure games include mysterious machines that are clearly just a puzzle, not a realistic part of their world.

➤ **Obtaining inaccessible objects.** In this kind of puzzle, there's an object—whether it's a treasure or something needed for some other purpose—that the player can see but not reach. The solution is often to find a clever way of reaching the object, perhaps by building some device that will give access to it.

➤ **Manipulating people.** Sometimes an obstruction is not a physical object, but a person, and the trick is to find out what will make the person go away or let the player pass. If it's a simple question of giving him something he wants, then it's really just a lock-and-key puzzle. A more creative approach is to create a puzzle in which the person must be either defeated or distracted. The player should have to talk to him to learn what his weakness is.

➤ **Navigating mazes.** This is an area that's deliberately confusing to move around in so that it's hard to know where you are and to get where you want to go. Use mazes sparingly. They're easy to make badly but difficult to make interesting. A maze should always contain cues that an observant player can notice and use to help her learn her way around.

➤ **Decoding cryptic messages.** Many players enjoy decoding messages, as long as there are sufficient clues to help out.

➤ **Solving memorization puzzles.** These puzzles require the player to remember where something is—a variant of concentration. She can usually defeat these by taking notes, but that's reasonable enough; it's how we remember things anyway. The real challenge for you as the designer is to create a realistic reason for the puzzle to be in the game.

➤ **Collecting things.** This is really a compound version of other puzzles; the player's job is to find all five of the pieces of the magic whatchamacallit.

➤ **Doing detective work.** The basis for lots of police-procedure games, detective work is great fun. Instead of solving a "puzzle" per se, the player has to figure out a sequence of events from clues and interviews with witnesses. It doesn't necessarily have to be a crime; it could be any unknown event.

➤ **Understanding social problems.** No, we don't mean inflation or unemployment. The challenges of understanding, and perhaps influencing, the relationships between people is a little-explored aspect of adventure game design. Most of the people in adventure games have very simple, mechanical states of mind. If we devote a little more effort to it, people, rather than objects, could become the primary subject of adventure games, and this would make the games much more interesting.

Only playtesting can tell you whether a puzzle is too hard or too easy, and unlike other genres, you can't adjust an adventure game's difficulty by tweaking some numbers. When designing puzzles, we encourage you to try to allow for lateral thinking of the players. If there's more than one way to solve a puzzle, don't arbitrarily restrict the player to *your* preferred method. Obviously, you can't build in multiple solutions to every puzzle, but if the player tries something entirely logical and there's no good reason why it doesn't work, she's going to be frustrated.

User Interface Design

Adventure games, more than most other genres, try to hide the fact that the player is using a computer. By comparison to vehicle simulators, sports games, or RPGs, the user interfaces of adventure games are very simple. The player needs to move through the world, talk to NPCs, and manipulate or collect objects in an intuitive way that does not interfere with his sense of immersion in the story.

Avatar Movement

The movement interface that you design depends considerably on the perspective you choose. In first-person and third-person perspectives, the player needs a way of steering her avatar around the world, as in an action game. We suggest that you look at Chapter 9, "Action Games," for a discussion of avatar movement in first- and third-person perspectives.

In a context-sensitive perspective, there are two common user interfaces: *point-and-click* and *direct control*.

Point-and-Click Interfaces

In this user interface, the player clicks somewhere on the screen. If the corresponding location in the game is accessible, the avatar walks to it. If the player clicks an active object, the avatar walks to it and picks it up or manipulates it in an appropriate way.

Object management is discussed more extensively in the "Manipulating Objects" section later in this chapter. The disadvantage of point-and-click is that the player can easily point to areas that aren't accessible to the avatar (halfway up a wall, for example), and sometimes an area that looks as if it should be perfectly accessible isn't. This can be frustrating for the player. Nevertheless, the point-and-click interface is the de facto standard for adventure games.

Direct Control Interfaces

In a direct control user interface, the player's commands say "Walk in this direction" rather than "Walk to this point," as they do in a point-and-click interface. In these kinds of games, such as *Grim Fandango*, from LucasArts, the player "steers" the avatar around the screen. Direct control can be awkward in a context-sensitive perspective because the camera angle changes from scene to scene.

Movement Speed

No matter what perspective or user interface you choose, we strongly suggest that you implement both a "walk" and a "run" movement mode so the player can move slowly through unfamiliar spaces and quickly through familiar ones. If the game requires the player to move repeatedly through areas he already knows well, it gets very boring to watch the avatar walk deliberately from place to place. On the other hand, if your world is rich and detailed and your game expects the player to examine everything closely for clues, the user interface must make it possible to move around slowly and accurately.

Manipulating Objects

One of the great challenges in designing an adventure game is in determining how the player should manipulate objects in the world. In many games, the player must figure out what to do with particular objects to solve puzzles and advance the game. In text adventures, this amounted to guessing the correct verb. You often got interchanges that looked like this:

```
> OPEN DOOR
The door is locked, but it looks pretty flimsy.
> BREAK DOOR
I don't know how to do that.
> SMASH DOOR
```

```
I don't know how to do that.
> HIT DOOR
I don't know how to do that.
> KICK DOOR
The door flies open.
```

Sometimes this was fun; a lot of the time it wasn't. In graphic adventure games, in which the player is using the mouse or a handheld controller, designers can solve this problem in a variety of different ways.

Identifying Active Objects

Not every object in the game world can be manipulated or picked up; some are just part of the background scenery. The player needs a way of recognizing the active objects in a particular location. Text adventures used to print a list of them. Graphic adventures have typically used one of four mechanisms:

➤ **Hunt and click.** Active objects don't look any different from anything else; the player simply has to click everything in the scene to see if it's active. This makes the scene look realistic, but it's annoying for the player, especially if some of the objects are small or partially hidden. This mechanism has generally been abandoned in favor of the following ones.

➤ **Permanently highlighted objects.** The active objects in a scene are permanently highlighted in some way—either they're slightly brighter than the rest of the scene or they're surrounded by a line of light or dark pixels, to make them stand out against the background. The moment the scene appears on the screen, the player can tell which objects are active. It's convenient, if artificial.

➤ **Dynamically highlighted objects.** The active objects in a scene normally look like part of the background, but they are highlighted when the mouse cursor passes over them. Either the object lights up or the cursor changes shape. It still means that the player has to do some hunting, but it's much easier than hunting and clicking; a quick wave of the cursor tells the player if there's an active object nearby.

➤ **Focus-of-attention highlighting.** This mechanism is typically used with handheld controllers when the player doesn't have a mouse cursor. As the avatar moves around in a scene, his focus of attention changes depending on the direction he is looking. Whatever active object is directly in front of him is the focus of his attention and is highlighted. When he turns away, its highlighting disappears again. The disadvantage of this mechanism is that if two active objects are close together, it can be tricky to point the avatar in exactly the right direction to put the focus of attention on the desired object.

One-Button Actions

In a graphic adventure game played with a handheld controller, designers often assign one button of the controller to a generic "use" or "manipulate" function: The player moves the avatar near the object and presses the "use" button for obvious functions such as opening a door or throwing a switch. The player can always count on the button to do the right thing with an object, whatever that might be. Some mouse-based games use a similar mechanism: Clicking an object does something appropriate with it. This makes the game very easy to play because there's no guessing about what you should do. The disadvantage of this system is that there can be only one action per object, so it doesn't allow the designer to challenge the player's lateral thinking.

Menu-Driven Actions

A number of games use a menu to allow the player to select the action he wants to take and the object that he wants to manipulate (see Figure 15.9). This gives the player a clear picture of his choices, but it does feel a little "computery."

Figure 15.9   The action menu in *The Secret of Monkey Island.*

In another variant, the player places the mouse cursor over the desired object and right-clicks it. A pop-up menu appears, showing a series of icons that represent the actions "take," "use," "examine," and possibly others (see Figure 15.10). The player left-clicks one of the icons, and the desired action is performed. This mechanism, in effect, shows the player all the available verbs that can be used with that particular object and lets him pick one.

Figure 15.10 The pop-up menu in *The Longest Journey* (at right, under tent). Note that the icons are an eye, a mouth, and a hand, meaning "look at," "talk to," and "manipulate."

Managing Inventory

Picking things up and carrying them around until they're needed later has been a major feature of adventure gaming since its beginning. Most games implement a limit on the amount of stuff the player can carry. (However, a few did not, for humorous effect: In *Haunt*, a noncommercial text adventure, the player could be walking through a haunted house wearing a wetsuit and carrying around a stereo, an antique chair, and an oil painting, along with an unlimited number of other items.) With the arrival of graphics, the inventory is usually handled as a pop-up box that shows everything the player is carrying whenever she asks to see it. If the box has a fixed size on the screen, it creates a natural limit on the amount a player can carry. When the box is full, she can't put anything else in it unless she takes something out first.

Inventory management is something the player will need to do frequently, so you should make it as easy as possible. One possibility is to devote a part of the screen to the inventory all the time. This is very easy to work with, although it tends to remind the player that he's using a computer. Its biggest disadvantage is that, unless you sacrifice a lot of screen area or implement a scrollbar, it can't be very big.

The more common solution is to give the player an inventory menu that she can open and close on demand. She should be able to do this with a single keystroke or button click. It should not obscure the whole screen—that feels like a mode change and tends to destroy suspension of disbelief. Instead, the box, bag, or whatever the inventory looks like should allow the player to drag objects in and out of it, from the game world to the inventory, and vice versa, quickly and efficiently. *The Longest Journey* included shortcut keys that allowed players to change the object currently being held in the avatar's hand without opening the inventory box, which was very convenient. Managing the inventory this way also means that you won't have to create animations of the avatar picking up and dropping every possible item in the game. *Asheron's Call*, an online RPG, includes "pick up" and "drop" animations, but they don't actually show the object in the avatar's hand.

One design error to avoid in adventure games is requiring the player to pick up everything she sees. Early adventure games listed the "live" objects in a room separately from the room's description, and there was a common tendency to give every object in a game a particular function. This meant that players had to pick up everything they could, often carrying it around for hours without having any idea what it was for. With the advent of 3D-modeled objects, everything in the whole world is (theoretically) available for the player to pick up.

The inventory is a typical feature of adventure games, but it is not absolutely required. One game, in particular—the LucasArts adventure *Loom*—was designed without an inventory. The player performed all actions in the game by "spinning" musical spells on a distaff, which was the only thing he carried (see Figure 15.11). *Loom* was designed to be especially accessible to people who were not already familiar with adventure games. Although it was short and considered by die-hard adventurers to be too easy, it was one of the most imaginative and beautifully executed adventure games ever created.

Figure 15.11 *Loom.* Note the musical distaff at the bottom of the screen, used for all actions other than movement.

Special Design Considerations

The following special considerations apply especially to adventure games, although there is some crossover with RPGs as well.

Conversations with NPCs

From the original *Adventure* onward, adventure games have always faced the problem of how to create realistic NPCs in the game world. RPGs have this problem, too, but in most of them, the NPC's conversation is defined by the role to which he's assigned: blacksmith, healer, tavern keeper, and so on. The player doesn't expect to be able to discuss arms and armor with a tavern keeper (although the games might be more interesting, and certainly less formulaic, if he could). But because adventure games are interactive stories, players expect the characters in them to be more human and less mechanical.

A good many games have tried to sidestep the problem entirely by setting the game in a world where there are extremely few people or none at all. This certainly creates a mysterious atmosphere, but it's suitable only for a limited range of stories. Imagine how Rick's bar in *Casablanca* would feel if it weren't full of people drinking and gambling. A world with no people in it is artificial and sterile.

A few early text-based games tried to implement parsers that could understand limited English sentences as typed by the player, but these seldom succeeded. You got either an NPC saying "I don't understand that" when you had asked a perfectly reasonable question, or an NPC whose answers weren't quite to the point, giving the impression that he was drugged or mentally ill.

Scripted Conversations

In the end, most adventure game designers gave up on trying to create the impression that you could talk to anyone about anything and devised the *scripted conversation*, a mechanism that has become the de facto standard for both adventure games and RPGs. A scripted conversation is a branching-tree structure in which each node represents an opportunity for the player to select one of several fixed lines to say from a menu of choices (see Figure 15.12). Depending on which line the player chooses to say, the NPC responds appropriately, and the conversation moves on to a new node in the tree. The contents of the menu change as the conversation progresses; as the NPC says things the player hasn't heard before, the player gets opportunities to ask for elaboration, end the conversation, or switch the subject to a different topic. Another common choice is "Tell me again about…," which enables the player to return to an earlier point in the conversation and go through it again, if he didn't pay close enough attention the first time.

Figure 15.12 The conversation menu in *The Lost Files of Sherlock Holmes.*

Benefits of Scripted Conversations

Although the scripted conversation forces the player to say only the things in the script, it does produce natural-sounding conversations, in which the sequence of remarks and replies is plausible. It also gives you, the designer, a way to illustrate both the avatar's and the NPC's character through something other than their appearances. You can write their lines in such a way that you give them distinct personalities of their own. For example, Guybrush Threepwood, the hero of the *Monkey Island* games, is a wise guy type who seldom takes anything seriously. The character's vocabulary, grammar, dialect, and—if the game has recorded audio of the conversation—tone of voice and accent are all important cues.

In addition to letting the player discuss a variety of topics with a given NPC, the menu system allows the player to choose a variety of different attitudes in which she says the same thing: aggressive, deferential, formal, or flippant, for example. The NPC can then respond to each of these in whatever way his character dictates. For example, a powerful character who brooks no nonsense might be offended by wisecracks and refuse to talk to the player anymore. (If you do this and the NPC's information is vital to the plot, make sure that either the NPC gets over his snit after a while or there's some other way for the player to obtain the information.)

The scripted conversation is not merely a mechanism for giving the player information, however. It's a real part of the gameplay, and the player's choices can have a distinct effect on the progress of the game. For example, an NPC could ask the player to entrust him with a valuable secret. The player's decision, whether to tell or not to tell, could have far-reaching consequences. The player has to choose based on her assessment of the NPC's character—to which you, the designer, must provide clues.

Mapping

When playing text adventures, players usually needed to make a map for themselves as they went along. Because the rooms were not physically modeled but were only described, it was difficult for the players to remember how the rooms were related to one another. A lot of text adventure worlds were also purposefully illogical, so a map was really important for keeping track of the relationships between different areas.

With the arrival of graphic adventures, mapping became less critical because the graphics provided cues about where the player was and how his current location related to other areas in the world. However, we think it's a good idea to give the player a map. A few games deliberately deny the player a map to make the game more difficult, but this is usually poor design—an obstacle that slows down the player without providing any entertainment value. There's not a lot of fun in being lost. If you force the player to make his own map, he has to constantly look away from the screen to a sketch pad at his side; that's a tedious business that rapidly destroys suspension of disbelief.

The map that you give the player doesn't have to be complete at the beginning of the game; it can start out empty and be filled in as the player moves around, a process called *automapping*. The player should be able to refer to his map conveniently at any time. It's also a good idea to give the player a compass to tell him which direction he's facing.

Automapping destroys the challenge imposed by mazes, but we think mazes are one of the most overused and least-enjoyed features of adventure games. Unless you have a good reason for including a maze and can construct one that's really clever and fun to be in, don't do it.

Journal Keeping

Another common feature of adventure games—one that is conceptually similar to automapping—is automatic journal keeping. The game fills in a journal with text as the player goes along, recording important events or information she has learned. If the plot is convoluted or there are large numbers of characters in the game, the journal is an invaluable reference tool for the player. Let her call it up and look at it at any reasonable time (though not, perhaps, while hanging over the edge of a cliff or being interrogated by a mean bad guy). As with conversations with NPCs, the journal gives you an opportunity to define the avatar's character through her use of language.

A Few Things to Avoid

As adventure games have evolved, their designers have created many different kinds of puzzles and experiences for the player. Some of these are extremely clever, such as the insult-driven sword fight in *The Secret of Monkey Island*. A good many others, however, proved to be only tiresome time wasters, obstacles that added no entertainment value to the game.

Puzzles Solvable Only by Trial and Error

If you give the player a puzzle that has a fixed number of possible solutions of equal probability (in effect, a combination lock), but no hints about which one is right, then the player simply has to try them all. The Infocom text adventure *Infidel* included a puzzle like this: Four statues of Egyptian goddesses had to be lined up in the correct order, but there were no clues about what it might be. The player simply had to try all 24 possible combinations and keep track of the ones she had already done. There's not much fun in that.

Conceptual Non Sequiturs

This is a variant of the trial-and-error puzzle, a problem whose solution requires thinking so lateral that it's completely irrational. A conceptual nonsequitur is something along the lines of "Put the lampshade on the bulldozer" or "Sharpen the headphones with the banana." A few games try to get away with this by claiming that it's surrealism, but true surrealism is informed by some kind of underlying point; it's not just random weirdness.

A variant of this is the opposite-reaction puzzle, one whose solution turns out to be the exact opposite of what you'd expect. You could give the player a rubber dagger and then have it turn out to be a deadly weapon after all. In the original *Adventure*, the player could drive away a menacing snake by releasing a little bird from its cage. Fortunately, at this point in the game, the player didn't have many options, so he usually found the solution soon. But unless you design an entire game on this principle, it's just an annoying gimmick.

Illogical Spaces

Illogical spaces were a classic challenge in text adventures. If you went north from room A, you got to room B, but if you went south from room B, you didn't go back to room A. Their modern equivalent is teleporters that give you no idea of where you have teleported to. The player simply has to wander around taking notes until she can figure out the relationships among the various locations. Unless you offer some clues, this is another problem that can be solved only by trial and error.

Puzzles Requiring Outside Knowledge

Many adventure games rely on some occasional oddities, especially for comic effect, but the player must have a realistic chance of figuring them out. If a game requires information from a source other than itself, it's unfair to the player. For example, *Haunt* had puzzles that could be solved only if the player was familiar with the 1960s-era cartoon series *Beany and Cecil* ("Help, Cecil, help!") and with the movie *Monty Python and the Holy Grail*. It didn't really matter because *Haunt* was distributed for free and was mostly a joke anyway, but in a commercial game, such puzzles would be unreasonable unless you explicitly made it clear that knowledge of trivia was required. If you want to make humorous references to popular TV shows, movies, and so on, do them in narrative or in an NPC's conversation rather than as solutions to puzzles. Beware, though: Cultural references age very quickly and will make the game seem dated after a few years.

You have to be even more careful when developing games for foreign markets because other countries don't always have the same idioms. For example, the action "Wear the lampshade on my head" could cause other characters in the game to assume that the player's avatar is drunk, which might be desirable in the context of the story. However, wearing a lampshade as a sign of drunkenness is an American cultural idiom that might not be understood in Japan, for example. Again, it's okay to make cultural references in your game; just be careful about requiring the user to understand them to win.

Click-the-Right-Pixel Puzzles

A few adventure games with point-and-click user interfaces require you to click on a tiny and inconspicuous area of the screen to advance the story, for no particular reason except that it's difficult to find. This is lazy design—a cheap way of creating an obstacle for the player without any entertainment value.

Backward Puzzles

A *backward puzzle* is one in which you find the solution before you find the puzzle itself. For example, you find a key, but you don't know of any locked doors. However, you carry it around with you all the time, just in case. When you do eventually find a locked door, you immediately have the solution, which means it's not much of a puzzle. It's not always possible to prevent the player from finding a solution before he finds a puzzle because the solution has to be available, but it can be inconspicuous— for example, a poster on a wall full of posters, or an object in a trash can. Be aware, however, that "inconspicuous" is not the same as "obscure" or "nonsensical." If the key to a puzzle involves finding a live monkey, the monkey shouldn't turn out to be locked in a freezer.

Too Many "FedEx" Puzzles

A *FedEx puzzle* is one that you solve by picking up an object from one place and bringing it to a different place, as if you were a Federal Express driver. Of course, carrying objects around until you find a place to use them is a common feature of adventure games, but some games consist of little else. This gets dull after a while, especially if the solution to a puzzle consists only of fetching and carrying without any lateral thinking or other activity. Liven up the game with a variety of puzzles and tasks. It's fun to include objects that have a variety of different uses, such as Indy's bullwhip in *Indiana Jones and the Infernal Machine*, or objects that are left over from one puzzle but have a part to play in another.

Adventure Game Worksheet

When beginning the design of an adventure game, consider the following questions:

1. Who is the central character in the game, the player's avatar? What is the avatar's sex? (For the purposes of this worksheet, we'll assume that the player is male and the avatar is female.) What does she look and sound like? What are her personal qualities, strengths, weaknesses, interests, likes, and dislikes? What sort of vocabulary and grammar does she use? What are her ethnic, social, religious, political, and educational backgrounds? What is her personal history? What is her family like?

2. What is the story of the game? What is the avatar's ultimate goal? What will occur at the dramatic climax? What things must she collect, learn, or achieve for the dramatic climax to take place?

3. Where does the game take place? What sort of a world is this? Is the player free to move around these areas continuously throughout the story, or do one-way elements prevent him from returning to earlier areas?

4. What other characters are in the game? What functions do they serve? How do they look and act? How do they respond to the avatar? Can she affect their moods and attitudes?

5. How is conversation implemented? What consequences can arise from it? Can the player choose a variety of attitudes in which to speak?

6. What kinds of puzzles are in the game? What obstacles will the player encounter, and what actions will he be able to take to overcome them? Is this a pure adventure game or an action-adventure? If it's an action-adventure, what are the action elements like?

7. What graphics technology will be used to display the world? 2D backgrounds? Real-time 3D? How will this affect the look and richness of the world?

8. What perspective will the player have on the game setting? Context sensitive? First person? Third person?

9. What is the user interface for moving the avatar around the game world? Will it be point-and-click, direct control, or some other mechanism?

10. How does the player recognize active objects in the world? How does he command the game to manipulate them? What verbs are available for each object?

11. Is there an inventory, and, if so, how is it displayed and used? How does the player pick things up and put them down again? Can objects be combined or used together? How is this handled?

12. Does the player need a map? If so, will it be static or maintained automatically?

13. Should the game keep a journal to help the player remember things?

Putting It Together

Adventure games are seldom a technological challenge to build unless you're trying to include powerful artificial intelligence techniques—natural language recognition or generation, for example. They rarely demand a lot of CPU power. But what they lack in technological challenges they make up for in creative ones. As the designer of an adventure game, it's your job to bring not just a story, but a world to life—a world in which a story is taking place. Your talents at creating places, characters, plots, dialogue, and puzzles will be tested as in no other genre. Because the adventure game is not bound to flying or shooting or commanding troops in battle—indeed, not to any particular mode of interaction at all—it has the greatest potential for design creativity of any genre.

All computer games are made to realize dreams. Adventure games realize the strangest dreams of all.

Chapter 16

Artificial Life, Puzzle Games, and Other Genres

This chapter is about a few game genres that aren't as popular as the ones we've already covered: artificial life, puzzle games, and games for girls. That doesn't mean there's anything wrong with them; they have produced some extremely successful games. In fact, because there are fewer games in these categories, the market isn't crowded with look-alike products. Working in one of these genres, you actually have a better chance of creating something distinctly new. However, you might have trouble persuading a conservative producer that a really good puzzle game is a better bet than yet another first-person shooter.

Because we're covering several genres in this chapter, we don't have room to explore the elements of each one; instead, we'll just hit the highlights.

Artificial Life Games

Artificial life is a branch of computer science research, just as artificial intelligence is. Artificial life, or *A-life*, as it is sometimes called, involves modeling biological processes, often to simulate the life cycles of living things. A-life researchers hope to discover new ways of using computers by using biological mechanisms—mutation and natural selection, for example—rather than algorithmic ones. In particular, A-life is the study of *emergent properties*, unanticipated qualities or behaviors that arise out of the interaction of complex systems. Life itself is considered an emergent property of the planet Earth.

The most famous (though not the first) A-life game is called simply *Life* and was created by a mathematician named John Conway. It depicts *cellular automata*, simulated beings that "live" on a grid. All they do is survive, reproduce, and die according to three very simple rules. When people first began playing with the game, they quickly discovered that it had a number of emergent properties even though it had such simple rules. Certain patterns of cells could move across the grid ("gliders"), and some ("glider guns") could even generate an endless stream of new cells.

Because they're intended for entertainment rather than research, commercial A-life games implement only a subset of what A-life research investigates. There aren't any commercial A-life games about observing thousands of generations of one-celled animals evolving in an environment, for example. Typically, A-life games are about maintaining and growing a manageable population of organisms, each of which is unique.

Artificial Pets

One subcategory of artificial life game is the *artificial pet*. Artificial pets are simulated animals that live on your computer, either in an environment of their own or on your desktop. They can be simulations of real animals, as in the *Petz* series developed by P.F.Magic, or fantasy ones like the Tamagotchi, a tiny and very simple computer game built into a keychain.

Artificial pets are almost always cute. The nature of their gameplay concentrates on training and maintenance, and watching them do endearing things. They seldom reproduce or die, and the player usually wants to interact with only one or two at once. (Games about whole populations of organisms, in which they do reproduce and die, are discussed in the section "Genetic A-Life Games," later in this chapter.)

If the player is going to spend much time looking at an artificial pet, then the pet needs to have quite a lot of AI: a variety of things that stimulate it and behaviors that it exhibits. An artificial pet should have a number of emotions, or moods, that the player can learn by observation and can influence by interacting with it somehow. It also needs to interact meaningfully with others of its own kind: teasing, playing, grooming, fighting, and so on. Above all, it needs to be able to learn, so there must be a way for the player to show it how to do things. The learning process must not be too long (or the player will get frustrated and think his pet is stupid) or too short (or the player will run through everything he can teach it very quickly). (Tamagotchi, being so tiny and inexpensive, are obviously an exception to this principle!)

This quality of rich artificial intelligence distinguishes artificial pets from other kinds of A-life, in which individuals have simple rules but the population as a whole develops emergent properties. Artificial pets can have properties that appear only after they have been around for a while, but typically these are preprogrammed and are not truly emergent.

Because an artificial pet doesn't have much of a challenge or a victory condition (apart from training it to do something specific), it's a *software toy* rather than a game. ("Software toy" is a term coined by Will Wright, the original designer of *Sim City,* for entertainment software that you just play around with, without trying to defeat an opponent or achieve victory.) The entertainment of an artificial pet comes from watching it do things and interacting with it. In *Petz,* shown in Figure 16.1, you can see three cats, all of which are interacting with things in their environments. One is simply sitting on a rug, but it knows that it is a rug and has chosen to sit on it rather than somewhere else. An artificial pet has a large number of behaviors that the player sees repeatedly, and others that occur more rarely. Part of balancing it—making sure that the player doesn't get bored with it—is making sure that these rare behaviors occur often enough that the player does get to see them but doesn't take them for granted.

Figure 16.1 *Petz* from PF.Magic.

The Sims

The Sims is almost the only game of its kind. There was one game a bit like it, *Little Computer People*, many years ago on the Commodore 64, but it wasn't nearly as rich as *The Sims*. If *The Sims* can be said to belong to a class, it is a virtual dollhouse: It simulates a family in a suburban home. You can make the people move around, cause them to complete certain tasks, tell them when to go to bed and when to get up, and so on. You can indirectly influence their relationships by making them talk to each other—the big difference is that you can't decide what they say, and you can't guarantee that they will like each other. Each simulated person has her own personality, likes, and dislikes.

One of the best things about *The Sims* is that there are multiple ways to play with it. It's sort of a cross between an artificial pet and a construction and management simulation. You need money to build additions to the house and to buy new furniture for it. The family has to earn that money by at least one member having a job. You can spend quite a lot of time in the buying-and-building mode, if you can afford it, which has nothing at all to do with artificial life. Some players, the particularly goal-oriented ones, really concentrate on this aspect, working hard to construct a mansion and fill it with luxuries. Others are more interested in the interactions among the people. In Figure 8.11 in Chapter 8, "The Internal Economy of Games and Game Balancing," you can see two sims dancing in their kitchen. This might have been spontaneous behavior, but it was more likely in response to an instruction given by the player.

Needs

The main challenge of *The Sims* is to manage this group of slightly incompetent people and to improve their career prospects by teaching them things that will help them get better jobs. Each person, called a "sim," has eight needs that she must meet on an ongoing basis: hunger, comfort, hygiene, bladder, energy level, fun, social interaction, and room (which, in effect, means uncrowded, attractive surroundings). These needs drive her behavior. When a sim feels a need, she takes actions to meet it somehow. If the need goes unmet for too long, the sim becomes unhappy and can even die (in the case of hunger). Each sim always has a queue of things to do to meet her current needs, unless they're all met at the moment. The player can also give the sim orders, in effect inserting a behavior at the front of the queue. This need-based AI is at the heart of most simple behavior simulations, whether of people or animals; if implemented properly, it works very well.

Skills

Unlike with an artificial pet, it isn't necessary to teach the sims by repeatedly showing them something. Instead, the trick is finding the time for them to improve their skills, which they can do by a variety of means. The sims have six skills: cooking, repair, charisma, body (physical strength and dexterity), logic, and creativity. These skills influence the jobs that they can take and, consequently, the amount of money that they can earn. Unfortunately, the sims are so busy and do everything so slowly that often they don't get enough leisure time to study or work out. The game is very much an exercise in time management.

Personalities

Unlike almost every other computer game, *The Sims* tries to simulate relationships among individual people. These relationships are not terribly sophisticated, but they do include such concepts as jealousy, anger, and love. Each sim's personality is defined by five key variables: neat, outgoing, active, playful, and nice. These determine how they react to one another and whether they're likely to get along. *The Sims* also encourages the player to develop friendships among his fellow sims because career advancement is conditional upon having a certain number of friends.

The Success of *The Sims*

The Sims has been a huge success, which we believe it owes to two things. First, it enables the player to exercise his creativity in a familiar sphere: the ordinary suburban home. In addition to building and furnishing a house, players can design their own "skins" for the sims, creating people who look like themselves (or anyone else). The game actually offers more creative play than *Sim City* or *Sim Tower*, for example, just because there are more different kinds of things to do. Players can also take photographs of their houses and store them in albums, along with written commentary that they supply, effectively creating illustrated stories. And they can share all these things over the Internet. The game offers more scope for personal creativity on the part of the player than just about any other on the market.

The second reason for the success of *The Sims* is that it is about human relationships. The player's immediate objective in playing *The Sims* is to make sure his sims' physical needs are met, but his secondary, longer-term objective is to meet the sims' mental or emotional needs: fun, social interaction, and quality living space. The need for social interaction is considerably more complex because it involves building relationships with other people rather than simply interacting with objects, and those social interactions can produce emergent properties. Players enjoy watching and influencing these interactions. In fact, the player's imagination plays a very large role in the game, just as it does in playing with dolls. The sims are not terribly complex simulations, but players give them names and personalities and ascribe many more characteristics to them than they actually possess. This quality of imaginative play is actually another form of creativity that contributes strongly to its success, especially among female players.

Genetic A-Life Games

Some A-life games are about managing a population of creatures over time. Rather than concentrating so much on individuals, the object of the game is to achieve certain things with the population as a whole. By far, the most successful of these is the *Creatures* series from Creature Labs (formerly Cyberlife). In *Creatures*, you manage a small group of beings called Norns. Norns have a certain amount of AI, and they can be taught things through repetition, like the animals in *Petz*. Norns also have distinct genetic characteristics. Unlike either the people in *The Sims* or the animals in *Petz*, they have a limited life span, so the game is about breeding generation after generation of Norns and exploring and manipulating their world indirectly through them.

Designing a Genome

To create a game in which you crossbreed creatures and get new, unique individuals, you need to devise a *genome*: a set of descriptors (genes) that define all the important characteristics of the creature. These characteristics should include everything about the creature that can vary from individual to individual: shape, size, coloration, and so on. You can leave out details that are common to all creatures. For example, if all your creatures will have two eyes and that will never change, there's no need to store a gene called Number of Eyes. Genes can have any number of possible values, from two (striped or spotted?) to floating-point numbers (height of creature in meters).

When two individuals reproduce, they mix their genes somehow, and you will need to define how this is done. For a quantitative value such as height, the initial temptation is to average them. Don't do this. Within a very few generations, all your creatures will be the same height, or very nearly. In fact, human genetics works differently. We have not one value for each characteristic, but two, one inherited from the mother and one from the father. These two values are called *alleles*. If a person's two alleles for the same trait don't match, one of them dominates according to a rule (the allele for brown eyes dominates the allele for blue, so people with one brown allele and one blue allele will have brown eyes). When a human reproduces, one of the two alleles is chosen at random to go on to the next generation. This means that it's possible for a brown-eyed person to still pass on the allele for blue eyes. Otherwise, the allele for blue eyes would disappear from the population almost immediately.

As for quantitative values such as weight, in humans, they tend to be controlled by multiple genes and influenced by environmental factors as well. You can define these mechanisms any way you like; you certainly don't have to do it the way humans do. As research goes on, geneticists are finding that mechanisms for genetic recombination and expression are quite complex and vary a lot even within a single species.

Mutation

Mutation is a change to a gene that occurs as a result of some environmental factor. Radiation is well known as being mutagenic; so are some chemicals. Mutation has the benefit that it introduces random new values into the gene pool. Bear in mind that mutation doesn't normally affect the individual whose genes are mutated; it affects only his offspring. Of course, some of these changes can be detrimental or even lethal to the individual that inherits them. For the purposes of your game, you probably don't want to allow lethal mutations—those that produce miscarriages or stillborn offspring. If your creatures' gestation period is long, it wastes time and doesn't add anything of value to the gene pool.

Life Span, Maturity, and Natural Selection

Each of your creatures needs a natural life span, or your population will explode. (In *Creatures*, the life span of a Norn is about 30 real-time minutes.) If you want your population to evolve through natural selection—that is, to become better adapted to its environment—then your creatures also need a period of immaturity, when they are not fertile, followed by a period of maturity, when they are. Natural selection works only if it kills off creatures with maladaptive genes before they are old enough to reproduce. If creatures could reproduce immediately after they were born, maladaptive genes would never leave the gene pool. For example, suppose that a creature's genes are such that it is unable to recognize food. This creature should die of starvation very soon. Whatever genetic values determine its food-recognition ability are clearly maladaptive. However, if it can reproduce immediately, those genes will be passed on. For natural selection to take place, you will have to design environmental hazards or other mechanisms (such as starvation) that tend to kill off young individuals with poor genes before they get the chance to pass on those genes.

(One of the reasons there are so many diseases associated with aging in humans is that those diseases catch you only *after* you have had the chance to reproduce. There's no natural selection against genes for arthritis and osteoporosis because those are diseases that occur later in life, after people have already had children.)

If there's one thing we know about evolution, it's that it's very slow—at least, if it works purely through random mutation and natural selection (evidence is growing to suggest that it's more complex than that). The life span of the Norns in *Creatures* is really too long for the player to breed hundreds of generations. If you want evolution to be a part of your game, you'll need to find ways of making it work nonrandomly or keep the life span of your creatures very short. Of course, the shorter the lifespan is, the less chance a given creature has to exhibit an interesting behavior, so there's a balance to be struck.

Inheritance of Acquired Characteristics

Long ago, in the morning of the world, the first zebra was pure white. But one day, there was a great fire amid the grasses of the savanna. The zebra stood deep in a pond for safety. When she came out, she was very wet. And as she passed through the burned grasses and reeds on the shore of the pond, the cinders left black stripes all along her sides. And from that day to this, all zebras have had black stripes along their sides.

Inheritance of acquired characteristics is a fancy term for this old children's-story idea. People used to think it was how evolution worked—if giraffes stretched up their necks to get food, the next generation of giraffes would have slightly longer necks, and so on. In fact, the opposite is true: Giraffes with short necks tend to starve without reproducing, leaving only giraffes with long necks in the gene pool. The outcome is the same, but the mechanism is entirely different. Stretching your neck doesn't change your genes.

However, you're designing a computer game. There's no reason you can't include inheritance of acquired characteristics if you want to. If the player pours blue ink over one of his creatures, that could change the creature's genes to produce blue offspring. In fact, this provides a convenient way for the player to do his own genetic engineering. Instead of fiddling with the creature's genes in a rather artificial user interface, he can fiddle with the creature directly to change its genes.

Learned Behavior

Notice that learned information is also an acquired characteristic. Humans are not born knowing arithmetic; they have to be taught it. When you teach a human arithmetic, unfortunately, that doesn't cause her children to be born knowing it because the learning goes into her brain, not into her genes. In a game, however, there's a good reason for storing learned behavior in genes as well. If your creatures need to learn something important to survive, it's unlikely that the player will want to teach each individual one by one. It would be better for the player to teach one individual and then for that learning to be expressed in the genes of its offspring so that the player never has to teach them again.

Alternatively, the creatures could store the information in their brains and then begin to teach each other. Of course, you could allow the content of the teaching to change over time, producing behaviors slightly different from what the player originally intended. If certain teachings produce adaptive behavior, they themselves could be selected for, just as genes are. (The notion that ideas behave the way genes do is called *memetics* and is a highly controversial topic in academic circles. We're talking about computer games, however, and we can do whatever we like.)

How Many Sexes?

Sexual reproduction has the advantage over asexual reproduction in that it mixes up the genes and creates unique new individuals, which might be better adapted to their environment. You don't have to restrict your number of sexes to two, but it is the most efficient mechanism. Two is a convenient number of sexes because it has the maximum probability that two individuals of opposite sexes will find each other when roaming around their habitat.

Here's an example. Let's assume that you have equal numbers of each sex in the population, and it takes a certain amount of time for a given individual to find another one and determine whether it is a member of the opposite sex. In a two-sex species, there's a 50-50 chance that any other individual is of the opposite sex; that's not bad odds. But if three sexes are required for reproduction, it is harder for all three to find each other. A given individual would need to find two others, which takes longer, and the odds aren't as good, either. Suppose that I'm of sex A, and I need to find two other creatures of sexes B and C, respectively. When I find the first one, the chance is one third that it is also of sex A (no use to me) and two thirds that it is of sex B or C, either of which will do for now. Let's suppose that it's of sex B. Now the two of us have to go hunt for another creature of sex C. The chance of any given creature being of sex C is only one third. So, the total probability that I'll find members of the sexes I need when I bump into two random individuals is only two ninths (2/3 × 1/3) instead of 50%. And of course, it gets worse the more sexes you have.

You don't have to stick to that rule of having equal numbers of each sex, however. Beehives contain one fertile female (the queen), hundreds of infertile females (the workers), and a few fertile males (the drones). The sex of creatures need not be determined by their genes, either. The sex of many reptiles is determined by the temperatures of their eggs during gestation. Eggs at the top of the pile, nearer the sun, develop into females; the cooler ones at the bottom develop into males.

What Does the Player Do?

A genetic A-life game might not seem to have much for the player to do: Wind it up and watch it go. However, there is actually a fair number of things she might do. For example, she can create completely new individuals and add them to the population to observe how their genes influence the population. She can add and remove environmental hazards that would tend to weed out certain genes. She can play with the rate and nature of mutation by adding or modifying mutagenic objects or areas of the environment. She can also mate particular individuals to select for particular characteristics (with animals, this is considered useful and is called *breeding*; with people, it is considered evil and is called *eugenics*).

Puzzle Games

Many single-player computer games contain puzzles. In action games, you often have to figure out the boss opponent's weakness. Adventure games are full of puzzles, frequently about obtaining inaccessible objects or getting information from other people. Even first-person shooters have the occasional puzzle, figuring out how to get past locked doors and other obstacles. Puzzle design is an essential element of game design, and it's harder than it sounds.

Puzzle games are games that are primarily about puzzle solving, sometimes without incorporating the puzzles into a story line or larger goal. That doesn't mean that they're a random collection, however. Puzzle games are usually variations on a single theme. To be a commercial success, a puzzle game needs to be challenging (but not too hard), visually attractive, and, above all, enjoyable to play with. It also needs to be fresh and large enough to justify spending the money on. Although solitaire card games such as *FreeCell* belong in the class of puzzle games, unless you sell a lot of them together as a collection, people are unlikely to want to pay for them.

Scott Kim's Eight Steps

Scott Kim is a designer who creates puzzles for the print media, web sites, and computer games. He has worked in the field for many years and has identified eight steps in puzzle game design. The first four steps comprise the process of specifying the rules, while the last four comprise the process of building the puzzles and the game itself:

1. **Find inspiration.** This can come from a variety of sources, including other games. *Tetris*, for example, was inspired by a noncomputer game called Pentominoes. You can be inspired by a piece of art (the drawings of M.C. Escher have a very puzzle-like feel), a story, or some particular subject matter. Another source of inspiration is a play dynamic of some kind: flipping switches, turning knobs, sliding objects around, or picking them up and putting them down. Or, there are more complex dynamics among objects: balancing, reflection, connection, and transmission.

2. **Simplify.** Suppose you have an idea for a puzzle: efficiently parking vehicles of different sizes in a crowded parking lot so that when someone asks you to retrieve their car, you have to move as few other cars as possible. Part of making this task fun is simplifying it to its essentials. First, identify the essential tricky core skill (in this case, space planning on the fly) and concentrate on that. Second, eliminate any irrelevant details. Don't make your player worry about crashing the cars, for example. Third, make the pieces uniform. Instead of having cars with infinitely variable shapes and sizes, it's better to have several standard types that conform to a square grid. Finally, simplify the controls. Figure out what the essential moves are, and devise controls that implement them with a minimum of fiddling.

3. **Create a construction set.** The only way to be sure that a puzzle concept works is to play it, but obviously you don't want to code up the whole game before you know whether it's fun. You can build a paper prototype or a simple version in something like Macromedia Flash to see if it works. The rule designer can play with it to tweak the rules, and later the level designer can use it to build levels. You can also code a construction set into the final game so that players can construct puzzles for each other.

4. **Define the rules.** This is the key part of puzzle design. Most puzzles are characterized in terms of four things: the *board* (Is it a grid? A network? Is it irregular? Or is there no board at all?), the *pieces* (How are they shaped? What pictures are on them? What other attributes do they have? Where do they come from?), the *moves* (What is allowed and what is not? Are they sequential or simultaneous? What side effects do they have?), and the *goal* or victory condition (Does it have to be an exact match, or will a partial one do?).

5. **Construct the puzzles.** A puzzle challenges the player to get from a problem to a solution, but, of course, the path isn't simple. Every puzzle requires that the player make choices, some of which lead to dead ends. In an adventure game, each puzzle appears in a larger context (the story) that gives it meaning, and solving it advances the plot somehow. Some puzzle games also offer an overall plot of sorts or won't let you try the next puzzle until you've completed the current one. Good puzzles require insight from the player, that "Aha!" moment that occurs when the player realizes how the puzzle works and how to solve it. But you mustn't require an insight that's too obscure, or it will feel unfair. If you tell the player that he's in a maze, it's unfair for the only solution to be to knock down the walls unless you indicate somehow that this is possible.

6. **Test.** Testing tells you several things. It tells you whether the puzzle is too easy or too hard (this can be difficult to predict in advance), and it also tells you whether it's fun in the first place. It helps you find out if there are alternate solutions that you didn't think of, and it helps you discover errors in the rules. And, of course, it lets people try out the user interface. Because puzzle actions tend to be repetitive, it's important that the interface be smooth and not frustrating.

7. **Devise a sequence.** Now it's time to order all your puzzles into a sequence. The most obvious arrangement is a linear or accelerating sequence going from easy to difficult, but in practice, that becomes tiring and discouraging. A better arrangement is a sawtooth shape, which gets difficult for a while, then goes back to an easy puzzle, and so on, over and over. And, of course, you can give the player the freedom to play the puzzles out of order or let her earn it. You also need to think about transitions between puzzles, something that will keep her moving on to the next one. War games and role-playing games often do this with a story line. Or, the player can be working on a metapuzzle in between the regular puzzles, which motivates her to complete the whole game.

8. **Pay attention to presentation.** Finally, of course, there are all the other details of game design: sound, graphical style, animation, user interface elements, story line (if any), and so on. If you're used to designing other kinds of games, it might be tempting to move this to an earlier point in the process, but with puzzle games, the puzzles are 90% of the battle. Get them right first, and the rest won't be nearly as hard.

What Computers Bring to Puzzles

Computers enable us to make a lot of puzzles that would be impossible or very expensive to create in the real world—all the mechanical parts in *The Incredible Machine*, for example. But even if a puzzle is physically possible, the computer can add a number of useful features to make the gameplay easier and more enjoyable.

➤ **Enable nonphysical or awkward moves.** The computer can let players do things that don't correspond to physical actions in the real world—for example, changing the color of something. You can also let the player control several things at once with just one key, something that would be awkward to do in a physical implementation.

➤ **Include computation features.** You can use the computing power available to automatically generate new puzzles, find solutions to the current puzzle, or generate hints about what the player should do next.

➤ **Enforce the rules.** In a lot of physical puzzles, it's up to the player to enforce the rules on himself. Sometimes players make mistakes and break the rules accidentally. A computer game can make sure that never happens.

➤ **Undo and record moves.** This very useful feature for games involves moving objects around in a sequence, as in Solitaire.

➤ **Structure the experience.** The computer allows you to present the experience in a particular order, if necessary, passing automatically from one phase to another, if that's what your game requires. In the real world, the player would be looking at the instructions and saying, "Let's see, what am I supposed to do next?"

➤ **Teach.** You can include tutorial modes and step-by-step instructions to help your player get into the game.

➤ **Utilize bells and whistles.** Obviously, with sound and animation, you can make a puzzle much more aesthetically interesting on the computer than it would be as a physical object.

➤ **Enable online play.** The computer lets players compete against one another, compare solutions, and be part of a puzzle-solving community.

Checking the Victory Condition

Bear in mind that players don't always find the solution to a puzzle the same way that you did when you invented it. There might be more than one path to the goal. When your game is checking to see whether the puzzle has been solved, you should test only to see if the player has met the victory condition you gave her, *not* that she has done it in the way you expected. Otherwise, you've cheated her, and she'll be very frustrated. She's managed to get to the correct solution state, but your game refuses to recognize it.

This problem occurred in the game *Interstate '76*. It wasn't a puzzle game, but one of the levels did contain a puzzle of sorts. The player was driving an armed and armored car around in an area enclosed by a concrete wall, and the victory condition for winning the level stated that (among other things) it was necessary to get out of the enclosed area somehow. The game's designers had put in a hidden ramp, which they wanted players to find and use to drive out of the area. However, players of the game discovered that there was another way to get out. If a player dropped a land mine near the wall and then drove toward it at full speed, the force of the explosion would lift the car high enough to clear the wall, and the car would fly over it and out. Unfortunately, the software didn't test for the solution state given: Is the car outside the wall? Instead, it tested to see if the ramp was being used. If a player got out without using the ramp, it didn't know that the level was finished, even though the victory condition had been met.

Of course, sometimes games contain bugs that allow a player to cheat in some way and reach a solution by a means that's completely outside the rules. In *Interstate '76*, however, the trick with the land mine wasn't a bug; it was just an innovative solution that the designers didn't consider. When the software is checking the victory condition, be sure it's checking the solution state that you told the player to achieve, not the way in which he achieved it.

Case Study: *The Incredible Machine*

The Incredible Machine is an excellent example of a puzzle game that is imaginative and clever and that has sold really well. In fact, it's not just a game, but a whole game franchise, with five editions so far. The current version is called *Return of the Incredible Machine: Contraptions*, and it's published by Sierra Entertainment (formerly Sierra On-Line).

continues

continued

The game consists of a series of puzzles, each of which involves building a Rube Goldberg–like machine to accomplish a certain task. Each machine is constructed in a two-dimensional space upon which a variety of mechanical devices can be placed. (Some of these devices are actually animals, which can be frightened by noises or lured by food.) A few objects are already in position at the beginning of the puzzle, and the victory condition states what the player is trying to accomplish (for example, pop the balloon). The player is given a limited number of additional devices to place in the area. The object is to place them and hook them up in such a way that when the machine is set in motion, the goal is achieved. Playing the game consists of adding elements to the machine, trying them out, adjusting them, trying again, and so on. Figure 16.2 shows one of the scenarios in *The Incredible Machine*. The goal is given at the left. Available parts are in the area beneath the main workspace.

Scott Kim has identified three key design decisions that he feels have made *The Incredible Machine* the prototypical construction puzzle game.

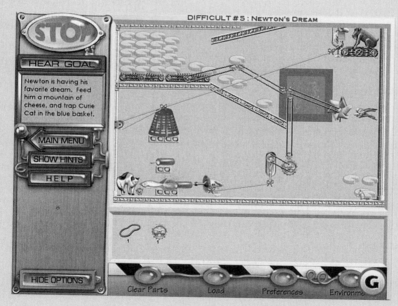

Figure 16.2   *The Incredible Machine.*

1. **Allow the player to build things.** This makes *The Incredible Machine* a construction game and differentiates it from, say, *Tetris* (an action puzzle game) or *Marble Drop* (a logic game in which you decide where and when to drop marbles into a mechanism). The player feels as if he is exercising his creativity.

2. **Include no real-time decision making.** Constructing the machine and running it take place in separate modes. The player can take as long as he wants to think about what he's doing. This is in contrast with *Lemmings*, which is also an excellent game but requires the player to solve the puzzle on the fly. Often if the player didn't get it figured out in time, he had to start over.

3. **Allow players to design their own puzzles.** Any time players can build their own elements, it adds value to the game and helps create a community of devoted fans. Players can exchange their puzzles by email, post them on web sites, run tournaments, and enjoy all kinds of other activities, all of which is free publicity for the game.

Games for Girls

The game industry has always been overwhelmingly male, and male developers have tended to design games that they themselves would like (or would have liked when they were boys). For most of the industry's history, no one made an effort to design games specifically for girls, or to even to think much about what kinds of games girls would like. It was a *Catch-22* situation: If you proposed a game for girls to a publisher, you would be met with the reply, "Girls don't play video games." But, of course, the reason they didn't play video games was that there weren't many games they liked to play—or, at least, that was the general perception. (Further research showed that this was an unfounded stereotype; far more girls played games than people realized, even though no one was considering their interests.)

In the mid-1990s, a number of people realized that girls represented an untapped market, and several companies were set up to exploit it. One in particular, Purple Moon, did a great deal of research to try to discover how girls play games and what kinds of games they would like. Unfortunately, the games that Purple Moon published on the basis of this research took little time to finish, and they offered less value for the money than most other games did. They didn't sell very well, and eventually Purple Moon got into financial trouble and was sold to Mattel, the toy company. Industry attention waned, and games for girls ceased to be a major subject of debate.

However, we think it's an area worth discussing because some people are continuing to make money with games for girls, and this remains an underserved market. Remember, however, that we're talking about *girls*, not women. Adults are more diverse than children are: They live in a larger world, and they've been exposed to more things and have a wider variety of interests. Don't make the assumption that what applies to girls also applies to women generally.

Mattel's Approach

If you want to make games specifically for girls, as opposed to games that appeal to children of both sexes, you have to ask yourself what girls are especially interested in—and, perhaps more important, what they're *not* interested in. For the answer, you need look no farther than Mattel. Mattel is the manufacturer of Barbie®, the single most famous toy for girls in the world. Mattel has had great success developing games for girls because it understands its target market. (Mattel doesn't publish software itself anymore, but it licenses its brands to others.)

Part of the reason for Barbie's success is that she follows a proven, time-tested formula. She is aimed a core age group from four to eight years old; after that, girls' interests change, and Mattel does not try for a one-size-fits-all approach. The company has no social agenda and makes no claim of political correctness.

Jesyca Durchin is the owner of the consulting company Nena Media (www.nenamedia. com), which creates media content for young girls, and is a former executive producer for Mattel. At the 2000 Game Developers' Conference, she gave an extremely useful summary of what she had learned about how girls in this age group play games:

Developing Games for Girls

Girls Have a Wide Variety of Interests
It is *vital* to identify what type of girl is interested in your type of game. Girls are much more fragmented in their interests than boys. Girls change more rapidly, and their emotional and intellectual growth happens differently. A girl will have different needs in her playtime almost every year of her childhood—loosely defining childhood to be ages 4 to 14.

Hinge Interactivity on Proven Play Patterns
A play pattern is a traditional and almost instinctual way a child will approach an object or an activity to entertain her. Girls traditionally value the following:

- Fashion play
- Glamour play
- Nurture play
- Adventure play
- Action/twitch play
- Collection play
- Communication/social play

As well as exercising their own imaginations, girls like to reproduce daily life in play. Barbie is a vehicle for projecting adult activities into a child's world. Don't be afraid of open-ended or non–goal-oriented play.

Girls Like *Stuff*
Stuff is what the girl can collect, display, or take away from the product. It is incredibly important for the girl to feel there is a reason for her to play. In some ways, collecting stuff replaces the concept of scoring in traditional boy's software. Collecting each one of a variety of shells, for example, is more interesting than trying to achieve a high, but abstract, numerical score.

Create Environments That Are Attractive to Girls
Girls like environments that are reality-based but either are beautiful or make sense to the story line. Symmetry and color coherency are important to girls. Not everything has to be pink, purple, and pretty, but each environment should give the girl the feeling of being in another place. Girls (and boys) are highly imaginative, and they will create alternative story lines in their own heads. Be aware that the girl's imagination will influence her view of your environment.

Girls Appreciate Sensual Interfaces
Girls tend to respond more positively to what I refer to as the sensual interface. They need colorful, sound-driven interfaces that "feel" good. The interface needs to feel magical and needs to have what I call the *brrrring* factor. Don't give girls a group of identical gray pushbuttons, no matter how logically organized they may be; give them buttons that ring and change shape and color.

Extend the Play from Existing Toys or Media into Software
Branding is becoming more and more important in the business of software. It is doubly important in the girl's software business because girls are still just getting involved in viewing the computer as an entertainment tool. Branding is important to rising above all the muck.

continues

continued

> **Don't Be Ashamed of Your Work**
> If you're embarrassed by what you're doing, it will show. Do it wholeheartedly or don't do it at all. Girls can tell if you're ashamed of making games for them. If you're uncomfortable using terms like "hair play" or "relationship games," don't bother.

A Few Misconceptions

Because people see fewer girls playing hard-core games than boys, they have tended to jump to conclusions about what girls want.

➤ **Girls don't like computer games because computers are techie.** This is patently false. Although most girls and women generally are less fascinated by the technical details of computers than boys and men are, that doesn't discourage them from playing computer games any more than automotive specifications discourage them from driving cars.

➤ **Girls don't like violence.** No, what girls don't like is nonstop, meaningless violence. It's not so much that they're repulsed by it as that they're bored by it. It doesn't stimulate their imaginations. If you've seen one explosion, you've seen them all.

➤ **Girls want everything to be happy and sweet.** Not true. Ever see a group of girls setting up a party and planning to exclude someone? Girls are perfectly capable of being deliberately hurtful. If you read books written specifically for girls, you'll see that they're not just saccharine from one end to the other. Girls like stories filled with mystery, suspense, even danger—but again, it has to be meaningful, not just random or pointless.

➤ **Girls don't like to be scared.** This is only partially true. Jesyca Durchin makes a useful distinction between *spooky* and *scary*. Girls like things that are spooky but not scary. The abandoned house that contains a clue to the mystery, or the carnival at night, are spooky. Walking through dark streets with a murderer on the loose is scary. Spooky is about the possibility of being startled or frightened; scary is about the possibility of being hurt or killed.

A Final Note

Bear in mind that these are generalities. In her 1989 book *Gender Blending*, Holly Devor quoted studies that showed that as many as 50% of heterosexual women identified themselves has having been tomboys as children. We wouldn't claim that the characteristics described previously appeal to all girls, but they certainly appeal to many. You should take them into consideration if you're trying to make a game for them.

Some developers, both male and female, are repulsed by the idea of making games about hair and clothing and makeup; they feel that this perpetuates a stereotype of femininity. Although there's some merit in that argument, goodness knows that a vastly larger number of games perpetuate a much more unfortunate stereotype of masculinity: They depict men (and reward players) who are violent, greedy, wanton, and monomaniacal. To condemn games for girls on the basis that they're stereotypical is to establish an unfair double standard.

Putting It Together

We've divided our book into genres because there are distinct differences in the ways various genres are designed. An action game for the Nintendo GameCube has very little in common with a construction and management simulation for the PC: The target market is different, the user interface is different, and the internal economy of the game is different. This chapter has been a bit of a catchall for other categories that don't get as much attention.

We strongly encourage you not to become a slave to these divisions. It's true that some genres don't mix well—an adventure gamer will be annoyed if you suddenly make her play an action game—but we will only fully exploit the possibilities of our medium by testing its boundaries, not by remaining within safe little pigeonholes. Ultimately, what matters is that your game is entertaining and rewarding to play. If you have a game in mind that doesn't fit one of these categories, you might have a harder time persuading jaded industry executives to fund it, but try not to compromise your vision if you can. Both your game and the players will be better off for it.

Chapter 17

Online Games

Over the last seven years, online gaming has gone from a tiny fraction of the interactive entertainment business to a major market in its own right. It has many unique qualities, both good and bad, as well as unique design challenges. Because it's a technology rather than a genre, we don't look for design patterns in this chapter the way we did in the earlier ones. Instead, we address some of the design considerations that are peculiar to all kinds of online games, no matter what genre they belong to. It's a huge topic, however; we could probably write an entire book about it. Unfortunately, we can cover only the highlights here.

The second half of the chapter is devoted to *persistent worlds*, also known as massively multi-player online role-playing games, or MMORPGs (although persistent worlds need not necessarily be about role playing). We're particularly indebted to Raph Koster, lead designer of both *Ultima Online* and *Star Wars Galaxies*, and Tess Snider, a long-time online role player and member of the WorldForge Project, for their help with this material. In his many years of working with online games, Koster has assembled a valuable collection of "laws" or observations about this particular form of interactive entertainment, and with his permission, we're going reprint many of them here. Some of these laws are originally his; others are credited to his colleagues. You'll see them scattered throughout this chapter like this:

> ***Ola's Law About Laws:*** Any general law about virtual worlds should be read as a challenge rather than as a guideline. You'll learn more from attacking it than from accepting it.

You can read the complete set of laws at Koster's web site at `www.legendmud.org/raph`.

Advantages of Online Games

As we said, online games have many positive qualities. Some of them are advantages to us as game developers; others are features that attract players who might not otherwise play computer games.

Player Socializing

The single greatest benefit of online play, as far as the players are concerned, is that it offers opportunities for social interaction. Of course, they can't talk as well as if they were in the same room together, and they can't give each other the high five, but these are minor considerations. The social aspect doesn't affect the internal economy of the game much, but it has a distinct effect on the players' enjoyment of the experience. One of the reasons that girls and women have traditionally been less interested in interactive entertainment, especially games for personal computers, is that it is often a solitary activity. But women represent a much greater proportion of the online game market than they do the single-player game market, chiefly for this reason: They enjoy interacting with others.

At the moment, this capability is usually limited to typing text ("chatting"), which is awkward while trying to play a fast-paced game, but a few games are beginning to include voice communication. When enough people get broadband access, they will probably include video as well. A time might come when we see players dressing appropriately to their roles in the game so that they'll look cool on camera.

The social element makes online games more than just games. They become clubs, cafés, casinos—places where people get together for fun. As the creator of such spaces, you're more than just a game designer; you must also be a social architect. This is actually your toughest challenge, far more difficult than designing the core mechanics of a single-player game. An online game isn't an experience that you lead a player through; it's a Petri dish for growing social situations, and it's nearly impossible to predict in advance what will happen there. For further discussion of this topic, please read the excellent and insightful *Community Building on the Web* by Amy Jo Kim.

Human Intelligence Instead of Artificial Intelligence

In single-player games, the player competes against the computer, so the computer has to have enough artificial intelligence to be a good opponent. If the game is complex, building the AI is a huge programming task and is difficult to get right. If the players are competing against each other, as they are in most online games, you don't need any AI. The players provide all the intelligence required. This feature of online play is second only to the social aspect in terms of the benefit provided to the player.

Of course, you can still design the game in such a way that AI is required: You might have nonplayer characters (NPCs) who need to behave intelligently, or you might design a game in which all the players play cooperatively against an artificial opponent. But many online games rely on their players to provide the intelligence in the game, and this can make the game easier to develop.

Psychological Tactics

Intelligence, in gameplay terms, means more than just smarts; it means an understanding of human behavior. Computer software is particularly poor at this; humans are particularly good at it. Playing against other people, you can bluff, feint, ambush, lure opponents out of hiding with lame-duck tactics, and try all manner of *ruses de guerre* that would never work against an AI opponent (or, worse yet, would work consistently every time). You can learn another player's style and look for ways to exploit his tendencies—while being aware that he is learning from yours, too. Except in simple games, playing against human opponents is a richer, more subtle experience.

Online Gameplay Versus Local Multi-Player Gameplay

Multi-player gameplay offers great flexibility to the game designer: It allows purely competitive ("everyone for himself"), purely cooperative ("It's us against the machine"), or team-based play. Multi-player play can be either online or local. In online play, players are linked by a network and are (generally, but not necessarily) in separate locations. In local play, all the players sit in the same room, playing the game on the same machine and, most important, looking at the same screen. For the last 30 years, local play has been the standard mode of interaction for multi-player console games: Each player has a controller, and they all look at the TV. That could change as the new generation of consoles introduces network capability, but it's likely to remain the most common way people use them: It costs nothing and lets people play together in social groups.

Problems with Local Play

From a design standpoint, however, local multi-player play has serious drawbacks. For one thing, because all the players share the same TV, any user interface elements have to be duplicated for each of them, taking up valuable screen space. If every player has a separate point of view, the screen must be subdivided into little windows. Each individual window is harder to see, and the other players' windows are a distraction.

More important, however, in local play there is no hidden information. Each player can see what the others are doing. This is fine for fighting games, but not so good in any game in which players might want to keep their activities secret—war games, for example.

(The Nintendo GameCube does allow players to plug in a Game Boy Advance and use it as a controller; the Game Boy's screen is then available for displaying hidden information to the player. However, this feature requires players to own both devices as well as the necessary cable. Although it solves the problem in theory, in practice any commercial game that requires it as a gameplay mechanism limits its market to those players who actually own all the gear.)

Finally, local play necessarily imposes limits on the number of people who can participate at once. Consoles seldom support more than four players; PCs support even fewer. Even if you could add players indefinitely, the machine itself would be bogged down as the computing task grows.

Benefits of Networked Play

Online gaming solves all these problems. Each player has her own screen, and the entire area is dedicated to supporting her gaming experience. The game can present her with her own unique perspective, including exactly as much information as she is supposed to have, and no more. And online games can support any number of people (although, if they require a central server, there are still some limits)—it's not uncommon for some games to have tens of thousands of players online at a time. With an online game, you can always find other people to play with at any hour of the day or night.

Of the three forms of player interaction (single-player, local multi-player, and online multi-player), online playing offers you the most flexibility as a designer. However, it is not without its problems, as we'll see in the next section.

Disadvantages of Online Games

Playing games over a network, especially the Internet, creates technical challenges that single-player or local multi-player games don't face. Playing with anonymous strangers can cause social friction, and if you provide an online game, you might have a serious legal obligation to make sure people don't use it to abuse children.

Technical Issues

Because this is a book about design, we won't go into the technical issues in detail, much less try to provide solutions for them. However, we think it's worth listing a few just to let you know what you're up against.

> *Murphy's Law:* Servers crash and don't restart only when you go out of town.

Communication Models

Your programming team will need to choose a communication model for the game. Two communication models are used in network gaming. One is *client/server,* in which each player runs a program, called the *client,* on his computer that communicates with a central program, the *server,* on a computer owned by a company providing the game service. In the client/server model, the server "owns" the game and the clients merely present it to the players. The other model is *peer-to-peer,* in which players' computers communicate directly with each other. Peer-to-peer (sometimes abbreviated P2P) is quite straightforward for two-player games, but it becomes more complicated as more players are involved. The players must somehow decide that one machine is the "host," controlling the game, and the others are guests; but if the host logs out of the network, one of the guests must take over and become the new host—preferably automatically and without anyone noticing (this is known as "automated host migration" and is already supplied by Microsoft's DirectPlay facilities). Some companies also operate "matchmaking" services in which the company server's only function is to allow players to find one another and connect together in peer-to-peer networks. All of this is programming work that offline games don't have to bother with.

Transmission Delay Times

The Internet was designed for redundancy rather than speed, and it doesn't make any guarantees about how long a given packet of data will take to get from one point to another. In many games, a faster connection translates into a gaming advantage, so players with high-speed connections are more likely to win the game. There are ways of designing around this: You can make your game turn-based or try to match opponents up on the basis of their connection speed. At the moment, however, there is no one satisfactory answer.

Dropped and Garbled Packets

What happens to your game if it doesn't get some of the information it needs? Your system will require a mechanism for detecting that a packet has gone missing or contains bad data, and requesting that it be resent from the server. Packets can also arrive out of order, which can be confusing if your client receives information that a race car is about to cross the finish line, but the next packet tells it that the car is 100 yards back up the track instead. Every packet must have a unique serial number so that you can tell if one is missing or if they are arriving in the wrong order.

It's Harder to Suspend Disbelief

For some players, gaming is a form of escapism. They want to go away to a magical place, and they want it to stay magical while they're there. To them, it's particularly important that nothing occur in the game to break their suspension of disbelief. This is substantially harder to accomplish with online games because there will always be players who won't stay in character or who will talk about real-world issues and events while they're in the game. Unless there's a strong (and enforced) ethos of in-character role-playing, people who play in an online game have to accept that their imaginary world includes a lot of entirely real people.

> ***Koster's Law:*** The quality of role playing is inversely proportional to the number of people playing.

> ***Enforcing role playing:*** A role play–mandated world is essentially going to have to be a Fascist state. Whether or not this accords with your goals in creating such a world is a decision you will have to make.

Misbehavior

Unfortunately, playing with strangers—particularly anonymous strangers—creates opportunities for a variety of types of misbehavior that can ruin the game for others. These range from simple rudeness to harassment, cheating in various forms, and outright fraud. Rudeness might not sound very serious, but it does drive away other customers. (Raph Koster has stated, only partly joking, that the sole rule in *Star Wars Galaxies* is, "Any behavior that hurts business is bad behavior.") Furthermore, if you want children to play your game, it is particularly important to make sure they have a safe environment to play in—and that means hiring customer service people to monitor them. Self-contained networks such as America Online have some tools at their disposal to manage these problems, but on open networks such as the Internet, it's much harder. We address some of these issues in the section on design issues, later in the chapter.

> ***John Hanke's Law:*** In every aggregation of people online, there is an irreducible proportion of [jerks].

The Need to Produce Content

When you're building a game sold in retail stores, the project is over when the gold master disc goes off to manufacturing. The players buy the boxes, and you can go off to work on another project.

Online games don't work this way; they earn money either through advertising revenue or subscriptions (or both). To keep people interested, you have to change things, and that means producing new content on an ongoing basis. This is expensive to the service provider and ties up skilled development staff. The problem is most obvious with persistent worlds, but even simple games need to be kept fresh somehow. America Online used to run a suite of games called *RabbitJack's Casino* (no real money was awarded as prizes). Although the graphics didn't change, the game's managers held theme nights and gave away additional prizes when particular combinations of events occurred.

> ***Persistence means it never goes away:*** When you open your online world, expect to keep your team on it indefinitely. Some of these games have *never* closed. And closing one prematurely could cost you the faith of your customers, damaging the prospects for other games in the same genre.

Customer Service

All game companies require customer service staff to help players with problems, but online games need far, far more of them. With offline games, players mostly need help with technical difficulties; for gameplay problems, they can buy strategy guides or find hints on the Internet. But in a live, online environment, players expect to get help immediately, and they demand help for a much larger range of issues than they do in offline games. Players expect customer service people not only to solve technical problems, but also to explain the user interface, answer questions about game content, and enforce justice by investigating and punishing misbehavior by other players. With thousands of players logged on at any one time, it can become very expensive to provide these services.

> ***Anonymity and in-game administrators:*** The in-game administrator faces a bizarre problem. He is exercising power that the ordinary virtual citizen cannot, and he is looked to in many ways to provide a certain atmosphere and level of civility in the environment. Yet the fact remains that no matter how scrupulously honest he is, no matter how just he shows himself to be, and no matter how committed to the welfare of the virtual space he might prove himself, people will hate his guts. They will mistrust him precisely because he has power and they can never know him.

Design Issues for Online Gaming

In this section, we're going to address a hodgepodge of design issues that are peculiar to online games.

Arriving Players

Players can log on wanting to play your game at any time, and the game has to be capable of dealing with them intelligently. In most noncomputer games, all the players must be present at the beginning of the match, or it won't be fair. In *Monopoly*, for example, anyone who entered the game late would be at a significant disadvantage—the others would have already grabbed the best properties, and the game's built-in inflation would swiftly bankrupt them.

The usual solution is to start new matches at frequent intervals and to have a waiting area or "lounge" where the players can hang around while they wait for it to begin. If a game can be played with any number of players (bingo is a good example), you can simply start a new match every three minutes, say, with whoever is around to play. In games requiring a fixed number of players, such as bridge, you will need to establish a matchmaking service that allows them to form groups and to wait (more or less patiently) for enough players to join a particular group; the game begins as soon as the required number has arrived. The number of players needed for a game should be small, however, so that they don't have to wait too long. Any game that requires more than about eight players will have difficulties in this respect.

In some games, players can join almost immediately without any disadvantage—poker, for example. Each hand takes little time, and new players can join as soon as the current hand is over. For games of indefinite duration, such as persistent worlds, nothing can be done about the fact that some players are ahead of other players. The players who were there the earliest and who have the most time to play will always have an advantage (unless you allow players to purchase prebuilt characters for real money on eBay, but that just shifts the advantage from players who have the most time to players who have the most money). There are a few ways of preventing this from spoiling the game for the players, however:

> ➤ **Get rid of the victory condition.** Without winners and losers, it ceases to be a game, per se, and becomes a different kind of entertainment. The player focuses on her own achievements rather than on defeating all the others. In this case, the old cliché becomes true: It's not whether you win or lose, but how you play the game. Persistent worlds, which we address later in the chapter, work like this.

> ➤ **Discourage competition between old-timers and newcomers.** You can measure the progress of your players and see to it that only those who are fairly matched come into direct conflict. This is why tournament chess has a ranking system. An old-timer who beats a newcomer gets little or no reward for it. The cliché description for this solution is, make players "pick on someone their own size."

> ➤ **Be sure that direct competition is consensual.** If old-timers do get the chance to compete directly with newcomers, the newcomers should have the option to refuse to play. No one should be forced to take part in an unfair competition.

Disappearing Players

Just as players can appear at any time, they can log off at any time. If possible, your game should deal with this neatly and with minimal disruption to the other players. Obviously, in games that require a fixed number of participants, your only options are to include an AI element that can take over for the missing player, or to shut down the game.

However, in many games, such as racing games, players compete against one another in a free-for-all. The disappearance of one player doesn't make that much difference—his car vanishes from the track, and that's that. It's as if he pulled out with mechanical trouble. In effect, the player forfeits the race and the others continue. On the other hand, if the game is played in teams, the disappearance of one player could put his team at a serious disadvantage.

Logging Out as a Form of Cheating

Tournaments are another matter, though. If players are competing to get the best win-loss ratio, one might deliberately choose to log out rather than lose the game—which also denies the other person victory. Should the vanishing player be forced to forfeit? What if the disconnection was an accident, caused by a bad line? Unfortunately, there's no way to tell which it was.

In baseball, if a game is called off due to rain, it is considered finished if five or more innings have been played (four and a half, if the home team is ahead). Unlike baseball, however, most computer games don't have a distinct way of counting progress toward completion.

Responses to Vanishing Players

Here are a variety of alternative suggestions for dealing with vanishing players:

➤ **The vanishing player forfeits.** Obviously, this is hard on players for whom it was an accident. Unless connections are extremely reliable and unlikely to break (such as in a game played on a local area network), you have to consider the possibility that it was unintentional.

➤ **Institute a penalty for disconnections, less severe than forfeiture.** If you disconnect in the middle of combat during an *EverQuest* session, your avatar remains in the game for a minute, taking additional damage. Unfortunately, it doesn't fight very well by itself!

➤ **Award victory to whoever is ahead in the game.** The problem with this is that the moment someone goes ahead, she can disconnect to prevent her opponent from having a chance to catch up. Again, you should consider this only in circumstances in which it is difficult or impossible to disconnect intentionally.

➤ **Record it as a tie.** Obviously, this motivates a player who is behind in the game to disconnect intentionally. It is a fairly neutral solution, however.

➤ **Record it as a "disconnected game."** You then have to decide exactly what this means in the context of a tournament, say. If the records are visible to the players, they might notice when someone has a suspiciously high number of disconnections and avoid playing with that person.

➤ **Abandon the game entirely.** This is the fairest solution in the case of accidental disconnections, but it is unfair to whoever is leading if the player who is behind pulls the plug.

> **Questions to Ask Yourself**
>
> There's no one right answer to this problem; it depends too much on the nature of the game. It's up to you as the designer to think about it and try to decide what's fair. Here are some questions to ask yourself:
>
> 1. What will happen to the gameplay when a player vanishes? How will it affect the other players' experience of the game (what they see and hear)? Does it disrupt the balance of the game? Will it make the challenges easier or harder? Is the game even meaningful anymore?
> 2. What happens to the score when a player vanishes—the players' relative progress toward victory? Is the game still fair?
> 3. Does your game offer a player an advantage of some kind for intentionally disconnecting himself (whether by preventing himself from losing or by sealing his own victory)? Is there any way to minimize this without penalizing players who are disconnected accidentally?

Real-Time Versus Turn-Based Games

Many online games take place in real time, with each player acting simultaneously. This offers them maximum freedom; they always have something to do and can order their activities any way they like. It's also more immersive than turn-based gaming. Waiting your turn while other players act harms suspension of disbelief. Unfortunately, real-time gaming tends to make a strategy game into an action game. Whichever player moves his pieces fastest has the advantage. In games such as *Command & Conquer*, victory becomes a matter of establishing an efficient weapons-production system as quickly as possible.

Turn-based games seem rather old-fashioned nowadays, but there is still a demand for them. Many simpler online games are automated versions of noncomputerized card games and the like, and they still require players to take turns. For this to work smoothly, you must include certain features:

> ➤ **Limit the number of players in one game.** Four or five is a good maximum. With more than this, players will have to wait too long between turns and will grow impatient.

> ➤ **Set a time limit on the length of a player's turn.** They mustn't be allowed to hold up the game while taking their turn. Both the player whose turn it is *and* all the other players should be able to see a countdown timer. The length of time

will naturally vary depending on the sort of game it is; for a card game such as Hearts, we recommend no more than 10 seconds.

➤ **Determine a reasonable default action if the player runs out of time.** In games in which it's allowed, this might simply be to pass without acting, but in a game such as checkers, in which a move is required, the game will have to choose one. It doesn't have to be a very smart move, however. It's up to the player to supply the intelligence; if he doesn't, it's his own fault.

➤ **Let players do other things while waiting their turn.** They should definitely be allowed to chat with one another, study the battlefield, organize their units, or do anything else that doesn't actually influence the gameplay.

➤ **Allow simultaneous turns.** This might sound like an oxymoron, but a few games, such as *Age of Wonders II*, allow all the players to take their turns simultaneously. The turn ends, and the results are computed and displayed when all of the players have input their moves.

Chat

Every multi-player game for machines that have a keyboard should include a chat feature—a mechanism that enables players to send messages to one another. Depending on the nature of the game, players should be able to send private messages to one other individual, messages only to members of their own team (if any), or general broadcast messages to all other players who might reasonably be interested. Obviously, if there are thousands of players in a game, any one player should be able to broadcast messages only to those in his "local vicinity," whatever that might mean in the context of the game.

Unfortunately, chat brings problems with it: rude, abusive, or harassing behavior. People who are paying to play your game have expectations that others will meet certain minimum standards of behavior. In a sporting event, this is enforced by the referee or, at minimum, by the collective authority of the other players. Online, it's much more difficult to enforce.

> *Psychological disinhibition:* People act like jerks more easily online because anonymity is intoxicating. It is easier to objectify other people and, therefore, to treat them badly. The only way to combat this is to get them to empathize more with other players.

Dirty-Word Filters

Dirty-word filters have been tried, but they never work—and they sometimes produce laughable results. Words such as *damn* and *hell* are perfectly legitimate in a religious context, even if they're considered swearing in another context. In any case, people always get around such filters by misspelling the words. Don't bother trying to implement a dirty-word filter unless you also back it up by other means, such as online customer service representatives.

Complaint and Warning Systems

Some chat systems include mechanisms designed to discourage online rudeness. A complaint system enables players to push a "complain" button whenever they receive an offensive message. The message is automatically forwarded to someone with authority over the game (usually an online customer service person), who can then investigate and take appropriate action: warn the offender to mend his ways or even kick him offline.

The America Online Instant Messenger includes a fully automated system that allows users to warn each other, either anonymously or openly, when one of them is behaving badly. A user can be warned once per message that he sends; the more warnings he receives, the less frequently he is allowed to send messages. If he receives enough, he is unable to send any for several hours. The effect of the warnings fades over time.

Ignoring Other Players

A useful feature of some chat mechanisms is the capacity to ignore other people who are being offensive. The player simply selects the name of a person he wants to ignore, and he no longer receives chat messages from that person. You can permit this to take place silently (the other player doesn't know she's being ignored) or automatically send a message telling her that she has been ignored—the online equivalent of deliberately turning your back on someone. This is one of the most efficient mechanisms available because it doesn't require staff intervention.

Moderated Chat Spaces

The most effective, but also the most expensive, way of keeping order in a chat space is to give one person authority to discipline the others at all times. This feature is used on Internet Relay Chat, in which the creator of a chat room has the authority to kick people out of it. It is, however, subject to abuse. In a game that people are paying for, you can't safely hand over that authority to one of the players; the moderator has to be an impartial representative of the game's provider—a customer service agent, in effect, whether paid or unpaid.

Collusion

Most games—true games, in which players compete for victory—are designed with an assumption that the players will try to beat one another and that there is never any reason for them to help each other. Often this assumption is formalized in the rules. For example, in *Monopoly*, one of the rules states, "No player may borrow from or lend money to another player." *Collusion* is a form of cheating in which players who are supposed to be opponents work together in violation of the rules. In *Monopoly*, what prevents collusion is the players' agreement to abide by the rules, the potential damage to their friendship if they don't, and the fact that they're all watching each other to prevent it. Unfortunately, you can't count on any of these factors in an online game. Some players will join a game with a deliberate, even avowed, intent to cheat. Because they're playing with strangers, there's nothing at stake, and because they're physically miles apart, no one can see them do it. If you cheat at a board game, you'll most likely be thrown out of the game and your friends won't ever play with you again. Unfortunately, these kinds of penalties are difficult to enforce in online games.

Examples of Collusion

Computer games seldom have written rules because the designers assume that the game will enforce the rules automatically: The players simply can't make illegal moves, for example. However, there's no way for the software to detect certain kinds of collusion between players. Consider an online multiple-choice trivia game. Each question has three possible answers. Each player receives the same question from the server and has a fixed length of time in which to enter an answer. When he enters it, he immediately learns whether he was right or wrong. Correct answers earn points, and the player with the largest number of points at the end of the game is the winner.

Four players can easily collude at this game to guarantee that one of them will win. They all play on different machines in the same physical location—an Internet café, for example. When a question appears, three of the players immediately enter a different response—A, B, or C—and the fourth one waits. When the software informs one of three players that she is correct, she immediately calls out her letter, and the fourth player enters it before the time runs out. This way the fourth player always enters the correct answer.

This form of collusion is easily defeated: You simply don't reveal the correct answer until the time has run out to enter it. Players who enter an answer early simply have to wait to find out whether they were right. But other forms of collusion can be more insidious. If you offer a prize for the player who wins the greatest number of chess games in a certain length of time, for example, two players can collude to play each other, with one always trying to lose to the other as quickly as possible.

Designing to Reduce Collusion

Part of your job as a designer of an online game is to try to anticipate collusion as much as possible. Unfortunately, experience has shown this to be an extremely difficult thing to do. There are no limits on players' ingenuity or the lengths to which some will go, and, of course, there are thousands of them to only one of you. Even if your game doesn't offer a chat feature, players can play from two machines in the same room or call each other on cellphones to collude.

You can't prevent players from colluding, but you can design the game to minimize its effects. Here are some types of collusion to consider:

➤ **Sharing secret knowledge.** Does the player ever have secret knowledge that she can share to someone else's benefit? In the trivia game described previously, some players are given the correct answer before the time runs out. Withholding this information makes collusion pointless.

➤ **Passing cards (or anything else) under the table.** Does the game include mechanisms to transfer assets from one player to another? Is there any way to abuse these mechanisms?

➤ **Taking a dive.** What are the consequences if one player deliberately plays to lose? Obviously, this makes a huge difference if you allow gambling on matches (even if only with "play" money).

If you're designing a game in which it's supposed to be every player for herself, try imagining what would happen if you made it a team game in which players were supposed to collaborate. If it's already a team game, try to imagine what would happen if one player on the team were a spy for the other team.

Technical Security

For some reason, people feel a strong impulse to test the limits of computer software—to see what it will do with nonsensical data, for example. In playing a war game, it is a rare player who will not at some point try to order his troops to fire on his own side, just to see what will happen. Similarly, players often think of ways to do things in a manner that the designers never intended or expected. Sometimes these unanticipated maneuvers, such as using the rocket launcher to propel yourself upward in *Quake*, even become standard tactics.

Making unexpected but legal moves is still fair; one can argue that the designers should have anticipated these tactics or that the testers should have discovered them for themselves. Other forms of cheating, such as hacking the game's software or data files, are clearly unfair. In a single-player game, it doesn't really matter, however. It's rather like cheating at solitaire, and it says more about the player's character than anything else. It is a peculiarity of modern computer games that they are often so difficult that they must come with built-in cheats. Originally these cheats were built in during development to make testing easier and were removed when the game shipped, but now they are often left in for the public to use as well.

The issue of cheating in multi-player games is considerably more serious. People who wouldn't dream of cheating their close friends in person—say, playing poker around the living room table—are happily willing to cheat strangers when protected by the distance and anonymity that an online game offers. There's still that temptation to try to break the software, especially because players have gotten used to the notion that computer games will enforce the rules for them. They assume that anything that they can do, they are allowed to do.

This is a grave problem. Players have a moral right to expect a fair game when they're playing against other people, and they have a legal right to it as well if they're paying for the privilege of playing. This becomes even more true if they're playing for prizes.

Although all game software comes with a disclaimer that it's sold "as-is" and without any warranty, the moment you start to give out prizes of real monetary value, you have to be very careful to make sure the game is fair.

Use a Secure Telecommunications Protocol

It takes an extremely dedicated hacker to tamper with the data stream between the client software and the server, but it takes only one. If the stakes are high enough, it can be well worth it. To foil this, your software must use a secure telecommunications protocol. Designing such a thing is a programming problem and is beyond the scope of this book, but we include a few suggestions.

➤ First, all data should be encrypted to prevent users from understanding its contents. It should also include a suitable checksum, which will enable the software to detect whether it has been garbled in transmission.

➤ Second, you might want to consider a "heartbeat" mechanism in which your client software sends a short packet to your server at regular intervals, even when there is no data to be transmitted, simply to tell the server that the client is still present.

➤ And as we described earlier, all packets should include a unique serial number to indicate what order they belong in and to prevent spurious packets from being inserted by unauthorized means.

Don't Store Sensitive Data on the Player's Computer

Typically two kinds of data about a player exist in a game. One kind is settings or preferences about the way the player appears and likes to play. The other is information that's actually relevant to the game state: the player's position, score, possessions, and so on. In *Monopoly*, for example, the player's playing piece (hat, shoe, car, and so on) belongs in the former category; it doesn't matter which token the player is using. However, the player's properties, cash, and position on the board belong in the latter; changes to them affect the player's status in the game.

This second kind of information shouldn't be stored on the player's own computer. Even with encryption techniques, you have to assume that any data kept on the player's machine is subject to tampering and could be used to give the player an unfair advantage over others. If there's really too much sensitive data about each character to store it all on the server, at least store a checksum over the data when the player logs out so that when he logs back in again, you can check over his data and see if it has been improperly modified in the meantime.

Don't Send the Player Data He Isn't Supposed to Have

A common characteristic of real-time strategy games is the "fog of war," in which unexplored areas of the map are dark and the movements of the enemy are not visible unless a friendly unit is nearby to see them. In single-player games, all this information is in the player's computer, of course; it's just not visible to the player. In an online game, any hidden information should not be sent to the player. If the player hacks the game to lift the fog of war, he can see unexplored areas and watch the movements of enemy units, which gives him a significant advantage over his opponents.

Don't Let the Client Perform Sensitive Operations

If you're designing a client/server game, there is always a balance to be struck between the amount of processing that the server does and the amount that the client does. It's clearly cheaper for you to offload as much of the processing work onto the client that you can. However, it isn't always safer. Suppose, for example, that you're designing a very simple role-playing game in which the player occasionally encounters monsters and must do battle with them. It's cheapest for the server to send the client some information about the current monster, and let the fight take place entirely on the player's computer. When the fight is over, the client sends a message back to the server saying whether the player won, lost, or ran away. However, this is obviously very dangerous. If the player has hacked his client, he could program it to report that he wins every fight. In fact, the server, not the client, should act out the fight and determine whether the player won or lost.

> **Never trust the client:** Never put *anything* on the client. The client is in the hands of the enemy. Never ever forget this.

The legitimate players aren't the enemy, of course, but the handful of cheaters are. We lock our doors at night not to protect us from the honest majority of the population, but to protect us from the dishonest minority. You will have to design your game with the same consideration in mind.

Persistent Worlds

A game, as we defined it earlier, is a contest with rules and a winner. However, a good many online "games" are not really games at all. *Asheron's Call, EverQuest, Anarchy Online*, and so on are actually persistent worlds: permanent environments that players can play in, retaining the state of their avatar from one session to another. Persistent worlds have a number of special problems and design requirements, which we discuss here.

The Origins of Persistent-World Gaming

Persistent worlds have been around for much longer than the graphical MMORPGs that are so popular right now. Since 1978, a small but dedicated community of developers has been building, playing, and studying text-based persistent worlds called *MUDs* (multi-user dungeons or domains, depending on who you talk to) that could be played by groups of people over the Internet. In these worlds, everything was accomplished by typing commands, and a rich culture of online role playing evolved. MUDs have since fragmented into subcategories: MUSHes (multi-user shared hallucinations, dedicated primarily to personal interaction rather than combat), and MOOs (MUDs, object-oriented, in which people can use a scripting language to design their own objects for use in the environment), and others even more esoteric.

We won't go into MUD design in any detail here; they're not a commercial market, and a vast amount of literature on them already is available on the Internet. However, many of the design problems of today's MMORPGs, particularly those relating to social interactions among players, were already solved—or at least studied—long ago in the MUD community.

How Persistent Worlds Differ from Games

Computer games appeal to players in a variety of ways. Part of the appeal is the environment in which the player finds herself: a fantasy world where magic really works, for example, or behind enemy lines in World War II. Another part is the role the gamers will play in the game: detective or pilot or knight-errant. Yet another is the gameplay itself, the nature of the challenges the player faces and the actions she may take to overcome them. And, of course, there is the goal of the game, its victory condition: to halt the enemy invasion, for example. The victory is usually the conclusion of a story that is told partly through narrative supplied by you, the designer, and partly through the player's own actions.

Story

Because persistent worlds have so many players, and because they are intended to continue indefinitely, the traditional narrative arc of a single-player game doesn't apply. You can't take the player by the hand and lead her through an experience of your designing. A persistent world is not a story, but a playground. It's up to you to build the environment and to give the players things that they may do, but how they spend their time is for them to decide.

You can still incorporate two elements from storytelling in a persistent world. One is the setting itself and the overall conditions of life in the world. It can be a dangerous place or a safe one, a rich place or a poor one, a tyrannical place or a democratic one. You can slowly change these conditions or introduce threats from the outside that challenge players to respond to them.

> ***Elmqvist's Law:*** In an online game, players find it rewarding to save the world. They find it more rewarding to save the world together, with lots of other people.

The other element is a quest or errand that the player undertakes as an individual or collectively with others. These can be small-scale (eliminate the pack of wild dogs that has been marauding through the sheep flocks) or large-scale (everyone in the town gets together to rebuild the defenses in anticipation of an invasion). Most persistent worlds have large numbers of these quests available for players.

> ***Storytelling versus simulation:*** If you write a static story (or, indeed, include *any* static element) in your game, everyone in the world will know how it ends in a matter of days. Mathematically, it is not possible for a design team to create stories fast enough to supply everyone playing. This is the traditional approach to this sort of game nonetheless. You can try a sim-style game that doesn't supply stories but that instead supplies freedom to make them. This is a *lot* harder and, arguably, has never been done successfully.

The best emergent stories occur in purely role-playing environments with almost no game-like elements, such as in MUSHes. These aren't profit-making enterprises, however, and they work because they have a small population of unusually dedicated players. As a designer, there's no way to force this to happen; it depends too much on the imagination and talent of the participants.

The Player's Role

In a single-player, plot-driven game, the player's role is defined by the actions he is allowed to take and is constrained by the requirements of the story. In a persistent world, the player doesn't have a single storyline to follow, so he needs a larger variety of things to do. Most persistent worlds are science fiction or fantasy role-playing environments, and they tend to define the choices available. Some of the early ones were designed like traditional single-player RPGs, in which the only role to play is that of mercenary adventurer, but thankfully that has changed somewhat in recent years.

As the designer, it is up to you to supply an assortment of possible roles the player may play and to make them meaningful in your world. You should also give the player the freedom to change her role (though not always easily or immediately) as she sees fit. Because the world continues indefinitely without coming to a narrative conclusion, you can't expect the player to want to play the same way forever. Just as people change careers and hobbies over time, players need to be able to change roles.

Gameplay

Finally, there's the question of the gameplay. Without a victory condition, you have to decide what challenges the player does face and what kinds of things she can achieve. Most persistent worlds are designed like role-playing games, and the player's objective is to advance her character. This is (usually) accomplished by fighting AI-controlled "monsters." However, there are many other things she might attain as well: wealth, political power, fame (or notoriety), and so on.

> ***If your game is narrow, it will fail:*** Your game design must be expansive. Even the coolest game mechanic becomes tiresome after a time. You have to supply alternate ways of playing or alternate ways of experiencing the world. Otherwise, the players will go to another world where they can have new experiences. This means new additions or, better yet, completely different subgames embedded in the actual game.

In a single-player game, the player is, to some extent, trying to read the designer's mind, to figure out what you want him to do and then do it. His play is often reactive, a response to challenges thrown at him. In a persistent world, the player is deciding for himself what he wants to do. He seeks out challenges if he feels like it, but he can spend all his time socializing if he prefers. His gameplay—and, indeed, the entire nature of the experience—is *expressive* and active rather than reactive. Role playing, especially when it's taken seriously by the players, has qualities in common with live theater and improvisation. This characteristic of persistent-world play has profound effects on their design, as you will see later in this section.

> **Schubert's Law of Player Expectations:** A new player's expectations of a virtual world are driven by his expectations of single-player games. In particular, he expects a narrow, predictable plot line with well-defined quests, carefully sculpted for himself as the hero. He also expects no interference or disruption from other players. These are difficult and sometimes impossible expectations for a virtual world to actually meet.

The Four Types of Players

In 1996, a MUD developer named Richard Bartle wrote a seminal article called "Hearts, Clubs, Diamonds, Spades: Players Who Suit MUDs" for the first issue of the *Journal of MUD Research*. He proposed that MUD players fall into four categories depending on whether they enjoy either *acting on* (manipulating, exploiting, or controlling) or *interacting with* (learning about and communicating with) either the world or the other players (see Figure 17.1). Those who enjoy acting on other players he dubbed Killers, or clubs; those who enjoy interacting with other players he called Socializers, or hearts. Those who enjoy acting on the world he described as Achievers, or diamonds; those who enjoy interacting with the world he referred to as Explorers, or spades.

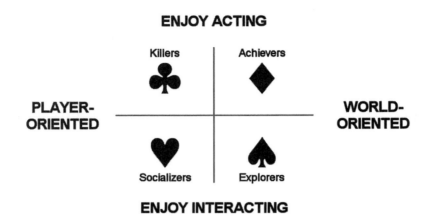

Figure 17.1   Bartle's four types of players.

Bartle went on to claim that a healthy MUD community required a certain proportion of each of these types of players and that adjusting the game design to attract or discourage any given type of player would tend to influence the numbers of others as well. In effect, a persistent world is a sort of ecology in which the players' styles of play influence their population. Bartle's data was drawn from personal observation rather than rigorous statistical analysis, so his conclusions are certainly arguable. However, his grouping of player types has been found to be useful not only in the design of MUDs, but in graphical persistent worlds as well.

Creating an Avatar

As we said earlier, playing in persistent worlds is more than merely a form of game-play; it's also a form of expression. The first thing a player does in joining a persistent world is to create an avatar, or character who represents her in the game, so this is one of the most expressive things she can do. The avatar is a mask she's going to wear throughout the game.

The avatar is defined by both tangible and intangible attributes (Koster's terminology). The tangible attributes are those that the game software recognizes and makes use of in gameplay—physical attributes such as strength and speed, and mental attributes such as training and experience. The intangibles include some that are part of the software, cosmetic things such as clothing color, and others that are really defined by the way the player plays: vocabulary, prejudices, and attitudes.

If you're making an online role-playing game that includes traditional avatar attributes such as speed, strength, and so on, consult Chapter 11, "Role-Playing Games," for more information.

The Avatar's Profile

In addition to their tangible attributes associated with gameplay, players like to have a profile that identifies and describes them to other players. This profile can include such things as these:

➤ **Unique name or handle.** Unless your game allows totally anonymous play, people will need some way of identifying their avatars by name. That way, a player's name can appear in documents, on leader boards, in chatrooms and bulletin boards, and so on.

➤ **Physical appearance.** People clearly have to be able to tell one character from another on the screen. The physical appearance of avatars should be as customizable as you can afford to make it. Even if it has no impact on gameplay, players identify with and respond to physical appearances.

➤ **History or experience.** This is simply a record of the player's achievements for others to see. It could be experience levels, quests undertaken, kills in battle, or any other accomplishments the player might be proud of. You'll have to decide whether players might want to keep some of these things private and, if so, whether they should be allowed to.

➤ **Reputation.** Players can get positive or negative (or even multi-dimensional) reputations based on their behavior in the game. Some games use the reputation mechanism as a way of tagging players who frequently take advantage of others somehow. The reputation attribute warns other players "This person is dangerous" or "This person is trustworthy." Beware, however: This system is subject to abuse through collusion if you don't place limits on it.

➤ **Player autobiography.** It's fun for a players to make up a history for his character, a background that will introduce him to others in the world. It's another form of self-expression. If children have access to your world, you will need to have a real person approve them for suitability.

You might or might not want to include important gameplay attributes in the player's public profile; it depends on how this affects the gameplay. If a player wants to hide his attributes from the world, is that a legitimate part of gameplay or is it an unfair advantage? (*Monopoly* players are not allowed to hide their property cards under the table—everyone is allowed to see what they own.)

> *Modes of expression:* You're trying to provide as many modes of expression as possible in your online world. Character classes (a mechanism classifying characters according to their attitude toward the world) are just modes of expression, after all.

World Models

Unless your world is really only a chatroom, it's going to give players something to do. The things that you give them to do, and the rewards they earn for doing it, constitute the *world model*. We don't mean this in the genre sense of "killing monsters" versus "battling enemy spacecraft," but rather in the sense of how the world wants the player to live and grow in it.

Raph Koster has identified five classic world models, although there are undoubtedly more. Some include elements from more than one of these:

➤ **Scavenger model.** Players collect things and return them to places of safety. The game is primarily a large treasure hunt, and they don't risk losing anything they've collected. Such games usually need to be reset to their initial state from time to time because players are hoarding too much stuff.

➤ **Social model.** The world is primarily an expressive space. The fun comes from role playing in character; most forms of achievements are social achievement (political power, adulation, notoriety, and so on). Players rely primarily on intangible attributes—their degree of leadership, charisma, or duplicity, for example. The normal tangible attributes, such as strength, are used as a basis for role playing rather than computer-managed combat.

➤ *Dungeons & Dragons* **model.** This is the best-known model. The player is primarily in conflict with the environment, fighting NPCs for advancement and doing some scavenging along the way. It relies heavily on the tangible attributes of the avatar for its gameplay and includes an element of positive feedback: defeating enemies advances the character, which requires the game to offer tougher enemies next time. Such worlds tend to include quests as a form of narrative and a way of offering challenges to the players.

> ➤ **Player-versus-Player model.** In this sort of world, players advance by defeating one another at contests of some kind, often characterized as combat. Players advance through a combination of their natural skill and rewards from winning battles. For this to work successfully, they need to be reasonably evenly matched; you can't have the old-timers beating up the newcomers all the time.

> ➤ **Builder model.** This somewhat rare sort of world enables players to construct things and actually modify the world in which they play. It's a highly expressive form of entertainment. People get kudos not for their fighting skills, but for their aesthetic and architectural ones, both intangible qualities.

Avatar Death

In any persistent world that includes combat, you have to decide if it's possible for the player's avatar to die and what will happen if he does. Most role-playing games treat character death in certain standard ways; these are addressed in Chapter 11. As with other games, avatar death must be accompanied by a disincentive of some kind, or players won't care if they die. The trick is to find a disincentive that is appropriately proportional to the likelihood of their dying—to put it in simpler terms, it's a balance problem. If the avatar can easily be killed through no fault of the player (such as through ignorance or bad luck), then the cost of dying—the disincentive—should be low. If the player really has to be stupid to get his avatar killed, the cost can be high.

Permanent Death

Here's the most extreme case: The avatar is destroyed and loses all property that he owns (in which case the system has to decide what happens to it). The player is forced to start over from scratch with a new avatar. This makes sense in games of short duration, but not in persistent worlds. Players put too much time and effort into building up their avatars to do this to them.

Resurrection with Reduced Attributes

Bringing the avatar back to life with reduced tangible attributes—strength or skills, for example—is a common way of penalizing death. In effect, it sets the player back a bit in her quest to grow a powerful avatar. Players find it irritating, of course, and it discourages risky play, but it makes a certain amount of sense. If you've just been beaten to death by a gang of club-wielding trolls, you ought to feel pretty lousy for a while when you come back to life!

Resurrection with Some Property Missing

Here's another classic disincentive for dying: When a player dies, he loses his money, gear, clothes, and other items that he has on him at the time. How much of it he loses and what becomes of it can vary considerably from game to game. You can also allow players to have a vault in the game where they can safely keep items that they're not carrying around with them, and these items can be there when their avatar is resurrected. You might as well include this feature because if you don't, the players will create a second character that they never play with, known in MMORPG parlance as a "mule," to hold their primary avatar's things for them.

The Player-Killer Problem

No aspect of the design of persistent worlds has been debated more than this one simple question: Should players' avatars be allowed to kill one another? We won't offer a definitive answer here, but instead we'll try to summarize some of the issues so that you can make an informed decision for your own game.

Most persistent worlds are designed as role-playing games in which players advance in skill and power through combat. It's generally more interesting if this combat occurs against another player rather than against an NPC, as Koster observes:

> *It is always more rewarding to kill other players than to kill whatever the game sets up as a target.* A given player of level x can slay n creatures of level y. Therefore, killing a player of level x yields $n \times y$ reward in purely in-game reward terms. Killing players will therefore always be more rewarding in game terms than monsters of comparable difficulty. However, there's also the fact that players will be more challenging and exciting to fight than monsters no matter what you do.

The *Ultima Online* Experience

Ultima Online was initially designed in such a way that players could kill one another without restraint (except in towns), and the designers hoped that they would establish their own justice mechanisms within the game. Unfortunately, the world quickly began to resemble Afghanistan after the Soviets left: unremitting random violence, feuds, continual victimization of the weak by the strong, and petty warlords or gangs of bandits controlling areas of turf. No satisfactory solution arose from the players, partly because the software did not offer any genuinely painful punishment mechanisms for them to take advantage of. (In real life, we either lock murderers away for a very long time or kill them permanently, neither of which any for-pay persistent world can afford to do.) A variety of different automated mechanisms for encouraging justice were tried, but most were subject to some kind of exploitation. In the end, the developers threw up their hands and divided the world into "shards" with different rules for each. Some allowed player-versus-player (PvP) combat, and others did not. Approximately 80% of the players chose to play in non-PvP shards.

Justice Mechanisms

Koster offers the following summary of approaches to regulating PvP combat:

> ➤ **No automated regulation.** Anyone can attack anyone, and only administrators or social mechanisms (vigilante justice) are available for dealing with rogue players. Koster estimates that as many as 40% of the potential audience will avoid this type of game because they don't like PvP.

> ➤ **Flagging of criminals.** The server automatically detects criminal behavior and flags the criminals, who become fair game for others to attack. The system can also reduce the attributes of criminals, in effect penalizing them for their behavior. This can be used for thievery and other crimes as well as murder.

> ➤ **Reputation systems.** This is similar to flagging, except that players decide when to "report" someone for criminal behavior and can choose not to do so. In practice, they almost always do, however.

> ➤ **"PK switch."** Players can indicate whether they are willing to fight other players; those who are not are invulnerable to attack as well. This can also be used to give temporary consent for duels and arena-based combat. Unfortunately, this

mechanism creates suspension-of-disbelief problems when wide-area spells are being used: Three PK players get roasted by a fireball, while an adjacent non-PK player is untouched because the fireball was cast by another PK player.

> ➤ **Safe games; no PvP allowed.** This is the least troublesome solution, but even it is not without its hazards. Players will still find ways of abusing one another—for example, by luring an unsuspecting newcomer into an area where he will be attacked by a monster. Koster estimates that this approach will cost you up to 20% of your potential audience, those who like PvP.

You can also divide the world into safe and dangerous geographic zones, but in practice, people tend to either stay in the safe zones or play near the edges, hoping to lure a potential victim over the line without his realizing it.

Faction-Based PvP

A solution that has become more common in recent years is to allow players to belong to factions. These can be as small as gangs or as large as entire nations at war. The rules enable players to attack members of enemy factions but not members of their own faction—in effect, it's team play. Different regions are under the control of different factions, so players generally know which areas are safe and which are not. For the most part, this arrangement solves the random violence problem that plagued *Ultima Online* at first.

Star Wars Galaxies further extends the faction concept to allow players to be overt or covert members of a faction. Overtly declared members are at constant risk of being attacked by members of a hostile faction, so they receive certain advantages to compensate. Covert members don't run the risk but are not allowed to do certain things. Players can also be neutral.

The Bottom Line on Player Killing

You cannot please everybody, so you are really better off deciding *who* you want to please and tailoring your environment to them. A good many player-killers are cowards, undesirable players who enjoy exploiting their superior strength to victimize weaker ones without ever putting themselves at risk. You can't please them without also providing them with victims who *won't* be pleased, so it's not worth trying. Ultimately, you need to bear two things in mind:

1. **It's a fantasy-world.** That means it's supposed to be enjoyable, escapist entertainment. People don't fantasize about being harassed, bullied, or abused. A fair contest among consenting players is one thing; perpetual harassment or an ambush by a gang is quite another.

2. **People are paying to play.** This makes your world distinctly different from the real world. The real world doesn't owe us anything; we have to survive as best we can. But as a game provider, you've taken the players' money, so you have obligations to them. Just exactly what those obligations are is open to debate, of course, but if players don't feel that you are meeting them, they will leave.

    Players have higher expectations of the virtual world than of the real world. For example, players will expect all labor to result in profit; they will expect life to be fair; they will expect to be protected from aggression before the fact, not just having to seek redress after the fact; they will expect problems to be resolved quickly; and they will expect that their integrity will be assumed to be beyond reproach. In other words, they will expect too much, and you will not be able to supply it all. The trick is to manage the expectations.

The Nature of Time

In a single-player computer game, you have a great deal of control over the relationship between "game time" and "real time." Most games run at many times the speed of real time, and a simulated "day" in a computer game often takes an hour or less of real time to experience. You can also hand over control of the speed of time to the player when you want to; it's not uncommon for players in combat flight simulators to speed up time when flying to and from the combat zones, and then slow it down to real time when they get there. Finally, you can skip time entirely during periods when the player's avatar is supposed to be asleep, for example. You can blank the screen for a moment and then put up a text message that says "8 hours later…" and continue with the game.

None of these options is available in multi-player games. You obviously can't have some players moving through time at different speeds than others, and you can't skip time unless you somehow force all players to skip it together. Although game time might be faster than real time, it must proceed at the same fixed pace for everyone.

As a result, you must be careful about designing time-consuming activities. *EverQuest*, for example, has a mechanism called "meditation" in which players simply have to wait around for a while to restore their magic powers. There's no way to speed up this process—it literally does involve waiting. Nor can they log out of the game while meditating and log back in again later to find that it's done. They can't even switch to a different process on their computer! Verant, the developers, eventually built in a mini-game for players to play while they were waiting, but this is clearly a patch, not a real solution. If your game contains features that are so boring that you have to distract the players, you need to rethink the features.

Time Is Irreversible

One of the key design considerations of single-player games is that they can be stopped and restarted at the player's discretion. If the player can save the game, he can essentially "reverse time" by going back to a previous point in the game and replaying it from there. This robs single-player games of the emotional impact of events: Anything that happens, good or bad, can be reversed by reloading a saved version of the game. You can design the game so that some events are inevitable, but, of course, the more of them there are, the less interactive the game is.

In an online game, time is irreversible. Even if there were a convenient way to do it, you can't reasonably ask all your players to agree to reverse time to an earlier point (although the managers of some persistent worlds have had to "roll back" to a saved state when the game got into problems). In the ordinary course of events, when a thing happens in an online game, it's done and can't be undone. It might be repaired, but it cannot be made as if it had never happened.

Persistent World Economies

If the players in a persistent world can collect and trade things of value, then the world has an economy. We discussed economies in some detail in Chapter 14, "Construction and Management Simulations." Economies are *much* easier to design and tune in a single-player game than they are in a persistent world. You can control the actions of a single person fairly strictly; in a persistent world, you have thousands of people interacting in ways that you might not have anticipated.

Ultima Online was originally designed to have a completely self-contained, closed economy with a fixed number of resources that flowed around and around. For example, you could mine iron ore, smelt it into iron, and forge the iron into weapons. Using the weapons would cause them to deteriorate, and when they wore out, they would return to the pool of raw iron ore available for mining. This last step wasn't strictly realistic, but it did close the loop.

What the designers didn't count on was that players would hoard objects without using them. Because they didn't go back into the pool, the iron ore was quickly mined out, and as resources dwindled, inflation ran rampant. The players had literally cornered the market and could charge extortionate fees for anything. Eventually, *Ultima Online* was forced to adopt an open economy in which new resources are dumped in at intervals by the servers.

It's particularly essential in any economy that players not find a way to create something for nothing; that is, to return a resource back to the system for more than they paid for it in the first place. Otherwise, they'll find a way to automate this process and generate an unlimited stream of gold. Koster observes:

> ***Online game economies are hard:*** A faucet/drain economy is one where you spawn new stuff, let it pool in the "sink" that is the game, and then have a concomitant drain. Players will *hate* having this drain, but if you do not enforce ongoing expenditures, you will have Monty Haul syndrome, infinite accumulation of wealth, an overall rise in the "standard of living" and capabilities of the average player, and thus produce imbalance in the game design and poor game longevity.

Final Thoughts on Persistent Worlds

Here are a few more of Raph Koster's observations on persistent worlds, to wind up this section:

> The secrets to a really long-lived, goal-oriented, persistent world of wide appeal:

> ➤ Have multiple paths of advancement (individual features are nice, but making them ladders is better).

> ➤ Make it easy to switch between paths of advancement (ideally, without having to start over).

➤ Make sure the milestones in the path of advancement are clear and visible and significant (having 600 meaningless milestones doesn't help).

➤ Ideally, make your game not have a sense of running out of significant milestones (try to make your ladder not feel finite).

Ownership is key: You have to give players a sense of ownership in the game. This is what will make them stay—it is a "barrier to departure." Social bonds are *not* enough because good social bonds extend outside the game. Instead, it is context. If they can build their own buildings, build a character, own possessions, hold down a job, feel a sense of responsibility to something that *cannot* be removed from the game—then you have ownership.

J.C. Lawrence on utopias: Don't strive for perfection, strive for expressive fertility. You can't create utopia, and if you did nobody would want to live there.

Putting It Together

Multi-player games are harder to design than single-player ones; online games are harder still, and persistent worlds are the hardest of all. It's a bit like the difference between cooking for yourself and planning a dinner party. When you're cooking for yourself, you decide what you want, make it, and eat it. When you're planning a dinner party, you have to take into account more variables: who likes what food, who gets along with whom, and what people are going to do besides just eat. A dinner party requires more work ahead of time—but it's a lot more fun than eating by yourself, too. The flexibility and power of online gaming enables you to create entertainment experiences that you simply can't produce in other forms.

Chapter 18

The Future of Gaming

For our last chapter, we're going to indulge in a little blue-sky speculation about what the future of gaming might hold. It's clear that the commercial game industry has only begun to scratch the surface of what interactive entertainment can do. We are still a long way from exploiting the full potential of this medium.

Gaming Hardware

Many aspects of game design are independent of the hardware running the game: subject matter, theme, and art style, for example. Nevertheless, the future of interactive entertainment is closely tied to the future of computing hardware. At the moment, the principal emphasis in hardware design is on making games look and sound better, and, indeed, the amount of audiovisual improvement in the last 20 years has been astonishing. But game hardware does much more than that: It determines how complex and how smart the games can be. And that, in turn, affects the kinds of games that we can make. We have just started to build games that simulate the behavior of humans, for example, at a level above the trivial. For more powerful simulations, we need more powerful machines.

Specialized game hardware might include dedicated neural network processors and voice-recognition or speech-synthesis chips. We might see special chips dedicated to solving path-finding problems or to simulating thousands of cellular automations such as ants in an anthill or soldiers on a battlefield. In the farther future, there could be chips that know the grammatical rules of a language and can generate real dialogue on the fly rather than prerecorded responses. Whether such gear gets out of the laboratory and into consumer products is another story; it depends more on what it costs to build than on how useful it is to games. But hardware R&D for games is already taking place, and it will increase now that game development is starting to be recognized as a legitimate subject of academic study.

In the next few sections, we talk about some of the game hardware that's commonplace today and where we see it going.

Location-Based Entertainment

Location-based entertainment is a fancy term for any kind of computer gaming in which you play somewhere besides your own home. Typical kinds of location-based entertainment are video arcades, group ride simulators, and individual networked simulators.

Video Arcades

Video games were first introduced to the public as arcade machines because their computing hardware was too expensive for ordinary people to afford. These were extremely popular, and video arcades proliferated throughout the 1980s and early 1990s. However, as microprocessors and memory became cheaper, the home video game console appeared and offered serious competition to the arcades. Parents liked home consoles, too; kids could play at home rather than down at the mall, and although there was a higher up-front cost to buy the machine and games, you could play them endlessly for free. The arcade game format is also very limiting for the game designer because the games have to be designed to make money every minute or two.

The heyday of big video arcades is over, except in entertainment locations such as movie theaters and theme parks, and in places where kids are likely to be stuck for a while with nothing to do, such as airports or hotels. This doesn't mean that arcade machines are dead—only that they will never again occupy the niche that they did when video games were new. They now have to compete with home console machines. Many arcade machines create their appeal by offering something that you can't get at home, such as expensive hardware—a driving simulator with a force-feedback steering wheel, pedals, and a gearshift, for instance. Such games will certainly continue to exist, but the high cost of manufacturing them means that they will have to charge a lot to make back their initial cost.

Group Ride Simulators

A *group ride simulator* is a room designed to give a small audience—typically 20 or 30 people—the impression of riding in a vehicle. The floor is actually a large platform, typically fitted with theater seats mounted on pistons. The audience faces a large movie screen on which a story is shown, and the pistons cause the floor to move up and down to increase the feeling of movement. Surround-sound speakers complete the effect.

Ride simulators are extremely expensive, costing several million dollars to build. Most are not interactive at all, but they just consist of a short movie with an accompanying script that controls the movement of the floor. However, it wouldn't be difficult to make these simulators interactive by giving the viewers something to do that affects what they see on the screen. At the moment, the movies are mostly made on film to present a high-quality cinematic experience, but they could easily be replaced by a computerized 3D environment. The audience can be given weapons or other controls whose effects are seen on the screen. These could also have an effect on the platform. If some of the players handle a large gun, for example, the pistons could simulate the gun's recoil. We can certainly expect to see continuing advances in the realism of the experience.

Ride simulators won't ever become a large-scale phenomenon like video arcades were; they're just too expensive. Because they have to admit people in groups for short periods, they require a large audience who can afford the time and who are willing to wait in line for a while. This makes them perfect for theme parks and resorts. The future of such simulators is dependent on the economy in the same way that tourism and all forms of expensive leisure entertainment are.

Individual Networked Simulators

Individual networked simulators are groups of small enclosed cubicles, sometimes called "pods" or "cockpits," each designed for one person or perhaps two. The pods are networked together to play a single game so that people can compete against each other alone or in teams. These simulators are not usually owned by individuals. They are installed in shopping malls and similar places, and players pay to play for a certain amount of time. They offer high-quality, multi-player gaming, usually of vehicle-based action games such as flight simulators or mechs. Because the player is usually completely enclosed, these games also offer a highly immersive experience. The BattleTech Centers (`www.virtualworld.com`) are a good example.

The arrival of the Internet—and especially broadband connections—has reduced some of the demand for these centers. Although the quality of the experience playing on a PC is not as immersive, it's also much cheaper, and you don't have leave home to do it. We expect that networked simulators will remain a small niche market with demand proportionate to their price. They will, of course, continue to benefit from improvements in computing hardware, but as with ride simulators and the fancier arcade games, the majority of their production cost is in the mechanical rather than the electronic gear, and that's not going to change as rapidly.

Home Video Game Consoles

Game consoles have won the hearts of consumers, and they're here to stay. Designing a game console is tricky business because the manufacturer has to balance the console's cost against its computing power, to compete against other consoles on both price and performance. Unlike PCs, consoles can't be customized over a whole range of performance characteristics. Instead, all consoles of a given model are identical (or nearly so) so that any game made for that model is guaranteed to run correctly. This means that the manufacturer gets only one chance to design it properly. We see a number of trends in console machine design that will affect gaming in the future.

Consoles Get More PC-Like

There's no doubt that home game consoles will continue to take advantage of the growth in computing power: faster CPUs, more memory, better audio and video technology. These will have the greatest impact on the look and feel of the games we play. More important, however, home game consoles are starting to take on some of the characteristics of their more powerful cousin, the PC: disk drives and networking capability. It won't be long before this also includes such things as video cameras and voice-recognition facilities, with all the implications for multi-player gaming that those represent. These features will enable console players to have game experiences currently available only on PCs: to download and store game upgrades or new scenarios on a disk drive, for example, and to play against other people around the world. As consoles get more PC-like hardware, we can expect to see an ongoing convergence between console and PC games.

The Relationship of Consoles to Other Media Players

Game consoles are now capable of playing audio CDs and video DVDs, which means that there's little need to own a separate media player for each of those devices if you already own a console. We don't expect that game consoles will entirely supplant standalone versions of those devices because some people will want media players without the gaming capability. Nevertheless, we believe that consoles will be an increasingly important part of the family's "entertainment center," the cluster of equipment located underneath the TV. One game console with a built-in DVD drive and hard disk drive could replace four separate dedicated machines: the CD player, the DVD player, the VCR, and a digital video recorder such as the TiVO service. Consoles have the potential to become complete computerized "entertainment managers," if their manufacturers want to take them in that direction.

Add-On Devices

We believe that the market for add-on devices such as dance mats and other specialized controllers will continue to grow. As game playing occupies an increasingly larger slice of people's leisure-time entertainment, they will invest in gear accordingly. Although only a minority of gamers will buy them, these devices' profit margins are much higher than those of the base machines, making them a lucrative source of revenue for the hardware manufacturers. And such gadgets do make the experience of playing games designed to take advantage of their particular features much more enjoyable.

HDTV

The Achilles' heel of all home console machines is their output device, the conventional television. The television's low-resolution, 25- to 30-frames-per-second refresh rate and 4:3 aspect ratio are just adequate for displaying movies and TV shows, but they don't allow either the detail or the speed available on personal computer monitors.

We think that the growing popularity of high-definition television (HDTV) will significantly improve home console gaming. A wide screen offers a more natural viewing experience, allowing events to take place in the player's peripheral vision. The higher resolution will allow for more detailed images and more complex user interfaces. A number of Xbox games already support HDTV resolutions, and as HDTV becomes the standard, all new generations of consoles will certainly do so.

Personal Computers

The personal computer is a little more than a quarter of a century old now, and it looks set to be here for a while. Although the appearance and capabilities of the PC (by which we mean all personal computers, not just the IBM PC and its clones) might change, even a hundred years from now people will still want a computing device on which they can read and write, do research, and process information. There's no reason that that device shouldn't also provide them with interactive entertainment.

Of course, personal computers are going to become more powerful. They will get better sound systems and larger, higher-resolution monitors. Development of graphics hardware will continue to drive—and be driven by—computer games, and this will enable richer, more detailed scenes. As with home consoles, sheer computing power will make the biggest difference in the way games look and feel on the PC.

Add-On Devices

Over the last few years, we've seen a variety of specialist hardware for serious gamers: force-feedback joysticks and steering wheels, automotive and airplane pedals, and so on. Those will continue to sell—there's no particular reason for them to die out—but they won't ever routinely be bundled with PCs because the demand for them is too small to justify the expense. Virtual reality gear fits into this category as well. It's expensive and unnecessary for most personal computing tasks, so it is unlikely to ever be routinely bundled with personal computers.

Even with advances in handwriting recognition, the pen will not replace the keyboard as the primary interface for the personal computer. The typewriter superseded the pen as a means of creating text because it was faster and less tiring to use, and that won't change. The combination of keyboard and mouse is perfect for most applications except actual drawing. Professional artists use digital pens (graphics tablets) with personal computers, but few other people do, and pens certainly have little use in gaming. There has been a certain amount of debate about gesture-recognition devices, but they, too, have the disadvantage that they're tiring. Nobody wants to have to wave his hands around for hours at a time. This is exactly why the mouse was invented in the first place: Early researchers recognized that the touch screen, or any system that requires you to lift your hands from the desk, was impractical for prolonged use.

Voice recognition, on the other hand, has tremendous potential in gaming—more even than in business applications. Although dictation is faster than using a keyboard, talking eventually becomes tiring and makes for a noisy, distracting office environment. But games are noisy anyway, and suspension of disbelief will be greatly enhanced by being able to shout "Group one, charge!" rather than pressing the 1 key and clicking a menu item labeled "Charge." And, of course, microphones are already very much in use for communication between players in multi-player gaming; this will only increase with the growth of broadband Internet connections.

Why Consoles Won't Kill Off the PC

Every time a new generation of consoles comes out, a number of pundits pop up on the Internet and in the gaming magazines to proclaim that the PC is dead as a gaming platform. They're thinking about the fact that the game console now closely approaches, or even surpasses, the computing performance of the PC at a much lower price. And as we said in the previous section on consoles, we can expect to see a growing convergence between console games and PC games as console hardware begins to include such features as disk drives and Internet access.

Nevertheless, the PC is here to stay as a gaming device because its appeal is not based on its performance characteristics alone. The most important difference between the PC and the console is not its hardware, but simply where you sit when you use it. The PC is designed to be used at close range by a single person because that's how we need to use it when we're working on documents or surfing the Internet. Certain games—construction and management simulations, for example—are best played that way as well. The game console, on the other hand, is designed to be used by one or more people, sitting farther away so they all can see. This is great for multi-player experiences such as sports or fighting games, okay for flight simulators and action games, and terrible for any game with a complex, multi-level user interface. That's the area in which PCs excel.

Controversial Subject Matter

Another reason why consoles won't kill off the PC as a game platform is that the PC is the only platform on which you can explore controversial subjects. To publish a console game, you have to obtain the approval of a publicity-conscious hardware manufacturer. Recently, Canadian artist Robin C. Pacific

continues

continued

produced *Babes in the Woods*, a game whose object, among other things, was to find pubic hair for a Barbie doll and whose culminating reward was to enter The Great Yoni. You probably won't see this particular title on the Nintendo GameCube anytime soon. The best thing about the PC is that anyone who has one can create a PC game. Neither a profit-gobbling license nor a hugely overpriced development kit is needed, which is why the PC is where the most cutting-edge work is always done.

Continuous Technological Advancement
Finally, the technical quality of PC games will always eventually surpass that of the games on any given console machine. This is because a console machine is an inexpensive device that remains technically static from its launch until it is finally superseded by a new model. The PC, on the other hand, is an expensive device that continues to improve year on year. (There have been a few efforts to construct console "upgrades," such as the Sega 32X and CD drive add-ons for the Genesis, but none was really successful—people don't seem to want to upgrade their game consoles.) If you have a game design that demands the very latest technology, the PC is the only place you can put it.

Handheld Game Machines, PDAs, and Telephones

From the simplest toys that play only one game on a black-and-white LCD screen, to the latest color cartridge-based machine, handhelds are a hugely popular gaming medium, especially for children. Rugged, portable, and relatively cheap, they offer increasingly sophisticated games that until recently could only be played on much more expensive machines.

There's a lot of talk about the convergence among handheld devices, and although it's bound to happen, that doesn't mean that all handheld devices will merge into a single, universal portable computer. There will always be mobile telephones without any real game-playing facilities for people who only want a telephone, and there will always be low-end handhelds with no wireless capability. Nobody wants their four-year-old racking up long-distance charges by accident.

The practical limitations of handheld devices are not in their computing power, which will continue to grow, but simply in their physical dimensions. A handheld can't get bigger than a certain size without becoming a nuisance to carry around. Although you can get a very enjoyable gaming experience from a handheld device, it will never be as immersive as sitting in front of a high-resolution monitor with big speakers and a subwoofer jarring your bones.

We expect to see a slow but steady growth in gaming for handheld devices. Telephones and phone-equipped PDAs offer the most potential because players can compete against each other. Single-player PDA games and dedicated handhelds of various sorts will necessarily remain fairly lightweight. Without a CD-ROM or DVD drive, handhelds can't produce the "big" gaming experiences of a *Baldur's Gate*. But handhelds offer excellent growth potential for games for the casual gamer—someone who wants to play for 10 or 20 minutes as a break from the daily routine.

Virtual Reality

Virtual reality is a term for a technology that tries to make the player forget where he really is and to feel as if he's in the game instead. In practical terms, this means loading him down with a helmet that includes earphones and a pair of miniature liquid-crystal displays for stereo vision, as well as a position sensor that can determine what direction he's looking. VR was considered something of a holy grail for gaming a few years ago, but it has almost dropped out of sight again. The gear is expensive, and unless it's carefully calibrated to the individual user, it tends to give people motion sickness.

Still, there's a lot of potential for the technology. If you've ever seen a really good 3D movie—one projected with polarized light, not the old red-and-green glasses—then you know how powerful the effect of stereo vision is. On a big screen, occupying all your peripheral vision, it really does make you feel as if you're in the scene. To do this on a computer means computing two different images, one for each eye—and, of course, that requires twice as much graphics processing power. To reduce what's called "visual stress"—making the eye work harder than it normally does—VR gear must operate with high resolution at a high frame rate and with sharp focus.

We think there's a future for virtual reality in games, but it's several years off yet. The quality of the helmets needs to get much, much better, and the cost needs to get much, much lower. In any case, VR is unlikely to become the standard way of playing. Many people like to play console games in groups, and they enjoy interacting with their friends as they play. Shutting out the rest of the room with a VR helmet will significantly degrade that experience. VR will probably be at its best in single-player or multi-player networked games.

The Future of Game Programming

The way we program computers, even after 50 years of doing it, is still slow, exacting, and error-prone. Almost all the efforts to devise better kinds of programming languages and better ways of programming have been ignored by the industry in general and game programmers in particular, who usually trade convenience and even reliability in exchange for execution speed without a second thought. Game programmers are notoriously conservative; it took many years to persuade them to program in high-level languages rather than "down on the bare metal," and it took many more to use object-oriented techniques and project-management tools. Even today there's still something of a cult of machismo among the more hard-core programmers, each trying to outdo the others to squeeze a few more instructions per millisecond out of the hardware.

Most game machines contain a single general-purpose central processing unit and one or more dedicated graphics processing units. Their CPUs follow the traditional one-instruction-at-a-time model that goes all the way back to the Jacquard loom. This design was originally intended for computing ballistics tables for artillery guns, not for simulating complex scenes or looking five moves ahead in a chess game. However, it seems firmly entrenched, and we believe that until there is a completely new paradigm in computer hardware design, software will continue to be programmed in much the same way that it has been for the last 20 years. Because computers are designed to perform mathematical calculations, our models are all still mathematical rather than, say, neurological. Mathematics has the advantage that it's highly abstract and can be applied—with varying degrees of accuracy—to nearly anything.

However, despite the fact that the near future doesn't look as if it will offer any major changes to the way computers are built and programmed, we do expect to see a number of advances in computer programming, and these will have a distinct effect on game development as well.

Scene Representation

We've separated scene representation from animation because they represent two different kinds of programming problems. The current state of the art is to represent a scene as a set of textured surfaces whose shapes are defined by a database of polygons. 3D graphics-acceleration hardware is essential for doing this quickly. It works very well for the simple problem of displaying objects in a room, so now most of the graphics programming effort has turned to harder challenges: creating lighting effects, particle effects, fog, and so on.

As for the future, there could come a time when hardware support for drawing polygons seems as antiquated as hardware support for drawing lines does now. There are at least three other ways in which scenes can be displayed, and there might be more that we haven't envisioned.

Mathematical Representations

At the moment, scenes are represented as data: thousands or millions of points in 3-space that define the corners of the polygons that make up the surfaces that we see. This data normally is created in a 3D scene editor such as Maya, and they take up a lot of memory. They're particularly expensive as a way of representing curved surfaces because they have to break down the curve into a large number of straight lines.

Another way of representing a scene is by describing it as a series of mathematical equations that describe the surfaces, whether curved or flat. Two techniques currently under investigation are nonuniform rational B-splines (NURBS) and Bézier patches. Program code uses the equation to calculate the shapes of the surfaces and project them onto the screen. It takes more computing power than drawing polygons, but it allows the artist to represent more curves in less memory.

Procedural Scene Representation

Instead of storing a database of points or mathematical equations, you could "paint" a scene algorithmically by writing program code that generates an image on the fly—a chair subroutine would draw a picture of a chair, for example. This extends traditional object-oriented programming, in which programmers write code that determines how objects behave, to include the concept of code that determines how they look as well. Unlike raw image data, a drawing algorithm can be given new parameters to tell it to draw things in a variety of ways. A program called AARON has already used this technique to create 2D paintings of people and objects.

Real-Time Ray Tracing

Ray tracing is an extremely slow but powerful technique in which the color of each pixel on the screen is computed, one by one, from a three-dimensional model of a scene, including its light sources. The idea is that each pixel is hypothetically "lit" by a ray of light coming from within the scene somewhere, and the process computes where it originated and what happened to it. Because it computes each ray of light individually, ray tracing can display the effects of mirrors, lenses, translucent surfaces, and anything else that affects light as it travels. The process normally takes many hours to generate a single still frame. Ray tracing is often used to create special effects in movies because for each frame of the movie, it has to be done only once. In a computer game, in which things are changing on the fly 30 times a second or more, it's much too slow—for now. But there could be a time when real-time ray tracing is made possible by hardware accelerators.

It's impossible to predict which lines of research will prove fruitful. One thing is certain: Whatever is the hottest, most exciting state-of-the-art technique today will be yesterday's news a few years from now. This is one of the reasons a designer should avoid creating designs dependent on a specific piece of hardware—they age too quickly.

Animation

In film and television, animation is pre-rendered and can be refined in the studio until it looks right in every scene. In computer games, however, animation must be displayed on the fly, often without any way to adjust it to account for differences between one scene and another. This is fairly easy when animating rigid mechanical objects such as machines, and it is very difficult with soft, deformable objects such as people and animals. When the action being animated is self-contained and has a natural cycle, such as a person running in a straight line along a flat surface, it looks pretty good. However, there are a number of ways in which computer game animation can be improved in the future.

Facial Animation and Speech Generation

The human brain contains special neurological wiring that responds specifically to faces, and the face transmits a huge amount of data about the emotional state of the speaker. Obviously, prescripted facial animation performing in conjunction with fixed audio clips of the character speaking is already commonplace, but the holy grail of facial animation is on-the-fly lip synchronization with artificially generated speech. We've reached the point at which we can do this with rather wooden, robotic-seeming characters, but truly natural-sounding speech will come in time. The other aspect of facial animation, emotional display, also shows great promise. At the moment, a few games are doing this in a fairly clumsy way—a raised eyebrow or a frown—but before long we will be able to do more subtle expressions.

Inverse Kinematics

Computer animation involving interactions between two objects often doesn't look right. Consider the simple motion of walking uphill. With each step, the walker's forward foot should stop descending at a point higher than his rear foot because the ground is higher there. The angle of his ankles should also be different from what it is on flat ground because his feet are sloping upward from back to front. If you use the same walk cycle that you would use on flat ground, the walker's forward foot will appear to descend into the earth, and his ankles will be at the wrong angle. To correct these errors, it's possible to use a programming technique called *inverse kinematics* to compute where the heel and toes should stop based on the height of the ground it will contact. The data for the position and orientation of the legs is then modified to account for the different height of the surface. This has to be done at every step, to compensate for changes the angle of the surface. If the terrain flattens out or starts to slope downhill, the positions of the legs must change to reflect that.

Inverse kinematics have a great many uses besides walking. In reaching out to pick up an object, for example, the distance the character's arm extends naturally depends on how far away the object is. If the animation for extending the arm is fixed, the model must be the same distance from every object it is going to pick up. If the model is too far away, its arm will stop moving before the hand reaches the object, which will then appear to float up in midair. If the model is too near, its hand will appear to pass through the object. By using inverse kinematics, the model's arm can be made to stop extending at the point at which the hand touches the object.

Inverse kinematics are computationally expensive compared to using fixed animation, especially when there are large numbers of animated people moving around in complex environments such as a cocktail party. But research is underway, and as processors become more powerful, we can expect to see more of this technique.

True Locomotion

At the moment, most computer animation moves a 3D model rather the way a marionette moves. A marionette wiggles its legs back and forth to look as if it's walking, but the puppet isn't really moving by pushing its feet against the ground. The same is true of computer models: The movement of the model through an environment is actually computed by a mathematical formula unrelated to the movement of its legs. Typically, the speed of the model either is fixed or varies according to a straight-line acceleration, as with a rocket. But if the movement of the legs doesn't actually match the speed of the model over the ground, it produces a visual anomaly: The character looks as if she is ice skating. This often appears in sports games because different athletes run at different speeds depending on their ability ratings, but they all use the same animation cycle for running. In most other games, all characters move at the same speed or at a few fixed speeds, each of which has its own properly tuned animation cycle. For now, only sports games have a wide and continuous range of speeds for all their athletes.

The solution to this problem, even more processor-intensive than inverse kinematics, is *true locomotion*—that is, simulating the movement of a body according to real physics acting on the body, involving its mass, strength, traction on the ground, and many other factors. If done properly, calculations should also take into account such features as the swaying of the person's body as weight shifts and the flexing and deformation of the feet under the changing load conditions of walking. True locomotion is common in pre-rendered animations such as the dinosaurs in the film *Jurassic Park*, but it has yet to be seen in computer games because we just don't have the processing power to do it in real time, especially for a whole field full of athletes. But it won't be long before we do. It's another thing to look out for in the coming years.

Natural Language Processing

Not long after computers were invented, early artificial intelligence researchers confidently predicted that they would have programs speaking and understanding English within 10 years. Fifty years later, we're not significantly closer to that goal. Computers do use language to communicate with their users, but it's almost entirely by means of prescribed sentences. Few programs have been devised that can express meaning by generating sentences from individual words, and those few usually do so over a very limited domain.

It turns out that generating and understanding natural language is an exceedingly hard problem. Large areas of the human brain are devoted to it. Language comprehension involves much more than understanding the dictionary definitions of the words and the rules of grammar; it also takes into account the relationships between the speakers, their physical circumstances, the sorts of routine conversational scripts that we follow, and many other variables. To give an extremely simple example, a person who is drowning might shout "Help!" to those on shore, and a person on shore who can't offer help himself for some reason might also shout "Help!". The first person obviously means "help *me*" while the second means "help *him*." It's up to the listener to observe the situation and draw the correct conclusion about who needs help. Most of us could do this in a fraction of a second, but at the moment, no computer program can do so at all. A great deal of natural language comprehension is tied into something called "common sense," but common sense is so enormous and illogical that we don't even know how to start to teach it to computers.

Nevertheless, natural language processing will be extremely significant in the games of the future. There are two problems to solve: language recognition and language generation.

Language Recognition

Language recognition isn't the same as voice recognition, which we've already dealt with in the section on gaming hardware. *Language recognition* is the process of breaking down sentences to decode their meaning, and it is also called *parsing*. Computers aren't too bad at parsing sentences that refer to a tightly restricted subject. This is what compilers do as the first step in processing program source code. Source code, however, has extremely rigid rules and an unambiguous meaning for everything. English is much more complex, fluid, and illogical. Consider the sentence, "Alice told Betty that she would have to leave." Who would have to leave?

Giving orders in English will be a lot of fun, as long as it doesn't prove to be less efficient than doing it by other means. Most games provide a fairly restricted domain, so orders such as "Attack," "Hold your ground," and even "Start a diversion on the west side of the enemy base" won't be too difficult to interpret. But the real challenge for language recognition will be in games with simulated characters, with whom the player wants to have conversations. Early text-based adventure games did a certain amount of this, but most of that work was abandoned with the arrival of graphical adventure games and scripted conversations. For the moment, most programs that try to do language recognition sort of fake it, guessing what the player means from keywords in the input and responding more or less appropriately depending on how good the guess was. It will probably require several more decades of AI research before we can do language recognition well.

Language Generation

Simple language generation—assembling prerecorded phrases into sentences—is less difficult than language recognition. Unlike parsing user input, which could be anything, as designers we can limit the scope of what a game character says and guarantee that it's grammatically correct. We're already starting to get good doing this and play it back smoothly, and this will continue to improve.

In the near future, we can't expect to have wide-ranging conversations with artificial characters, but we ought to be able to simulate reasonable interactions in stereotypical sorts of situations: bartenders, gas-station attendants, invading aliens, and so on. For now, these will probably remain scripted conversations, but we might be able to replace the current mechanism, in which the game just delivers a canned piece of dialogue, with a sentence assembled from semantic fragments that vary somewhat depending on the character's state of mind. To give a trivial example, take the sentence "I don't know" as a response to a question to which the character doesn't have the answer. If the character feels sympathetic to the player, the software could add "I'm sorry, but" before the sentence; if the character feels unsympathetic, it could add, "and I don't care" at the end.

Real language use, in the sense of converting a character's mental desire to make a "speech act," along with the semantic content of that act, into an actual utterance, is a far harder problem. Games will undoubtedly be able to do it someday, but, as with language recognition, this is primarily a subject for AI research at the moment.

Game Genres

It's nearly impossible to predict what new genres of games might arise in the future. American designers never anticipated the dance simulations that have recently come from Japan. *Rez*, the abstract music/shooting game from Sega, could be the first in another. There will undoubtedly be more as the medium expands.

One thing is certain: For interactive entertainment to grow, we have to be open-minded and willing to explore. Why didn't American game designers invent the dance simulation themselves? Probably because the idea of making a game about little girls dancing was just too uncool. The notion that gamers are all adolescent boys is clearly outdated, yet many designers persist in building games as if they were the only market.

To invent a game in a genuinely new genre, you have to throw out all your preconceived notions about computer games and start from scratch with two simple questions: *What activities do people think are fun?* and *Can that activity reasonably be turned into a computer game?*

In the meantime, we'll discuss what we think will happen in some existing genres.

Action Games

The challenges in action games arise mostly from their twitch elements: motor skills, coordination, and timing. To a lesser extent, they also include puzzle solving and exploration—figuring out where to go and what to do to survive and pass through the level. These are well-understood elements of an action game's design. Most of the advances in action gaming in recent years have been in the game's content rather than in the nature of the challenges it offers. *Banjo-Kazooie*, for example, was a very successful game about a bear (Banjo) carrying a bird (Kazooie) around in his backpack. This peculiar bird-bear avatar enabled the designers to create a number of unique moves that would have been incongruous if the avatar were just a bird or just a bear. *Soul Reaver* was a game about a maimed vampire with only a limited ability to fly. *Toy Story*, of course, was based on the movie and was all about toys in a suburban environment. This kind of imaginative thinking will keep action games moving forward rather than stagnating.

First-person shooters represented a big leap forward when they appeared, but what was new about them was mostly the quality of the display and the richness of the environment rather than the concept itself. Multi-player first-person gaming goes back at least as far as the early 1980s, when a game called *MazeWars* was programmed for the short-lived Xerox Alto workstation. Since then, most of the advances have been evolutionary rather than revolutionary: nonrectilinear rooms and stairs (the biggest differences between the original *Castle Wolfenstein 3D* and *Doom*), a greater variety of weapons and enemies, and so on. We can expect to see continuing evolutionary advancements in the first-person shooter genre, providing better graphics, better sound, and especially better enemy AI.

Thief, one of the most innovative action games in recent years, turned the shooter on its head by actively discouraging shooting. It was still a first-person game in which the player was armed with a variety of weapons, but the goal was to steal things rather than to kill people, to get through as much of the game as possible without firing a shot. Stealth, not violence, ensured success, but the game still required both hand-eye coordination and puzzle solving in the best traditions of the action genre. We hope to see more action games that explore alternative kinds of actions and approaches to victory.

Strategy Games

By far the largest unexplored area of strategy games is the human factor. Armies are led by generals, and generals have human strengths and weaknesses that have a profound influence on their performance in the field. Determination, imagination, daring, lateral thinking, personal courage, and sheer analytic intelligence all play important roles in military capability. So does the indefinable quality of leadership, an attribute that determines whether men risking their lives will be confident or fearful, which can sometimes turn the tide of battle all by itself.

There have been efforts to quantify and simulate some of these qualities. As far back as *The Ancient Art of War*, players could choose to fight against simulated versions of Julius Caesar, Genghis Khan, or Napoleon Bonaparte, each of whom was characterized as representing certain military attributes. We've also worked on simulating the psychological condition of soldiers themselves: Microsoft's *Close Combat* gave each soldier a state of mind that varied from courageous and confident to cowering in terror, unable to obey any order.

Nevertheless, there's a great deal more to be done in this area. In most computer strategy games, there's no such thing as psychological operations, nor do they simulate the element of surprise, diversionary tactics, bluffing, feigned retreats to draw out the enemy, or lame-duck tricks to give an impression of weakness. Computer games tend to simulate soldiers as robotic killing machines, obeying whatever order they're given, even if it is suicidal, and unflinchingly standing their ground to the last man. With more processing power and richer, deeper simulations of human reactions, we will start to see war games that depict battles as they are really fought.

Another weakness of real-time strategy games at the moment is an overemphasis on economic production models. Players concentrate on achieving economic efficiency rather than strategic or tactical superiority. They treat their units as cannon fodder, relying on overwhelming the enemy with sheer numbers rather than with military skill—a tactic uncomfortably reminiscent of Field Marshal Haig at the Somme. Because they're only simulated soldiers, we don't have to care how many of them die, except insofar as it gives us fewer units to fight with. This represents an inaccuracy in the simulation. Real soldiers' morale is hurt when their leaders exhibit a flagrant disregard for the value of their lives, and their performance suffers accordingly. In the future, we can expect to see these details simulated properly, and players will have to take care of their soldiers to win.

Role-Playing Games

Computerized role-playing games still bear the marks of their heritage as pencil-and-paper, dice-based games. Many players like RPGs this way and enjoy fiddling around with their weapons, armor, and magic items to find the optimal combination of attack and defense potential.

Although there's a definite market for such games, we feel that the emphasis on statistics discourages a larger market, the casual player, from playing RPGs. Casual players want to have adventures and collect loot without having to study all the peculiar capabilities of their equipment or to spend a lot of time shopping for it at the local arms merchant. Other genres—action games and action adventures—offer that kind of gameplay, but for the most part, they have thin plots and little character development. We expect that the traditional numbers-oriented RPG will continue to exist but that a new type of RPG, a sort of hybrid between the action-adventure and the traditional RPG, will emerge over time to satisfy the needs of the casual player. It will have the plot and character-interaction elements of the RPG, along with the usual quest structure and character-growth components, but it won't require so much fiddling or buying and selling.

Sports Games

As we've said elsewhere, sports games don't have a lot of room for creative growth. The game is defined by the nature of the sport. There are new sports from time to time, but they're created by their enthusiasts, not by computer game designers.

Sports games, of course, will continue to benefit from improvements in display technology and other kinds of hardware, and voice recognition could be a lot of fun when you're able to call plays and shout to your "teammates" on the field. But the greatest challenge in creating sports games, and the place where we can expect to see the most improvement in the future, is in artificial intelligence, especially in team games such as soccer. Two areas in sports games need AI: strategy, which we might also call play-calling or coaching, and tactics, the AI that controls the behavior of individual athletes on the field, especially in response to changing or unexpected play situations. Athlete AI is starting to improve already. We seldom see athletes doing things that seem to be patently stupid anymore—at least, not much more often than real athletes do things that seem to be patently stupid! Coaching is another matter, however. Games don't yet have the smarts to make up the tricks and clever moves that real coaches can devise, but perhaps they will in the future.

Vehicle Simulations

Although complacency is risky, if any genre of computer gaming can be said to be stable, it's probably vehicle simulations. Of course, there's much more that can be done, mostly in physics simulations and display technology, but, for the most part, vehicle simulations already offer all the gameplay that their fans could want. The aerodynamic models aren't realistic, but they're enough to provide all but the most demanding players with a feeling of authenticity. We could accurately model *all* the switches and levers in an F-15 fighter jet rather than just some of them, but doing so would make the game harder to play without adding enjoyment to the process.

The quality of the driver AI in racing games is pretty good at the moment. In racing, it's mostly every car for itself, and the cars have to stay in a restricted area, so the AI is chiefly needed for strategic decisions involving refueling, changing tires when rain is threatening, and addressing similar questions. We can probably expect to see this kind of decision making improve in the future. The casual player isn't likely to notice it very much, however.

Pilot AI in flight simulators could be improved somewhat, especially in cooperative missions. It's practically a foregone conclusion that if you're given an AI-controlled wingman in a computer game, he'll get shot down. It's not clear why wingmen seem to be so vulnerable. It could be that they're mostly designed to assist you rather than to protect themselves, so they take unnecessary risks.

Construction and Management Simulations

For the most part, construction and management simulations don't use 3D engines, but they demand a lot of processing power from the CPU to simulate whatever system they're modeling. As computing power increases, we can expect to see such games modeling larger systems, or the same kinds of systems but in more detail. We also expect that they will eventually switch from the isometric perspective that seems to be the current standard, to a fully 3D perspective that enables players to zoom right in on the world and observe things at close range.

As the demand for games grows, we might also start to see simulations for niche markets: small groups of people interested in a particular subject that doesn't necessarily have broad appeal. For example, there could be simulations about gardening, automobile traffic, wildlife conservation, or electrical power distribution. What really limits growth in this area is the cost of development.

Adventure Games

Adventure games have stagnated somewhat in recent years. They don't get as much adrenaline flowing as action games or vehicle simulations, and they cost more to develop than other slow-paced games such as war games or city simulations. Nevertheless, we're confident that they won't disappear entirely. A small but distinct market wants games with strong plots and interesting characters, and as gaming matures, this market will grow.

Part of the appeal of adventure games is in the beauty of their locations. Because they move more slowly, players have the time to admire the details of their worlds. As a result, many of them still use painted 2D locations rather than 3D environments. The best 3D engines still can't reproduce the lush detail of an open-air market, for example, in which every pomegranate and bolt of silk is lovingly rendered. However, this will change, and we expect that, in time, more adventure games will be moving to 3D-rendered worlds simply because they offer more freedom to the player and more camera angles to the designer. With a 2D background, every change of perspective requires a new painting; with a 3D engine, the perspective can be adjusted easily to fit the circumstances in the game.

Adventure games will benefit more than any other genre from advances in artificial intelligence. Good stories require believable characters, and to be believable, characters must speak and act normally.

Broadband Networking

At the moment, the Internet is both slow and unreliable for gameplay use. It's slow because most players' connections are still made with modems over ordinary telephone lines, which can't transmit much data per second. It's unreliable because the Internet doesn't provide a continuous guaranteed amount of bandwidth to each user. Instead, packets of data on the Internet compete for transmission priority, and there is no way to be certain what route they will take or how long it will take to get there. This means that gamers can't play equally; those with longer "ping times" are at a disadvantage.

The arrival of asymmetric digital subscriber lines (ADSL), cable modems, and, above all, fiber-optic links (all collectively called *broadband*) will give users a much faster connection to the Internet, although this will still not guarantee a particular minimum speed. This will have two significant effects on the games of the future: electronic distribution and higher-speed gaming.

Electronic Distribution

Our current method for distributing computer and video games is ridiculous. The object is to transfer a string of bits from the publisher's computer to the player's, in exchange for some money going from the player back to the publisher. At the moment, this is done by pressing a plastic compact or DVD disc, putting it in a cardboard box, selling it to a middleman who operates a retail store in a shopping mall, and attracting a player who drives down to the mall and buys the cardboard box with the disc inside from the retailer. The player then puts the CD in her computer, transfers the bits onto her hard drive, and throws away the cardboard. A few weeks or months later, she's done with the game and throws away the CD as well.

Electronic distribution will eliminate most of the waste that this entails. No cardboard boxes; no plastic disks; no heat, light, and security guards for the retail store; and, above all, no cars and trucks driving around the country emitting pollution just to carry the bits (at 60 miles per hour) between point A and point B. Instead, those bits will travel directly from the publisher's computer into the player's computer. In theory, we could eliminate the retailers entirely.

Benefits of Electronic Distribution

Apart from eliminating the manufacturing waste, the single greatest benefit to electronic distribution is that it ends the battle for shelf space. At the moment, too many games are being developed for all of them to fit into a reasonably sized retail store. This means that the competition to sell them to retailers is fierce, and the biggest distributors have by far the best chance of getting their products on the shelves. Small-time developers and publishers simply don't have the sales and marketing clout to compete.

Electronic distribution will help to level this playing field. You need only one copy of a game on the distribution server, no matter how many people you sell it to, and you don't have to take down one product to make room for another one. Shelf space on the Internet is effectively unlimited. Furthermore, small developers can have attractive web sites just as easily as large publishers can. Without the need to develop expensive in-store displays or to commit marketing development funds to retailers, developers can run a very efficient sales operation directly to the consumer.

This doesn't mean that small publishers will drive the giants out of business, however. The majority of a computer game's cost is not in the goods or the distribution, but in the marketing and development—paying all those creative people to build the game in the first place. Bigger publishers can afford to make bigger games, and bigger games will generally sell better than small ones. Bigger publishers can buy advertising space in magazines and on TV that small publishers couldn't begin to afford, and advertising sells games. They'll always have that advantage. But by taking away their control over retail sales, electronic distribution will improve the odds for small developers a little.

Piracy

The game industry loses billions of dollars every year to piracy, and many people are concerned that electronic distribution will make piracy even easier. At the moment, sophisticated large-scale piracy requires fairly expensive machinery to counterfeit the specialized compact discs that most game machines require. Publishers will be reluctant to embrace electronic distribution if it makes work easier for the pirates. We believe that this problem is solvable, but further work must be done to do it. The game industry will have to find a way to digitally "tag" each unique copy of a game and to make sure that no two identical copies can run at once. It's likely that before long, games will require an Internet connection and will not run without one—which might not sit well with players.

Speed of Delivery

The length of time it takes to drive to a retail store and buy a game is typically 30 to 60 minutes for people living in suburban areas. If you develop a severe hankering for a game, you can usually buy it and be playing it within an hour or so. You can't do that with the Internet as it exists today; the download speeds are too slow. For electronic distribution to offer real competition to retail shopping, it must be able to gratify that desire at least as quickly as shopping does.

Benefits of Retail Shopping

There are certain benefits to selling games at retail that electronic distribution won't provide. One is that the perceived value of a retail product is proportionate to the quality of its packaging. A beautifully printed box with a heavy manual inside gives the customer a warm feeling that she is getting her money's worth. (One of the reasons that cassette tapes didn't drive LP records out of the market was that customers liked the album art on LPs—and some mourned its passing with the arrival of the compact disc.) A CD in a jewel case alone feels cheap. A downloaded executable file on a computer doesn't feel like anything at all—although you can see the game running on your machine, there's no sense of having purchased something that you can hold in your hand.

Although you might think that this shouldn't matter, we feel that it will have a significant psychological impact at the one time of the year more important to the game industry than any other: Christmas. The interactive entertainment business is heavily dependent on Christmas gift giving, and the fact is that people like to see actual boxes under the Christmas tree—the bigger, the better. A slip of paper giving a web address where software can be downloaded isn't going to feel like much of a gift.

Retailers would also argue that buying in a store gives players the opportunity to look at games side by side and to ask questions of the staff. Although you can get more information by comparing game reviews online than you can by holding a box in either hand, many casual gamers don't bother to do that much research. Retail shopping offers the chance to browse in a way that online shopping simply doesn't. For all its convenience and efficiency, online shopping doesn't feel the same as running your eye over shelves full of games.

High-Speed Online Gaming

Online games currently suffer a great deal from bandwidth bottlenecks. They have to be carefully designed to eliminate any advantage that one player might get by having a faster Net connection than another player. They also have to prioritize their data transmission so that the most important data has the highest chance of being delivered rapidly, while less important data is delivered later and can be dropped altogether if bandwidth conditions deteriorate. The Swedish company Terraplay has created an entire software system to manage this problem for game developers.

As with everything else they use—memory, processor speed, disk space—computer games expand to consume the bandwidth available, and this problem will not go away simply by increasing the available bandwidth a hundredfold or even a thousandfold. But more bandwidth will change the kinds of games that we can play and the ease with which we play them online. Right now, when players start playing large online games, they must either buy a CD full of the graphical data or download it all, a very time-consuming process. When the game's provider wants to make a whole new region available to the players, those players are forced to download the new graphics. Either they can do it all in one chunk, which means they have to sit around and twiddle their thumbs until it's done, or they can download it in the background as they play, which hurts gameplay performance. Having more bandwidth will certainly make this a more pleasant process.

Ultimately, speeds will get so high that players don't even notice them. Network connections will be as ubiquitous as electric lights are now. (Microsoft's Xbox Live network is already broadband-only.) When this happens, we can expect to see not just games, but entire online environments that people pop into and out of continuously during both their work and leisure time. We have the capacity to create part of William Gibson's vision of cyberspace right now—a "consensual shared hallucination"—but only slowly and, for the most part, in two dimensions. Extremely fast communication will enable us to make it a reality, whether for gaming, working, shopping, or doing any other activity. The technology isn't in doubt; the more important question is, who will control it?

The Distant Future

In the TV show *Star Trek: The Next Generation*, Captain Picard relaxes by playing a computerized role-playing game in the holodeck, a place capable of temporarily creating (somewhat) solid matter, up to and including living things. While it's anyone's guess whether we'll ever develop the holodeck, Picard's "holonovels" have a lot in common with games that already exist: simulated characters, a fantasy setting, and a plot whose progress is influenced by the player. They do contain a few improvements over current games, however. Picard can interact with the people in the story in all the same ways that he could with real people, he isn't perpetually stopping to look at his statistics, and he doesn't have to stuff everything he sees into his pockets in case it might be useful later.

In this section, we'll talk about some of the things that might make Picard's experience come true.

Automated Programming

Most game machines are single-CPU computers with dedicated graphics and sound-processing units. Their CPUs follow the traditional one-instruction-at-a-time model that, as we said earlier, was originally intended for computing ballistics tables for artillery guns. In the more distant future, it is bound to be replaced, although with what isn't at all clear. Neural networks hold a certain amount of promise for pattern recognition; so does massively parallel computing. Molecular transistors are a certainty; quantum computing is probably not far behind. We might begin to see programming by evolution, using the principles of natural selection to create programs without human intervention. This has already been done to create simple electronic circuits, with successful but startlingly peculiar results.

It seems certain that eventually computers will learn to program themselves, although by that time they might bear no more resemblance to the machines we know today than the aircraft carrier does to the trireme—and probably less. For that to happen, computers will need a fundamental understanding of the nature of information and the way that it can be stored and manipulated. In particular, they'll have to be able to make the abstractions that human programmers do all the time. Teaching a computer to program itself to calculate mathematical formulas probably won't be that hard because most mathematical formulas are calculated using fairly simple algorithms anyway. The bigger challenge is to teach a computer to model imaginary situations mathematically, to solve the "story problems" that we remember from algebra class. The hardest part of a "story problem" was not solving the algebraic equations, but determining how the situation described could be modeled mathematically in the first place.

Intelligent Design Tools

Automated programming doesn't mean, however, that game designers are doomed to extinction. Captain Picard's Dixon Hill stories are written by real people; they're just executed by a computer. People will always want to design games, and that's not going to change. What will change is the way we do the work. Rather than collaborating with a large team of programmers, artists, writers, and audio engineers, the game designer of the far future could be collaborating with a game-design tool, a program specifically constructed to assist in creating games. We can easily imagine a conversation that goes like this:

Designer: "We're going to want three kinds of aerial units: fighters, bombers, and transports."

Computer: "OK. Have you figured out their operational parameters and combat capabilities?"

Designer: "Not yet. But fighters are designed to attack anything in the air; they won't be able to attack ground targets. Bombers can attack both air and ground units. Transports have no weapons."

Computer: "Why would you ever want fighters if bombers have more functionality?"

Designer: "Because bombers will be slower and less maneuverable than fighters, and also more expensive. Compare the performance characteristics of the World War II B-17 with the P-51 Mustang. Also notice the manufacturing time and cost of each."

Computer: [*reads history for a nanosecond*] "Okay, I understand the principle. Do you want me to use those numbers as a baseline?"

Designer: "Sure, what the heck? It'll do for now."

Self-Adjusting Plots

One of the many weaknesses that computerized role-playing games suffer in comparison to tabletop RPGs is that their plots are fixed, designed in advance by the developer. As a player, you can ignore the plot if you like, but the game won't be very interesting and you won't go far. To see everything that the game has to offer, you have to meet the challenges that it presents. If you don't, nothing happens. Larger games typically offer several subplots to choose from, so you don't have to do everything in a strictly linear order; nevertheless, what you bought is what you get.

On the other hand, live role playing with a human dungeon master frees players to ignore the dungeon master's intended plot, wander around on their own, and explore areas of particular interest to them. Although this might be frustrating for the dungeon master—particularly if he has spent a lot of time devising an adventure for the party, only to have them completely ignore it—a good DM is capable of adjusting the game to suit the circumstances. The players are much more the masters of their own fates in live role playing. The DM also has the ability to adjust the nature of the challenge to suit the nature of the party—if it is badly damaged, he can surreptitiously see to it that they don't meet anything capable of wiping them out in an instant.

This ability to devise new adventures on the fly and to adjust the difficulty of the game to match the abilities of the players is bound to appear in games in the future. At the moment, we have randomly generated adventures in games such as *Diablo*, but this really applies only to the layout of the rooms and the number of creatures in them. It doesn't change the personalities or dialogue of the nonplaying characters.

Artificial People

In 1950, the English mathematician Alan Turing proposed a famous test for determining whether computers are really thinking. Let a computer and a human each chat with another person, the Interrogator, in another room via teletype (today we would use instant messages). The Interrogator must ask them both questions and, on the basis of their responses, try to decide which is the human and which the computer. However, both are trying to persuade the Interrogator that they are human. If in a series of five-minute conversations the Interrogator correctly identifies the real human less than 70% of the time, the computer can be said to be thinking. (Turing's definition was slightly more complicated than this, but this is the generally accepted formulation.) Although it was largely abandoned as a serious goal of AI research, the Turing Test remains a popular informal standard for artificial intelligence.

In game development, we have a similar challenge, but the bar is far higher. Turing's test required only that the computer converse in typed text. We hope someday to be able to simulate credible artificial humans, computer-generated characters who look, act, and speak just like real people. Doing this successfully requires vast improvements in many different areas: graphics, animation, physics, simulation, and, of course, many kinds of artificial intelligence. A computer-generated person should be able not only to converse in natural language, but also take part in a political debate or interpret another person's mood just as well as an ordinary human would.

Computer games don't need to have artificial people, of course, any more than the telephone company has to have artificial operators. We can let human players play against one another, just as the phone company can hire real people to answer the phone. But artificial people are a key part of the "holodeck" fantasy and are probably its biggest challenge—perhaps even bigger than creating the mechanics of the holodeck itself. It's still a worthwhile goal for game development, even if the solution is centuries off.

Interactive Entertainment as an Art Form

In thinking about the future of interactive entertainment, it would be a mistake to consider only the advances that are likely to take place in the world of commercial, mass-market gaming. That would be like assuming that the potential of cinema was limited to what you see in Hollywood blockbusters, or that the written word was capable of no more than Danielle Steel novels. Interactive entertainment is an art form, just as filmmaking and writing are. Unlike filmmaking and writing, however, it has not yet been recognized as an art form by the public at large.

Film has the advantage that it is an outgrowth of drama, and, of course, drama was recognized as an art form by no less a figure than Aristotle. It took film a little while to achieve this status, but it is now unshakable. Computer games' roots are not in drama, however, but in gameplay. Their nearest noncomputerized parallels are board games and fairground shooting galleries, neither of which are or ever will be recognized as art forms. As a result, we face an uphill battle for recognition.

Part of the reason that board games and shooting galleries aren't art forms is that they contain very little expressive content. Graphically, they're abstract and minimal, requiring a lot of imagination on the part of the players to pretend that the little cardboard counters are really troops and tanks. They also seldom include any narrative or characters. Computer games, on the other hand, have a lot of content, both visible and audible; they have a distinct artistic style; and they often have a great deal of characterization and narrative.

Interactive Artwork

Most works of art require only passive observation, especially in traditional media such as painting, sculpture, and music. The observer brings his own knowledge and personal history to it, and these color his understanding and interpretation of the work, but the influence is entirely inside his own mind. He isn't asked to take an active, participatory role in creating the aesthetic experience.

There's no reason why works of art can't be interactive, however, and some are. In San Francisco, a science museum called the Exploratorium considers its exhibits to be works of art, and it actively seeks out artists to design them. Most of the exhibits are interactive, offering a learning experience as well as an aesthetic experience; they illustrate principles of nature, but also principles of design.

Not all interactive entertainment is art, but then, neither are all movies or all novels. Most movies—and most novels, too, for that matter—are merely light entertainment, popular culture. But just because James Bond novels and James Bond movies aren't generally considered to be art doesn't mean that film or the novel isn't an art form. Interactive entertainment is a collaborative art form in the same way that movies are, and it can be judged according to a variety of aesthetics the way movies are.

Requirements for Recognition

For interactive entertainment to be recognized as an art form, it must do some of the things that other art forms do, the things that people expect of art forms. We believe that game developers and publishers, and people who write about the game industry, can take several concrete steps to help it achieve that status.

We Must Devise Principles of Aesthetics

More than 20 years ago, Chris Crawford mentioned in his book *The Art of Computer Game Design* that the interactive entertainment medium needs principles of aesthetics. It remains true today. We're not much farther along than when he wrote that, though, for two reasons.

First, the serious study of computer games has only just begun. The commercial world is too busy churning out games as fast as it can to think deeply about them, and until recently, the academic world has ignored them as childish toys rather than important elements of popular culture. This is starting to change, and as we begin to see real analysis of computer games, principles of aesthetics will arise.

Second, computer games have been a rapidly moving target. Games have changed, at least in appearance and depth, far more in the last 20 years than movies or television did in any 20-year period of their history, partly because of the rapid development of new hardware. The principles of interactive entertainment aesthetics should perhaps be independent of hardware developments, but this is easier said than done. It took 20 millennia to go from cave paintings to color photography; computer games have made a similar journey in two decades.

However, we're already on the right track. We've all seen games that were clunky and awkward to use and others that were smooth and seamless. We've all noticed games with tacky, slapped-together graphics and others with elegant and atmospheric graphics. These are good first approximations for game aesthetics. At the moment, they are purely surface impressions, the equivalent of showing basic competence at oil painting or music composition. To be a great painter or a great composer, you must go beyond basic competence; you must reach out and touch your audience's soul. Interactive entertainment is capable of doing this, but it seldom does, and we have yet to devise an aesthetic for it.

Our Awards Must Change

The game industry is ridiculously full of awards, mostly given by magazines or web sites, some by trade associations and parents' pressure groups. Within the industry, however, we have a problem: We tend not to distinguish between art and craft in our awards.

In the film industry, the Academy Awards are actually presented at two different ceremonies. One is the glittering spectacle that everyone knows, broadcast live on TV and attended by movie stars and Hollywood bigwigs. The other is for the technical awards. It's a much smaller affair, usually held in a hotel ballroom, and attended only by technical people, the film industry's craftsmen. The "big" Oscars that everyone hears about are all about art: acting, storytelling, art direction, music composition, and so on. The technical Oscars are all about craft: new equipment and techniques that have advanced the craft of moviemaking.

We, on the other hand, have muddled this important distinction. You often see awards for "best graphics," but they don't state whether they're being given for technology or aesthetics. Some people think that "best graphics" means graphics that are displayed at the highest frame rate, or that use the most polygons, or that use sophisticated lighting and shading effects. That isn't good graphics, it's good graphic technology—good craft, but not good art. It's the same with sound; one award for "best sound" is supposed to encompass both music composition (an art) and 3D spatialization of ricocheting gunfire (a craft). As for those elements that Hollywood makes the most of—acting and storytelling—we typically give no awards at all. Small wonder, then, that these remain the weakest and most underappreciated parts of games.

To be recognized as an art form, our awards must change to value the artistic merit of computer games, not merely their technological prowess or craft.

We Need Critics, Not Just Reviewers

Like awards, the game industry is full of game reviews. In fact, that's where most of the awards come from: reviewers. But there's an important difference between reviewing and criticism. A review is a short essay whose purpose is to tell you about the game, to compare it with other similar games, and to give you an idea of whether you might like it and whether it's good value for the money. As they would say in the world of management consulting, it's a decision-support tool—it helps you decide whether to buy the game.

Criticism is not a decision-support tool. Criticism does discuss the basic competence of an art work, but it seldom goes into the question of whether it's good value for the money. The purpose of criticism is to increase understanding, to interpret a work of art in light not only of other, similar works, but also of the larger cultural and historical context in which it appears. It's not enough for critics to know all about other games. Critics must bring to their work a wide reading and an understanding of aesthetics, culture, and the human condition.

The movie *2001: A Space Odyssey* is a perfect example of why an art form needs critics as well as reviewers. *2001* left the movie reviewers severely confused because it was almost impossible to compare to other movies. It had very little action: no car chases, no fight scenes, no romance, and almost no discernible plot. In fact, it contained very little *acting* either: The characters in it were intentionally dull and wooden. Movie reviewers simply didn't know what to say about it, and quite a few of them panned it because it didn't contain any of what they thought were "essential" elements of a movie. The film critics, on the other hand, had a field day. *2001* was rich with ideas, crammed with them right to the final frame. It provoked thought about everything from the origin of human intelligence (and perhaps human violence) to our ultimate destiny in the universe. Along the way, it looked at the sterile lives of astronauts and bureaucrats, poked fun at the way we eat, and raised questions about the wisdom of placing human lives under the control of artificially intelligent machines.

2001: A Space Odyssey is a great work of art and one of the most important movies ever made. But by conventional movie reviewers' standards, it was just a curiosity, perhaps even a failure. That is why the interactive medium needs critics as well as reviewers.

Breaking New Ground

Ultimately, the greatest works of art are those that break new ground. They change the rules, challenge the established order, create new principles of aesthetics, and force the viewer to see something in a new way. But how to do it?

Some works of art deserve high praise because they are masterpieces of technique, taking a medium right to its physical limits while still demonstrating superb aesthetic feeling. Michelangelo's colossal statue of David is a good example. But although it's occasionally useful to take a medium to its limits as a technical exercise, it doesn't necessarily produce great art, especially if aesthetics are sacrificed or ignored for the sake of technical achievement. And the problem with doing this in computer games is that the limits are always changing. The challenge that Michelangelo faced, working in marble, is still the same for any sculptor working in the same medium. But in computer games, the medium changes almost week by week. Today's technical marvel is tomorrow's irrelevancy.

Michelangelo's most important achievement in sculpting *David* was not technical, but artistic. The traditional way of portraying David was as victorious, armed and holding Goliath's severed head. Michelangelo chose instead to depict David before the battle, vulnerable but filled with a fierce courage. This had never been done before, and it set the work dramatically apart from its predecessors.

The Impressionist movement in painting is another useful example of what breaking new aesthetic ground is about. Impressionism challenged existing notions of what painting was for and what it was supposed to do. It asserted that the eye is not a camera, that painting need not be a photographic reproduction of reality. Yet Impressionism was not a new technology of painting; its tools were still canvas and paint. Rather, Impressionism was a new way of seeing.

Interactive entertainment needs an Impressionism of its own, a daring, risk-taking movement to break through the tired old tropes—not a new way of seeing, but a new way of playing. We hope that you, our reader, might be our new Monet or Cassatt.

A Few Final Words

This book doesn't include everything there is to know about game design—that would be a work of many volumes. Instead, we've tried to cover the key tasks in designing computer games, and to identify the recurring elements in the most common commercial game genres. We hope that our book has given you the foundations on which to build the design for the great game that you have in your head.

Computer games are the most important new entertainment medium since the invention of motion pictures. Uniquely among all forms of entertainment, they combine the interactivity of traditional gaming with the visual impact and narrative power of the movies. Put simply, computer games enable players to live out fantasies that they could never experience in real life, and this is the source of their enduring appeal. It is your task as a designer to turn those fantasies into immersive and rewarding games. Go to it, and good luck!

Part III

Appendixes

Appendix A

Sample Design Documents

Creating and Using Design Documents

Game design documents actually have two roles. Everyone is familiar with their *development role*: Design documents help a team of people to create a game. As we said in Chapter 1, "What Is Game Design?," one of the stages of game design is communicating the design to others, and that's what design documents do. Even if you're developing a game all by yourself, it's useful to write down the things you've decided on, to make notes and lists of features that you want to include in the game.

Design documents also play a *sales role*. This doesn't mean selling the game to the public; it means selling the idea of the game to a publisher. The document is crafted to convince someone at a publishing company, probably a producer, to fund development of the game. The document should be attractive, easy to read, and upbeat about the idea. It should get the publisher excited about the game and at the same time show that you know your business.

Using Pictures in a Document

As a general rule, the more pictures you include in a design document, the better, especially if it's going to be used to sell the game. The game industry is extremely visually oriented, and pictures are what make executives, producers, marketing staff, and salespeople sit up and take notice. The old cliché about a picture being worth a thousand words holds true when you're trying to pitch a game to someone: You can save yourself a heck of a lot of talking with a single concept drawing. Consider including character sketches; user interface diagrams; special type fonts; screenshots from your prototype, if you have one; and anything else that might please the eye and support your message. In the early stages, before you've had a chance to create any images of your own, search the Internet for "graphic scrap"—pictures that give an idea of what you're hoping to accomplish.

Don't expect pictures to replace explanation, however. Every now and then, somebody—usually an artist or graphic designer—creates a game design document that's almost all pictures, with only the vaguest description of the gameplay. The author clearly knows what he wants the player to see but has very little conception of what the player is going to do. Pictures can illustrate and clarify, but they can't show the heart of the game: the player's motivation, objectives, and actions. For that, you need words as well.

Protecting Your Rights

If your design documents are only for your own use, then all you need to do to protect them is lock them up. However, if you're going to give copies to potential publishers, developers, or investors, you should take some simple steps to protect your intellectual property:

➤ Clearly identify them as yours. Put your name on the title page and in the header or footer of each subsequent page. This ensures that even if the copy is taken apart for some reason, your ownership is recorded on every page.

➤ Include a statement that asserts that you own the copyright, in the form "Copyright © <year> by <your name or company name>."

➤ If you don't want the document spread around, put "Confidential—Do Not Redistribute" on the title page and in the header or footer of each page.

➤ Don't hand out copies to all and sundry unless you don't care who sees it or makes use of it. If it's important to you to control access to your ideas, make a record of the name and address of every person to whom you gave a copy.

➤ Request that the person or company that you want to show the document to sign a *nondisclosure agreement* (NDA) before you give it to them. An NDA is a very short contract in which no money changes hands. Instead, the signer promises to keep your document and other information confidential, in exchange for being allowed to see it. This is an extremely common business practice, and you can find many sample NDAs on the Internet. Consult a lawyer to adapt one to your own use.

It is extremely unlikely that a reputable publisher will steal your document and use it to make a game without paying you. Even so, it's important that you take steps to protect your intellectual property because if a dispute arises, you need to be able to demonstrate that you considered your work valuable and tried to prevent its uncontrolled dissemination.

About These Templates

In this appendix, we have provided templates for three types of design documents: the *high-concept document*, the *treatment*, and the *design script* (sometimes called a *bible*). Each has a different function in the process of designing a game and pitching it to a publisher. However, the templates we're suggesting are by no means universal. Unlike Hollywood, which has had 80 years to work out a standard format for screenplays, there is no standard format for design documents in the game industry. Nor is there any rule about which ones you should create. Some developers might not bother to write high-concept documents at all, for example, and they might use other types of documents that we haven't discussed. It's up to you to determine what your project needs. You should feel free to adapt these templates any way you like, as long as the resulting document gets your message across and answers the questions in the reader's mind.

The High-Concept Document

A high-concept document is primarily a sales tool, although you can write one for yourself as well, just as a way of keeping a record of ideas you've had. Think of it as a résumé for a video game. The point of a résumé is to quickly convey a job applicant's qualifications and try to get him an interview with the hiring manager. The point of a high-concept document is to try to get a meeting with a producer, the chance to "pitch" the game. It should communicate rapidly and clearly the idea of the game—to whet her appetite and make her want to hear more about it. It doesn't matter that you haven't thought through all the details. You'll almost certainly end up changing several of the features during development anyway. The real point is to convey how much fun the game is going to be.

A high-concept document should be two to four pages long and should take no more than 10 minutes to read. The longer it is, the less likely it is that the producer will finish reading it. It shouldn't have a title page; the title and your name appear at the top of the first page, and the text begins immediately. Its most important material must appear on the first page.

In the sections that follow, we describe the key elements of a high-concept document.

High-Concept Statement

After the title and your name, the document should begin with no more than two lines that state the idea of the game. In a commercial environment, it is imperative that the idea be instantly comprehensible because everyone's most precious commodity is time. If the producer doesn't get the idea in a sentence or two, he's going to worry that the publisher's sales staff, the wholesale buyers, and, most important, the retail customers won't get it either.

Of course, there are exceptions to this, and those exceptions are often some of the greatest and most innovative games. In *Pac-Man,* for example, the player is a circle that eats dots and fruit and is chased by ghosts in a maze—not exactly an obvious idea. However, *Pac-Man* is an arcade game, which means that people can actually watch it playing by itself before they commit their money. If you're going to propose something really strange for a retail game, you need to be very good at explaining it!

Features

The rest of the first page should be devoted to a bulleted list of the key features of the game. Each item should consist of two or three sentences, no more. Remember that unless you have included a concept drawing, your reader doesn't have a mental picture of the game, so this section needs to build one for him. It's much more important at this point to convey the game's look and feel than to give the details about how it works. You're not selling the game's internal economy or its AI; you're selling the player's experience.

Avoid letting the feature list run on to the next page, if you can. More than about 10 bullet points in a row starts to look like a mass of text to read and discourages the eye. You might want to put the items that you think are the most fun, the most innovative, or the most important in bold type, just as you would in a résumé.

Overview

In this section, beginning on the second page, you summarize the key commercial considerations about the game: what machine it's for, who would buy it and why, and what you're hoping that the game will achieve. Consider including any or all the following items:

➤ **Player motivation.** This is a short statement that indicates what the player is trying to accomplish in the game—its victory condition. This helps indicate what sort of person the player is. He can be driven by a desire to compete, to solve puzzles, to explore, or whatever.

➤ **Genre.** Indicate the genre of the game, or if it is a mix of genres, indicate that.

➤ **License.** If you intend for the game to exploit a licensed property, say so here. Also include any facts and figures about the property's popularity, recognition value, and appeal to particular markets—but no more than a sentence or two.

➤ **Target customer.** What kind of person will buy this game? If age or sex is relevant, indicate that; more important, tell what other kinds of games they like to play.

➤ **Competition.** Are there already games on the market like this one? If so, list their names and indicate how this one is different or better than they are. This section isn't absolutely necessary, but it can reassure your reader that your game isn't just a copy of something else.

➤ **Unique selling points.** What's new in this game? How will it stand out from what has gone before?

➤ **Target hardware.** Tell what machine the game is intended for. Also indicate whether the game requires or can make optional use of any special hardware or accessories.

➤ **Design goals.** In this section, list your aims for the game as an experience. Don't just say "fun"—that's too broad. Be more specific. Are you trying to provide pulse-pounding excitement? Tension and suspense? Strategic challenge? Humor? A heartwarming story? The ability to construct or create something of the player's own? For each item, indicate in a sentence or two how the game will achieve the goal.

Further Details

In the last section, you can include additional material that you think the reader will enjoy learning about the game. You might include notes about the characters, the artwork, the music, the plot, or anything else that might pique his interest. Don't add so much that it makes the document too long, however.

A Sample High-Concept Document

The following is an old high-concept document for a simple console or arcade game. It was written before the currently popular "extreme" sports games existed, so although this game was never made, some of its ideas did find their way into other games.

Street Football—2 on 2!

Ernest W. Adams

High Concept

The game at its grittiest. No pads, no helmets, no refs, no field. It's just you and the guys, a ball, and a lot of asphalt. Choose up sides and go for it, two on two.

Features

- The point of view is derived from fighting games, with large, detailed players.
- You choose teams just like in real sandlot football, taking turns picking players from the neighborhood crowd. Each person has a different look, attributes, and set of skills. Not all the kids are available all the time.
- The "field" is an urban alley about 50 yards long. Sidewalks are out of bounds. Garbage cans, potholes, and junked cars create additional obstacles. Tin cans mark the yard lines.
- As in a fighting game, it's the personal interactions that count. Dodging, ducking, faking, jumping, diving, and tackling are all essential parts of the game. Certain players have special moves or abilities.
- Five pass plays, five running plays, and the field goal make up the whole playbook. Field goals and extra points are kicked through two guys holding their arms out and up like goalposts.
- Health meters show the players' level of injury and fatigue. If you lose a player, you can pick another one, but you forfeit two touchdowns.
- Rules are adapted for street football: You have four downs to get into your opponent's territory, and four more downs to score. Otherwise, you turn over the ball—no punting. No penalties except offsides, but expect a fistfight if it gets too rough.

- Lots of comedy touches: ball breaks a window—player flies into garbage can—player slips and skids on oil slick—van drives down alley and flattens football—little kid rides tricycle across the field—rival gangs appear and tag buildings, and then disappear—nerdy bystander gets called home to supper.

Player Motivation

Players pick teams and try to win a 20-minute game of street football. In tournament mode, two-player teams made up of all available players compete for the championship.

Genre

Sports arcade action with strong fighting-game overtones.

Target Customer

Sports arcade players looking for something new.

Competition

None

Unique Selling Points

- Fighting moves in a sports game
- Fighter-type personalities in a sports game
- Comedy in a sports game
- Team selection process

Target Hardware

Sega Genesis or Super Nintendo

Design Goals

Simple: Very simple play-calling combined with fighting-game controls makes this an easy game to learn and play.

Hot: Fast, arcade-style action. No timeouts, no players running on and off the field, no stats or halftime summaries: just raw football.

Deep: Because teams are made up of pairs of different individuals, lots of possible teams are available. It takes a while to find the best pairings, not to mention playing your way to the top of the championship tree.

continues

continued

Characters

Each of the characters has certain attributes that define how well he or she plays, and each player also has a relationship with the others in the group. Characters who are not playing can be seen watching from the sidelines, and the observant player will notice things going on that give hints about them. Here are a few possible characters:

Joey: All-American guy, a natural quarterback. Great passing accuracy, good scrambling, good pass distance, very good speed. Not a great receiver or blocker. Good stamina.

Butch: The bruiser on the block. Big and strong, hard to tackle, but slow. Great pass distance, but poor accuracy. A fair receiver. Excellent stamina. A loner, he usually stands by himself—he's not especially good with any other player.

Dana: She's lithe and agile, a good scrambler, and the fastest runner of the bunch. A good receiver and a fairly accurate passer, but her range is short. Fair stamina. Dana is Joey's girlfriend and stands with her arm around him, so they make a good team.

…etc.…

The Game Treatment

So you've shown your high-concept document to a number of producers or potential investors, and now one of them wants a meeting to hear more about it. (It can take quite a while before you find a producer who's interested enough to give you the time. Be persistent!) For that meeting, you'll normally bring along the key members of your development team and do a PowerPoint presentation showing the main features and concept art for the game. It would also be good to have some prototype code running that you can show; producers want proof that you can deliver. But after the meeting is over, people's memory of what you said will start to fade and get mixed up with impressions of other developers' pitches for their products. To keep your game fresh in the producer's mind, you need to leave something behind to remind them of it.

This is where the *game treatment* comes in. A treatment is a longer document, typically 10 to 20 pages long. Again, it's a selling tool whose function is to show off your idea in the best possible light. The text and images should echo the images you used in the

PowerPoint presentation. It should be attractively produced: printed on good-quality paper and bound in a report cover with a clear transparent front so people can see the picture on the title page. You want the treatment to say "Pick me up!" to anyone who sees it lying around, and it should be substantial enough to discourage throwing it away.

Take copies of the game treatment to the meeting, but don't hand them out at the beginning—people will flip through them instead of paying attention to you. Hand them out to everyone after the meeting is over so that they'll have something to take away with them. And be sure you bring enough copies for everyone—the more that are floating around the publisher's offices, the better.

What follows is a template for a game treatment. We don't have room to include an entire sample game treatment document here, but where it's helpful, we've included an excerpt from a hypothetical game treatment called *Psychic Warriors* to give you an idea of how it might read. Bear in mind that these excerpts are only partial, just to give you the flavor.

Title Page

The title page includes the game's title and a short tagline to indicate what it's about. As usual, it should also give the author's name, the date, and any necessary copyright or confidentiality information. Don't overemphasize this material, however; you want it to look attractive and fun, not like a legal document. If at all possible, include a big color picture.

Psychic Warriors
Supernatural Combat Against the Forces of Evil

Jeff Haas and Ernest W. Adams
August 16, 2005

Executive Summary

Like the features list in the high-concept document, this is a one-page bulleted list of the most important things to know about the game. In effect, it copies all the best points from later in the document onto the first page. It doesn't matter that the text duplicates that found elsewhere; that's why it's called a summary.

Psychic Warriors is an exciting new 3D action game from Foo Bar Productions. With an original and compelling storyline, *Psychic Warriors* combines paranormal and real-world combat against humans and huge morphing monsters. **The psychic + military combat theme is not found in any product currently on the market.**

Game Overview

This is the first major section of the document, and it discusses what the game itself will be like. It is broken up into several subsections.

High Concept

The high-concept statement is identical to that in the high-concept document. You can include a little more introductory material here, however.

Diablo meets *The X-Files* in 3D.

A new threat has appeared on the streets of America: a mysterious drug code-named Indoctrinol. No one sent to investigate it has ever come back, and it's clear that something sinister is going on. To neutralize this menace, you're given command of a super-secret team of four psychic warriors—psychically talented and superbly trained individuals drawn from the Special Forces of the U.S. Armed Services.

Genre

This is similar to the genre statement in the high-concept document. Because this document is a little longer, you can afford to go into more detail—a short paragraph, if necessary—perhaps referring to other games that this game is similar to.

➤ **Mission-based small-squad action/tactical game** combining psychic and real-world combat with a variety of weapons against humans and huge morphing monsters.

Hooks

A hook is any element—graphical, auditory, gameplay, storyline, theme—that will attract the player to the game and, you hope, keep her there. In effect, this section is the answer to the question "Why would anyone buy this game?" Don't throw in the kitchen sink; choose your five or six best features to emphasize here.

➤ **Psychically skilled characters** go beyond usual military weapons. Many opportunities for exciting special effects here. There are no current competitors in this arena.

➤ **Third-person, squad-oriented perspective** permits simultaneous control over the team. This allows for interesting tactical behaviors such as covering fire and performing leapfrog maneuvers, which are more difficult to control in first-person games.

➤ **Morphing enemies** add visual variety and an element of suspense—is that a human or a monster in disguise?

License

If this game will use licensed property, indicate which one and how the game will exploit the features and public recognition value of the license. What you choose to include here depends a lot on the nature of the license. For example, in a driving game featuring sports cars, you'll want to emphasize the performance characteristics of the actual car brands you've licensed. In a game based on a movie, you should talk about the characters and locations that appeared in the movie.

Gameplay Highlights

This section is a further list of elements that describe the experience of playing the game. Include anywhere from 10 to 20 different items. You don't have to present detailed lists of characters, places, or objects at this point; just say what sorts of things and features you want to include in the full design.

➤ **Very large variety of animations,** to allow for a vast number of specialized activities.

➤ Many different **richly detailed environments** from around the world.

➤ **Intelligent situation-based movement** by AI-controlled characters, implementing proper tactics and muzzle discipline.

Online Highlights

If the game will include an online or multi-player element, it will be useful to break it out into a separate section. Online play adds a whole new dimension to the game (unless it's online *only*, of course!) and brings its own challenges and rewards to both the publisher and the players.

➤ **Cooperative multi-player play** via Internet, LAN, or modem.

➤ **Web server offering matchmaking/team-assembly service** (à la *BattleNet*), tournaments, chat areas, and bulletin boards.

➤ **Unique missions available online** that are not provided in the retail product. A scoring system will allow for **competitive team play.**

Technology Highlights

This is where you talk about the great technology that your game will include, particularly anything innovative. If you're planning to license a game engine from a third party, name it here and indicate what it brings to the project. Don't go into programming details unless you're sure you audience will understand them; instead, discuss how the software will enhance the game. Technology doesn't necessarily mean only programming, either. Include anything that uses or requires advanced technology.

➤ **Morphing** polygonal enemies. Humans transform into hideous zombies and other monsters as they run at you.

➤ **Voice-recognition** of commands in single-player mode. In multi-player mode, players can **talk to other team members live** using speakers and a microphone.

Art and Audio Highlights

If there are any special details about the art or audio that you want to include, do so here. Many games now feature soundtracks by pop or rap groups, or dance tracks by famous DJs. These are obviously big selling points for the product, so be sure to mention them prominently. Likewise, if your art or animation includes anything special or unusual, point it out.

> ➤ Motion-captured animations drawn from **ex–Delta Force personnel** (for characters), **actors, dancers, and gymnasts** (for enemy humans and monsters).

Hardware

As in the high-concept document, state your target platform. If it is a personal computer rather than a console, also state the minimum configuration required to play the game.

Production Details

If you're writing a treatment as part of a pitch to a publisher, it's essential to say not only what the game will be like, but who will develop it and when, and what it will cost to develop. Good game ideas might be common, but good development teams are rare; the publisher will want to see evidence that you have the resources and experience to get the job done.

Current Status

Start by letting the publisher know where you are now. If you have actually begun some prototype work or proof-of-concept work, say so and indicate what features it contains. If the game is still no more than a gleam in your eye, leave this section out.

Completed prototype demonstrating military (but not psychic) game features. Includes:

> ➤ 3D landscape with moving water and foliage, bridges, buildings, vehicles.

> ➤ Player characters with visible differences, motion-captured animations, variety of movement modes.

Development Team

List the names and qualifications of your key people. Indicate what role each will play in the project. Don't include their entire résumés; nobody will read all that. Instead, give a one-paragraph synopsis of each person's history, including who they've worked for, in what position, and what games they already have credited to them. Include their education only if it's relevant and recent; producers are much more interested in knowing that someone has shipped a successful product than in where he went to school.

Don't include more than about six people here. If you have a big team, list only your managers and star performers.

Budget

Budgeting game development is a black art indeed and is far beyond the scope of this book. At this point in the process, without a signed contract, it's not worth trying to figure out a detailed budget—you can't know what everything will cost until you and the publisher have agreed on what all the game will include. However, you can give a rough estimate of how much you expect to spend overall. This lets the publisher know approximately how big your ambitions are. If you say $500,000 here, they'll know you're talking about a small project; if you say $5 million, they'll know you want to build a blockbuster.

At this point, nobody will hold you to whatever number you put down; it's only a guideline. The number that really matters will be the one in the contract.

Schedule

As with budgeting, there's no point in scheduling tasks in detail until you know what they're going to be. However, you can offer a proposed ship date for the product and some key milestones here, if you want to. Again, this information just serves as a guide to the publisher to indicate how ambitious the project is. The real schedule will be the one built into the development contract.

Competition

The section on competition was optional in the high-concept document, but at this point it's essential. A publisher will want to know what other games this product will be going up against in the marketplace, and how to position yours to beat them. Bear in mind that you're talking about a time 12 to 24 months in the future, depending on how long it will take to build your game. Games that are already on the market are unlikely to be its competition unless you expect their publishers to issue sequels or updates to them. The competition you need to list are the games that are under development at the same time as yours. Because they won't be advertised yet, you'll have to read the trade press and industry web sites to find out what features they're expected to include.

For each competing product, list its name, who makes it, what machine it's for, and when it's expected to ship, along with a summary of its key features. Then indicate clearly what will make your game different from it and, above all, better.

Game World

In the last major section in the document, you can include anything else that's likely to get your reader fired up about the product. You've already discussed the gameplay, technology, and general features of the game, so this is the time to include background material that draws the reader deeper into your world.

Backstory

If your game has a story and characters, then presumably something has happened that created the game's primary challenge. Tell your reader briefly what happened in the days (or geologic ages, depending!) leading up to the beginning of the game.

> The appearance of Indoctrinol has thrown America's national security apparatus into a panic. Everyone sent to investigate it has disappeared, including the elite Delta Force and Seal teams. It's clear that something special is called for. Searching the entire U.S. military, the government has found four—only four—superb soldiers who also have latent psychic abilities. After a few days of training, they're sent on their way: strangers to one another on a mission to the unknown.

Objective

What is the player's overall objective, the thing she is trying to achieve to complete the game? This doesn't have to be the "true" objective, however—the player can find evidence of a deeper and more serious problem as he plays.

> Follow the trail of Indoctrinol back to its source, and wipe it out. This will take you to locations around the world, operating undercover to perform missions against Third-World dictators, drug lords, terrorists, organized crime, and anyone else who has anything to do with Indoctrinol.

Characters

If you've already defined the game's characters and they are important enough to help sell the game, include their names, pictures, backgrounds, and special abilities here.

> ### Paul "Mayhem" Jackson
>
> *Psychic ability:* Shield. Can project a protective shield around teammates.
>
> *Weapons:* Chain gun, grenade launcher. Mayhem is a heavy-weapons expert.
>
> *Armor:* Very heavy, which makes him relatively slow-moving.
>
> *Personality:* Angry and ruthless over some event in his past.

Mission or Story Progression

Lay out the game's narrative arc as far as you know it. Document the twists and turns that the story might take, and indicate the way in which the player's success or failure will affect her progress through the game. For example, if the story is linear and the player must accomplish each scenario in order to proceed, say so; if it is branching, say that and explain how the player goes down one branch or another. Don't write a novel—this isn't the design script—but rather provide an outline for a novel, listing the key events in the plot.

> In the single-player game, missions will progress from easy to hard as the team follows the drug back to its source. Initially dealing only with human drug dealers on a local scale, they will eventually take on smugglers, distributors, and manufacturers of the drug.

In later missions, it will become clear that there are demonic creatures among the humans, for reasons that are not initially clear. They will remain in human form for as long as possible, but when attacked hard enough, they will morph into their original demonic forms, huge and terrifying.

To combat these creatures, additional psychic training and nontraditional weapons will be provided to the team as the game goes on....

The Design Script

This is the real McCoy—the document that officially, formally records your game's design. Whereas the high-concept document and the treatment are primarily sales tools, the script is primarily a development tool (although publishers often want to see a completed script before funding the next phase of a project). As we said in Chapter 1, it is a record of decisions made (and not yet made), a way of transmitting the design to the rest of the team, and a reference work for bringing new people up to speed as they join the team late in the development process.

If you already have a design script, even a partial one, bring it along to the pitch meeting to show how far along you are. Although it's not intended as a sales tool, a producer will appreciate getting a look at a well-organized design script. The producer might also bring along a programmer as a technical advisor to the meeting, who will ask you questions about your development plans.

How Big Should It Be?

In the earliest days of computer gaming, there were no design scripts. A programmer had an idea for a game and started coding it immediately. In a few weeks or months, it was done and that was that. The program code was all of the design document that there would ever be, but because games were very small and usually were built by one person, it didn't matter much.

As games and their development teams grew in size, people started to realize that they needed careful planning. Publishers began to insist that a game have an entirely comprehensive script before any programming or other work began. The script became the deliverable at the first milestone in the project. Design documents grew enormously, especially if the publisher was relying on an outside developer that it couldn't keep a close eye on. Scripts went from 50 to 100 to 200 pages in the early 1990s.

Since then, scripts have shrunk somewhat and also have become fragmented. Instead of one single monster document, many development groups create smaller documents to cover particular areas of the game: character design, for example, or core mechanics. There are a couple of reasons for this. Now that many games are using licensed game engines, there's no need to document the functional characteristics of a 3D environment in excruciating detail—this material is provided for you in the engine. Second, the last 10 years has seen tremendous growth in the use of level-editing tools to create the game's missions or scenarios. It used to be that the progression of a game was hard-wired into the code, so it was also documented extensively in the design script. Games have now become *data-driven;* that is, the software implements the AI, user interface, and core mechanics of the game, but the actual experience of playing each level—its appearance, challenges, and victory condition—are stored in data files created by the level editor. As a result, there's no need to define these things in advance in a design document. The script can focus on the elements that make up the game, and the level designers create the concrete challenge of playing it.

In short, there's no longer a clear rule about how many pages long a script should be. If a script is a part of a milestone deliverable, though, the fatter it is, the more likely it is that the publisher will think you've done your homework. A game that claims to offer 50 or 60 hours of gameplay and a vast number of characters, locations, weapons, and player options had better have more than 20 pages of documentation. Obviously, you shouldn't pad it out with fluff, but thoroughness is always appreciated by people who are expecting to invest a million dollars or more in a product.

The Design Web Site

Unless you have a particular need for paper copies, you might consider writing not a document, but a design web site. The web site has many advantages. For one thing, multiple people can work on different parts of it at the same time. It's very easy and convenient to add material to in a nonlinear fashion. It's also easy to add pictures. Hyperlinks enables you to cross-reference one page with another.

The disadvantage of a design web site is that it's difficult to take home and mark up with a pencil, and if your material is sensitive, you had better be darn sure that the site is secure. A Microsoft Word or Adobe Acrobat file can be protected and encrypted easily; a web site is vulnerable to being hacked if it's stored on a server available to the Internet.

Chris Taylor's Template

A great many game design templates are available on the Internet, in varying degrees of detail. Rather than write yet another one of our own, we've chosen to refer you to a template from a famous game designer with a string of hits to his name. Chris Taylor was the man behind *Total Annihilation, Fallout Tactics,* and *Dungeon Siege.* We think that his template is the most comprehensive (and also the funniest) currently available. It's primarily intended for a large game in a big world, with many characters, weapons, monsters, and so on, so obviously much of it will be unnecessary if you're designing a 10-minute Java-based trivia game. However, you can ignore anything that you don't need.

Chris Taylor's template is too long to include here, and you wouldn't want to type it all in anyway. You can download a copy in Microsoft Word format at `www.designersnotebook.com/ctaylordesign.zip`.

Appendix B

Bibliography

Now that you've read our book on game design, you might want to look into some others as well. Here we offer an eclectic selection of works for further reading. Some of them are specifically about games, but most are about other subjects that we believe a game designer should know something about; books that complement this one. We have not tried to be comprehensive, but rather to include works we have personally found to be useful.

Game Design

There aren't a great many other books on game design (that's part of why we wrote this one), but we think some of the following offer useful perspectives:

Art of Computer Game Design, The. Crawford, Chris. Probably the first book in the field, and a classic. This book is no longer in print, but may be read online at http://www.vancouver.wsu.edu/fac/peabody/game-book/Coverpage.html. Crawford will also soon be publishing a new work, *Chris Crawford on Game Design* (©2004, New Riders Publishing), to which we look forward with interest.

Creating Emotion in Games: The Art and Craft of Emotioneering. Freeman, David; New Riders Publishing; ISBN: 1592730078 (due out Fall 2003).

Community Building on the Web: Secret Strategies for Successful Online Communities. Kim, Amy Jo; Peachpit Press. Although this isn't technically a game design book, it is a highly regarded work on online communities and should be considered required reading for anyone who wants to build an online game or persistent world.

Elements of User Experience, The. Garrett, Jesse James; New Riders Publishing; ISBN: 0735712026.

Emergence: The Connected Lives of Ants, Brains, Cities, and Software. Johnson, Steve; Scribner; ISBN: 068486875X.

Game Architecture and Design. Rollings, Andrew and Dave Morris. Originally published by The Coriolis Group and soon to be reissued by New Riders. A giant tome on designing and building computer and video games from start to finish. It is the companion volume to this one.

Game Design Perspectives. Laramee, Francois Dominic (editor); Charles River Media; ISBN: 1584500905. This is an extensive collection of essays by a variety of people on different topics, not all of them game design.

Game Design Secrets of the Sages. Saltzman, Marc (editor); Brady Games. A collection of interviews with some of the top people in the business. In this form, it's more useful as background reading than how-to material, but it's a good way to see inside the heads of some of the industry's best designers.

Game Design: The Art & Business of Creating Games. Bates, Bob; Premier Press; ISBN: 0761531653. More of an introduction to the entire game business than a game design book. It's easy to read and nicely illustrated, and Bob Bates' credentials are impeccable.

Swords & Circuitry: A Designer's Guide to Computer Role-Playing Games. Hallford, Neal and Jana Hallford; Premier Press; ISBN: 0761532994.

Game Theory

Formal game theory is too abstruse for day-to-day use in game design, but some of the following works offer a lighter analysis:

The Compleat Strategyst: Being a Primer on the Theory of Games of Strategy. Williams, J. D.; Dover Publications; ISBN: 0486251012.

Fun and Games: A Text on Game Theory. Binmore, K. G.; D C Heath & Co; ISBN: 0669246034.

Game Theory: Analysis of Conflict. Myerson, Roger B.; Harvard University Press; ISBN: 0674341163.

History and Sociology of Video Games

Video games are currently the fastest-growing form of entertainment in America. They've permanently redefined the way we use our leisure time. The following books are good background reading on the video game phenomenon, if you want to understand not only the games, but their place in the world:

ARCADE FEVER: The Fan's Guide to The Golden Age of Video Games. Sellers, John; Running Press; ISBN: 0762409371.

Game Over: Press Start to Continue. Sheff, David; GamePress; ISBN: 0966961706.

High Score! The Illustrated History of Electronic Games. DeMaria, Rusel and Johnny Lee Wilson; McGraw-Hill Osborne Media; ISBN: 0072224282.

Joystick Nation: How Videogames Ate Our Quarters, Won Our Hearts, and Rewired Our Minds. Herz, J. C.; Little, Brown & Company.

Killing Monsters: Why Children Need Fantasy, Super Heroes, and Make-Believe Violence. Jones, Gerard; Basic Books; ISBN: 0465036953.

Phoenix: The Fall & Rise of Videogames. Herman, Leonard; Rolenta Press.

Supercade: A Visual History of the Videogame Age 1971-1984. Burnham, Van; MIT Press; ISBN: 0262024926.

Trigger Happy: Videogames and the Entertainment Revolution. Poole, Steven; Arcade Publishing; ISBN: 1559705396.

Ultimate History of Video Games, The: From Pong to Pokemon—The Story Behind the Craze That Touched Our Lives and Changed the World. Kent, Steve L.; Prima Publishing; ISBN: 0761536434.

Architecture and Graphic Design

Not being artists or graphic designers ourselves, we don't have an extensive list of suggestions; but we have found the following useful or inspiring:

A Pattern Language. Alexander, Christopher, et al. Oxford University Press; ISBN: 0195019199. This work created something of a revolution in architectural theory when it appeared, adopting a practical/psychological approach to the way people use buildings. Some of its ideas formed the basis for *The Sims.*

The Grammar of Ornament. Jones, Owen. Various editions exist, including one on CD-ROM. A massive collection of decorative elements.

L'Ornement Polychrome. Racinet, Albert. Various editions. Another massive collection of decorative elements. Don't worry about the fact that it's in French—just look at the pictures.

The next three books comprise a series and should be read in this order. Don't be put off by the long-winded titles. They are invaluable tools for learning to express numeric quantities visually, something every game designer must do:

The Visual Display of Quantitative Information. Tufte, Edward; Graphics Press; ISBN: 0961392142.

Envisioning Information. Tufte, Edward; Graphics Press; ISBN: 0961392118.

Visual Explanations: Images and Quantities, Evidence and Narrative. Tufte, Edward; Graphics Press; ISBN: 0961392126.

Writing and Narrative

Game designers spend most of their time writing, and they have the primary responsibility for creating a game's story if it has one. Most of the stories in games at the moment are pretty mediocre, but we think some of the following can help to correct that situation.

Characters and Viewpoint (Elements of Fiction Writing). Card, Orson Scott; Writer's Digest Books; ISBN: 0898799279.

Hamlet on the Holodeck: The Future of Narrative in Cyberspace. Murray, Janet Horowitz; MIT Press; ISBN: 0262631873.

Hero with a Thousand Faces, The. Campbell, Joseph; Princeton University Press; ISBN: 0691017840; reprint edition.

Myth and the Movies: Discovering the Mythic Structure of 50 Unforgettable Films. Voytilla, Stuart; Michael Wiese Productions; ISBN: 0941188663.

Pause & Effect: The Art of Interactive Narrative. Meadows, Mark S.; New Riders Publishing; ISBN: 0735711712.

Wizardry and Wild Romance: A Study of Epic Fantasy. Moorcock, Michael; Books Britain; ISBN: 0575041471.

The Writer's Journey: Mythic Structure for Writers. Vogler, Christopher; Michael Wiese Productions; ISBN: 0941188701; 2nd edition.

Index

N

Maximize Your Impact

0735700443
George Maestri
US$50.00

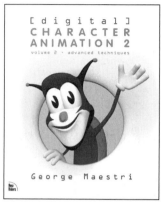

1562059548
Jeremy Birn
US$50.00

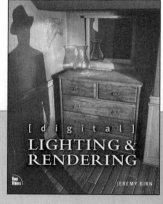

0735709181
Owen Demers
US$55.00

1562059300
George Maestri
US$50.00

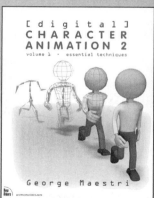

0735712581
Dan Ablan
US$45.00

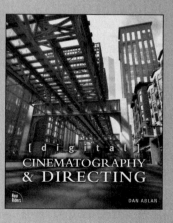

New
Riders

Leading game books
where game books
have never gone before...

New Riders presents

As THE game resource,
NRG books explore
programming, design, art,
and celebrity savvy.
NRG takes you behind
the scenes... revealing
insider secrets
like never before.

New
Riders

Designing Virtual
Worlds
0131018167
Richard Bartle
US$49.99

Andrew Rollings
and Ernest Adams
on Game Design
1592730019
Andrew Rollings
and Ernest Adams
US$39.99

The Fat Man on Game
Audio: Tasty Morsels
of Sonic Goodness
1592730094
George "Fat Man" Sanger
US$35.00

Creating Emotion
in Games: The Art and
Craft of Emotioneering
1592730078
David Freeman
Foreword by Wil Wright
US$39.99

Get in the Game!:
Careers in the
Game Industry
0735713073
Marc Mencher
US$29.99